The Aramaic Levi Document

Edition, Translation, Commentary

by

Jonas C. Greenfield, Michael E. Stone
and Esther Eshel

BRILL
LEIDEN • BOSTON
2004

This book is printed on acid-free paper.

Library of Congress Cataloging-in-Publication Data

Levi document. Polyglot.
The Aramaic Levi document : edition, translation, commentary / edited by Jonas C. Greenfield, Michael E. Stone, and Esther Eshel.
p. cm. — (Studia in Veteris Testamenti pseudepigrapha, ISSN 0169–8125 ; v. 19)
Text in Aramaic and Greek with English translation; commentary in English.
Includes bibliographical references and indexes.
ISBN 90–04–13785–8 (alk. paper)
1. Levi document. 2. Manuscripts, Aramaic. I. Greenfield, Jonas C., 1926– II. Stone, Michael E. III. Eshel, Esther. IV. Title. V. Series.

BM488.L48A116 2004 2004051984
229'.914—dc22

ISSN 0169–8125
ISBN 9004 137858

PRINTED IN THE NETHERLANDS

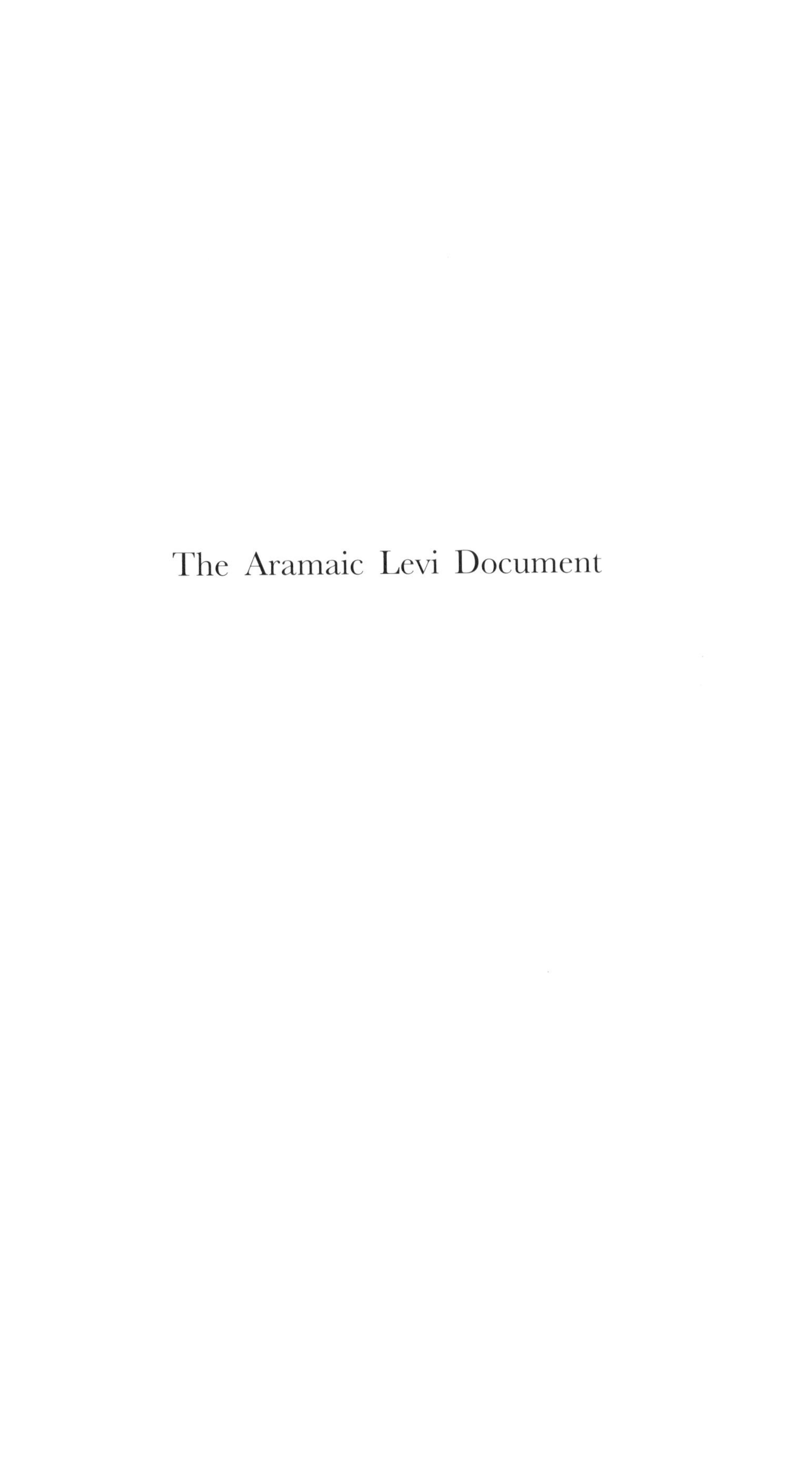

The Aramaic Levi Document

Studia in Veteris Testamenti Pseudepigrapha

Series Editors

Michael Knibb, Henk Jan de Jonge,
Jean-Claude Haelewyck, Johannes Tromp
Ediderunt

VOLUME 19

Dedicated to the Memory of
Jonas C. Greenfield ז״ל
Scholar, Colleague and Friend

בקר ובעי ודע מא יונא בעה
Examine and seek and know what *Jonas* sought

4QApocrypon of Levi[b] 24:4

CONTENTS

List of Illustrations and Tables ix
Preface xi
Acknowledgements xiii

Introduction 1
1. The Witnesses 1
2. Principles of Present Work 6
   The Present Work 7
   The Apparatus of Variants 9
   The Data Block and Versification 9
   Parallels 10
   The Translation 10
3. The Original Order of *ALD* 11
4. The Date and Provenance of *ALD* 19
5. Notes on Language of *ALD* 22
6. Testaments and Other Associated Works from Qumran 25
   Texts Related to the Testaments of the Twelve Patriarchs 26
   Other "Testament" Texts 28
   The *Testament of Qahat* and the *Visions of Amram* 29
   An Apocryphal Text Apparently Related to *ALD* 31
7. Some Specific Aspects of *ALD* 32
   TPL 4:2 and *ALD* 32
   The Two Spirits 33
   Sapiential Characteristics of the Priesthood 34
   Levi's Special Role in *ALD* 35
   Levi in *TPL* 8:14 39
   The Travels of Levi and Jacob in *ALD* and *TPL* 39
   The Sacrificial Ordinances and Measures 41
      1. The Sacrificial Ordinances 41
      2. The Metrological List in 9:17–18 42
   Postscript 45

Critical Signs and Abbreviations 46
Journals and Publications 46
Citations of Dead Sea Scrolls 47
Appendix 48

Text & Translation 56
Commentary 110
Unplaced Fragments 216
Aramaic Concordance 235
Greek Concordance 250

Bibliography 260
Indexes 271

ILLUSTRATIONS AND TABLES

1. Codicological Layout of the Geniza Manuscript xiv

2. Cambridge Ms ms T.S. 16, fol. 94 recto 52
Columns Cambridge a, f and e

3. Cambridge Ms ms T.S. 16, fol. 94 verso 53
Columns Cambridge d, c and b

4. Bodleian Ms Heb. c. 27 recto 54
Columns Bodleian b and a

5. Bodleian Ms Heb. c. 27 verso 55
Columns Bodleian d and c

6. Genealogical Table .... opposite p. 181

PREFACE

The *Aramaic Levi Document* was the object of long-standing joint research for Jonas C. Greenfield and Michael E. Stone. They published several studies of it, individually and together, and had undertaken to prepare a full edition and commentary on the whole work for the series *Studia in Veteris Testamenti Pseudepigrapha*. In addition to their published papers and to the publication of the Aramaic Levi fragments from among the Dead Sea Scrolls, they had assembled notes and parts of a preliminary draft of the edition of the Geniza fragments. With the sudden death of Jonas Greenfield on March 13, 1995, Michael Stone completed the edition of the Dead Sea Scrolls fragments which were eventually published in DJD. He then laid aside the accumulated results of almost thirty years' joint research for four years. In 1999 he invited Esther Eshel to join him in bringing this labor to completion and her contribution has been invaluable in finishing this book. Michael Sokoloff kindly reviewed the translation and made a number of acute and apposite comments. Vered Hillel who worked as our research assistant has played a major role in coordinating and finalizing the diverse materials. A grant from the Israel Science Foundation enabled Stone and Eshel to carry out this work and we gladly acknowledge the support of ISF. A number of colleagues have graciously advised us on specific matters and their contributions are acknowledged as appropriate.

ACKNOWLEDGEMENTS

The Scripture quotations contained herein, unless marked otherwise, are from the New Revised Standard Version Bible copyright ©1989 by the Division of Christian Education of the National Council of Churches of Christ in the USA. Used by permission. All rights reserved.

The citations from the works of Hollander and de Jonge are given by permission of E.J. Brill, Leiden. Those from VanderKam's *Jubilees* are given by permission of the author and the publisher, Peeters, Leuven. These permissions are gratefully acknowledged.

The pictures of Bodleian Ms Heb. c. 27 are published by permission of the Bodleian Library, University of Oxford. The pictures of Cambridge Ms ms T.S. 16, fol. 94 are published by permission of Cambridge University Library, University of Cambridge.

All other quotations are acknowledged at the appropriate point.

Reconstruction of the Geniza Manuscript Fascicule

p. 1		p. 12		
missing	missing / Camb a	Camb f	Camb e	Bifolium 1a Camb outer side
p. 11		**p. 2**		
Camb d	Camb c	missing / Camb b	missing	Bifolium 1b Camb inner side
p. 3		**p. 10**		
missing	missing	Athos	Athos	Bifolium 2a Athos outer side
p. 9		**p. 4**		
Athos	Athos	missing	missing	Bifolium 2b Athos inner side
p. 5		**p. 8**		
missing	missing	Bodl d	Bodl c	Bifolium 3a Bodleian outer side
p. 7		**p. 6**		
Bodl b	Bodl a	missing	missing	Bifolium 3b Bodleian inner side

Table based on calculation that Athos Greek without Aramaic = 4 columns

INTRODUCTION

We refer throughout to the work being presented here as *Aramaic Levi Document*. In previous generations it has been called *Aramaic Testament of Levi* or *Aramaic Levi*. We chose this title, following usage of recent years, because it is not clear that the work is a testament and the inclusion of the word "Testament" in the title inevitably leads to the idea that this is an Aramaic version of *Testament of Levi* found in *Greek in Testaments of the Twelve Patriarchs*. The choice of a title for thc document in Modern Hebrew proved difficult, and Professor M. Bar Asher has proposed כתב לוי, based on both Hebrew (Ezekiel 13:9 ובכתב בית ישראל לא יכתבו "and they will not be inscribed in the register [book] of the house of Israel") and Aramaic, as in 1QapGen 5:29 [פרשגן] כתב מלי נׄוׄחׄ "[A Copy] of the Book of the Words of Noah".[1]

1. *The Witnesses*

At the end of the nineteenth century, the first part of the *Aramaic Levi Document* from the Cairo Geniza was identified in the Cambridge University collection, where it is now known as Cambridge ms T.S. 16, fol. 94. H.L. Pass made this identification and published the first edition of the fragments in 1900.[2] He describes the manuscript as follows:

> The fragment consists of one complete leaf, and attaching to it a very small portion of a second leaf of a two-column vellum ms, written in an Oriental hand, which can scarcely be later than the eleventh century. The leaf is ten inches square, and is in some places so severely mutilated as to be entirely illegible.[3]

Each folio of the manuscript contained two columns on each side and so, in the Cambridge fragment, parts of six columns survive,

[1] Steiner, 1995, 66–71, especially pp. 68–69. The title *Aramaic Levi Document* is used, for example, by DiTommaso, 2001. See previously Stone, 1988.
[2] Pass and Arendzen, 1900, 651–661.
[3] Pass and Arendzen, 1900, 651–52.

known as Cambridge cols. a–f (see Figs. 2–3). The first two columns (a–b) are very partially preserved, each including only parts of nine lines of text, Pass's "very small portion of a second leaf". From the shape of this fragmentary leaf, we may speculate that it came from the bottom of a pile where it suffered more degeneration, though it is also possible that it was torn.

Another single leaf was discovered among the Bodleian library lot of Geniza fragments and published by Cowley and Charles in 1907 (see Figs. 4–5).[4] Designated Bodleian ms Heb c 27, fol. 56 it preserves four almost complete columns. The Cambridge and the Oxford leaves were written by the same scribe and they derive from the same manuscript.

Between the end of Cambridge col. a and the beginning of Cambridge col. b at least two columns and 14 lines are missing. Charles also stated that four columns are missing following Bodleian col. a.[5] This is incorrect and, in fact, eight columns (4 pages) are missing.[6]

The script was characterized by Pass and Arendzen as oriental and was dated to the eleventh century.[7] Beit-Arié dates the fragments to the oldest layer of Geniza material, prior to 1000 CE.[8] Vertical as well as horizontal rulings can still be seen and on some of the pages remains of ink coming from the other side of the page can be detected; e.g., on Cambridge col. c. The manuscript has 23 lines per column. The left-hand ends of the lines are ragged, length varying as much as four or five letters in some cases. The columns are about 80 mm. wide and the interlinear space is 8 mm.[9]

Scribal marks and peculiarities of the layout have been noted as follows:

- Cambridge col b, line 20, end—unusual elliptical sign.
- At the end of short lines, single or double sloping, hooked lines have been written to fill out the line.[10] Instances of double lines

[4] Cowley and Charles, 1907.
[5] Cowley and Charles, 1907, 569.
[6] See Kugler, 1996, 231–33.
[7] Greenfield and Stone, 1979, 216.
[8] Greenfield and Stone, 1979, 216.
[9] For a detailed description of the Geniza manuscript and its dimensions, see Puech, 2002, 513.
[10] See Beit-Arié, 1993, 83, plate 5.

are in Bodleian a, line 3 (4:9), Cambridge c, line 14 (11:8), Cambridge e, line 5 (13:1) and Cambridge e, line 14 (13:3). Instances of single lines are in Bodleian a, line 17 (5:3), Bodleian b, line 6 (5:8), Bodleian b, line 22 (6:5), Bodleian c, line 10 (7:4), Bodleian c, line 21 (8:1), Bodleian d, line 9 (8:4), Cambridge d, line 19 (12:7).

- Like Torah scrolls, the text is written with "open" and "closed" section endings (פרשות פתוחות וסתומות), i.e., cases in which the end of a section is marked by a space reaching to the end of the line of writing ("open") and cases where a space is left in the middle of a line of writing ("closed"). We have usually followed these section divisions in our versification. In the lists here, we have also recorded the word starting the new verse, when it also serves to mark a new section.
- Closed sections occur at the end of our verses: 4:11, 5:1, 5:8, 6:1, 11:7, 11:8 (+ בשנת), 11:11 (+ בשנת), 12:1, 12:2, 12:2, 12:6, 12:7, 12:9, 13:5. In 13:9 a closed section occurs in the middle of our verse.
- Open sections occur in 11:6 (+ בשנת), 11:10 (+ בשנת), 13:3 (+ וכען).
- Indentation occurs before 13:4 (+ וכען).[11] In 4:14 there is an unclear indentation in the middle of the verse.

The text is written basically in Standard Literary Aramaic[12] but there are errors and orthographies which are due to the medieval copyist, some of them the result of Hebrew influence (see section on Language, below).[13] Some Hebraisms have also been detected in the copies of the work discovered among the Dead Sea Scrolls. However, after the study of the whole work, it is the view of the present editors that it is unlikely to be a translation from Hebrew into Aramaic,

[11] There is an unexplained indentation in the Bodleian fragment c (7:5), probably the result of scribal inattention.

[12] Compare Grelot, 1983, 103–04.

[13] These remarks are based on pp. 227–29 of Greenfield and Stone, 1979 which were written by J.C. Greenfield. In the course of subsequent work, no decisive evidence emerged to prove or disprove the hypothesis of a Hebrew source, although we should stress that "[t]he 'Hebraisms' noted by Charles and others are not an isolated phenomenon any longer, since similar Hebraisms may be detected in the published Qumrân Aramaic texts" (Greenfield and Stone, 1979, 228: cf. Cowley and Charles, 1907, 567–69). The case for a Hebrew original was urged most energetically by Grelot, 1955.

and that the Hebraisms found in the text are probably to be attributed to the use of both Hebrew and Aramaic by an educated Jewish author of the Second Temple period. In the course of the commentary, Hebraisms have been noted in the following verses: 3:10, 5:8bis, 6:3, 6:4, 7:1, 7:3, 8:6, 11:2, 11:8bis, 11:11, 12:14, 13:5 and 13:16. Rather often, these are evocations of biblical phrases. Moreover, the Hebraising onomastic midrashim fall into a special category and are discussed in the commentary to chapter 11. They do not witness to an underlying Hebrew text of *ALD*.

In addition to the textual evidence from the Geniza manuscript, seven fragmentary copies of *ALD* were discovered among the Dead Sea Scrolls. These are enumerated, with reference to the *editiones principes*, in the following list. The dates are indicative.

1QLevi (1Q21), late Hasmonean (100–1 BCE), DJD 1, Milik, 87–91.
4QLevi[a] (4Q213), late Hasmonean-early Herodian (50–25 BCE), Stone and Greenfield, DJD 22, 1–23.[14]
4QLevi[b] (4Q213a), late Hasmonean (75–50 BCE), Stone and Greenfield, DJD 22, 25–36.[15]
4QLevi[c] (4Q213b), late Hasmonean (75–50 BCE), Stone and Greenfield, DJD 22, 37–41.[16]
4QLevi[d] (4Q214), late Hasmonean (75–50 BCE), Stone and Greenfield, DJD 22, 43–51.[17]
4QLevi[e] (4Q214a), late Hasmonean or early Herodian (50–25 BCE), Stone and Greenfield, DJD 22, 53–60.[18]
4QLevi[f] (4Q214b), Hasmonean (150–30 BCE), Stone and Greenfield, DJD 22, 61–72.[19]

In addition to these Aramaic manuscripts from Qumran, the work is cited by the *Damascus Document*, as was discussed by J.C. Greenfield.[20] He regards the reference to the "words of Levi son of Jacob" in CD

[14] See previously Stone and Greenfield, 1994.
[15] Previously discussed in Stone and Greenfield, 1996a, 1–15 and earlier by Milik, 1955, (fragments 1 and 2) and Stone and Greenfield, 1993.
[16] Previously discussed by Stone and Greenfield, 1996b, and see also Greenfield and Stone, 1979.
[17] Milik, 1976, 244 says that 4QLevi[b], which for him must mean 4Q214, was written by the same hand as 4QEnoch[f]. Milik would date the writing to the early Hasmonean period (150–125 BCE). Now we have distinguished three manuscripts among the fragments assigned the number 4Q214. The hands are indeed quite similar but not identical.
[18] See previously Stone and Greenfield, 1997.
[19] See previously Stone and Greenfield, 1997.
[20] Greenfield, 1988.

4:15 as an allusion to *ALD* 6:3, although the text has been corrupted.

Extracts from a Greek translation of *ALD* have also been interpolated into one Greek manuscript of *Testaments of the Twelve Patriarchs*. This is manuscript Athos, Monastery of Koutloumous, Cod. 39 (catalogue no. 3108), of the 11th century. Into the *Greek Testament of Levi* (*TPL*) it inserts three passages that are not part of the text of *TPL*. The first two are parallel to Aramaic Levi material known from the Geniza and from Qumran. The first of these, containing the *Prayer of Levi* and two preceding verses (*ALD* 2:4–3:18), is included following *TPL* 2:3 although the motive for its introduction was surely the latter part of *TPL* 2:4.[21] The second is a long passage extending from *ALD* 5:6 to 11:8 and is inserted in the manuscript following *TPL* 18:2. The third interpolated passage, following *TPL* 7:2, apparently is of Christian origin and deals with various doctrinal and other matters.

Two Greek citations attributed to Levi are to be found in the writings of Ammonas, a fourth century monastic author. The two citations are: καθὼς καὶ ὁ Λευΐ φησι· καὶ τὴν ἡδονὴν τοῦ πνεύματος τίς ἔγνω, εἰ μὴ ἐκεῖνος εἰς οὓς κατεσκήνωσεν. "As Levi says, 'And who knew the delight of the spirit, except that one among whom he/it has dwelt?'."[22] The second citation is: Ὅτε γοῦν κατηξιώθη αὐτοῦ ὁ Λευΐ, μεγάλας εὐχὰς δέδωκε τῷ Θεῷ λέγων· Ὑμνῶ σε, ὁ Θεὸς ὅτι ἐχαρίσω μοι τὸ πνεῦμα ὃ ἔδωκας τοῖς δούλοις σου. "When, then, Levi had been deemed worthy of it, he gave great prayers to God, saying, 'I praise you, O God, because you graced me with the spirit that you gave to your servants'."[23] These quotations are not scriptural, nor are they drawn from the extant parts of *ALD*, or from *TPL*. Denis did suggest that they derive from the Prayer of Levi, but we fail to see the similarity.[24] Tromp, in his thorough study of these fragments, points out that the second of them, in particular, may well have been drawn

[21] Greenfield and Stone, 1990, 155. On the reasons for the location of these extracts, see de Jonge, 1988, 369 note 12.

[22] This verse attributed to Levi by Ammonas might be related to *Letter of James* 4:5: "Or do you suppose that the Scripture speaks in vain? Does the spirit he made to dwell in us crave enviously?" (πρὸς φθόνον ἐπιποθεῖ τὸ πνεῦμα ὃ κατῴκισεν ἐν ἡμῖν) (Randall Buth).

[23] Nau, 1915, 453.

[24] Denis and Haelewyck, 2000, 241–42.

from a prayer. After a careful analysis he concludes, "Given the facts that Ammonas quotes a prayer of Levi, and that the *Aramaic Levi Document* contained a prayer of Levi; considering, furthermore, that the subject matters of Ammonas' epistle and the Levi documents are closely related, we may conclude that there is a distinct possibility that Ammonas knew the Aramaic Levi Document in some Greek form, although not the Greek form that was probably known to the author of *T. Levi* and/or the copyist responsible for manuscript *e*. . . . It is most likely that Ammonas in his epistle referred to a prayer of Levi, actually existing in writing, although there is no writing extant from which the quotation demonstrably derives."[25]

A small Syriac fragment was printed by W. Wright in his renowned catalogue of Syriac manuscripts in the British Museum, copied from there by Pass and then by Charles, who re-collated it.[26] This fragment covers 12:6–9, part of the chronological summary, and was doubtless preserved for that reason in a miscellany dated 874 CE.[27]

2. *The Principles of the Present Work*

We are in the fortunate position of having reliable editions of almost all these diverse texts. The Qumran fragments have been published, first in articles, and then definitively in the relevant volumes of *Discoveries in the Judean Desert.*[28] The Athos Greek manuscript was re-edited by Marinus de Jonge and his collaborators in the *editio maior* of the Greek *Testaments of the Twelve Patriarchs.*[29] As noted above, Charles re-collated the Syriac. We have used all these sources freely. The main edition of the Geniza text is that of Charles.[30] This has been corrected by us from photographs and also by an autopsy examination. The Qumran fragments were also re-collated against pho-

[25] This is discussed by Tromp, 1997; quotation from pp. 246–47. Cited by permission.

[26] Charles, 1908a, 254.

[27] See Wright, 1871, 2.997: cf. also de Jonge, 1999, 78.

[28] See notes 14–19 above. Caquot, 1998 published French translations with some notes, just of the Qumran fragments, without relating these either to the Geniza text or to the Athos Greek.

[29] De Jonge, 1978.

[30] Charles, 1908a, 245–56. A new edition is Puech, 2002, containing many changes.

tographs of the manuscripts. The results of these re-collations have been incorporated here and we were able to recover some additional letters and words of the Aramaic text.

The Present Work

The primary purpose of the present work is not to prepare a new edition of the textual witnesses. It is to present *ALD* as a single literary work with a translation and commentary, so making it readily available to students of Ancient Judaism. Consequently, particularly as regards the fragmentary material from Qumran and the Geniza, we have limited our critical marking and remarks to signalling (a) damaged, but certain letters (supralinear dot) and (b) fragments of letters in the manuscript that are consistent with our readings (supralinear circles). Detailed notes on the physical preservation of the letters and the state of the parchment, etc., have not been made, and may be found in the DJD edition.[31]

The text in our edition is diplomatic, and is not an attempt to restore the spelling and grammar of the third-century BCE Aramaic in which the work was composed. In general, where the Aramaic text exists, it is taken as the dominant text. The only instances where this practice is not sustained are where the Aramaic text is very fragmentary and another, more complete witness exists. Moreover, where the Geniza manuscript does exist, it is taken as the dominant text, even if fragmentary Qumran manuscript(s) also survive. This is because it is usually less beset by lacunae than they are and because it is by far the most extensive of the textual witnesses. Where the Geniza text does not exist, but there is a Qumran witness, that Qumran witness is taken as the dominant text. Where the Greek text exists, it is given in smaller type, interlinear, unless it is the only witness. Then it is regarded as the dominant witness. The dominant witness is always printed in larger type.

No attempt has been made to standardize the orthography or morphology of the Aramaic throughout the document. When the Geniza manuscript is dominant, its practice is followed; where a Qumran manuscript is dominant, its practice is preserved. The Geniza

[31] See Kugler, 1996, 38–45 and Puech, 2002, 513 for a physical description of the Geniza manuscript.

text is characterized by many peculiarities in both respects and these have been allowed to stand as they occur in the manuscript. If a Qumran manuscript runs parallel to the Geniza and presents a different orthography or morphology, that is recorded in the apparatus of variants. The relegation of such readings to the apparatus does not express a view about originality, but follows from our diplomatic editorial practice. In the commentary, remarks are made about a number of such instances. We have refrained from introducting punctuation into the Aramaic text because of the danger of its confusion with diacritical marks. Our understanding of the semantic division of the text is reflected in the translation.

The following additional information is presented in the text itself.

1. Words extant in the Geniza text and for which Qumran manuscripts also exist are marked by **bold** type. This only indicates the existence of the Qumran manuscripts, but the readings of those manuscripts, if they differ from the dominant text, are recorded in the apparatus of variants.
2. When Aramaic and Greek both exist, words occurring in one and not in the other, are printed in *italic* type.
3. When more than one Qumran manuscript preserves a word or words, the different manuscripts are distinguished by overbar or underlining.
4. In a very few instances where different Aramaic recensions exist, they are printed one beneath the other.

It should be observed that, as far as can be discerned, in general the Geniza Aramaic text resembles that of the Qumran fragments. It differs from them in its late orthography and some grammatical forms. However, there are quite a lot of instances of textual variants, which have been recorded in the apparatus and occasionally, when they reflect different recensions, as inter-linear text, as we have noted (e.g., 4:11). There are two Aramaic Qumran manuscripts that preserve recensions differing from the dominant text: 4QLevi^{d} frag. 1[32] and 4QLevi^{e} the latter of which is quite certainly a shorter text than Geniza and 4QLevi^{f} with which it overlaps.[33] Thus we may

[32] Stone and Greenfield, DJD 22, 43–45.
[33] Stone and Greenfield, DJD 22, 54–60.

observe that considerable textual development had already taken place by the first century BCE. Because of the unfortunately fragmentary character of the Qumran manuscripts, we can only catch brief glimpses of the short recension and its impact on the text published here is very limited.

The Apparatus of Variants

At the end of each chapter of the work is an apparatus of variants. This apparatus contains four types of information:

1. All instances of variants between the manuscripts are recorded. This category does not include simple additions and omissions existing between a single Aramaic witness and the Greek text, when they are printed one beneath the other. Such cases, as noted above, are marked in the text itself by italics.
2. All cases in which the text has been emended by the editors, or in which the editors consider it to be corrupt.
3. A careful selection of the conjectures, emendations and readings proposed by previous scholars of the document.
4. Certain technical information pertaining to the manuscripts, such as special marks, etc.

The Data Block and Versification

At the beginning of each chapter, a Data Block is given in which we have given a table of concordance between our chapter and verse numbering and previous numberings by sections, columns, fragments and lines. This specifies which witnesses exist for the chapter and for which parts of the chapter. Following that, a concordance of the verse numbering is given.

Because of the complicated history of the book, various and conflicting forms of versification and reference have been used in the past. For the Geniza fragments both column and line numbers were current, as well as section numbers that were introduced by the early editors, starting from 1 in Cambridge col. a up to 94 in Cambridge col. f. Subsequent recognition of *Prayer of Levi* as part of the work led to its being assigned another set of numbers, extending from 1 to 19. The addition of Qumran fragments which are not parallel to either Geniza 1–94 or to Prayer 1–19, added a further dimension of chaos to the presentation of the book, for they are referred to by Qumran manuscript sigil, fragment number, column and line.

Our purpose in the present work is to present *ALD*, as far as the witnesses allow, as a single work. We have attempted to place all the textual material surviving in a sequential order that is either borne out by the physical remains of the manuscripts or else can plausibly be supported by arguments based on those parts of the book preserved sequentially. This order may be disputed in some instances, and doubtful cases are noted. Below, the reasoning behind our placement of the material will be set forth. Any textual material that cannot be placed by either means is put at the end of the work, in the Appendix "Unplaced Fragments". These fragments serve to remind us that the surviving text is only part of the document.

Once the sequential order was established, we divided the text into chapters and verses, usually starting new verses at the points of division which have been customary in scholarly usage. *Vacat*s in the manuscripts and marginal markings likewise assisted in this task. We are conscious of the problems that renumbering ancient texts creates, but this action was forced upon us by the multiple and conflicting numbering systems that had become customary.

Parallels

Because *ALD*, as has been recognized from its discovery on, was itself a source of *TPL*, or else very much resembles a source of *TPL*, the parallels in the latter work provide, on occasion, textual material bearing on the text of *ALD*. The same is true, to a lesser extent, of *Jubilees*. Consequently, at the end of each chapter, following the Apparatus of Variants, we have given the parallels detected and we have indicated to which chapter and verse of *ALD* they are relevant. We have given *TPL* parallels in Greek and English, drawing on de Jonge's *editio maior* and translation and *Jubilees* in VanderKam's English translation.[34]

The Translation

The translation is based on the dominant text. Below the translation of each chapter, we give translations of the parallels from *TPL* and other sources.

[34] VanderKam, 1989.

3. *The Original Order of* ALD

The order of the main body of the text, running from 4:9 to 13:16, is confirmed by the manuscript situation. Starting with the beginning of col. b of the Bodleian manuscript, it concludes with the end of 4QLevi[a] frag. 1, col. 2. It is all held together by overlaps[35] as is clear from the following table of sequential texts.

Geniza	*Greek*	*4QLevi*[a]
4:9–5:5		
5:6–9:1	5:6–9:1	
	9:1–11:4	
11:5–13:12	11:5–11:8	13:1 16

Because of the fragmentary folio that contains Cambridge cols. a and b, we know that we have the following sequence preceding this body of text:

1) lacuna of at least 14 lines, but most probably more
2) 1:1–3
3) lacuna of 2 columns and 14 lines
4) 2:1–3
5) lacuna of at least 4 columns

and then the major block of material starting in 4:9.

One more very substantial fragment exists, extending from 2:4–4:6. This is preserved in the Greek text called, not quite precisely, *Prayer of Levi,* that overlaps largely with 4QLevi[b] frag. 1 cols. 1–2. This fragment does not overlap with the Geniza-Athos Greek sequence listed above. The first and most central issue in the reconstruction of *ALD* is the placing of *Prayer of Levi.* Once that is resolved, certain of the other fragments can be placed, while yet others remain without definite location.

The *Prayer of Levi* sequence contains four incidents. These are the following:

a) 2:4–5 which describe a purification ritual;
b) 3 the actual prayer of Levi;

[35] Some fragments of Qumran manuscripts contain pieces of this body of text, but they teach us nothing about the sequence of events and are not shown in this table.

c) 4:1–2 which mention travel to Jacob "[ ] from Abel Mayyin";
d) 4:4 description of a vision mentioning something below Levi and high as heaven and then the gates of heaven and an angel.

The authors have reached the conclusion that this body of material from 2:4–4:4 originally stood in the lacuna between chapters 2 (Cambridge col. b) and 4:9 (Bodleian col. a), which is item no. 3 in the numbered list above.[36] The reasons for this conclusion are the following:

1. 2:4–5 are not part of the incident related in chapter 3, but the end of a preceding event. Note that both 2:4 and 3:1 start with τότε and nothing in the text indicates a necessary narrative continuity between them. This is enhanced by the fact that the laundering of garments and washing of the body, actions typical of Levitical purity (see Numbers 8:21), do not occur anywhere else preceding a prayer or an apocalyptic vision experience, but instead are usually related to a cultic, priestly act (see *ALD* 7:1–2, 8:2 and 10:6) or to ritual impurity. Two possibilities emerge. If, as we think, the text here refers to two different incidents, then this purification is the end of a ceremony. Alternatively, if the same incident is being described, then this passage shows the transfer of Levitical purity to the context of prayer. We think that the former alternative is the more probable since we tend to link chapter 2 with the Wars of the Sons of Jacob or some similar events.[37] Consequently, the impurity may have been the result either of the Shechem incident or of the wars of the sons of Jacob (if indeed they were included in *ALD*) or whatever other incident is referred to in Cambridge col. b.

J. Baumgarten has espoused the view that the ablution is connected with the prayer. He adduces only two examples of immersion before prayer, Judith 12:7[38] and *Sibylline Oracles* 4:165. Judith 12:7 is a specific narrative context while *Sibylline Oracles* "calls upon penitents to wash their whole bodies 'in perennial rivers' before stretching out their hands to heaven".[39] Yet an examination of the

[36] They are not the only persons to do so. For example, Philonenko, 1987, 834–36 actually introduces the prayer into his translation of *TPL* following 2:3.

[37] See below, commentary on 2:1. See Greenfield and Stone, 1990, 156–57 and in detail Stone and Greenfield, 1993, 249–250.

[38] See Grintz, 1957, ad loc. and references there.

[39] Baumgarten, 2003, 395.

whole context, lines 163–165, shows exactly the sequence of killing, immersion, stance and prayer that we are positing here. "Ah, wretched mortals, change these things, and do not lead the great God to all sorts of anger, but abandon daggers and groanings, murders, and outrages, and wash your whole bodies in perennial rivers and, stretching your hands to heaven, seek forgiveness for your former deeds, and with praises ask pardon for your bitter ungodliness."[40]

2. The second reason for placing this passage here is that it contains the beginning of a vision. This occurs in 4:3–6. Levi was in a prone position; he saw the heavens, apparently standing in his vision on a high place or mountain, and the gates of heaven were opened to him and one angel . . . and then the text breaks off. Now, the beginning of Bodleian col. a, 4:9–12, is the end of a vision. Levi received an eschatological prophecy. He is beloved more than all flesh and granted an anointing of eternal peace. Then, we are told, "the seven" (i.e., angels) left him (4:12) and he awoke from his sleep and hid the matter in his heart.

There has been considerable debate about whether *ALD* contained one vision or two. It is possible that one single vision was found here, starting in 4:3 and ending in 4:12 with the loss of substantial text between. The vision might have had two parts, one a vision of the heavens with a single angel and the other, a descent of seven angels to anoint and bless Levi. The other possibility is that there were two visions, one of the heavens and a second one of the seven angels and of Levi's anointing. There is nothing in the surviving text of *ALD* to incline us in one or the other direction.[41]

The chief witness invoked to resolve this conundrum is *TPL*.[42] The overall relationship between *ALD* and *TPL* is amply evident from the parallels that we give at the end of each chapter of *ALD* below, and we are far from being the first to observe the rather obvious

[40] Baumgarten, 2003, 393–97 speaks of the apparent similarities between blessings set after immersion at Qumran and the prayer preceeded by immersion in *ALD*. We fail to see the similarity and Baumgarten himself observes differences in both position and the content of prayer in *ALD* and the blessings at Qumran.

[41] See discussion by de Jonge, 1988, 375–76.

[42] This matter was particularly central to R. Kugler's thesis, put forward in his book, Kugler, 1996. See also de Jonge, 1999, 82–83. Hultgård, 1982, 2.93–123 analyses this relationship in detail. He concludes that *ALD* is a source document used, sometimes maladroitly, by *TPL*. See particularly pp. 106–07.

parallels between the two documents. In 1907 Cowley and Charles entitled their article, "An Early Source of the Testaments of the Twelve Patriarchs".[43] The scholarly discussion continues, however, on the issue of just how the author/redactor of *TPL* used *ALD* and, consequently, to what extent can we argue back from the structure of *TPL* to recover the structure of *ALD*.[44] It is not our intention here to attempt to resolve this issue, for such an attempt should form part of an overall study of the editorial techniques and composition of the *Testaments of the Twelve Patriarchs*.

In attempting to clarify the relationship between the two writings on the point at issue, M. de Jonge makes the following observations:

a. *TPL* omits the text of the prayer, though it has the phrase ηὐξάμην κυρίῳ ὅπως σωθῶ "I prayed to the Lord that I might be saved" (*TPL* 2:4), which may be a passing allusion to the extensive prayer found in *ALD*.

b. M. de Jonge considers, however, that there are definite points of contact between *ALD* 4:1–6 (the narrative following the prayer) and *TPL*. He points to *TPL* 2:5 τότε ἐπέπεσεν ἐπ' ἐμὲ ὕπνος "Then a sleep fell upon me" (cf. *ALD* 4:3) and *TPL* 5:1 τὰς πύλας τοῦ οὐρανοῦ "the gates of heaven". In full, *TPL* 5:1 reads: "The angel opened to me the gates of heaven, and I saw the holy temple and the Most High upon a throne of glory." De Jonge points out that the words τὰς πύλας τοῦ οὐρανοῦ are "in any case awkward after the descriptions of several heavens in the previous chapters" of *TPL*, thus strengthening the argument for the dependence of *TPL* 5:1 on *ALD*.[45] We have argued elsewhere that the vision of the heavens in *TPL* 3–5 is complex and contains various elements and that the section starting in 5:1 may be secondary.[46] Whatever view is taken of the growth of the vision of the heavens, however, it contains enough

[43] Cowley and Charles, 1907, 566.

[44] Compare de Jonge, 1988, 374–388; Kugler, 1996, 171–220. See most recently Stone, 2003, 429–437 and in further detail, Stone and Greenfield, 1993, 248–250. The discussion is summarized by de Jonge, 1999, 77–83, 87. Compare also Becker, 1970, 75.

[45] De Jonge, 1974, 138. For his most recent view, which is not very different, see de Jonge, 1999, 80–81. M.E. Stone has argued elsewhere that the transfer of "the gates of heaven" from before the vision, as in *ALD*, to the middle of it in *TPL* 5:1 is part of the reworking of *ALD* materials by the author redactor of *TPL*. On this issue, see Stone, 2003, 432–37. See in further detail, Stone and Greenfield, 1993, 248–250. Both Hultgård, 1982, 2.93–123 and Kugler, 1996, 171–220 have extensive comparisons between *ALD* and *TPL*.

[46] Stone, 2003.

elements from *ALD* to confirm, together with the explicit statement in *ALD* 4:5–6, that that work did contain a vision of the heavens.

Equally clearly, *ALD* 4:9–13 are the end of a vision in which seven figures (in all probability angels) leave Levi, blessing him and mentioning his anointing (4:9–12). Moreover, 4:7 (1QLevi frag. 1) at least, formed part of the vision of his investiture. The text then relates that Levi awoke and hid the matter in his heart (4:13). Moreover, in 5:2 Jacob learns in a dream that Levi is a priest. As a result, he gave him a tithe "in accordance with his vow". *ALD* does not tell us what the vow was, and it was probably contained in the lost text preceding 4:9.

It seems likely that the vow refers to Jacob's promise in Genesis 28:22 ". . . and of all that you give me, I will set aside a tithe for you" (JPS; and see *Jubilees* 27:27). Later, the biblical story relates, God sent Jacob to Bethel to build the altar there, which he did (Genesis 35:1–5).[47] According to *Jubilees* 31, Jacob urged his family to go to Bethel to fulfill his vow, building the altar and setting up a pillar "on the first of the seventh month" (*Jubilees* 31:3). Neither Genesis 35:1–5 nor *Jubilees* 31 mentions giving the tithe in this context. According to *Jubilees* 31:26, Jacob took his son to visit his parents, telling his father all his adventures, among them "the vow that he had made to the Lord, the vision that he had seen, that he had built an altar and everything was ready for offering the sacrifice before the Lord that he had vowed". Issac refused to come because of his age, but sent Jacob's mother with them, saying to him, "Be successful and carry out the vow that you made. Do not delay (in carrying out) your vow . . ." (verse 29). The following night Jacob stayed at Bethel, where "Levi dreamed that he—he and his sons—had been appointed and made into the priesthood of the Most High forever". The next morning, on the 14th day of the seventh month, Jacob "gave a tithe of everything which had come with him—from people to animals, from money to all utensils and clothing. He gave a tithe of everything" (32:2).

Thus, after Levi was anointed in his dream as a priest, Jacob fulfilled his vow and gave him the tithe. Later, after Jacob actually invested Levi in priestly garb (*Jubilees* 32:3), Levi started to sacrifice and Jacob gave him a second tithe (32:9), which was used by the

[47] See VanderKam, 2000 and Kugel, 1993, 2–3.

author of *Jubilees* to teach the laws of the second tithe (verses 10–15). The fulfilment of the vow through Levi shows, as suggested by VanderKam, that the author of *Jubilees* was using the tradition found in *ALD*, directly or indirectly, and in addition to making Levi the "the ancestor of the priest . . . he also had to document how his hero Jacob had in fact tithed and thus fulfilled his earlier vow".[48]

As a result, Levi and his descendants were recognized by Jacob as priests and Jacob invested him with the priestly garments. So, Jacob repeats in the real world the investiture that Levi had received in the vision. Then Levi became priest of God and offered sacrifices and blessed his father and brother, exercising the privilege of blessing that appertained to his priestly status. These three elements are preserved in a second vision in *TPL* 8. Considering the seven angels, the priestly associations of the blessing in *ALD* 4:11 and the fact that Jacob and Isaac subsequently recognize Levi's priestly status (5:2–8), it is reasonable to infer that the lost material between the 4:6 and 4:9 related a vision of Levi's priestly consecration and investiture parallel in import to *TPL* 8:2–17.

We must remark, however, that the wording of the benediction and prophecy in *ALD*, as far as it survives (4:9–11), differs from that of *TPL* 8, despite some overall resemblances.

To summarize our conclusions then:

a. *TPL* 2:4 knew the prayer of Levi, but only included a reference to it.
b. The vision starting in *ALD* 4:4 was of the heavens and its content was reworked by *TPL* 2:5–5:1.[49]
c. The vision ending in *ALD* 4:9–13 was a vision of Levi's consecration and investiture, on the whole resembling *TPL* 8:2–17. This vision ended with the words, "And those seven departed from me" (4:12). It included Jacob's vow.
d. It remains impossible to determine whether these two visions were part of a single, two-tiered vision experience or were two separate visions, linked by narrative. The loss of continuous text

[48] VanderKam, 2000, 551. See further in *Jubilees* 32:3, where Jacob counts his sons and Levi is the tenth, see discussion with parallel sources in VanderKam, 2000, 551–53.

[49] In Stone, 2003 we argued that the commissioning of Levi to destroy Shechem in *TPL* chapter 5 was probably introduced as part of the editorial reworking of the source material drawn from *ALD*.

between 4:6 and 4:9 prevents a determination of this point. If *TPL* is any indication, there were two separate but linked vision experiences.[50]

e. An additional complication is that 3:4 implies that Levi is surrounded by his children. This implies a narrative context not evident from the surviving textual material.[51]

The first editor of 1QLevi, J.T. Milik, proposed that two fragments of this manuscript precede 4:9, the beginning of Bodleian col. a. These are frag. 1 and frag. 7. These both are apparently part of the eschatological blessing, and seem not out of tune with what is to be found in 4:9–11. We have accepted Milik's proposal and regard the fragments as belonging in the lacuna between 4:6 and 4:9. We have numbered them 4:7 and 4:8 respectively.

In Bodleian col. a, and in the text preceding it, Levi is consecrated as a priest. This takes place on a visionary level in the dream vision described in *TPL* 8. It is quite bizarre to read in 4:13 "And I hid this too in my heart and I revealed it to nobody".[52] Then, in 5:1 "we" went to Isaac, who "כדן" blessed me. We translated "thus", but if this text was behind *TPL* 9:1 then Judah and Levi went to Isaac and "the father of my father blessed me according to all the words of my visions" (9:2).[53] So, perhaps the word כדן should be taken to mean "according to this (i.e., this vision)". Isaac knew that Levi had been consecrated even though Levi hid it "in his heart", and he blessed him. This is an anticipation of 5:7 and, in some ways, a doublet of it. One wonders what the actual function of this verse might have been.[54]

A final issue remains. Some have maintained that 4QLevi[b] frags. 3–4 relate to the Dinah incident. The name of Dinah is not mentioned, and what we have is third person narrative which refers to a woman who has desecrated her name and that of her father and brothers. The last three lines of this fragment are eschatological,

[50] Kugler, 1996, 47–50, 52–59 and 77–87 argues vigorously that there was only one vision experience. His arguments were not persuasive, and see the review by Morgenstern, 1999, 135–37.

[51] Greenfield and Stone, 1990, 155–56.

[52] This was the source of *TPL* 8:18–19.

[53] So Hollander and de Jonge, 1985, 155.

[54] For a review of scholarly opinion on the "scope and shape" and date of *ALD*, see Kugler, 1996, 28–33, 131–34.

saying that "the name of the righteous will not be wiped out from all her people for ever. [ ] for all the generation of eternity" and it then refers to "holy tithe a sacrifice for teaching (?)". Nothing we know about Dinah helps us to contextualize this material, nor does it have any sort of parallel or echo in *TPL*.[55] Therefore, we are not persuaded that it relates to Dinah and we have left it among the unplaced fragments.[56]

Now that these points have been clarified, we are in a position to present the structure of *ALD*, and with it our division of the material into chapters and verses.

- No chapter numbers assigned: Loss of an undefined body of material, at least 14 lines, but perhaps of considerably more, preceding Cambridge a. It must have contained part of the Dinah events.
- *Chapter 1* The Story of Dinah (Cambridge a)
- *Lacuna* of two columns and 14 lines in which there was the inception of whatever incident is referred to in Chapter 2, perhaps the Wars of the Sons of Jacob.
- *Chapter 2* (Cambridge b) In spite of the mention of Shechem, Cambridge b does not seem to accord with anything in the known versions of the Dinah incident. Shechem was in the area in which Jacob and his sons pastured. The fragment might be associated with the Wars of the Sons of Jacob or some other incident.
- *Lacuna* following this, in which we place: 1QLevi frag. 8 (2:2–3) and Athos Greek 1–2 (2:4–5). We regard these as part of Chapter 2.
- *Chapter 3* Levi's Prayer, placed in the same lacuna.[57]
- *Chapter 4* Travels and Vision(s) of Levi still mostly placed in the lacuna. It comprises part of 4QLevi^b frag. 1, col. 2 (4:1–6), 1QLevi frag. 1 (4:7), 1QLevi frag. 7 (4:8) and Bodleian a, lines 1–13 (4:9–13 old §§1–7). The text henceforth is all sequential.
- *Chapter 5* Levi's Priesthood, Blessing and Instruction (old §§8–13)
- *Chapter 6* Priestly Teaching—Purity (old §§14–18)
- *Chapter 7* Priestly Teaching—Wood Offering (old §§19–25a)
- *Chapter 8* Priestly Teaching—Sacrifices (old §§25b–31)

[55] But note the usage of חלל here, to be compared with טמא in 2:1.
[56] See Appendix "Unplaced Fragments".
[57] See Greenfield and Stone, 1990, 156–57. Stone and Greenfield, 1993, 249–250.
[58] Kugler, 1996, 28–33 and 171–74 reviews scholarly opinion on the overall form

- *Chapter 9* The Measures of Wood, Salt, Fine Flour, Oil, Wine and Frankincense (old §§32a–47)
- *Chapter 10* Concluding Injunctions and Blessing (old §§48–61)
- *Chapter 11* Birth and Naming of Levi's Children (old §§62–72)
- *Chapter 12* Levi's Grandchildren and Great-Grandchildren (§§73–81)
- *Chapter 13* Levi's Teaching—The Wisdom Poem (old §§82–95 + 4QLevi[a] frag. 1, 4QLevi[e], 4QLevi[f])
- *A lacuna of indeterminate length follows.*

There remain a number of unplaced fragments, which are all gathered in the Appendix.[58]

4. *The Date and Provenance of* ALD

There is good reason to date *ALD* to the third century or very early second century BCE. First, the date of the oldest manuscripts (4QLevi[f]—Hasmonean) provides us with a *terminus ante quem*. Second, *ALD* is cited in the *Damascus Document*, a foundational document of the Qumran sect, which was probably composed in the second century BCE. Thus, *ALD* is older than the *Damascus Document*.[59] Third, *ALD* (or something very like it) served as a source for *Jubilees*,[60] which is

of *ALD* and its relationship to *TPL*. The resolution of the latter issue stands outside our present purview and we are loth to speculate about the overall form of the work. This means, by the way, that we have no view on where to place the "Unplaced Fragments", except for the *Prayer of Levi*, whose location is argued here.

[59] Greenfield, 1988, 321–22.

[60] See also Grelot, 1991, 255; de Jonge, 1988, 373–76 for an overview. The date of *Jubilees* is debated, e.g., Nickelsburg, 1981, 78–79 and 1984, 101–03. He dates it slightly earlier than does VanderKam, 1977, 214–285. Both agree that it is earlier than the settlement at Qumran. See Stone, 1988, 159–160, 168. At one time, de Jonge claimed that there existed a source document upon which both *Jubilees* and *ALD* drew, that was called "original Levi" (1953, 39). Later his view changed, see 1999, 79 and 89 where he says that his view "has not much to recommend it". Similarly, Kugler, 1996, 138 claims that a document, which he calls "Levi-apocryphon", existed and served as a source for *ALD* and *Jubilees*. Kugler, himself, in a more recent study has claimed that "[i]n the end we can only say confidently that comparison of the testament's contents with the earlier traditions reinforces the conclusion that the *Testaments* included as much Levi material as possible, and that strategy explains much of the testament's peculiar appearance" (Kugler, 2001, 49). Becker, on the other hand, holds that *ALD* and *Jubilees*, as well as *TPL* go back to common oral traditions (1970, 86). His arguments are not convincing and, indeed, we have seen no considerations that compel us in the direction of either of these points of view. Milik, 1976, 24 has maintained that *ALD* is of exceptional antiquity

usually dated in the first third of the second century BCE. Its date makes *ALD* one of the most ancient of the Pseudepigrapha.[61] *ALD*'s original language has been debated but, despite some Hebraisms listed above, it seems to have been written in Aramaic.[62]

ALD says nothing directly about its provenance, nor would such statements be expected in a pseudepigraphon. Here we shall set forth a number of characteristics of the document that may hint at the character of the group that produced it. We list them in summary form, in order to give an overall view and they are analyzed later in this Introduction and in the Commentary.

First, it seems that *ALD* employs a solar calendar resembling that promoted by *1 Enoch, Jubilees* and the Qumran sectarian writings.[63] In the surviving fragments of *ALD*, however, no polemics surround the use of the solar calendar. This contrasts with the situation in *1 Enoch* and *Jubilees*.[64]

Second, it takes a very extreme position on the centrality of the priesthood. Both royal and priestly characteristics are attributed to Levi.[65] Royal language is used of the priesthood, and verses typical of Judah and the royal messiah are attributed to Levi. This is most unusual. Now, a dual Messianism is encountered in the Second Temple period, from Zechariah (4:14) and through a number of Second Temple period texts, such as 1QS 9:11. The dual role of Levi and Judah in *Testaments of the Twelve Patriarchs* is part of the same pattern. A single Davidic Messiah is encountered in other Second Temple period texts, such as *Psalms of Solomon* 18.[66] The third possibility, the combination of royal and priestly characteristics in a

---

and of Samaritan origin. This seems unlikely. See also Kugel, 1993, 52–58 and, for the summary of other scholars' opinion concerning this issue, see Kugler, 2001, 49. Wacholder, 1990 called some of the Aramaic texts "pre-Qumranic" and this idea has had some circulation.

[61] A more general argument is put forward by some scholars, who would place all the Aramaic narrative materials earlier than the Qumran Hebrew texts. A survey of opinion on the date of *ALD* is given by Kugler, 1996, 131–35.

[62] The existence of a Hebrew source was urged, *inter alios*, by Grelot, 1955, especially 96–97. His arguments for the Hebrew original are mostly drawn from the onomastic midrashim in chapter 11 and we have explored them in the commentary there.

[63] Greenfield and Stone, 1979, 224.

[64] Stone, 2000b, 486. On implications of this attitude see, Stone, 1988, 168.

[65] See Section "Levi's Special Role in *ALD*" below.

[66] On this see VanderKam, 2000, 462–475.

single Levitical messiah as found in *ALD* is most unusual. One is led to wonder, however, whether the expression "Messiah of Aaron and Israel" occurring in *Damascus Document* 12:23–13:1, 14:19 and 20:1; 4QD[a] (4Q266) 10 1:12, 4QD[d] (4Q269) 1 51:2 might not bear re-examination.[67]

A third characteristic is the stress on the purity of the levitical line and its descent.[68] Great importance is attributed to endogamy in the descent of those who were to become Aaronids.[69] This concern for the purity of descent is reflected more broadly in *Jubilees*, referring to various of the patriarchs.[70]

Fourth, *ALD* stresses the transmission of the priestly lore from generation to generation. Levi was instructed by Isaac (*ALD* 5:8); Isaac received the priestly teaching from Abraham (*ALD* 7:4) and Abraham's learning went back to Noah and the Book of Noah (*ALD* 10:10). This concern for the transmission of teaching from the generation of the flood and before, is to be encountered in various forms in the literature of the time.[71]

Fifth, *ALD* professes distinctive ideas about two spirits, apotropaic prayer and demonology.[72] It is the oldest work to speak of two spirits and to set them into opposition. It is one of the very first works to speak of "satan" as the name of a type of demon, and the terminology that it uses of the exorcism of such a demon stands squarely in the tradition of Jewish apotropaic prayer.[73]

Sixth, *ALD* already features the special, paradigmatic role of Joseph. He is attributed chiefly wisdom characteristics and serves as an example whom Levi presents to his offspring. This has two implications: first, a development of the wisdom dimension of the figure of Joseph,

[67] On Qumran Messianic views, see Ringgren, 1963, 167–182, especially 169–170, where he interprets the singular as a plural and Cross, 1995, 158–59 who does not specify the issue. A recent outline article with extensive bibliography is by Craig Evans, 2000, 1.537–542. On p. 540 he deals with what he calls "messianism as diarchy", implying that the single messiah pattern is standard. However, he offers no explanation of either the designation "of Aaron" or of the situation in the *Damascus Document*.

[68] See Stone, 1988, 169; Greenfield and Stone, 1979, 223–24.

[69] The same concern for endogamy is expressed in a different context in the genealogy of Bilhah in 4QNaphtali. See Stone, DJD 22, 73–82; Stone, 1996a.

[70] Halpern-Amaru, 1999, 9–31.

[71] Stone, 1999.

[72] Stone and Greenfield, 1993, 252.

[73] Flusser, 1966; Eshel, 1999.

which may be related to the growth of mantic wisdom during the Second Temple period. Second, that Joseph was paradigmatic at the indubitably Jewish level of the tradition, before the typology of Joseph and Christ came into play.[74]

Finally, *ALD* does not bear distinctive marks of Qumran sectarian language. Yet, in view of its calendar, two spirits and other similar features, it seems most likely that it should be attributed to the wing of Judaism in the third century BCE of which the Qumran sectarians were one group of descendants. This wing was priestly in character, though one might query whether *ALD* comes from a group connected with the Jerusalem temple, or an opposition group of some kind, though no polemical characteristics can be detected.

5. *Notes on the Language of* ALD

As early as 1953, de Jonge in collaboration with P.R. Weiss published their notes on the Aramaic of the *Aramaic Levi Document* from the Geniza.[75] They noted that in general its language resembles Targum Onqelos and the grammar and lexicography of the Babylonian Talmud, while noting some "forms peculiar to Biblical Aramaic" (among them the infinitive form לאלפותך with the ות- suffix, and the infinitive לפקדה, לאלפא without preformative *mem*). They also identified some Syriac words נחשירותא, נישפא and נצפתא).[76] According to their view, "[t]he original Testament of Levi to which the fragments as well as the Greek Testament go back was written originally in Hebrew" (they are referring, of course, to the "original Levi" work they assumed to have existed).[77]

In 1979, after examining the Geniza manuscript and the only fragment from Qumran that had been published at that time (4QLevi^b 1), J.C. Greenfield produced the first discussion of the language of the *ALD*. He focused mainly on the special grammatical forms introduced into the Geniza manuscript (e.g., the emphatic plural with *hē*

[74] See "General Notes" in the commentary to chapter 13.

[75] De Jonge, 1953, 129–131 and 169, note 7 where he acknowledges his dependence upon P.R. Weiss for most of the material concerning the type of Aramaic in *ALD*.

[76] De Jonge, 1953, 131.

[77] De Jonge, 1953, 131.

instead of the usual *aleph*; 3rd person singular feminine suffix ending with *hē* + *aleph* as well as some Hebraisms in vocabulary and syntax).[78] He concluded that, although the Qumran manuscripts were not yet fully published, one can see that in general, the morphology, lexicography and grammar of both Qumran and Geniza manuscripts are similar, and resemble those of Onqelos.[79] In his view, the copyist of the Geniza fragment was responsible for introducing *scripta defectiva* as well as some later forms. Thus, he concluded that *ALD* was composed in Standard Literary Aramaic and its medieval copyist introduced some later forms. In 1996, in their final edition of the Qumran manuscripts of *ALD*, Stone and Greenfield discussed some further issues concerning its grammar and added some new features concerning the relationship between the language of the Qumran fragment and that of the Geniza manuscript.[80]

Three years later, J.A. Fitzmyer contributed a study of the language of *ALD*.[81] According to Fitzmyer, as a result of the differences between the Qumran and the Geniza manuscripts of *ALD*, one should distinguish between Qumran "Middle Aramaic" (200 BCE and 200 CE) in which the Qumran texts are written (a slightly more developed language than the Imperial Aramaic of the Book of Daniel)[82] and the Geniza "Late Aramaic".[83] Other relevant studies of the Standard Literary Aramaic were carried out by E.M. Cook, M. Sokoloff and S.E. Fassberg.[84]

Today, although only 33 of the 115 Aramaic texts from Qumran remain to be published, and some of these are already in public domain in the various forms, still no comprehensive study of the Aramaic language of the Qumran texts has been published. The writers hope that this lacuna will soon be filled. The focus of this book, however, is not exclusively, or even mainly grammatical and

[78] Greenfield and Stone, 1979, 227–29.
[79] See also Stone and Greenfield, DJD 22, 4 note 9.
[80] Stone and Greenfield, DJD 22, 4–5, 27, 38, 44, 54 and 62–63.
[81] Fitzmyer, 1999.
[82] Fitzmyer, 1999, 459–464: see also his comments in 2000, 1.49. His characterization of the literary Aramaic of Qumran differs from that of Greenfield in a number of respects.
[83] This dialect includes, in addition to features noted by Greenfield and Stone, instances such as the shift of the pronominal suffix of the first person plural from *-na*ʾ to *-nan* (e.g. אחונן, אבונן), found also as a verb אמרנן, see Fitzmyer, 1999, 459–464.
[84] Cook, 1998, 359–378; Sokoloff, 2000b; Fassberg, 2002.

so the following remarks on the language of *ALD* are not intended to be exhaustive. We seek only to note some issues relating to the orthography and grammar of the Qumran and Geniza manuscripts, as well as some comparisons between these two Aramaic texts.

In orthography, the most striking phenomenon is the change from the *scripta defectiva* in the Qumran manuscripts to a full orthography in the Geniza copy. Comparing the Qumran manuscripts with one another reveals that 4QLevi[a], 4QLevi[d] and 4QLevi[f]—the last being the earliest copy and dated to the Hasmonean period—are all written in *scripta defectiva*; while 1QLevi, 4QLevi[b] and 4QLevi[c] use a fuller spelling.

Other orthographic phenomena of the Qumran manuscripts are the following: the emphatic state singular of both masculine and feminine ends with *aleph*, (e.g., קשטא, צדקתא 13:3 4QLevi[a], ב]אישא, זנותא 3:5 4QLevi[b] and ירכתא 8:4 4QLevi[d]); the masculine plural emphatic is יא- (e.g., ספריא 13:16 4QLevi[a]); the third person feminine singular possessive suffix with plural nouns is simply *hē*, rather than *hē ʾaleph* found in the 1QapGen and other Qumran Aramaic texts (e.g., ידעיה 13:10 4QLevi[a]). It is noteworthy that in two instances in 4QLevi[b] an *ʾaleph* was written following the *hē*, but subsequently removed: see also Geniza 13:10 קניהא.[85] In the Qumran manuscripts, in contrast to earlier Aramaic orthography, *waw* is found in the imperfect second and third person plural (e.g., יחזון and יעלון 13:12 4QLevi[a]). Note particularly תהוון (4QLevi[a] frag. 4:8). In 4QLevi[a] the *qal* infinitive למאלף preserves the radical *ʾaleph* (13:7), but in the same manuscript one can also find the form תתא without the *ʾaleph* (4QLevi[a] frag. 4:7).

Finally, the Qumran manuscripts add some unique lexicographical items, such as the nouns שיטו (13:5), מטמרה (13:13) and the verb מח״ל (13:7) in 4QLevi[a]; חסיה and חבל + שם (4QLevi[b] frags. 3–4:5–6); and the forms עע (7:5, see below), סינדה (7:6) and אדסא (7:6) in 4QLevi[f].[86]

In Qumran Aramaic we find a preference for *sin* rather than *samek*, e.g., שימה 13:10 (4QLevi[a]) and שניאין 13:9 (4QLevi[a], changed to סימא and סניאין in the Geniza as expected). In one instance, the reverse

[85] Frags. 3–4:6 אבוה there are signs of erasure after the *hē*; and in the same line we observe עמהא, but the *ʾaleph* is crossed out with a vertical line. The *ʾaleph* is found on the singular עמהא in 11:10 (Geniza).

[86] See discussion on these forms in Stone and Greenfield, DJD 22, 62–63.

shift occurs: לב[סרון in 4QLevi[a] is parallel to לבשרון in the Geniza manuscript (13:5). This is probably to be explained as a hypercorrection.

The Geniza manuscript, as expected in a medieval manuscript, includes many later Aramaic forms, e.g., התחמיון and not התחזיון (1:3), etc.,[87] yet it also preserves some old forms, such as the expression על[דברת די (1:1), found in Biblical Aramaic (Daniel 2:30) as well as some other archaizing language.[88] Note also the usage of the *haf'el* in the Geniza instead of the *'af'el* form (e.g., להנסקה 7:3 4QLevi[d] ל]אֿס[קה) and the noun אע (7:5–6) found in the Geniza, while in 4QLev[f] the parallel in 7:5 reads עע. The later form (אע) is also found in Targum Onqelos and Targum Jonathan, and is to be explained as a dissimilation of the first *'ayin*.[89]

In other words, the Geniza manuscript exhibits features which are to be expected in a medieval "modernization" of a text from antiquity.

6. *Testaments and Other Associated Works from Qumran*

In this section we shall present documents from the Dead Sea Scrolls which might be related in one way or another to *TPatriarchs*. Since *ALD* is a source of *TPL*, as is shown below, it is conceivable that among the Qumran manuscripts there exist other works which also served the author/redactor of *TPatriarchs*. Indeed, a number of scholars, including Milik, Baillet and Puech have regarded some small fragments as possible parts of *TPatriarchs*. Testamental compositions related to the patriarchs have been identified, including Hebrew *Testaments of Naphtali* and *Judah*, as well as Aramaic *Testaments of Judah* and *Joseph*. In this section, we will assess these identifications as well as enumerating other testamental texts related to the Levitical priestly line, particularly Kohath and Amram, and texts identified as an *Apocryphon of Levi*.

[87] See Commentary on 1:3, but חז"י is still the usual form.

[88] Greenfield listed the following words as archaic forms: אבוכון (13:2), לכון (13:2), עובדיכון (13:3), עמכון (13:3), קושטא (13:3), טאב (13:3), חוכמתָה (13:10), חוכמתה (13:9, 13:10), אליף (13:5), כולהון (5:5, 13:9), כולה (4:9, 4:11), עותר (13:10), הנון (13:1), הציתו (13:2), מהחוי (13:2), ת<הנ>עלון (13:3) and מהותבין (13:10). Note that almost all are found in the wisdom poem.

[89] Sokoloff, 2000b, 749.

Texts Related to the Testaments of the Twelve Patriarchs

4Q215 (4QNaph) is a Hebrew text dubbed *Testament of Naphtali* by Milik.[90] The official edition of this text was prepared by M.E. Stone,[91] who noted that it includes two separate narrative units. One, the birth and naming of Bilhah, closely resembles text found in the Greek *Testament of Naphtali (TPNaphtali)* 1:9–12. This text was also available to Rabbi Moses the Preacher of Narbonne (eleventh century) who included it in his *Midrash Berešit rabbati*. The second part, marked off by a blank line, relates how Laban gave Hannah, Bilhah's mother, to Jacob, and also mentions Dan's birth. The editor demonstrated that R. Moses had a Hebrew or Aramaic source document and that, at a number of points, his citation is closer to 4QNaph than it is to *TPNaphtali*. Thus he concludes, that "there existed developed traditions regarding Naphtali, but both their origin and the reason for their preservation over the centuries remain enigmatic".[92] Other than *ALD*, this is the only document from Qumran that seems to have served as a direct or indirect literary source of part of *TPatriarchs*.[93]

An additional Hebrew text, 3Q7, was identified by Baillet as related to the *Testament of Judah*.[94] This comprises six small fragments, on which only few complete words can be read;[95] and 4Q484 (4QTestament of Judah [?]), which he associates with it, includes nineteen even smaller fragments, yielding the name Issachar and some partial words.[96] Reading "the angel of presence" (מלאך הפנים) and the name of Levi (and reconstructing Zebulun and Issachar) in 3Q7, Baillet related this document to *TPJudah* 24–25. Yet, as Baillet himself admitted, "d'une part les lectures sont trop incertains, et de l'autre il est improbable que l'on puisse avoir à Q[oumran] un texte

[90] Milik, 1978, 97 also attributed a second plate to this manuscript, but it was shown to be from a different document called *4QTime of Righteousness*. See Chazon and Stone, DJD 36, 172–184.

[91] Stone, DJD 22, 71–82.

[92] Stone, DJD 22, 73–75. The quotation is from p. 75.

[93] See the general remarks in Hollander and de Jonge, 1985, 20–23. Nickelsburg, 1981, argues "that the existence of a testament of Naphtali would almost require the conception of twelve patriarchs, given the relative obscurity of that patriarch" (p. 234). See, however, the material assembled by Stone, 1988, which indicates that Naphtali may have had a more substantial role in antiquity.

[94] See Milik 1978, 98–99.

[95] Baillet, DJD 3, 99, plate 18.

[96] DJD 7, 3, plate 1.

très voisin du grec".[97] Later, in fact, 4Q484 was identified by E. Puech as parts of the *Book of Jubilees*.[98] We propose that 3Q7 should also be connected with the *Book of Jubilees* or another related composition, perhaps, as suggested by Baillet, "une source des Testaments".[99] Thus, no fragments of *TPJudah* or any obvious source of *TPJudah* have been identified at Qumran.

J. Starcky, in the card concordance of the Dead Sea Scrolls, first identified 4Q538, an Aramaic text, as *TBenjamin*. Subsequently Milik identified it as *TJudah*,[100] a title accepted by its editor E. Puech.[101] It is comparatively large in size[102] and speaks in first person singular of someone who "[. . . o]n my neck and hugged me" (4Q538 1:6). It also mentions Joseph twice. This was thought to refer to the story of Joseph in Egypt (Genesis 42–47; *Jubilees* 42–46) and particularly to his reunion with his brothers (Genesis 45; *Jubilees* 43). This text's identification as a *Testament of Judah* was based on the major role Judah plays in the biblical story and especially his speech at the brothers' reunion. Indeed, a short reference to the reunion is found in the Greek *TPJudah* 12:11–12, so *Testament of Judah* was seen to be an appropriate title for 4Q538. A closer examination uncovers problems with this identification:

a. In the Bible, Joseph ". . . embraced his brother Benjamin around the neck and wept, and Benjamin wept on his neck" (Genesis 45:14)—Benjamin and not Judah.
b. Other testaments in *TPatriarchs* mention Joseph's attitude toward his brothers, e.g., *TPZebulun* 8:4 and *TPSimeon* 4:3–7; but in neither of them nor in *TPJudah* 12:11, is the actual reunion described. In *TPJudah* 12:11 the event is summarized in a short sentence, "And after this we came into Egypt to Joseph, because of the famine". This sentence has no parallel to 4Q538.

Thus we may conclude (a) that there is no clear evidence that this text is a testament; and (b) there is no evidence for its connection with Judah. All we can say is that it is an Aramaic text, probably

[97] Baillet, DJD 3, 99.
[98] Puech, 1999.
[99] DJD 3, 99.
[100] Milik, 1978, 97–98.
[101] DJD 31, 191.
[102] DJD 31, 194–99.

referring to the reunion of Joseph with his brothers. It might conceivably have belonged to the pool of Jewish traditions upon which the author/redactor of *TPatriarchs* drew. It is certainly not a source of *TPJudah* and there is no reason to entitle it *Testament of Judah*.

Other "Testament" Texts

Milik suggested identifying 4Q539 as *Testament of Joseph*,[103] which identification was accepted by its editor, Puech.[104] However, this identification is also problematic. It is an address to the speaker's children, שמׄעו בני [. . . אצי]תו לי חביבי "Listen my sons . . . pay attention my beloved". In *ALD* very similar language precedes a wisdom hymn. Thus, the hortative opening is not necessarily part of a testament. A reference to בׄני דדי ישׄמׄעׄא]ל "the sons of my cousin Ishmae[l" (3:2) does not seem to refer to Jospeh's sale, as suggested by Puech.[105] Thus this document cannot be shown unambiguously to belong to the genre of testament, and *a fortiori*, cannot be shown to be a "Testament of Joseph".

Another problematic identification is the so-called *Testament of Jacob* (4Q537). As Puech noted,[106] this text resembles the angelic vision in *Jubilees* 32:17–19, foretelling Jacob's future as well as that of his sons. Perhaps this text is a source of the angelic vision in *Jubilees*, but several significant elements found in *Jubilees* are lacking here, including the specification of seven tablets and the opposition to Jacob's desire to build a temple at Bethel (*Jubilees* 32:21–22). Milik argues, not unreasonably, that in 4Q537 the tablets talk about Jacob's future and refer to the Exodus from Egypt.[107] Although Bethel is not mentioned in this fragment, it seems quite clear that the context is Jacob's vision. The place name Bethel does occur, moreover, in 4Q537 frag. 14 which refers to a battle and also mentions Beer Zaith and Rimmon.[108] Perhaps, 4Q537 expands the tradition about the wars of the sons of Jacob southwards,[109] or refers to the story

[103] Milik, 1978, 101–02.
[104] DJD 31, 201.
[105] DJD 31, 207.
[106] DJD 31, 173 and 176.
[107] Milik, 1978, 104.
[108] DJD 31, 183–84.
[109] Probably also the subject of *ALD* chapter 2 (see discussion there).

of the fight between the tribes of Benjamin and the other tribes of Israel, according to Judges 21. There is nothing in 4Q537 to indicate that it is a testament. It is best characterized as a vision and in our view, it should so be titled.

For completeness' sake, we should mention two additional texts dubbed "Testament (?)", 4Q526 of which only one fragment containing six words has survived, cannot be identified with any known work,[110] and 4Q581 which is still unpublished.[111]

Thus, the survey of the Qumran documents that have been identified in one way or another as parts of or sources of *TPatriarchs* yields only two such, *ALD* and 4QNaphtali. These are sources or very close to sources that were used by the author/redactor of *TPatriarchs*. None of the other works seems to be related in any direct way to *TPatriarchs*. Certain of them belong to the overall pool of traditions about the patriarchs that existed in the Second Temple period, while the relationship of others to the patriarchs is more tenuous.

The Testament of Qahat *and the* Visions of Amram

Two works from Qumran stand in a different relationship to *ALD* than that claimed for the documents mentioned above, *Testament of Qahat* and *Visions of Amram*. These two works have never been claimed to be sources of *TPatriarchs*, but share with *ALD* the association with the fathers of the priestly line.

Milik identified a text as *Testament of Qahat* (4Q542).[112] Addressed to "you, my son Amram" (4Q542 1 2:9), it resembles Levi's admonition to his sons (*ALD* 13:2) and is thus not necessarily part of a testament.[113] *ALD* and 4Q542 also share some ideas and phrases, such as the usage of the rare pair נכרי and כילי (see commentary to *ALD* 13:8). While in *ALD* it says that a wise man would be warmly welcomed everywhere, "and he is not li[ke] a stranger therein, and not like a scoundr[el . . .] in it" (13:8), in 4Q542 the listeners are warned not to give their heritage either to strangers or to scoundrels, because they will dishonor them. This heritage is identified as "all

[110] DJD 25, 179–181.
[111] The text is listed in Tov, DJD 39, 75.
[112] Milik, 1972, see also Puech, 1991.
[113] See Genealogical Table for the relationship between Levi, Qahat and Amram, and their wives.

my books as testimony" (4Q542 1 2:12). "The transmission of teaching to Amram from Abraham, via Isaac, Jacob and Levi is stressed."[114]

Ironically, the only real testament found among this group of texts is entitled *4QVisions of Amram*. Amram is prominent in a number of Second Temple writings such as Pseudo-Philo's *Biblical Antiquities* 9:1–10, while Josephus, *Antiquities* 1.212–217 knows of visions vouchsafed to Amram before the birth of Moses.[115] Yet, he has no prominent role in *Jubilees*, which is generally linked to *ALD* and *4QTestament of Qahat*.[116]

4QVisions of Amram was first published by J.T. Milik,[117] and later by E. Puech,[118] who thinks that the same scribe copied *4QTestament of Qahat* and *4QVisions of Amram*[a]. Remains of six and perhaps seven copies of *4QVisions of Amram* (4Q543–549) were found among the Dead Sea Scrolls. Milik dates the oldest manuscript *4QVisions of Amram*[b] to the second century BCE.

The beginning of the work has survived with the superscription: "Copy of the Book of the Words of the Visions of Amram" (4Q543 1a–c = col. 1). It is clearly a testament, being Amram's words to his children "on [the day of his death, in the year one hundred] and thirty-six, the year [of his death]".[119] Amram sees two angels in a dream vision (4Q544 1 = col. 2). One resembles a serpent and his garment is multicolored and dark, while the other has a smiling visage. They rule over all humans. These two beings were struggling over Amram and in a second, fragmentary column, Amram is called upon to make a decision between them. It identifies one figure as Malki-reša' associated with darkness, but the speaker is the angel who rules over light (4Q544 2 = col. 3). The name of the ruler of light has been lost from the manuscript, but it is often reconstructed as Malki-Ṣedeq. Other names found in the text are "ruler of light" and "ruler of darkness".

4QVisions of Amram refers to the dualism of light and darkness very typical of the Qumran sectarian documents, but the dualism of the

[114] See Stone, 2000c, 731. The preceding lines are much indebted to this article.

[115] Amram, together with Qahat and Levi, figures in the chain of transmission of *Sefer Harazim* from Adam to Noah (Morgan, 1983, 17).

[116] See Stone, 2000a, 23.

[117] Milik, 1972.

[118] DJD 31, 283–405.

[119] Puech, DJD 31, 322–334. Translation from García-Martínez and Tigchelaar, 1998, 2.1085.

two spirits is already present in *ALD* which clearly antedates both *4QVisions of Amram* and the Qumran sect. Thus, this element itself does not necessarily demonstrate that the document was written by the Qumran sect, and a pre- or extra-Qumran origin is quite possible.[120]

We should stress the relationship between *ALD*, *4QTestament of Qahat* and *4QVisions of Amram*, works associated with the generations of Levi down to Aaron, the direct father of the priestly line of Israel.[121] *ALD* is the oldest of these three and the other two works might be related to it and perhaps even depend on it to some extent. *4QTestament of Qahat* and *4QVisions of Amram* might have been written on the pattern of *ALD* to legitimate the continuity of the priestly line and its teaching.

An Apocryphal Text Apparently Related to ALD

Two manuscripts presumed to be copies of one composition dubbed *4QApocryphon of Levi* (4Q540–541), were first identified by Starcky as "Aharonique".[122] It was next titled *Testament* (or: *Visions*) *of Levi* by Milik and *Apocryphon of Levi* by Puech in the official edition.[123] 4Q540 is composed of three fragments, only one of which is sizeable, while 4Q541, comprises 24 fragments, some quite large, but none of which overlaps with 4Q540. Thus it would be wiser to speak of two distinct texts. The remains of 4Q540 speak of a period of stress and poverty, in which a figure will come, different from others. He will then leave the house where he was born; a temple is later mentioned. Some scholars have found correspondence between this text and *TPL* 17, but this is not convincing in our view.

4Q541 seems to be a part of an apocalyptic text, mentioning the Great Sea becoming red, and the wisdom texts being opened (frag. 7). Frag. 9, the largest preserved, speaks of a figure that will be sent to his people, referring to his divine teaching abilities. His task, among

120 See, Stone, 2000a.

121 Milik suggested, that the works of "the three patriarchs" τῶν γ′ πατριαρχῶν mentioned in *Apostolic Constitutions* 6.16.3 connected with the βιβλία ἀπόκρυφα, are the Levi, Qahat and Amram writings: Milik, 1972, 96–97. This is not generally accepted: see 4Q559 which presumably contains the chronology of Levi, Kohath and Aaron.

122 Starcky, 1963, 492. Fitzmyer, 1999, 457–58 notes that Levi's name is missing from the texts and says, "the absence of the name is a warning" (p. 458).

123 Milik, 1978, 95; Puech, 1992 and DJD 31, 213–16.

others, is to be an atonement for all his generation. His period is described as both evil and an age of everlasting sun which will make darkness disappear. 4Q541 also includes some references to the animal world, probably in a visionary manner. Frag. 24 of this text has been associated with *TPL* 18–19, but the common material is limited to a few shared phrases that can also be found in other related literature. Those who would associate it with *TPL* 18–19 would regard it as part of *ALD*. The text lacks its beginning and end, and has no clear testamentary features. Thus it can be concluded, that apart from the special teaching abilities of an unknown figure and the wisdom references that are shared by *ALD* and 4Q541, the texts are different. Thus 4Q541 cannot be identified as part of *ALD*.

7. *Some Specific Aspects of* ALD

TPL *4:2 and* ALD

Hollander and de Jonge point out that the *Prayer of Levi* or something very like it is implied by *TPL* 4:2, which seems to respond to it. That verse reads εἰσήκουσεν οὖν ὁ ὕψιστος τῆς προσευχῆς σου, τοῦ διελεῖν σε ἀπὸ τῆς ἀδικίας καὶ γενέσθαι αὐτῷ υἱὸν καὶ θεράποντα καὶ λειτουργὸν τοῦ προσώπου αὐτοῦ "The Most High, therefore, has heard your prayer to separate you from unrighteousness and that you should become to him a son and a servant and a minister of his presence." This verse claims that God has granted three petitions which Levi made in his prayer, (a) "to separate you from unrighteousness"; (b) "that you should become to him a son"; (c) "and a servant and minister of his presence".[124] Yet, if the prayer found in *ALD* is examined, only element (a) is to be found. Thus we read: "Make far from me, O Lord, the unrighteous spirit, and evil thought and fornication, and turn pride away from me" (3:5) while the second and third elements of the prayer to which *TPL* 4:2 refers do not seem to occur in the *Prayer of Levi*. While the third element, a reference to the Levitical and priestly functions of Levi, seems to be commonplace, the same can scarcely be said of the second element, "that you should become to him a son".

[124] Hollander and de Jonge, 1985, 141.

In fact, both the second and third elements in *TPL* 4:2 do derive from *ALD*, but they reflect a misconstrual of its text.[125] In *ALD* 3:18 we read: לבר עבדך מן ק]דם אנפך כל ימי עלם (the latter part is reconstructed on the basis of Greek) and the Greek text of *ALD* reads here καὶ μὴ ἀποστήσῃς τὸν υἱὸν τοῦ παιδός σου ἀπὸ τοῦ προσώπου πάσας τὰς ἡμέρας τοῦ αἰῶνος. The words מן ק]דם אנפך = ἀπὸ τοῦ προσώπου of *ALD* are reflected by the words "of his presence" of *TPL* 4:2. Equally, the word עבדך (rendered in the Greek of *ALD* as τοῦ παιδός σου, a common enough translation) stands behind the words θεράποντα καὶ λειτουργόν "a servant and a minister" of *TPL* 4:2. It remains only to suggest that the reworker of the *ALD* materials in *TPL* misconstrued לבר as "for a son". He might have read this word as if there were a final *kap* on it, "for your son", or read the next word as if a *waw* preceded, "for a son and for". It is not our claim, of course, that this understanding or interpretation of the Aramaic text is correct; to the contrary. It serves, however, to clarify how the text of *ALD* might have been utilized by the translator or the redactor of the materials in *TPL* in this instance.[126]

The Two Spirits

Levi prays to be separated from one series of features and to be made close to another (3:5–6). He formulates his petition in a contrastive style not unlike that of some Essene documents,[127]

Make far from me	Show me
the unrighteous spirit	the holy spirit
and evil thought	and counsel
and fornication	and wisdom
	and knowledge
and turn pride away from me	and grant me strength to do that which is pleasing before you

This is certainly one of the oldest passages in which two spirits are contrasted and, if a third century BCE date for *ALD* is accepted, then this concept, so characteristic of the Qumran texts, must be put back to that date. The terminology used here, however, is not typical of

[125] Greenfield and Stone, 1990, 153–161, especially p. 157 upon which much of this paragraph draws.

[126] See on this Greenfield and Stone, 1990, 157–58.

[127] See Stone, 1987, especially 576.

the sectarian writings from Qumran.[128] It is related to the idea of the two ways, one good and one bad, that is discussed in the commentary on 3:4, but is distinct from it in its use of the idea of the two spirits.

Sapiential Characteristics of the Priesthood

ALD particularly emphasizes the sapiential characteristics of the priesthood (13:4). In addition to the instructional aspect of the priestly learning that is stressed, a participatory aspect of wisdom is prominent. Levi wishes to be protected, pure, and endowed with wisdom as to be able to participate in divine words and do true judgment for all time. This aspect of the priestly function in the third century BCE has not previously been taken into account.

Below, we discuss how Levi urges his children to cultivate wisdom like Joseph, and how this parenesis resembles other sapiential materials.[129] Deuteronomy 33:10 is doubtlessly the ultimate source of the attribution of such characteristics to priestly figures.[130] The verses in Malachi 2:6–7 clearly interpret Deuteronomy 33:10. They read, "True instruction was in his mouth, and no wrong was found on his lips. He walked with me in integrity and uprightness, and he turned many from iniquity. For the lips of a priest should guard knowledge, and people should seek instruction from his mouth, for he is the messenger of the Lord of hosts." Most significantly, wisdom language functions alongside terminology of priestly teaching.[131]

The latter part of the wisdom poem combines a number of familiar features. We may compare the reading of books (13:16) with the "numerous eschatological prophecies drawn in *TPatriarchs* from a putative 'Book of Enoch'" (e.g., *TPL* 10:5, 14:1 and 16:1).[132] *TPL*

[128] See Stone and Greenfield, 1993, 251–52.

[129] The wisdom poem (chapter 13) is discussed below and in Stone, 1987, 579.

[130] The relationship of priestly sapiential functions in *ALD*, *TPL* and ben Sira, is discussed by Stone, 1987, 580–81. See also Stone and Greenfield, 1993, 253.

[131] The pair תורת אמת "true instruction" and עולה "wrong" in Malachi 2:6 evoke later sectarian language: compare Fuller, 1993, 31–44. These verses also recall Numbers 25:6–13 and Exodus 32:25–29 relating to the covenant with Levi. Kugler, 1996, 18–22 discusses the passage from Malachi. Knibb, 1995, 183 observes that the eschatological figure in 4Q540 and 541 is presented "as a sage, and as a priest who makes expiation." It is intriguing to note the connection of these texts with *ALD*: Puech, 1992, published these texts and discussed them extensively and sometimes quite speculatively. He regards them as part of *ALD*, a position that has been rejected for lack of proof by de Jonge, 1999, 77–78; see also our comments above.

[132] Stone and Greenfield, DJD 22, 20.

16:1 is followed by an eschatological prophecy (chapters 16–18). *ALD* 13:16, following the reference to books, also gives an eschatological prediction.[133]

The relationship between the priestly role described in the wisdom poem in *ALD* chapter 13 and the characteristics of the sage described in ben Sira 39, is striking.[134] The instructional features of the priest in *ALD*[135] became imbued with features of the sage.

Levi's Special Role in ALD

It was observed by Greenfield and Stone that two peculiarities of *ALD* indicate that it attributes a particularly central status to the figure of Levi and the Levitical line.[136]

a. The first of these features was the transferral of Judah's royal blessing to Kohath, Levi's second son and the ancestor of the High Priestly line. This is clearly implied in the name midrash connecting Kohath with Genesis 49:10, which verse is a blessing pronounced upon Judah: see commentary on 11:6–9.

b. The second of these features was the use of the 364-day calendar and the setting of the birth of Levi's children upon particularly significant days and parts of the day according to that calendar. The date of Kohath's birth is the first day of the first month at the rising of the sun, surely a promising and auspicious date (*ALD* 11:5–7).[137] Gershom was born in the tenth month, another important date: see 11:4,[138] and Merari in the third month (11:9).

c. In addition, we noted the special tradition of wisdom attributed to Levi (*ALD* 13:15) which accords with the particular teaching role attributed to the priest in *ALD* 13:2–11 from which *TPL* 13:1–5 was derived. "The circles responsible for Aramaic Levi laid a very strong emphasis on the instructional function of the priesthood and this aspect of the priesthood attracted sapiential motifs. This process was fully developed by the third century BCE at the latest. As a result of

[133] See Collins, 1990. This article discusses how the role of sage changes in apocalyptic literature to reflect mantic wisdom.

[134] See *ALD* chapter 13 and its recording in *TPL* 13:4–5. The matter is discussed in full detail in Stone, 1987.

[135] See de Jonge, 1988, 379.

[136] Greenfield and Stone, 1979.

[137] See below, commentary on 11:7 for a detailed discussion of the calendar.

[138] See Ben Dov and Horowitz, 2003, 16.

it the figure of the ideal priest became imbued with features of the sage."[139]

As well as being instructional in character (cf. Deuteronomy 33:10), priestly wisdom involved participation in purity, in the divine words (*ALD* 3:17). Hence we arrive at an explicit formulation of the idea implied by the expression in Deuteronomy, that a major function of priestly wisdom is the ability to do true judgment for all time.[140] The development of Levi's sapiential and even judicial role may be summarized by saying that he does not just "teach Jacob Torah", but becomes a central sapiential figure, instructing, teaching and participating in divine wisdom.

d. Furthermore, certain other features of the Levitical role as presented in *ALD* serve to expand the areas of life and teaching over which Levi and the Levites have authority. *ALD* obviously attributes a cultic role to Levi, yet it stresses the transmission of cultic teaching and lore from the antediluvian Book of Noah (*ALD* 10:10) to Abraham (*ALD* 10:3 and 10:10), to Isaac (*ALD* 5:8) and then to Levi. Thus it sets the Levitical priesthood in the sacerdotal line reaching back to Adam.[141] It is significant for our discussion that Levitical cultic authority and teaching is anchored in prior tradition and in recognition by the patriarchs rather than in Levi's consecration to the priesthood as such. His consecration makes him fit to receive the teaching. This strategy concentrates the antique traditions of priesthood in the Levitical line.[142] Thus, the tendency to establish Levi as an ideal priest from the past is already to be found in Malachi 2:4–9.[143]

The main texts in *ALD* showing the combination of royal and priestly language applied to Levi are the following (each of which is

[139] Stone, 1987, 580. On the functions of Levi in the chief biblical passages and at Qumran, see Fuller, 1993. Levi at Qumran is discussed by Kugler, 1999; see especially 472–73.

[140] Cf. Solomon's prayer in 1 Kings 3:9.

[141] See Stone, 1999, 133–140.

[142] Clearly, *ALD* could not anchor Levi's authority in the Mosaic revelation, which would have been a gross anachronism.

[143] See Fuller, 1993, 37–40. He says "The figure of Levi/the Levites fulfill three functions: (1) they observe the covenant, presumably the covenant between God and Israel not the special covenant with Levi; (2) they teach the ordinances and the Torah; and (3) they offer incense and sacrifice to God" (p. 36). These same characteristics are found in *ALD* and are biblically rooted.

expounded in detail in the commentary). To the explicit texts we add instances of the absence of Judah from contexts in *ALD* in which he is found in the corresponding text in *TPL* (see below, item 2).[144]

1) 4:7 (1Q Levi, frag. 1), which was placed here by J.T. Milik because it evoked the language of 4:9.

[. . .]מ֯ן די ל֯הוין תליתין[. . . לב]ניך מלכות כהנותא רבא מן מלכות֯[. . .]ל֯[א]ל֯[ע]ל֯[יון]

]from that they were third[to your so]ns the kingdom of priesthood is greater than the kingdom[ ]to the [Most Hi]gh G[o]d.[145]

This matter is discussed in detail in the commentary on 4:7–8.

2) 5:5–6 refer to Levi alone, while in *Jubilees* 31 the same incident, which is recited in much greater detail, is attributed to Levi and Judah.[146]
3) 11:6–7 see commentary below.
4) In the name midrash of Kohath, *ALD* 11:6 says ". . . he would have the high-priesthood; he and his seed will be the beginning of kings, a priesthood for [all Is]rael".[147]

[144] See de Jonge, 1960, 212, 217–18.

[145] See *TPL* 8:11–14. An alternative translation might be "to your] sons is a high-priestly kingdom rather than a [ ] kingdom[". See commentary on 4:8.

[146] Greenfield and Stone, 1979, 219. It is interesting to contrast the stark separation of royal and priestly persons in 1QM 67:12–15; this is equally stressed in *TPJudah* 21. See also 1QSa 2:12–15 and 4QTestimonia 12–16. Observe that, on its own, 5:5–6 does not show the combination of royal and priestly characteristics, but its unique stress on Levi is highlighted by comparison with *Jubilees* 31.

[147] This neatly contrasts with the blessing of Reuben according to Targum Neofiti and Vatican and Paris manuscripts of the Fragmentary Targum to Genesis 49:3: לך הויא חזיא למיסב תלתא חולקין יתירין על אחך בכירותא ומלכותא וכהונתא רבתא. ועל דחבתא ראובן איתיהיבת בכירותא ליוסף ומלכותא ליהודה וכהונתא רבתא לבני שבטוי דלוי "It would have suited you to receive three portions more than your brothers, the first-born rights, the kingship and the high priesthood. But because you sinned, Reuben, the first-born rights were given to Joseph, and the kingship to Judah, and the high priesthood to the members of the tribe of Levi." See Klein 1980, 1. 65–66; 2. 30. *Jubilees* 16:18 says of Isaac's seed that "he would become the share of the Most High. All his descendants had fallen into (that) share which God owns so that they would become a people whom the Lord *possesses* out of all the nations; and that they would become a kingdom, a priesthood, and a holy people." That is, the royal and priestly lines and the holy nation of Israel would all be descendants of Jacob. Compare also *Jubilees* 33:20. In all these instances, the royal and priestly offices are kept distinct, a contrast with the view expressed in *ALD*.

5) In 13:16, in a sadly fragmentary context, we find the collocations, "priests and kings" and "your kingdom".[148]

De Jonge points out the statement about Phineas in ben Sira 45:24 (ms B), which forms a nice contrast to the material we have discussed here.[149] On the one hand, reflecting the pre-Hasmonean situation, it regards the priest as leader of the people, but on the other, it does not introduce any royal language touching on the Levitical line.

לכן גם לו הקים חק ברית שלום לכלכל מקדש
אשר תהיה לו ולזרעו כהונה גדולה עד עולם

διὰ τοῦτο ἐστάθη αὐτῷ διαθήκη εἰρήνης προστατεῖν ἁγίων καὶ λαοῦ αὐτοῦ,
ἵνα αὐτῷ ᾖ καὶ τῷ σπέρματι αὐτοῦ ἱερωσύνης μεγαλεῖον εἰς τοὺς αἰῶνας.

Therefore a covenant of friendship was established with him,
that he should be leader of the sanctuary and of his people,
that he and his descendants should have
the dignity of the priesthood for ever.

e. This remarkable concentration of themes in Levi presumably relates to and perhaps reacts against other views of the priestly, royal and sapiental roles and their players in Judaism of the third century BCE. We lack the information, however, to paint the social contexts in which such varied views may have been cultivated.[150]

This constellation of features around Levi is combined with the claim of antiquity for *ALD*'s priestly instruction. The detailed priestly teaching in chapters 6–10 is quite unparalled in ancient Jewish literature. It is accompanied by a very determined attempt to root this teaching in the most ancient and authoritative sources (see above, "Sapiential Character of the Priesthood"). Abraham's teaching is drawn from the Book of Noah (10:3 and 10:10).[151] *Testament of Qahat* (4Q542) stresses the transmission of teaching from Abraham through Isaac, Jacob, Levi and Kohath (col. 1).[152]

[148] On these passages, see also Stone, 1999, 134–35.

[149] See de Jonge and Tromp, 1998, 231.

[150] The article of Smith, 1959 still has much valuable minatory comment on the variety of messianic figures.

[151] Stone, 1988, 168–69; Stone, 1999 deals in detail with the issue of transmission from antiquity. Caquot observes that Jacob is left out of the line of transmission, which passes from Isaac to Levi: see 1998, 4.

[152] Compare also *Jubilees* 45:16. The fragmentary list of high priests in 4QPseudo-Daniel[c] (4Q245) starts with Levi (or earlier; the manuscript is lacunose). See Collins

Levi in TPL *8:14*

A further remark concerning priesthood is found in *TPL* 8:14. It reads:

> ὁ τρίτος, ἐπικλήθησεται αὐτῷ ὄνομα καινόν, ὅτι βασιλεὺς ἐκ τοῦ Ἰουδὰ ἀναστήσεται, καὶ ποιήσει ἱερατείαν νέαν, κατὰ τὸν τύπον τῶν ἐθνῶν, εἰς πάντα τὰ ἔθνη.
>
> The third will be called with a new name,
> because a king will arise from Judah
> and will establish a new priesthood after the fashion of the Gentiles
> for all the Gentiles.

Above we have said that in *ALD* Levi combines the priestly and the royal functions and consistently applies royal terminology to the priesthood. This feature may help explain *TPL* 8:14. *TPL* 8:11 says that Levi's seed will be divided into three ἄρχας, but the description of the third ἄρχη is a prophecy not about Levi's seed at all, but about Judah and the eventual establishment of a new priesthood.[153] As well as the application of royal, i.e., Judahite, terminology to Levi in *ALD*, Judah is omitted from contexts in *ALD* in which he is found in *TPL*. Since *ALD* is much older than *TPL*, this suggests that Judah's role in *TPL* may have been introduced by editorial activity stimulated by the apparent "omission" of Judah from *ALD*.[154]

The Travels of Levi and Jacob in ALD *and* TPL

Some unclarity surrounds the travels recorded in *ALD* 5. In 5:1 "we" went to "my father" Isaac and he blessed "me" (i.e., Levi). This action followed immediately on Jacob's recognition of Levi's priesthood

---

and Flint, DJD 22.156–161; Stone, 1999 and compare also *Jubilees* 31. What Kugler regards as a list of high priests in 4Q225 (= 4QPsJub[a]) 2 2:11–12 includes Abraham, Isaac, Jacob and Levi and compare 4Q226 7:4 (4QPsJub[b]): Kugler, 1999, 472. *ALD* omits Jacob from the list of priestly teachers, see commentary on 5:4, below.

[153] Hollander and de Jonge do not broach this problem in their commentary to this passage.

[154] As has been noted above and in the commentary below, there are many points at which a careful reading of *ALD* can explain aspects of *TPL*. A full and careful comparison of the two documents would throw much light on the work of the author/redactor of *TPL*. Such a comparison, however, would be a different project to the present one and we limit ourselves to a few remarks which may help enhance our understanding of *ALD*.

by giving him tithes, "in accordance with his vow" and investing and consecrating him.[155] Upon this Levi offers sacrifices and blesses his father and brothers. In other words, in 5:2–5 Jacob carried out the investiture and consecration of Levi which had been recounted in Levi's vision in chapter 4.

In 5:5 Jacob and the brothers bless Levi and Levi completes the sacrificial offerings in Bethel. The significance of this reciprocal blessing of Levi is not clear. However, after Levi was installed as priest, they went to "the residence (enclosure) of Abraham" to Isaac's place. And Isaac saw them all and blessed them. He recognized Levi's priestly status and commenced instructing him about the priestly law (5:6–8).

There is a problem in the text here that was recognized by the author of *TPL*. If Isaac was at "Abraham's residence (enclosure)" to which they journeyed in 5:6, how and where did he bless Levi according to 5:1? It says, "we went to my father Isaac" (5:1) and so, after the dream, "we" (Judah and Levi if we follow *TPL* 9:1) went to Isaac, received the blessing, and returned or went to Bethel where Jacob was. Therefore, the editor of *TPL* added, "he would not come with us to Bethel" (*TPL* 9:2). This is related to Isaac's refusal, at an earlier point in the narrative, described in *Jubilees* 31:26–27.[156]

Isaac seems to have been at "Abraham's residence (enclosure)" for, when they went there (5:6) they found him there. Isaac blessed his grandchildren when they arrived (5:7) and no mention is made of the fact that he blessed Levi in any special way.

The only odd thing in this narrative structure so far is the double trip to Isaac. Isaac blessed Levi in the intermediate state between his dream of investiture and the actual investiture. He did this in accordance with the contents of Levi's dream, which he knew by some special means, for Levi concealed the contents of the dream. This special knowledge of Isaac's contrasts strongly with Jacob, who later learned of Levi's election in a dream of his own.

It seems that Isaac plays a special role here; after the dream Levi goes not to Jacob but to Isaac. By then, Jacob has invested him with the priestly garments, recognized his priestly role by giving him tithes, and Levi blesses Jacob with a priestly blessing. Why, one might ask, did not Jacob, his father, who invested him as priest, also give him

[155] See above, pp. 15–16.

[156] See commentary on 5:6.

instruction? The answer might be a simple one, that Isaac was the oldest patriarch alive. In addition, it has been observed that the priestly line skipped over Jacob. Therefore, it is Isaac who is Levi's teacher.[157] This teaching derived from Abraham and, ultimately, from Noah and so the privilege of teaching it belonged to the oldest living patriarch.

The Sacrificial Ordinances and Measures

1. *The Sacrificial Ordinances*

The proper order of sacrifice and the quantities of wood, of salt, of fine flour, of oil, and of frankincense are adumbrated in 8:7–9:16. In the Table here we set forth the various amounts of wood, salt, flour, oil, wine and frankincense for the different sacrificial animals:

animal	wood *minas*	salt *satons*	flour *satons*	oil & wine *satons*	frankincense *shekels*
1. large bull	60	1	1	$\frac{1}{4}$	6
fat alone	6				
2. bullock (second bull)	50	$\frac{5}{6}$	1		
fat alone	5				
3. calf	40	$\frac{2}{3}$	1		
4. ram or he-goat	30	$\frac{1}{2}$	$\frac{2}{3}$	$\frac{1}{6}$	3
fat alone	3				
5. lamb kid	20	$\frac{1}{3}$	$\frac{1}{3}$	$\frac{1}{8}$	2
fat alone	2				
6. unblemished, one-year old lamb or kid	15				
fat alone	1.5				
7. meal offering					2

The offerings listed here are burnt offerings, עולה, in which the animal, after being butchered, is offered whole upon the altar.[158] Leviticus 1 deals with this subject. The offering of the "fat alone" refers to

[157] See 5:4 and commentary. See also Kugel, 1993, 22–24; VanderKam, 1999, 503–04.

[158] This excursus has benefitted from the lecture of L.H. Schiffman, "Sacrificial

the "sacrifice of well-being" or "peace offering" (שלמים or *šĕlamîm*), which involves offering only the fat and the internal organs on the altar, as described in Leviticus 3:3–4.

The weights and measures are of some interest. In the early Roman period, one mina was approximately 403 gr.,[159] thus 60 minas are 24.18 kg. This weight is reasonable for the amount of wood required to burn a large animal, while the "fat alone" of this animal, sacrified as a peace offering, requires only about 2.4 kg. The smallest animal, an "unblemished, one-year-old lamb or kid" needs only 15 minas of wood, that is about 6 kg.

As noted by Schiffman, the only indication in Rabbinic literature of the amount of wood required for any part of the sacrificial service is in *m. Tamid* 2:2, where the quantity of coals necessary for the fire used for the incense altar is mentioned. Sufficient wood must be put on the altar to produce five seahs of ashes, yet the Mishnah does not specify how much wood that is. *ALD* sets forth how much wood must be used to burn for each type of animal or its fat and innards. *ALD* lays upon each person who brought a sacrifice the obligation to provide the required wood for it (see 10:5). In the same sections of *ALD*, the required amount of salt for the various animals offered is discussed and its same requirement for provision of salt is made, although earlier *ALD* stated that all parts of an animal being sacrified must be salted. This is also the case for the fine flour, the wine and the frankincense (so 10:5).[160]

2. *The Metrological List in 9:17–18*

> And a third of a saton is a third of an ephah and two parts of a bath, and of the weight of the mina, it is fifty shekels.
> And the fourth of the shekel is the weight of four *thermoi*.
> The shekel is about sixteen *thermoi* and of one weight.

Halakhah in the Fragments of the Aramaic Levi Document from Qumran, the Cairo Genizah and Mt. Athos Monastery", delivered at the Orion International Symposium, Hebrew University of Jerusalem, in January 2002. We would like to express our thanks to him for sharing his paper with us.

[159] See Kloner, 1990, 64–65 and bibliography there.

[160] Grelot, 1991, 258 observes that the cultic regulations are reduced to a few vague words in *TPL* 9:7–14. They were known to *Jubilees* as Abraham's teaching to Isaac (*Jubilees* 21:5–19).

After the above lists of quantities of wood, salt, and so forth for the various sacrifices, in 9:17–18 the text, which is preserved only in Greek, presents this list of measures and their equivalents. The connection between this metrological list and the preceding list of quantities is not clear. The measures mentioned in this list are: saton, ephah, bath, mina, shekel and θερμός. This paragraph contains three measures used in the preceding sacrificial ordinances, viz. the saton, mina and shekel. It also contains three measures, the ephah, bath and θερμός which are absent from the preceding list of sacrifices. This suggests that this list is introduced from an external source.

According to *ALD*, "The shekel is about sixteen *thermoi* and of one weight". The θερμός might be identified with Greek τριμήσιον,[161] Latin *tremis* and Syriac *trymysyn*. The *tremissis* was a small golden coin of an average weight between 1.3 gr. and 1.45 gr. It was in use in the eastern Roman Empire from the last quarter of the fourth century CE, having been "introduced by Theodosius I (379–395) to replace the $1\frac{1}{2}$ *scripulum* of Constantine's system".[162] D.R. Sear explains that "The coinage of the fifth century consisted mainly of the *solidus* and the two smaller gold denominations, the *semissis* ($\frac{1}{2}$ *solidus*) and the *tremissis* ($\frac{1}{3}$ *solidus*)."[163]

The tremissis is mentioned in a statement attributed to Rav (ca. 200–220 CE) in the Palestinian Talmud, *Gittin* 47b (35).[164] This text was probably re-edited at the end of the fourth or the beginning of the fifth century and at that time the mention of this coin was introduced. No denomination of $\frac{1}{16}$ of a *tremissis* is known to date.

161 LSJ, *s.v.* 9 p. 1820), according to which it is a coin equivalent in value to the aureus (golden dinar), 3.14 gr. (1 aureus = 24 dinar), documented from the fourth century CE.

162 Sear, 1988, 14.

163 Sear, 1988, 14.

164 One tremissis (טרימיסין) contributions are mentioned in four synagogue inscriptions in Palestine, dated to the fifth century CE, three from Hamat Gader and one from Eshtemoa; see Sukenik, 1935, 138–143; Hirschfeld 1993, 2.565–66; nos. I–III and nos. 33–35 in Naveh 1978, 57–63. At that period the tremissis was worth a third of an aureus (a golden denarius), see Yeivin, 1993, 2.425, and in *t. Baba Batra* 5,11–12 which records two currency systems of coins, see Lieberman, 1988a, 147; *idem*, 1988b, part X: Order Nezikin, 393, where he identifies טורמוסין with tremissis, as 'small coins'. In a hoard of golden coins found in the Khirbet Rimmon synagogue, 32 out of a total of 47 coins were identified as tremissis coins, which shows that it was a regular denomination in Palestine during the fifth century; see Kloner and Mindel, 1981, 60–68.

Consequently *ALD*'s saying: "The shekel is about sixteen *thermoi*" remains unclear.[165]

ALD 9:17 says, "and a third of a saton is a third of an ephah". This appears to be corrupt as we note in the commentary. From the Bible we learn that a saton is actually a third of ephah (see Genesis 18:6, 1 Samuel 25:18, 1 Kings 18:32, etc.). Therefore, we propose to read: "and a saton is a third of an ephah". The genitive "of the mina" seems difficult and perhaps the last part of the verse should be read "and the weight of the mina, it is fifty shekels" which equivalence also occurs in the Bible.[166] "And two parts of a bath" is inexplicable. In fact, from the Bible it is clear that an ephah is equivalent to a bath.[167]

As we have seen, the list of the metrological equivalents found here is corrupt, but with some emendations can be partly understood. In addition to measures, some of which are related to the preceding list of sacrifices but others not, it also contains some monetary terms. These stem from the Roman period, which date stands in tension with the third century BCE dating of *ALD*. Yet the early date of *ALD* is quite certain, and there are manuscripts of it from Qumran that are older than the period in which the use of the monetary terms became current.

Clearly then, part or all of this metrological list is later than the surrounding text. We propose that the list was inserted into an older text in the Roman period. This list even includes some of the measures with a biblical basis that do not occur in the extensive preceding sacrificial ordinances, not to speak of the monetary terms. Consequently, we regard the whole of the list of 9:17–18 as a later gloss. Alternatively, it might be suggested that an earlier metrological list dealing with the measures mentioned in the sacrificial ordinances was glossed and updated in the Roman period.

We are equally unable to tell whether this process of updating took place at the Greek or the Aramaic stage of the transmission. Because of this uncertainty, the metrological list does not necessarily provide a *terminus post quem* for the Greek translation of *ALD*.

---

[165] We would like to express our gratitude to Professor D. Barag for his important contribution to our study of this coin.

[166] Apart from the Book of Ezekiel where, based on the Mesopotamian measurement, it equals 60 shekels: Powell, 1992, 905–08.

[167] Powell, 1992, 903–05.

Postcript

After the manuscript of the present work was completed, the edition of the Geniza fragments by Emile Puech appeared.[168] Puech is a scholar of great experience in the decipherment of ancient Hebrew and Aramaic manuscripts, and in his edition he proposes a variety of readings and of reconstructions of the text. At many points he differs from the readings proposed by Greenfield and Stone in their various publications over the past 25 years, and it would be surprising if he were not able to improve the text at many points, as indeed he does.

We have considered each of Puech's proposals carefully and have accepted a number of readings into the text or apparatus, in each case attributing to him the reading accepted. We are grateful to Emile Puech for these improvements to the text. There are, naturally, a number of instances in which we do not accept Puech's readings. We have discussed certain of these instances in the Commentary as appropriate.

In going through his article, however, a disturbing matter came to our attention. There are quite numerous instances in which Puech has incorporated into his text readings proposed by Greenfield and Stone, mostly drawn from their article published in 1979.[169] Puech accepts almost 20 of the readings, reconstructions and emendations of Charles's edition proposed by Greenfield and Stone in that article.[170] Yet, he only attributes 3 of them to Greenfield and Stone, and presents the others unattributed, implying by this that they are his own. This goes, in our view, beyond normal scholarly practice. This is particularly so when it is complemented by a careful documentation and attribution of more than 40 places at which he differs from Greenfield and Stone, often stressing their faulty scholarship.

[168] Puech, 2002.
[169] Greenfield and Stone, 1979.
[170] See, for example, Cambridge col. a, lines 18, 20, 21, 22, 23, Cambridge col. b, lines 19, 20, 20, 23, 23, Bodleian col. a, 2, 8, 8, 9, etc.

Critical Signs and Abbreviations

ẋ	a dot over a letter signifies a partly preserved letter whose reconstruction is certain
x̊	a circle over a letter signifies a reconstructed letter not incompatible with the surviving fragmentary sign(s)
.	a dot on the line signifies that a sign can be seen but cannot be identified
{ }	corruption in text
< >	editors' emendation of corrupt text
[ ]	editors' reconstruction of missing text
( )	addition in the translation for stylistic reasons
[*italics*]	conjectured sense of word or words lost in a lacuna
[font]	words extant only in Greek, where Aramaic is the dominant text.
|	end of a line in the manuscript

ALD	*Aramaic Levi Document*
b.	Babylonian Talmud, followed by treatise name
col., cols.	column, columns
fem.	feminine
j.	Jerusalem (Palestinian) Talmud, followed by treatise name
l., ll.	line, lines
m.	Mishnah, followed by treatise name
ms	manuscript (only used with a sigil)
sing.	singular
TPL	*Testament of Levi in Testaments of the Twelve Patriarchs*
TPName	*Testament of Name in Testaments of the Twelve Patriarchs*
t.	Tosefta, followed by treatise name

The names of biblical and apocryphal books and treatises of Mishnah, Tosefta and Talmud are given in full, except that in certain cases, diacritical marks are omitted for typographic simplicity.

Journals and Publications

AbrN	*Abr-Nahrain*
ActaOr	*Acta Orientalia*
AGAJU	Arbeiten zur Geschichte des antiken Judentums und des Urchristentums
BDB	Brown, Driver and Briggs, *New Hebrew and English Lexicon of the Old Testament*
BETL	Bibliotheca ephemeridum theologicarum lovaniensium
BZ, NF	*Biblische Zeitschrift, Neue Folge*
CBET	Contributions to Biblical Exegesis and Theology
CRINT	Compendia rerum iudaicarum ad Novum Testamentum
CSCO	Corpus scriptorum christianorum orientalium
DJD	Discoveries in the Judean Desert (see below)
DSD	*Dead Sea Discoveries*
HTR	*Harvard Theological Review*
HUCA	*Hebrew Union College Annual*
IDB	Interpreter's Dictionary of the Bible

IEJ	*Israel Exploration Journal*
INJ	*Israel Numismatic Journal*
JANESCU	*Journal of Ancient Near Eastern Society of Columbia University*
JBL	*Journal of Biblical Literature*
JJS	*Journal of Jewish Studies*
JPOS	*Journal of the Palestine Oriental Society*
JPS	Jewish Publication Society
JQR	*Jewish Quarterly Review*
JSJ	*Journal for the Study of Judaism in the Persian, Hellenistic and Roman Period*
JSP	*Journal for the Study of the Pseudepigrapha and Related Literature*
JSPSup	Journal for the Study of the Pseudepigrapha and Related Literature Supplement Series
JSS	*Journal of Semitic Studies*
LSJ	Liddell-Scott-Jones, *Greek-English Lexicon*
NT	*Novum Testamentum*
PVTG	Pseudepigrapha Veteris Testamenti graece
RB	*Revue biblique*
RÉJ	*Revue des études juives*
RQ	*Revue de Qumran*
SBLEJL	Society of Biblical Literature Early Judaism and Its Literature
ScrAeth	scriptores aethiopici
SCS	Society of Biblical Literature Septuagint and Cognate Studies
STDJ	Studies on the Texts of the Desert of Judah
SVTP	Studia in veteris testamenti pseudepigrapha
TDNT	Kittel, *Theological Dictionary of the New Testament*
UF	*Ugarit-Forschungen*
VT	*Vetus Testamentum*
VTSupp	*Vetus Testamentum Supplement*
ZAH	*Zeitschrift für Althebraistik*
ZNW	*Zeitschrift für die Neutestamentliche Wissenschaft*

Citation of Dead Sea Scrolls

DJD	The volumes of the *Discoveries in the Judean Desert* series are cited by simple volume number, with no further details. Editors' names given are those who edited the particular work being cited. All these individual works and editors are not included in the Bibliography, but simply the series name.

Dead Sea Scrolls documents are cited in two ways:

If more than one fragment of the document exists, three numbers are given: fragment no., column no. and line no. in the following format: 1 1:1

If there is only one fragment, then two numbers are given: column no. and line no. in the following format: 1:1

APPENDIX

CONCORDANCE OF VERSIFICATION AND MAIN TEXTUAL WITNESSES TO *ALD*

		Geniza		
1:1	1	Cambridge a 1		
1:2	1	Cambridge a 1		
1:3		Cambridge a 2		
2:1	3	Cambridge b	**1QLevi 48**	
2:2		**1QLevi 8**		
2:3		8		
		4QLevi^{b} 1:1–4	unnumbered	
2:4	*1		Greek	
2:5	*2		Greek	
2:6		**4QLevi** ^{b} 1	Greek	
3:1	*3	b 1	Greek	
3:2	*4	b 1	Greek	
3:3	*5	b 1	Greek	
3:4	*6	b 1	Greek	
3:5	*7	b 1	Greek	
3:6	*8	b 1	Greek	
3:7	*9	b 1	Greek	
3:8	*9b	b 1	Greek	
3:9	*10	b 1	Greek	
3:10	*11	b 1	Greek	
3:11	*12		Greek	
3:12	*13		Greek	
3:13	*14	b 2	Greek	
3:14	*15	b 2	Greek	
3:15	*16	b 2	Greek	
3:16	*17	b 2	Greek	
3:17	*18	b 2	Greek	
3:18	*19	b 2	Greek	
4:1		b 2 11–12		
4:2		b 2 12–13		
4:3		b 2 14		
4:4		b 2 15–16		
4:5		b 2 17		
4:6		b 2 18		
4:7		**1QLevi 1**		
4:8		**1QLevi 7**		
		Geniza		
4:9	4	Bodleian a	**1QLevi 3**	**1QLevi 26**
4:10	5	Bodleian a	3	
4:11	6	Bodleian a	3	
4:12	7	Bodleian a	**4QLevi**^{c}	
4:13	7b	Bodleian a	c	

5:1	8	Bodleian a	c			
5:2	9	Bodleian a	c	**1QLevi 4**		
5:3	9b	Bodleian a	c			
5:4	9c	Bodleian a	c			
5:5	10	Bodleian a				
5:6	11	Bodleian b	**Greek**			
5:7	12	Bodleian b	Greek			
5:8	13	Bodleian b	Greek			
6:1	14	Bodleian b	Greek	**4QLevi^{f} 7**		
6:2	15	Bodleian b	Greek			
6:3	16	Bodleian b	Greek			
6:4	17	Bodleian b	Greek			
6:5	18	Bodleian b	Greek			
7:1	19	Bodleian c	Greek			
7:2	20	Bodleian c	Greek			
7:3	21	Bodleian c	Greek			**4QLevi^{d} 1**
7:4	22	Bodleian c	Greek			**4QLevi^{f}**
7:5	23	Bodleian c	Greek			f
7:6	24	Bodleian c	Greek		**4QLevi^{e}**	f
7:7	25	Bodleian c	Greek	d 2	e	f
8:1	25b	Bodleian d	Greek	d 2	e	f
8:2	26	Bodleian d	Greek	d 2	**1QLevi 45**	f
8:3	27	Bodleian d	Greek	d 2	45	f
8:4	28	Bodleian d	Greek	d 2		
8:5	29	Bodleian d	Greek	d 2		
8:6	30	Bodleian d	Greek	d 2		
8:7	31	Bodleian d	Greek			
9:1	32	Bodleian d	Greek			
9:2	33	Greek				
9:3	34	Greek				
9:4	35	Greek				
9:5	36	Greek				
9:6	37	Greek				
9:7	38	Greek				
9:8	39	Greek				
9:9	40	Greek				
9:10	41	Greek				
9:11	42	Greek				
9:12	43	Greek				
9:13	44	Greek				
9:14	44b	Greek				
9:15	45	Greek				
9:16	46	Greek				
9:17	46b	Greek				
9:18	47	Greek				
10:1	48	Greek				
10:2	49	Greek				
10:3	50	Greek				
10:4	51	Greek				
10:5	52	Greek				
10:6	53	Greek				
10:7	54	Greek				
10:8	55	Greek				
10:9	56	Greek				

10:10	57	Greek			
10:11	58	Greek			
10:12	59	Greek			
10:13	60	Greek			
10:14	61	Greek			
11:1	62	Greek			
11:2	63	Greek			
11:3	64	Greek			
11:4	65	Greek			
11:5	66	**Cambridge c**	Greek		
11:6	67	Cambridge c	Greek		
11:7	68	Cambridge c	Greek		
11:8	69	Cambridge c	**4QLevi[e]** 2–3		
11:9	70	Cambridge c	e 2–3		
11:10	71	Cambridge c	e 2–3		
11:11	72	Cambridge d			
12:1	73	Cambridge d			
12:2	74	Cambridge d			
12:3	75	Cambridge d			
12:4	76	Cambridge d			
12:5	77	Cambridge d			
12:6	78	Cambridge d	**Syriac**		
12:7	79	Cambridge d	Syriac		
12:8	80	Cambridge d	Syriac		
12:9	81	Cambridge e	Syriac		
13:1	82	Cambridge e	**4QLevi[a]**		
13:2	83–4	Cambridge e	a		
13:3	85–7	Cambridge e	a		
13:4	88	Cambridge e	a		
13:5	89	Cambridge e	a		
13:6	90	Cambridge e	a		
13:7	91	Cambridge e	a		
13:8	91b	Cambridge e	a		
13:9	91c-2	Cambridge e	a		
13:10	93–4	Cambridge e	a		
13:11	95	Cambridge f	a	**4QLevi[e] 2–3**	
13:12	96	Cambridge f	a	e 2–3	
13:13				e 2–3	**4QLevi[f] 8**
13:14			a		
13:15			a	e 2–3	
13:16			a		

Unplaced

1QLevi all fragments except for frags. 1–2, 3, 7, 26 and 45.
4QLevi[a], frag. 4 part of an eschatological address of Levi to his sons
4QLevi[a], frag. 5 part of an address
4QLevi[b], frag. 6 too small to provide context
4QLevi[d], frags. 3–4 too small to provide context
4QLevi[f], frag. 1 second person address

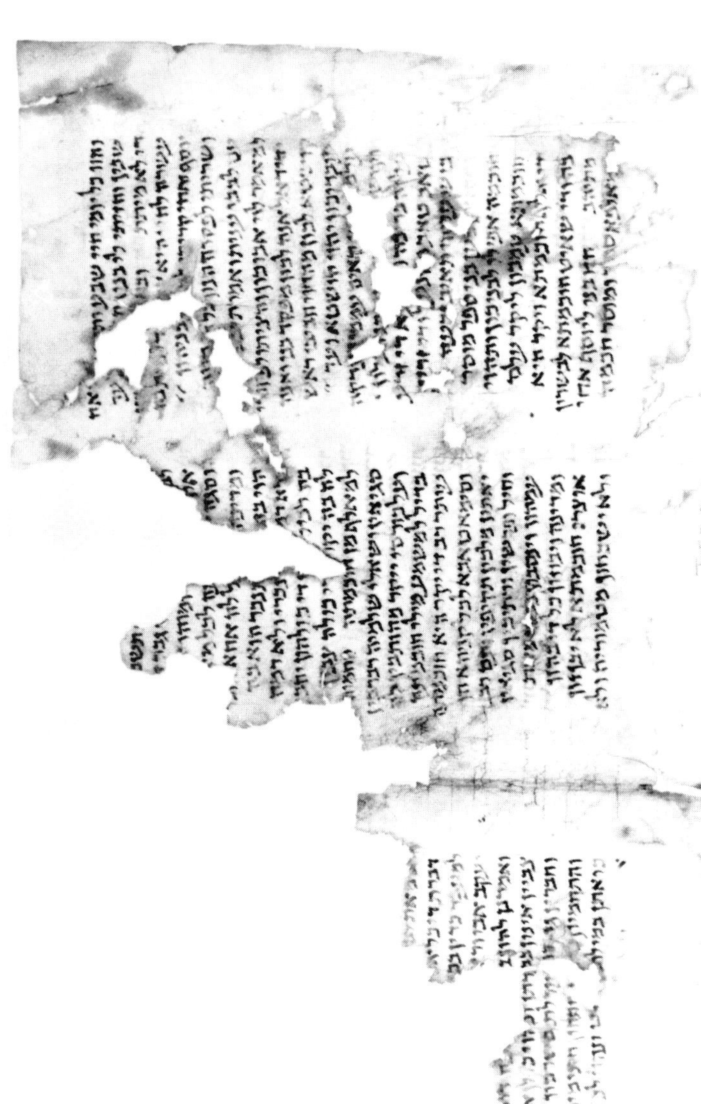

Cambridge Ms ms T.S. 16, fol. 94 recto
Columns Cambridge a, f and e

Cambridge Ms ms T.S. 16, fol. 94 verso
Columns Cambridge d, c and b

Bodleian Ms Heb. c. 27 recto
Columns Bodleian b and a

Bodleian Ms Heb. c. 27 verso
Columns Bodleian d and c

TEXT

Chapter 1: The Story of Dinah

Aramaic text is Cambridge, col. a, ll. 1–14 of the column are missing and, moreover, an indeterminate amount of text before that.

1:1–3 Cam a

1:1 ..טמאת לבנ̊[י על] | דברת די כל אנ̊ש̊ [ ] | למעבד כדין בכל̊ [ ] | יעקב אבי ורא̇[ובן אחי] |

1:2 ואמרנן להון ב̇[ ]..נ̇ה די ה̊[ן] | צביין <אנתון> בברתן ונהוי כולן א[חין] | וחברין

1:3 נזורו עורלת בשרכון | והתחמיון כו̊א̊ת̊ן̊ ותהון חתימין | כואתן במילת [קש]ו̊ט ונהוי לכ[ון] | א[חין ?]

Variants

1:1 ..טמאת לבנ̊[י—ד̊טמאת לבנ̊[י Puech ..מאת י̊ש[ ] Greenfield Stone כל א.[ ]—Puech כל אנ̊ש̊[| Beyer ל̊כ̊ל̊ מאת ומד̊[ינה Kugler [ו]ממאת למ[Greenfield Stone כלא... Charles כלא א̊[נון | Beyer בכל̊[—Puech Beyer בכ.[ ] Greenfield Stone | ורא̇[ובן אחי—ורא̇[ה] Charles **1:2** ..נ̇ה[—ו]ב̊י̊נ̇ה Puech כה.[Beyer נח.[ ] Kugler: in the lacuna preceding this, Puech conjectures ב[חוכמה | <אנתון>—eds. אינון manuscript | כולן—כ[ו]לן Charles **1:3** כו̊א̊ת̊ן̊—Puech כ[ואתן] Charles | [קש]ו̊ט—ט[Charles | א[חין]—single letter in line, probably an error and was the first letter of the next page; we conjecture אחין and cf. 1:2.

Parallels

TPL 6:3 resembling 1:3
ἐγὼ συνεβούλευσα τῷ πατρί μου καὶ Ῥουβὴμ τῷ ἀδελφῷ μου, ἵνα εἴπῃ τοῖς υἱοῖς Ἑμμὼρ τοῦ περιτμηθῆναι αὐτούς, ὅτι ἐζήλωσα διὰ τὸ βδέλυγμα ὅ ἐποίησαν ἐν Ἰσραήλ.

TRANSLATION

Chapter 1: The Story of Dinah

1:1 . . you / she defiled the so[ns of (?) ac-] | cording to the manner of all people [ ] | to do according to the law (*or*: to do so) in all [. . . *took counsel with*] | Jacob my father and Reu[ben my brother . . .] |
1:2 and we said to them:[. . .] | "[I]f <you> desire our daughter so that we all become broth[ers] | and friends,
1:3 circumcise your fleshly foreskin | and look like us, and (then) you will be sealed | like us with the circumcision [of tru]th and we will be br[others] | for y[ou] . ."

Parallels

TPL 6:3 resembling 1:3
I advised my father and Reuben my brother that he would tell the sons of Hamor to be circumcised, because I was zealous because of the abomination which they had wrought in Israel.

Chapter 2: The Wars of the Sons of Jacob (?)

Aramaic text of 2:1 is Cambridge col. b: two columns and 14 lines are missing between the end of Cambridge a and the beginning of Cambridge b.

2:1 = Cam b 1QLevi frag. 48
2:2–3 = 1QLevi frag. 8
2:4–5 = Athos Greek 1–2
2:4 = 4QLevi[b] frag. 1

2:1 15[ ].אחי בכל עד̇ן | [ ]א̇ די הוו בשכם|[ ]אחי ואחוי דן |[ ]בשכם
ומה |מי̇ת̊[עב]די חמסא ואחוי | 20אי̇נו̇ן יהוד̊ה די **אנה** ושמעון | אחי
אזלנא להן[ ]ר̊ד לראובן | אחונן די למדנ̊ח̊ א̊שר ושור | יהודה קדמא
[ל]מ̊שבק עאנא |

1QLevi frag. 8 may relate to the end of Cambridge b. Its place in the story is unclear. We have put it here and, because of the *vacat* in line 1, we regard it as a fragment of two different verses.

2:2 1[ו שלם *vacat*
2:3 ו̊אנה̇[| 2[שלם וכל אנש[| 3[ן̊ אנה [ ]ל̊[| 4[ל̊[

There is a lacuna of 4 lines at the start of 4QLevi[b], frag. 1, col. 1. There is a full Greek translation of this passage interpolated into ms e of *TPL* in *TPL* 2:3. Some tiny fragments of Aramaic occur in 4QLevi[b], frag. 1, col. 1, ll. 5–6. It cannot be determined how much text is missing between the end of Cambridge b and the beginning of this passage. Overall, based on the codicology of the Geniza manuscript, we know that at least four columns are missing between Cambridge b and the start of Bodleian a. The text of 2:4–5 and all of chapter 3 and the subsequent material down to the start of Bodleian b must have been in that lacuna. A further bifolium was probably lost which contained four more columns preceding Bodleian b and then the material preserved only in Greek preceding Cambridge c.

2:4 τότε ἐγὼ ἔπλυνα τὰ ἱμάτιά μου, καὶ καθαρίσας αὐτὰ ἐν ὕδατι καθαρῷ·

5[דן | 6[ ]א̊נה |

2:5 καὶ ὅλος ἐλουσάμην ἐν ὕδατι ζῶντι· καὶ πάσας τὰς ὁδούς μου ἐποίησα εὐθείας.

7אתרחע[ת וכל

Variants

2.1 מ̊י̇ת̊[—מ Charles | ר̊ד[—or ד̊ד[. . .] | די למדנ̊ח̊ א̊שר—Puech | יהודה—[י]הודה Charles | עאנא—after this word an elliptic sign is found | [ל]מ̊שבק—[די] שבק Charles

Chapter 2: The Wars of the Sons of Jacob

2:1 [. . .]. my brother(s?) at all times | [. . .] who were in Shechem, | [. . .] my brother(s?) and he told this | [. . .] in Shechem and that | [. . . do]ers of violence and Judah told | them that I and Simeon | my brother had gone [. . .] to Reuben | our brother, which is to the east of Asher, and Judah | leaped forward [to] leave the sheep |

2:2]peace *vacat*[

2:3 and I[ ] peace and all [. . .] people[1] [|] I [. . .]

2:4 Then *I* laundered my garments, and having purified them in pure water,

2:5 I also washed my whole self in living water, and I made all my paths upright.

[1] Or: men.

Chapter 3: Levi's Prayer

There exists a fragmentary Aramaic text of Levi's prayer in 4QLevi[b] which was filled out with a reconstruction by Greenfield and Stone based on the Athos Greek manuscript, which preserves the prayer in full. Here the Aramaic is given for each verse, followed by the Greek. Words additional in one version compared with the other are put in *italic* type. From the end of the Aramaic text in 3:10 (עבד), at the end of 4QLevi[b] frag. 1, col. 1, we use the Greek as the dominant text until the Aramaic resumes in col. 2, line 5 = 3:13. Aramaic is, moreover, very fragmentary for two lines at least after it resumes.

3:1–10 = 4QLevi[b] frag. 1, col. 1 and Athos Greek 3–11
3:11–13 = Athos Greek 12–14
3:14–18 = 4QLevi[b] frag. 1, col. 2 and Athos Greek 15–19

3:1 $_{8}$]אדין עיני ואנפי [נטלת לשמיא |]ופומי פתחת ומללת[

τότε τοὺς ὀφθαλμούς μου καὶ τὸ πρόσωπόν μου ἦρα πρὸς οὐρανόν, καὶ τὸ στόμα μου ἤνοιξα καὶ ἐλάλησα,

3:2 ואצבעת כפי וידי | $_{10}$]אושטת בקושטא קדם קדישיא וצלית ו[אמרת

καὶ τοὺς δακτύλους τῶν χειρῶν μου καὶ τὰς χεῖράς μου ἀνεπέτασα εἰς ἀλήθειαν κατέναντι τῶν ἁγίων. καὶ ηὐξάμην καὶ εἶπα.

3:3 מרי אנתה |]ידע כל לבביא וכל רעיוניא א[נתה בלחודיך ידע |

Κύριε, γινώσκεις πάσας τὰς καρδίας, καὶ πάντας τοὺς διαλογισμοὺς *ἐννοιῶν* σὺ μόνος ἐπίστασαι.

3:4]וכען בני קדמי והב לי כל [אׄרחת קשט

καὶ νῦν τέκνα μου μετ᾽ ἐμοῦ. καὶ δός μοι πάσας ὁδοὺς ἀληθείας.

3:5 ארחק |]מני מרי רוח עויה ורעיונא ב[איש^{א} וזנותא דחא |]מני

μάκρυνον ἀπ᾽ ἐμοῦ, κύριε, τὸ πνεῦμα τὸ ἄδικον
καὶ διαλογισμὸν τὸν πονηρὸν καὶ πορνείαν *καὶ ὕβριν* ἀπόστρεψον ἀπ᾽ ἐμοῦ.

3:6 אחזיני מרי רוח קודשא ועטה וח[כמה ומנדע וגבורה | $_{15}$]הב לי

δειχθήτω μοι, δέσποτα, τὸ πνεῦμα τὸ ἅγιον,
καὶ βουλὴν καὶ σοφίαν καὶ γνῶσιν καὶ ἰσχύν δός μοι.

3:7 למעבד די שפיר קדמך ולא[שכחה רחמי<ן> קדמיך |

ποιῆσαι <τὰ> ἀρέσκοντά σοι καὶ εὑρεῖν χάριν ἐνώπιόν σου

3:8]לשבחה מלליך עמי מרי[ ] [דׄשפיר ודטב קדמיך |

καὶ αἰνεῖν τοὺς λόγους σου μετ᾽ ἐμοῦ, κύριε. [*missing*]

Chapter 3: Levi's Prayer

3:1 Then I lifted up my eyes and my countenance to heaven,
and I opened my mouth and spoke.
3:2 And I stretched out the fingers of my hands and my hands
for truth over against (*or*: towards) the holy ones,
And I prayed and said,
3:3 'My Lord, you know all hearts,
And you alone understand all the thoughts of minds.
3:4 And now my children are with me,
And grant me all the paths of truth.
3:5 Make far from me, my Lord, the unrighteous spirit,
and evil thought and fornication,
and turn *pride* away from me.
3:6 Let there be shown to me, O Lord, the holy spirit,
and grant me counsel and wisdom and knowledge and strength,
3:7 in order to do that which is pleasing to you
and find favour before you,
3:8 and to praise your words with me, O Lord.
[. . .] that which is pleasant and good before you.

3:9 [ו]אֹל תשלט בי כל שטן | [לאטעני מן ארחך]

καὶ μὴ κατισχυσάτω με πᾶς σατανᾶς πλανῆσαί με ἀπὸ τῆς ὁδοῦ σου.

3:10 [ורחם ע]לׄיׄ מׄרׄיׄ וקרבני למהוא לכה | [עבד

καὶ ἐλέησόν με καὶ προσάγαγέ με εἶναί σου δοῦλος καὶ λατρεῦσαί σοι *καλῶς*.

3:11 τεῖχος εἰρήνης σου γενέσθαι κύκλῳ μου,
καὶ σκέπη σου τῆς δυναστείας σκεπασάτω με ἀπὸ παντὸς κακοῦ.
3:12 παραδοὺς διὸ δὴ καὶ τὴν ἀνομίαν ἐξάλειψον ὑποκάτωθεν τοῦ οὐρανοῦ,
καὶ συντελέσαι τὴν ἀνομίαν ἀπὸ προσώπου τῆς γῆς

3:13 לע[ ]

καθάρισον τὴν καρδίαν μου, δέσποτα, ἀπὸ πάσης ἀκαθαρσίας,
καὶ προσάρωμαι πρός σε αὐτός.

3:14 [אל תפנה אנפיך מבר עבדך יעקב
אנתה] | מרי ב[רכת לאברהם אבי ולשרה אמי

καὶ μὴ ἀποστρέψῃς τὸ πρόσωπόν σου ἀπὸ τοῦ υἱοῦ παιδός σου Ἰακώβ.
σύ, κύριε, εὐλόγησας τὸν Ἀβραὰμ πατέρα μου καὶ Σάρραν μητέρα μου,

3:15 וממלת די תיהב להן] | זרע דק[שט בריך לעלם

καὶ εἶπας δοῦναι αὐτοῖς σπέρμα δίκαιον εὐλογημένον εἰς τοὺς αἰῶνας.

3:16 ואף שמע לקל] | צלות עב[דך לוי למהוא קריב לך

εἰσάκουσον δὲ καὶ τῆς φωνῆς τοῦ παιδός σου Λευὶ γενέσθαι σοι ἐγγύς,

3:17 *one hemistich missing* למעבד] | דין קשט לכ[ל עלם

καὶ μέτοχον ποίησον τοῖς λόγοις σου

ποιεῖν κρίσιν ἀληθινὴν εἰς πάντα τὸν αἰῶνα,
ἐμὲ καὶ τοὺς υἱούς μου εἰς πάσας τὰς γενεὰς τῶν αἰώνων.

3:18 ואל תעדי | [ ]לבר עבדך מן ק[דם אנפך כל ימי עלם.

καὶ μὴ ἀποστήσῃς τὸν υἱὸν τοῦ παιδός σου ἀπὸ τοῦ προσώπου σου πάσας τὰς ἡμέρας τοῦ αἰῶνος.

καὶ ἐσιώπησα ἔτι δεόμενος.

3:9 And let not any satan have power over me,
to make me stray from your path.
3:10 And have mercy upon me, my Lord, and bring me forward,
to be your servant and to minister well to you.
3:11 so that the wall of your peace is around me,
and let the shelter of your power shelter me from every evil.
3:12 Wherefore, giving over even lawlessness,
wipe it out from under the heaven,
and end lawlessness from the face of the earth.
3:13 Purify my heart, Lord, from all impurity,
and let me, myself, be raised to you.
3:14 And turn not your countenance aside from the son of your servant Jacob.
$_{6}$ You, O, Lord, blessed Abraham my father and Sarah my mother.
3:15 And you said (that you would) give them a righteous seed blessed for ever.
3:16 Hearken also to the prayer of your servant
Levi to be close to you,
3:17 And make (me) a participant in your words,
to do true judgment for all time,
me and my children for all the generations of the ages.
3:18 And do not remove $_{10}$ the son of your servant
from your countenance all the days of the world.'
And I became silent still continuing to pray.

Variants

3:5 ב[אישא 4QLevi[b] with א2° above line | διαλογισμὸν τὸν πονηρὸν—de Jonge διαλογισμῶν τῶν πονηρῶν manuscript **3:7** τὰ—de Jonge τό manuscript | ל[שבחה—לא[שכחה Fitzmyer and Harrington | רחמיך—רחמי<ן> manuscript **3:13** לע[יניך]—לע] Fitzmyer and Harrington **3:16** צלות—צלת Beyer

Parallels

TPL 2:10 related to 3:16
ὅτι σὺ ἐγγὺς κυρίου στήσῃ, καὶ λειτουργὸς αὐτοῦ ἔσῃ, καὶ μυστήρια αὐτοῦ ἐξαγγελεῖς τοῖς ἀνθρώποις, καὶ περὶ τοῦ μέλλοντος λυτροῦσθαι τὸν Ἰσραὴλ κηρύξεις·

TPL 4:2 related to 3:16
εἰσήκουσεν οὖν ὁ ὕψιστος τῆς προσευχῆς σου, τοῦ διελεῖν σε ἀπὸ τῆς ἀδικίας καὶ γενέσθαι αὐτῷ υἱὸν καὶ θεράποντα καὶ λειτουργὸν τοῦ προσώπου αὐτοῦ.

Parallels

TPL 2:10 related to 3:16
For you will stand near to the Lord and will be his minister and will declare his mysteries to men and will proclaim concerning him who will redeem Israel.

TPL 4:2 related to 3:16
The Most High, therefore, has heard your prayer to separate you from unrighteousness and that you should become to him son and a servant and a minister of his presence.

Chapter 4: Travels and Vision(s) of Levi

Following the prayer in Chapter 3, Levi's travel to his father (4QLevi[b] col. 2, 11–14 = 4:1–3) and then a vision (4QLevi[b] col. 2 15–18 = 4:4–6) are recounted. We think that it is very likely that 1QLevi frags. 1 and 7 are also part of this chapter, though their order is not absolutely certain. 4QLevi[b] col. 2, 11–18 = 4:1–6 follow the prayer immediately. It is also possible that 1QLevi frag. 37 belongs to the vision of consecration, but this is not certain.

4:1–6 = 4QLevi[b] frag. 1, col. 2
4:7 = 1QLevi frag. 1
4:8 = 1QLevi frag. 7
4:9–13 = Geniza Bodleian a 4–7
4:9 = 1QLevi 26
4:9–11 = 1QLevi 3
4:12–13 = 4QLevi[c]

4:1 $_{11}$באדין נגדת ב[ ]|על אבי יעקוב
4:2 וכד[י] | מן אבל מין
4:3 אדין[ ] | שכבת ויתבת אנה ע[ל
4:4 *vacat* $_{15}$אדין חזיון אחזית[ ] | בחזית חזויא
4:5 וחזית שמ[יא] | תחותי רם עד דבק לשמי[א]
4:6 [ ] | לי תרעי שמיא ומלאך חד[

1QLevi (1Q21) frag. 1 is, in our view, to be located somewhere before the material with which Bodleian a opens. We have numbered this 4:7. Milik thought that frag. 2 of this manuscript, which contains a total of 3 letters, also belongs with frag. 1. We think this unprovable. It is possible, however, that frag. 7 col. 1 is associated with this same material and note particularly line 2. This fragment is numbered 4:8 below. Column 2 of frag 7 has only 2 letters surviving, לא.

4:7 $_{1}$]מׄן די להוין תליתין [
$_{2}$לב]נׄיך מלכות כהנותא רבא מן מלכותׄ[
$_{3}$]ל֯[א]ל֯[ע]ל֯[יון

1QLevi frag. 7 col. 1. Milik based his edition on a join which is unacceptable. Therefore, our edition omits several words that are on the wrongly placed fragment: see DJD 1, plate 17.

4:8 $_{1}$]ב֯תא עד[
$_{2}$]ת֯מלך עם[
$_{3}$]ם בעא[

The Geniza material resumes with col. a of the Bodleian fragment. Where Qumran fragments overlap with the Geniza text, we have put the text into bold type. Differences between the two texts are, however, listed in the Apparatus, which comes at the end of each chapter. In the following section, 4:9–11, fragments of two Qumran manuscripts, 1QLevi frags. 26 (4:9) and 3 (4:9–11) exist (marked with overstrike). In 4:11–5:4 we have 4QLevi[c]. In the text parallel to 4:11a, it is very different from the Geniza and both versions are given in our text. For the rest it is close, with some variants.

Chapter 4: Travels and Vision of Levi

4:1 $_{11}$Then I continued on[. . .] | to my father Jacob
4:2 and when [. . .] | from Abel Mayyin.
4:3 Then[. . .] | I lay down and I remained o[n
4:4 $_{15}$ Then I was shown visions[. . .] | in the vision of visions
4:5 and I saw the heaven[s] | beneath me, high until it reached the heaven[s
4:6 [ ] | to me the gates of heaven, and an angel[|
4:7]from that they were third [
$_{2}$to your so]ns the kingdom of priesthood is greater than the kingdom[
$_{3}$]to the [Most H]igh G[o]d
4:8 $_{1}$] until you [. . . $_{2}$]you will rule until[. . . $_{3}$]. ask[

4:9 שלמא וכל חמדת בכורי **ארעא** | כולה למאכל
ולמלכות ה**רבא** פגשא | וקרבא ונחשירותא ועמלא *vacat* | ונצפתא וקטלא
וכפנא
4:10 זמנין תאכול | וזמנין תכפן
וזמנין תעמול וזמנין] תנוח
וזמנין תדמוך וזמנין תנוד|שנת עינא
4:11 **Geniza** כען חזי לך הכין רבינך מן כולה|
4QLevi^{c} line 1 ה]**כה רעיתך מן כל בשר**[**א**
והיך יהבנא לך רבות **שלם** | **עלמא** |
4:12 *vacat* ונגדו שבעתון מן לותי
4:13 **ואנה אתעירת מן שנתי**
אדין | אמרת חזוא הוא דן וכדן אנה | מתמה די יהוי <לי> כל חזוה | **וטמרת**
| **אף דן בלבי ולכל אינש לא** גליתה|

Variants

4:1 marginal mark and indentation in manuscript **4:4** חזוין—חזין Fitzmyer and Harrington | בחזות חזונ̊א—בחזית חזויא Beyer | חזיוא—חזויא Milik **4:7** לב]ניך—לך ולב]ניך Grelot | מן]—[ד.] Beyer | מלכות [חרבא—מלכות] Grelot **4:8**]נתא—]ב̊תא Milik **4:9** כולא—כולה Charles | תעמל—תעמול 1QLevi frag. 3 | **4:11** כולא—כולה Charles | והך—והיך Charles **4:12** שבעתין—שבעתון Charles; שבעת<ה>ון Beyer **4:13** [ו]כדן <ו>אנה—וכדן אנה Beyer | <לי>—eds לה Geniza | בלבבי—בלבי 4QLevi^{c} line 3 | אנש—אינש 4QLevi^{c} line 3

Parallels

TPL 3:5–6 resembling 4:4–6
3:5 ἐν τῷ μετ᾽ αὐτὸν οἱ ἄγγελοί εἰσι τοῦ προσώπου κυρίου, οἱ λειτουργοῦντες καὶ ἐξιλασκόμενοι πρὸς κύριον ἐπὶ πάσαις ταῖς ἀγνοίαις τῶν δικαίων.
3:6 προσφέρουσι δὲ κυρίῳ ὀσμὴν εὐωδίας λογικὴν καὶ ἀναίμακτον προσφοράν.

TPL 5:1 resembling 4:6
Καὶ ἤνοιξέ μοι ὁ ἄγγελος τὰς πύλας τοῦ οὐρανοῦ· καὶ εἶδον τὸν ναὸν τὸν ἅγιον, καὶ ἐπὶ θρόνου δόξης τὸν ὕψιστον.

TPL 8:16 resembling 4:9
πᾶν ἐπιθυμητὸν ἐν Ἰσραὴλ σοὶ ἔσται καὶ τῷ σπέρματί σου· καὶ ἔδεσθε πᾶν ὡραῖον ὁράσει, καὶ τὴν τράπεζαν κυρίου διανεμήσεται τὸ σπέρμα σου,

TPL 8:18–19 resembling 4:13–14
8:18 καὶ ἐξυπνισθεὶς συνῆκα ὅτι τοῦτο ὅμοιον ἐκείνου ἐστίν.
8:19 καὶ ἔκρυψα καίγε τοῦτο ἐν τῇ καρδίᾳ μου, καὶ οὐκ ἀνήγγειλα αὐτὸ παντὶ ἀνθρώπῳ ἐπὶ τῆς γῆς.

4:9 peace, and all choice first-fruits of the whole | earth for food. And for the kingdom of the sword (there is) fighting | and battle and chase and toil | and conflict and killing and hunger.
4:10 Sometimes it shall eat | and sometimes it shall hunger,
and sometimes it shall toil and sometimes | it shall rest,
sometimes it shall sleep and sometimes lie | awake.
4:11 Now, see how we made you greater than all | (Geniza)
h]ow I loved you more than all flesh[(4QLevi[a])
and how we gave you the anointing (*or*: greatness) of eternal | peace.
4:12 And those seven departed from me. |
4:13 And I awoke from my sleep.
Then | I said, "This is a vision and like this (vision),[2] I am amazed that | <I> should have any vision at all." And I hid | this too in my heart and I revealed it to nobody. |

Parallels

TPL 3:5–6 resembling 4:4–6
3:5 In the (heaven) next to it are the angels of the presence of the Lord, those who minister and make propitiation to the Lord for all the sins of ignorance of the righteous,
3:6 and they offer to the Lord a pleasant odour, a reasonable and bloodless offering.

TPL 5:1 resembling 4:6
And the angel opened to me the gates of heaven, and I saw the holy temple and the Most High upon a throne of glory.

TPL 8:16 resembling 4:9
Every desirable thing in Israel will be for you and your seed; and you will eat everything beautiful to see, and your seed will divide among themselves the table of the Lord.

TPL 8:18–19 resembling 4:13–14
8:18 And when I awoke I understood that this (vision) was like the former.
8:19 And I hid this also in my heart and I did not tell it to anybody on earth.

[2] I.e., the first one.

Chapter 5: Levi's Priesthood, Blessing and Instruction

For this chapter we have the Geniza text and two Qumran fragments, 5:1–4 in 4QLevi^{c} and 5:2 in 1QLevi frag. 4 (see apparatus of variants). The end of Bodleian column a is the word ואשלמת in 5:5 and the subsequent text is from Bodleian b. From verse 6 on, the Athos Greek manuscript also exists.

5:1 = Bod a 8
5:1–4 = 4QLevi^{c}
5:2 = Bod a 9a; 1QLevi frag. 4
5:3–4 = Bod a 9b
5:5–8 = Bod a–b 10–13
5:6–8—Athos Greek 11–13

5:1 וע֯לנא על אבי יצחק ואף הוא כדן | [ברכ]ני *vacat*
5:2 אדין **כדי הוה יעקב** | [**אבי**]**מ֯ע֯שר** כל מה די הוה לה כנדרה |
5:3 [באדין] אנה הוית קדמי בראש | [כהנו]ת֯**ה ולי מכל בנוהי יהב** קרבן | מ֯ע֯ש֯[ר] לאל
5:4 ואלבשי לבוש כהונתא | ומלי ידי והוית כהין **לאל עלמיא** | וקרבית כל קרבנוהי וברכת לאבי | בחיוהי וברכת לאחי |
5:5 אדין כולהון | ברכוני ואף אבא ברכני ואשלמית | להקרבה קורבנוהי בבית אל
5:6 ואזלנא | מבית אל ושרינא בבירת אברהם | אבונן לות יצחק אבונה

καὶ ἀνήλθομεν ἀπὸ Βεθὴλ καὶ κατελύσαμεν ἐν τῇ αὐλῇ ᾿Αβραὰμ τοῦ πατρὸς ἡμῶν παρὰ ᾿Ισαὰκ τὸν πατέρα ἡμῶν.

5:7 <וחזא> | יצחק אבונא לכולנא וברכנא | וחדי

καὶ εἶδεν ᾿Ισαὰκ ὁ πατὴρ ἡμῶν πάντας ἡμᾶς καὶ ηὐλόγησεν ἡμᾶς, καὶ ηὐφράνθη.

5:8 וכדי ידע די אנה כהין לאל | עליון למארי שמיא שארי | לפקדה יתי ולאלפא יתי דין | כהנותא *vacat*

καὶ ὅτε ἔγνω ὅτι ἐγὼ ἱεράτευσα τῷ κυρίῳ δεσπότῃ τοῦ οὐρανοῦ, ἤρξατο διδάσκειν με τὴν κρίσιν ἱερωσύνης,

Variants

5:2 [אבי]מ֯ע֯שר—יעקב Geniza יעקוב אבי מעשר 4QLevi^{c} אבי יע[קב מעשר] 1QLevi frag. 4: Puech reads the מ of מעשר which Greenfield and Stone reconstructed | [אבי]מ֯ע֯שר—[...]עשר Charles **5:3** [באדין]—[וכדי] Charles; [לאל] Beyer | [כהנו]ת֯ה—Puech [כהונת]א Charles כה[נ֯י֯ה Beyer | מכל—מן 4QLevi^{c} | מעש[ר]— ... Charles **5:4** עלמיא—עלמא written over another word(s) | ומלי—[ומ]לי Charles | בחיוהי—בחיותי Charles **5:5** בבית אל—בביתאל Beyer **5:6** מבית אל—מביתאל Beyer **5:7** <וחזא>—Charles, cf. Greek, והוא Geniza

Chapter 5: Levi's Priesthood, Blessing and Instruction

5:1 And we went to my father Isaac, and he thus[3] [blessed] me. |
5:2 Then, when Jacob | [my father] tithed everything which he
possessed, in accordance with his vow, |
5:3 [then]I was before <him> at the head | of the [priesth]ood,
and to me of all his sons he gave a gift | of tit[he] to God,
5:4 and he invested me in the priestly garb | and consecrated
me and I became a priest of the God of eternity | and I offered
all of his sacrifices. And I blessed my father | during his lifetime
and I blessed my brothers. |
5:5 Then they all blessed me and my father also blessed me and
I finished | bringing his sacrifices in Bethel.
5:6 And we went | from Bethel and we encamped at the resi-
dence of Abraham | our father alongside Isaac our father. |
5:7 And Isaac | our father <saw> all of us and blessed us | and
rejoiced.
5:8 And when he learned that I was a priest of the Most High |
God, the Lord of heaven, he began | to instruct me and to teach
me the law | of the priesthood.

[3] Perhaps: "in accordance with this (i.e., vision)".

Parallels

TPL 9:1–2a resembling 5:1
9:1 Καὶ μεθ᾿ ἡμέρας δύο ἀνέβημεν ἐγὼ καὶ Ἰούδας πρὸς Ἰσαὰκ μετὰ τοῦ πατρὸς ἡμῶν.
9:2a καὶ εὐλόγησέ με ὁ πατὴρ τοῦ πατρός μου κατὰ πάντας τοὺς λόγους τῶν ὁράσεών μου ὧν εἶδον.

TPL 9:4 resembling 5:2
καὶ ἀναστὰς τὸ πρωὶ ἀπεδεκάτωσε πάντα δι᾿ ἐμοῦ τῷ κυρίῳ.

TPL 8:2b–3, 8:10b resembling 5:4
8:2 Ἀναστὰς ἔνδυσαι τὴν στολὴν τῆς ἱερατείας καὶ τὸν στέφανον τῆς δικαιοσύνης καὶ τὸ λόγιον τῆς συνέσεως καὶ τὸν ποδήρη τῆς ἀληθείας καὶ τὸ πέταλον τῆς πίστεως καὶ τὴν μίτραν τοῦ σημείου καὶ τὸ ἐφοὺδ τῆς προφητείας
8:3 . . . Ἀπὸ τοῦ νῦν γίνου εἰς ἱερέα κυρίου . . . ἕως αἰῶνος.
8:10b . . . καὶ ἐπλήρωσαν τὰς χεῖράς μου θυμιάματος, ὥστε ἱερατεύειν με κυρίῳ.

Jubilees 32:3 resembling 5:4
His father put priestly clothes on him and ordained him.

TPL 9:7a resembling 5:8
καὶ ἐδίδασκέ με νόμον ἱερωσύνης.

Parallels

TPL 9:1–2a resembling 5:1
9:1 And after two days I and Judah went up with our father to Isaac.
9:2 And the father of my father blessed me according to all the words of my visions which I had seen.

TPL 9:4 resembling 5:2
And after having risen early in the morning he paid tithes of all to the Lord through me.

TPL 8:2b–3, 8:10b resembling 5:4
8:2 Arise, put on the robe of priesthood and the crown of righteousness and the breastplate of understanding and the garment of truth and the plate of faith and the turban of (giving) a sign and the ephod of prophecy.
8:3 . . . From now on become a priest of the Lord . . . for ever.
8:10b . . . And they filled my hands with incense that I might serve as priest to the Lord.

Jubilees 32:3 resembling 5:4
His father put priestly clothes on him and ordained him.

TPL 9:7a resembling 5:8
9:7a . . . And he taught me the law of the priesthood.

Chapter 6: Priestly Teaching—Purity

This passage exists in Geniza Bodleian b, in the Athos Greek manuscript and apparently in 4QLevi^{f} frag. 7 = 6:1, though this identification is not certain: see commentary below. Bodleian b concludes at the end of 6:5.

6:1 = 4QLevi^{f} frag. 7
6:1–5 = Bod b 14–18
6:1–6 = Greek

6:1 ואמר לי לוי אזדהר | לך ברי מן כל טומאה ומן | כל חטא
דינך רב הוא **מן כל** | **בישרא** *vacat*

καὶ εἶπεν· Τέκνον Λευί, πρόσεχε σεαυτῷ ἀπὸ πάσης ἀκαθαρσίας. ἡ κρίσις σου μεγάλη ἀπὸ πάσης σαρκός.

6:2 וכען כרי דין | קושטא אחזינך ולא אטמר | מינך כל פתגם לאלפותך
דין | כהנותא

καὶ νῦν τὴν κρίσιν τῆς ἀληθείας ἀναγγελῶ σοι, καὶ οὐ μὴ κρύψω ἀπό σου πᾶν ῥῆμα. διδάξω σε.

6:3 לקדמין הי<ז>דהר לך | ברי מן כל פחז וטמאה ומן כל | זנות

πρόσεχε σεαυτῷ ἀπὸ παντὸς συνουσιασμοῦ καὶ *ἀπὸ πάσης* ἀκαθαρσίας καὶ ἀπὸ πάσης πορνείας.

6:4 ואנת אנתתא מן משפחתי | סב לך ולא תחל זרעך עם זניאן |
ארי זרע קדיש אנת וקדיש | זרעך היך קודשא
ארו כהין | קדיש אנת מתקרי לכל זרע | אברהם

σὺ {πρῶτος} ἀπὸ τοῦ σπέρματός <μου> λάβε σεαυτῷ καὶ μὴ βεβηλώσῃς τὸ σπέρμα σου μετὰ <πόρνων>.
ἐκ σπέρματος γὰρ ἁγίου εἶ, καὶ τὸ σπέρμα σου ἁγίασον *καὶ τὸ σπέρμα* τοῦ ἁγιασμοῦ σου ἐστίν. ἱερεὺς ἅγιος κληθήσεται τῷ σπέρματι Ἀβραάμ.

6:5 קריב אנת לאֹלֹ וֹקריב | לכל קדישוהי
כען אֹזדכי | בבשרך מן כל טומאת כל גבר

ἐγγὺς εἶ κυρίου καὶ σὺ ἐγγὺς τῶν ἁγίων αὐτοῦ. γίνου καθαρὸς ἐν τῷ σώματί σου ἀπὸ πάσης ἀκαθαρσίας παντὸς ἀνθρώπου.

Variants

6:1 ברי—ברי ברי Geniza: dittography | בישרא—בשׂר]א 4QLevi^{f} **6:2** כהנותא—כהונתא Charles | διδάξω σε—followed by an omission in Greek **6:3** הי<ז>דהר—היוהר ms: cf. 5:7 (Puech) | זנות—זנו{ת} Beyer **6:4** πρῶτος—corrupt de Jonge: perhaps from 6:3 | אנתתא—אנת{ת}א Beyer | <μου>—eds. Greek omits | <πόρνων>—eds. πολλῶν Geniza: corrupt de Jonge **6:5** לאֹלֹ וֹקריב—ל[אל ו]קריב Charles | וֹקריב—<אנת> וֹקריב Beyer

Chapter 6: Priestly Teaching—Purity

6:1 And he said to me, Levi my son, | beware of all uncleanliness and | of all sin, your judgment is greater than that of all | flesh.

6:2 And now, my son, I will show | you the true law and I will not hide | anything from you, to teach you the law | of the priesthood.

6:3 First of all, be<wa>re | my son of all fornication and impurity and of all | harlotry.

6:4 And marry a woman | from my family and do not defile your seed with harlots, | since you are holy seed, and sanctify | your seed like the holy place
since you are called | a holy priest for all the seed of | Abraham.

6:5 You are near to God and near | to all his holy ones.
Now, be pure | in your flesh from every impurity of man.

Parallels

ALD 9:9 resembling 6:3
πρόσεχε, τέκνον, ἀπὸ τοῦ πνεύματος τῆς πορνείας·

Parallels

ALD 9:9 resembling 6:3
Beware, child, of the spirit of impurity.

Chapter 7: Priestly Teaching—Wood Offering

This chapter is extant in Bodleian c, Athos Greek, 4QLevi[d] frag. 1 (7:3), 4QLev[f] frags. 2–6 (7:3–7: signalled in text by overbar), and in 4QLevi[c] frag. 1 (7:6–7).

7:1–7 = Bod c 19–25a and Athos Greek 19–25a
7:3 = 4QLevi[d] frag. 1
7:4–7 = 4QLev[f] frags. 2–6
7:6–7 = 4QLevi[c] frag. 1

7:1 וכדי תהוי קאים למיעל לבית אל | הוי סחי במיא ובאדין תהוי לביש לבוש כהנותא |

καὶ ὅταν εἰσπορεύῃ ἐν τοῖς ἁγίοις, λούου ὕδατι *πρῶτον* καὶ τότε ἐνδιδύσκου τὴν στολὴν τῆς ἱερωσύνης.

7:2 וכדי תהוי לביש | הוי תאיב תוב ורחיע ידיך | ורגליך עד דלא תקרב למדבחא | כל דנה

καὶ ὅταν ἐνδιδύσκῃ, νίπτου πάλιν τὰς χεῖράς σου καὶ τοὺς πόδας σου πρὸ τοῦ ἐγγίσαι πρὸς τὸν βωμὸν προσενέγκαι ὁλοκάρπωσιν.

7:3 וכדי תהוי נסב להקרבה | כל די חזה להנסקה למדבחה | הוי עוד תאב ורחע ידיך ורגליך |

καὶ ὅταν μέλλῃς προσφέρειν ὅσα δεῖ ἀνενέγκαι ἐπὶ τὸν βωμόν, πάλιν νίπτου τὰς χεῖράς σου καὶ τοὺς πόδας σου.

7:4 ומהקריב אעין מהצלחין ובקר | אינון לקודמין מן תולעא | ובאדין הסק אינון ארי כדנה | חזיתי לאברהם אבי מיזדהר |

καὶ ἀνάφερε τὰ ξύλα *πρῶτον* <ἐ>σχισμένα, ἐπισκοπῶν αὐτὰ πρῶτον ἀπὸ παντὸς μολυσμοῦ·

7:5 מן כל תריעשר מיני אעין אמר | לי די חזין להסקה מינהון למדבחה | די ריח תננהון בשים סליק

ιβ᾽ ξύλα εἴρηκέν μοι ἐπὶ τὸν βωμὸν προσφέρε<ιν> ὧν ἐστιν ὁ καπνὸς αὐτῶν ἡδὺς ἀναβαίνων.

7:6 ואלין | אינון שמהתהון ארזא ודפרנא | וסנדא ואטולא ושוהא ואדונא | ברותא ותאנתא ואע משחא | ערא והדסה ואעי דקתא
4QLev[f] frags. 2–6 ותככה̊

καὶ ταῦτα τὰ ὀνόματα αὐτῶν· κέδρον καὶ ουεδεφωνα καὶ σχῖνον καὶ στρόβιλον καὶ πίτυν καὶ ολδινα καὶ βερωθα {καν} θεχακ καὶ κυπάρισσον καὶ δάφνην καὶ μυρσίνην καὶ ἀσφάλαθον.

7:7 אלין | אינון די אמר לי די חזין להסקה | מנהון ל[ת]חות עלתא על מדבחא

Chapter 7: Priestly Teaching—Wood Offering

7:1 And when you are about to enter the Sanctuary, | wash in water and then put on | the priestly garment.

7:2 And when you are robed,[4] | lave your hands and feet again | before you approach the altar | at all.

7:3 And when you are about to sacrifice | anything fitting to offer up on the altar, | wash your hands and feet once again. |

7:4 And offer split wood, and examine | it first for worms | and then offer it up, for thus | I saw my father Abraham acting with care. |

7:5 Of any of all twelve kinds of wood which are fitting, he | told me to offer up on the altar, | whose smoke rises up with a pleasant odor.

7:6 And these | are their names—cedar and juniper, | and almond and fir and pine and ash, | cypress and fig and oleaster, | laurel and myrtle and asphalathos.

tkkh 4QLevi[f] frags. 2–6

7:7 These are | those that he told me are fitting to offer up | [be]neath the holocaust upon the altar. |

[4] Literally: will have put (it) on.

ταῦτα εἴρηκεν ὅτι ταῦτά ἐστιν ἅ σε ἀναφέρειν ὑποκάτω τῆς ὁλοκαυστώσεως ἐπὶ τοῦ θυσιαστηρίου.

Variants

7:1 לבית אל—ἐν τοῖς ἁγίοις | πρῶτον—Greek only **7:2** כל דנה—προσενέγκαι ὁλοκάρπωσιν **7:3** להנסקה—ל[אׄס]קה 4QLevi[d] **7:4** מהצלחין—מׄצׄלׄחׄין 4QLevi[f] | <ἐ>σχισμένα—de Jonge σχισμένα manuscript | כדנה—כדן 4QLevi[f] | חזיתי—חזית 4QLev[f] **7:5** אעין—עעין 4QLev[f] | להסקה—ל[אׄסקה 4QLevi[f] | προσφέρε<ιν>—προσφερε manuscript | מינהון—מנהון 4QLevi[f] | למדבחה—למדבחא 4QLevi[f] | תנהון—תננהון Charles | סליק—סׄלׄק 4QLevi[f] **7:6** ואלין—ואׄלן 4QLevi[f] | אינון—omit 4QLevi[f] | וסנדא—וסינדה 4QLevi[f] | ותאנתא—ותככׄה 4QLevi[f]: cf. Greek | והדסה—אדסא 4QLevi[f] | ואעי—ועעי 4QLevi[f] | דקתא—reading uncertain: might be רקתא, תׄאׄ.[4QLevi[e] | Charles omits μυρσίνην **7:7** אלין— אׄלן 4QLevi[f] 4QLevi[e] | אינון—אנׄון 4QLevi[f] | לת[חׄות]—Puech ל[תחו]ת Charles | מדבחא—followed by *vacat* 4QLevi[e]

4QLevi frag. 1 has some tiny morsels of text in lines 6–7 that differ from 7:4–5 here.

Parallels

TPL 9:11 resembling 7:1–2
καὶ πρὸ τοῦ εἰσελθεῖν εἰς τὰ ἅγια, λούου· καὶ ἐν τῷ θύειν, νίπτου· καὶ ἀπαρτίζων πάλιν τὴν θυσίαν, νίπτου.

Jubilees 21:16 resembling 7:3
21:16 And at all times be careful with respect to your body. Wash with water before you go to make an offering on the altar. Wash your hands and feet before you approach the altar (or: sacrifice). When you have finished making an offering, wash your hands and feet again.

TPL 9:12 resembling 7:5
δώδεκα δένδρων ἀεὶ ἐχόντων φύλλα ἄναγε κυρίῳ, ὡς κἀμὲ᾽ Αβραὰμ ἐδίδαξεν.

For comparisons to the list of trees in 7:6, see Commentary.

Parallels

TPL 9:11 resembling 7:1–2
And before entering the holy place, bathe; and when you offer (the sacrifice), wash; and when you finish again the sacrifice, wash.

Jubilees 21:16 resembling 7:3
21:16 And at all times be careful with respect to your body. Wash with water before you go to make an offering on the altar. Wash your hands and feet before you approach the altar (or: sacrifice). When you have finished making an offering, wash your hands and feet again.

TPL 9:12 resembling 7:5
Offer to the Lord of twelve trees which always have leaves, as also Abraham taught me.

For comparisons to the list of trees in 7:6, see Commentary.

Chapter 8: Priestly Teaching—Sacrifices

The Aramaic text is from Bodleian c and d; the Greek from Athos ms *e*; the chapter is also represented in 4QLevi[f] 3–6 = 8:1–3 and 4QLevi[d] 2 = 8:2–6 and 1QLevi frag. 45 = 8:2 (for which see the apparatus of variants). Bodleian c concludes with the word להדלקה in 8:1.

8:1 = Bod c 25b
8:1–3 = 4QLevi[f] 2–6
8:1–7 = Athos Greek 25b–31
8:2–3 = 1QLevi frag. 45
8:1–6 = 4QLevi[d] 2
8:2–7 = Bod d 26–31

8:1 וכדי הנסקת מן אעי אלין על | מדבחא ונורא ישרא להדלקא | בהון
והא באדין תשרא למזרק דמא | על כותלי מדבחה

καὶ τὸ πῦρ τότε ἄρξῃ ἐκκαίειν ἐν αὐτοῖς, τότε ἄρξῃ κατασπένδειν τὸ αἷμα ἐπὶ τὸν τοῖχον τοῦ θυσιαστηρίου.

8:2 ועוד רחע ידיך | ורגליך מן דמא ושרי להנסקה אבריה| מליחי<ן>

καὶ πάλιν νίψαι σου τὰς χεῖρας καὶ τοὺς πόδας ἀπὸ τοῦ αἵματος, καὶ ἄρξῃ τὰ μέλη ἀναφέρειν ἡλισμένα·

8:3 <ראשא> הוי מהנסק לקדמין | ועלוהי חפי תרבא ולא יתחזה לה |
דם נ<כס>ת תורא

τὴν κεφαλὴν ἀνάφερε πρῶτον καὶ κάλυπτε αὐτὴν τῷ στέατι, καὶ μὴ ὀπτανέσθω τὸ αἷμα *ἐπὶ τῆς κεφαλῆς αὐτῆς*·

8:4 ובתרוהי צוארה | ובתר צוארה ידוהי ובתר ידוהי | ניעא עם כן דפנא
ובתר ידיא | ירכאתא עם שדרת חרצא | ובתר ירכאתא רגלין רחיען
עם | קרביא

καὶ μετὰ τοῦτο τὸν τράχηλον, καὶ μετὰ τοῦτο τοὺς ὤμους, καὶ μετὰ ταῦτα τὸ στῆθος μετὰ τῶν πλευρῶν, καὶ μετὰ ταῦτα τὴν ὀσφὺν σὺν τῷ νώτῳ, καὶ μετὰ ταῦτα τοὺς πόδας πεπλυμένους σὺν τοῖς ἐνδοσθίοις,

8.5 וכולהון מליחין במלח כדי | חזה להון כמסתהון

καὶ πάντα ἡλισμένα ἐν ἅλατι ὡς καθήκει αὐτοῖς αὐτάρκως.

8:6 ובתר דנה נישפא | בליל במשחא ובתר כולא חמר נסך | והקטיר
עליהון לבונה ויהוון כן | עובדיך בסרך וכל קורבניך [לרע]וא | לריח
ניחח קודם אל עליון

καὶ μετὰ ταῦτα σεμίδαλιν ἀναπεποιημένον ἐν ἐλαίῳ, καὶ μετὰ ταῦτα οἶνον σπεῖσον καὶ θυμίασον ἐπάνω λίβανον {τὸ ηεεσθαι} τὸ ἔργον σου ἐν τάξει καὶ πᾶσα προσφορά σου εἰς εὐδόκησιν καὶ ὀσμὴν εὐδωδίας ἔναντι κυρίου ὑψίστου.

Chapter 8: Priestly Teaching—Sacrifices

8:1 And when you have offered up any of these woods upon | the altar and the fire begins to burn | them, you should then begin to sprinkle the blood | on the sides of the altar.

8:2 And once more wash your hands | and feet of the blood and begin to offer up the salted | portions (*or*: limbs).

8:3 Burn its head first | and cover it with the fat and so that the blood of the | slaughtered bull will not be seen on it.

8:4 After it, its neck | and after its neck its forequarters and after its forequarters | the breast with the side and after the forequarters | the haunches with the spine of the loin | and after the haunches the hindquarters washed, with the | entrails.

8:5 All of them salted with salt as is | fitting for them in their proper amount.

8:6 After that, fine meal | mixed with oil. After all that pour out the wine | and burn the frankincense over them; and thus let | your actions follow due order and all your sacrifices be [acceptable] | as a pleasing odour before the Most High God.

8:7 וׄ[כל די] | תהוה עביד בסרך הוי עבׄי[ד במדה] | ובמתקל **לא** תותר צבו די **לא** [חזה] | **ולא** *תחסר מן חושבן* חזתׄאׄ אׄעׄ[י]ן | <חזין> להקרבה **לכל** די סליק למדב[חא] |

καὶ ὅσα ἂν ποιῇς, ἐν τάξει ποίει *ἅ ποιῇς* ἐν μέτρῳ καὶ σταθμῷ καὶ μὴ περισσεύσῃς μηθὲν ὅσα οὐ καθήκει, καὶ {τῷ καθηκι τῶν}οὕτως ξύλα *καθήκει* ἀναφέρεσθαι ἐπὶ τὸν βωμόν·

Variants

8:1 הׄנׄסׄקׄתׄ—Puech [הסקת] Greenfield and Stone | אעי—אׄ[עי] 4QLevi[f] | אלין—אלׄ[ין 4QLevi[f] | על מדבחא—לׄמׄדׄבׄחׄ[א 4QLevi[f] **8:2** ועוד—ותובׄ 4QLevi[f] | אבריה—א]בׄ[ריה א 4QLevi[f] | מליחי<ן>—יׄן[4QLevi[d] מׄ[ל]יׄחן 4QLevi[f] ..]ין 1QLevi 45; so also Greek ἡλισμένα; the Geniza has מליחי and Beyer has מליחי<ה> **8:3** <ראשא>—Thus 4QLevi[d] 4QLevi[f] 1QLevi 45, Greek τὴν κεφαλήν, Geniza has ואשה: Charles emended to ראשא | הוי מהנסק לקדמין—4QLevi[d] must have read [ל]קׄ[דמין הוי מהנסק: Greek word order might reflect the Geniza text | מהנסק—מתנסק Charles | ולא יתחזי—ואל יתחזה 4QLevi[d] | נ<כס>ת—נסבת Geniza corrupt **8:4** צוארה—צור]אׄ 4QLevi[d] | ידוהי 1°—ידיא 4QLevi[d], Charles emends to ניעא, Cowley emends to דנא: see commentary | ובתר ידיא—ובת]רׄהן 4QLevi[d]: see commentary below | כן—בן Charles | ירכאתא—ירכתא 4QLevi[d], in the Geniza manuscript there is a dot over the final א | עם שדרת—ושדרתׄ 4QLevi[d] **8:5** וכולהון—וכׄלׄהׄ[ן 4QLevi[d] | כמסתהון—כ]מסתן 4QLevi[d] **8:6** כולא—כלא 4QLevi[d] | ויהוון—ו]הוא 4QLevi[d] | כׄןׄ—Puech [כל] Charles | עובדיך—עבדך 4QLevi[b] **8:7** וׄ[כל]—Puech [וכל] Charles | אׄעׄ[י]ן—חזתׄאׄ .. חזת אע[ין Charles, and he emends to חזי די אעין

8:7 And [whatsoever] | you do, do it in due order, [by measure] | and weight, do not add anything that is not [fitting] | and do not diminish from the amount . . . of wo[o]d | <fit> for sacrifice with everything that is offered up on the altar. |

Chapter 9: The Measures of Wood, Salt, Fine Flour, Oil, Wine and Frankincense

The Aramaic text of Bodleian d ends with the word סליק in 9:1. The rest of this chapter is extant only in the Mt. Athos Greek manuscript. The larger size Greek letters indicate that Greek is the only witness to those verses.

Wood

9:1a = Bod d 32a and Athos Greek 32a
9:1b–5 = Greek 32b–36

9:1 לתורא רבא <ככר> אעין ליה במתקל | ואם תרבא בלחודוהי סליק
שיתה |מנין ואם פר <תרין> הוא די סליק |

τῷ ταύρῳ τῷ τελείῳ τάλαντον ξύλων *καθήκει* αὐτῷ ἐν σταθμῷ, καὶ εἰς τὸ στέαρ μόνον ἀναφέρεσθαι ἓξ μνᾶς· καὶ τῷ ταύρῳ τῷ δευτέρῳ πεντήκοντα μνᾶς·
καὶ εἰς τὸ στέαρ αὐτοῦ μόνον πέντε μνᾶς·

9:2 καὶ εἰς μόσχον τέλειον μ´ μναῖ·
9:3 καὶ εἰ κριὸς ἐκ προβάτων ἢ τράγος ἐξ αἰγῶν τὸ προσφερόμενον ᾖ,
καὶ τούτῳ λ´ μναῖ, καὶ τῷ στέατι τρεῖς μναῖ·
9:4 καὶ εἰ ἄρνα ἐκ προβάτων ἢ ἔριφον ἐξ αἰγῶν κ´ μναῖ, καὶ τῷ στέατι
β´ μναῖ·
9:5 καὶ εἰ ἀμνὸς τέλειος ἐνιαύσιος ἢ ἔριφος ἐξ αἰγῶν ιε´ μναῖ, καὶ τῷ
στέατι μίαν ἥμισυ μνᾶν.

Salt

9:6–9 = Greek 37–40a

9:6 καὶ ἅλας {αποδεδεικτω} τῷ ταύρῳ τῷ μεγάλῳ ἁλῖσαι τὸ κρέας
αὐτοῦ, καὶ ἀνένεγκε ἐπὶ τὸν βωμόν. σάτον καθήκει τῷ ταύρῳ. καὶ ᾧ ἂν
περισσεύσῃ τοῦ ἁλός, ἅλισον ἐν αὐτῷ τὸ δέρμα·
9:7 καὶ τῷ ταύρῳ τῷ δευτέρῳ τὰ πέντε μέρη ἀπὸ τῶν ἓξ μερῶν τοῦ σάτου·
καὶ τοῦ μόσχου τὸ δίμοιρον τοῦ σάτου·
9:8 καὶ τῷ κριῷ τὸ ἥμισυ τοῦ σάτου καὶ τῷ τράγῳ τὸ ἴσον·
9:9 καὶ τῷ ἀρνίῳ καὶ τῷ ἐρίφῳ τὸ τρίτον τοῦ σάτου

Fine Flour and Oil

9:9b–13 = Greek 40b–44a

καὶ σεμίδαλις καθήκουσα αὐτοῖς·
9:10 τῷ ταύρῳ τῷ μεγάλῳ καὶ τῷ ταύρῳ τῷ β´ καὶ τῷ μοσχαρίῳ, σάτον
σεμίδαλιν·
9:11 καὶ τῷ κριῷ καὶ τῷ τράγῳ τὰ δύο μέρη τοῦ σάτου καὶ τῷ ἀρνίῳ

Chapter 9: The Measures of Wood, Salt, Fine Flour, Oil, Wine and Frankincense

Wood

9:1 For a large bull: a talent's weight of wood (is fitting) | for it; and if the fat alone is offered up, six | minas; and if it is the second bull that is offered up, fifty minas, and for its fat alone, five minas.

9:2 And for a full-grown bullock, forty minas.

9:3 And if that which is offered is a ram of the sheep or a he-goat out of the goats, for it thirty minas and for its fat three minas.

9:4 And if it is a lamb of the sheep or a kid of the goats, twenty minas, and for its fat two minas.

9:5 And if it is an unblemished lamb one year old or a kid of the goats (of the same qualities) fifteen minas, and for its fat one (and) one half minas.

Salt

9:6 And . . . salt upon the great bull to salt its flesh and offer it up upon the altar. A saton is the proper amount for the bull, and salt down the skin with whatever salt is left over.

9:7 And for the second bull, five sixths of a saton; and for the bullock, two thirds of a saton;

9:8 and for the ram half a saton; and for the he-goat the same;

9:9 and for the lamb and the kid a third of a saton.

Fine Flour and Oil

And the fine flour which is the proper measure for them:

9:10 for the great bull and for the second bull and for the bullock, a saton of fine flour;

9:11 and for the ram and for the he-goat two thirds of a saton, and for the lamb and the kid of the goats a third of a saton. And the oil:

καὶ τῷ ἐρίφῳ ἐξ αἰγῶν τὸ τρίτον τοῦ σάτου καὶ τὸ ἔλαιον·
9:12 καὶ τὸ τέταρτον τοῦ σάτου τῷ ταύρῳ ἀναπεποιημένον ἐν τῇ σεμιδάλει ταύτῃ·
9:13 καὶ τῷ κριῷ τὸ ἕκτον τοῦ σάτου καὶ τῷ ἀρνίῳ τὸ ὄγδοον τοῦ σάτου καὶ ἀμνοῦ

Wine and Frankincense

9:14–16 = Greek 44b–46a

9:14 καὶ οἶνον κατὰ τὸ μέτρον τοῦ ἐλαίου τῷ ταύρῳ καὶ τῷ κριῷ καὶ τῷ ἐρίφῳ κατασπεῖσαι σπονδήν.
9:15 λιβανωτοῦ σίκλοι ἓξ τῷ ταύρῳ καὶ τὸ ἥμισυ αὐτοῦ τῷ κριῷ καὶ τὸ τρίτον αὐτοῦ τῷ ἐρίφῳ. καὶ πᾶσα ἡ σεμίδαλις ἀναπεποιημένη.
9:16 ἥ<ν> ἂν προσαγάγῃς μόνον, οὐκ ἐπὶ στέατος, <προσχωθήσεται> ἐπ᾽ αὐτὴν λιβάνου ὁλκὴ σίκλων δύο·

Measures

9:17–18 = Greek 46b–47

9:17 καὶ τὸ τρίτον τοῦ σάτου τὸ τρίτον τοῦ ὑφή ἐστιν·
9:18 καὶ τὰ δύο μέρη τοῦ βάτου καὶ ὁλκῆς τῆς μνᾶς ν´ σίκλων ἐστίν· καὶ τοῦ σικλίου τὸ τέταρτον ὁλκὴ θερμῶν δ´ ἐστίν· γίνεται ὁ σίκλος ὡσεὶ ις´ θερμοὶ καὶ ὁλκῆς μιᾶς.

Variants

9:1 <ככר>—Charles כבר manuscript: cf. Greek τάλαντον | ליה—ליא Charles | <תרין>—eds. cf. Greek תורין Geniza **9:6** {αποδεδεικτω}—Charles says that this is a corrupt imperative form of ἀποδείκνυμι **9:16** προσχωθήσεται—de Jonge προσωχησεται manuscript

Parallels

The following two verses from *TPL* probably briefly reflect this long passage of sacrifical specifications:

9:13 καὶ παντὸς ζῴου καθαροῦ καὶ πετεινοῦ καθαροῦ πρόσφερε θυσίαν κυρίῳ.

9:14 καὶ παντὸς πρωτογενήματος καὶ οἴνου πρόσφερε ἀπαρχάς· καὶ πᾶσαν θυσίαν ἅλατι ἁλιεῖς.

9:12 and the fourth of a saton for the bull mixed up in that fine flour;
9:13 and for the ram, the sixth of a saton; and for the lamb the eighth of a saton, and of a lamb.

Wine and Frankincense

9:14 And wine: according to the measure of the oil pour out a libation for the bull and for the ram and for the kid.
9:15 Six shekels of frankincense for the bull and half of that for the ram and a third of that for the kid. And all the mixed up fine flour,
9:16 if you offer it up alone and not upon the fat, let a two shekels' weight of frankincense be poured out upon it.

Measures

9:17 And a third of a saton is a third of an ephah
9:18 and two thirds of a bath, and of the weight of the mina, it is fifty shekels. And the fourth of the shekel is the weight of four *thermoi*. The shekel is about sixteen *thermoi* and of one weight.

Parallels

The following verses from *TPL* probably briefly reflect this long passage of sacrificial specifications:
9:13 And offer a sacrifice to the Lord of every clean beast and clean bird.

9:14 And offer the first of all first fruits and of wine. And you shall salt every sacrifice with salt.

Chapter 10: Concluding Injunctions and Blessing

10:1–3 = Greek 48–50

10:1 καὶ νῦν, τέκνον μου, ἄκουσον τοὺς λόγους μου καὶ ἐνωτίσαι τὰς ἐντολάς μου, καὶ μὴ ἀποστήτωσαν οἱ λόγοι μου οὗτοι ἀπὸ τῆς καρδίας σου ἐν πάσαις ταῖς ἡμέραις σου, ὅτι ἱερεὺς σὺ ἅγιος κυρίου,

10:2 καὶ ἱερεῖς ἔσονται πᾶν τὸ σπέρμα σου· καὶ τοῖς υἱοῖς σου οὕτως ἔντειλον ἵνα ποιήσουσιν κατὰ τὴν κρίσιν ταύτην ὡς σοὶ ὑπέδειξα.

10:3 οὕτως γάρ μοι ἐνετείλατο ὁ πατὴρ Ἀβραὰμ ποιεῖν καὶ ἐντέλλεσθαι τοῖς υἱοῖς μου.

10:4–5 = Greek 51–52

10:4 καὶ νῦν, τέκνον, χαίρω ὅτι ἐξελέχθης εἰς ἱερωσύνην ἁγίαν καὶ προσενεγκεῖν θυσίαν κυρίῳ ὑψίστῳ, ὡς καθήκει κατὰ τὸ προστεταγμένον τοῦτο ποιεῖν.

10:5 ὅταν παραλαμβάνῃς θυσίαν ποιεῖν ἔναντι κυρίου ἀπὸ πάσης σαρκός, κατὰ τὸν λογισμὸν τῶν ξύλων ἐπιδέχου οὕτως, ὡς σοὶ ἐντέλλομαι. καὶ τὸ ἅλας καὶ τὴν σεμίδαλιν καὶ τὸν οἶνον καὶ τὸν λίβανον ἐπιδέχου ἐκ τῶν χειρῶν αὐτῶν ἐπὶ πάντα κτήνη.

10:6–10 = Greek 53–57

10:6 καὶ ἐπὶ πᾶσαν ὥραν νίπτου τὰς χεῖρας καὶ τοὺς πόδας, ὅταν πορεύῃ πρὸς τὸ θυσιαστήριον· καὶ ὅταν ἐκπορεύῃς ἐκ τῶν ἁγίων, πᾶν αἷμα μὴ ἁπτέσθω τῆς στολῆς σου· οὐκ ἀνήψῃς αὐτῷ αὐθήμερον.

10:7 καὶ τὰς χεῖρας καὶ τοὺς πόδας νίπτου διὰ παντὸς ἀπὸ πάσης σαρκός·

10:8 καὶ μὴ ὀφθήτω ἐπί σοι πᾶν αἷμα καὶ πᾶσα ψυχή· τὸ γὰρ αἷμα ψυχή ἐστιν ἐν τῇ σαρκί.

10:9 καὶ ὃ ἐὰν ἐν οἴκῳ {ουσης} σεαυτὸν πᾶν κρέας φαγεῖν, κάλυπτε τὸ αἷμα αὐτοῦ τῇ γῇ πρῶτον πρὶν ἢ φαγεῖν σε ἀπὸ τῶν κρεῶν καὶ οὐκέτι ἔσῃ ἐσθίων ἐπὶ τοῦ αἵματος.

10:10 οὕτως γάρ μοι ἐνετείλατο ὁ πατήρ μου Ἀβραάμ, ὅτι οὕτως εὗρεν ἐν τῇ γραφῇ τῆς βίβλου τοῦ Νῶε περὶ τοῦ αἵματος.

10:11–14 = Greek 58–61

10:11 καὶ νῦν ὡς σοί, τέκνον ἀγαπητόν, ἐγὼ λέγω, ἠγαπημένος σὺ τῷ πατρί σου καὶ ἅγιος κυρίου ὑψίστου· καὶ ἠγαπημένος ἔσῃ ὑπὲρ πάντας τοὺς ἀδελφούς σου.

10:12 τῷ σπέρματί σου εὐλογηθήσεται ἐν τῇ γῇ καὶ τὸ σπέρμα σου ἕως πάντων τῶν αἰώνων ἐνεχθήσεται ἐν βιβλίῳ μνημοσύνου ζωῆς·

10:13 καὶ οὐκ ἐξαλειφθήσεται τὸ ὄνομά σου καὶ τὸ ὄνομα τοῦ σπέρματός σου ἕως τῶν αἰώνων.

10:14 καὶ νῦν, τέκνον Λευί, εὐλογημένον ἔσται τὸ σπέρμα σου ἐπὶ τῆς γῆς εἰς πάσας τὰς γενεὰς τῶν αἰώνων.

Chapter 10: Concluding Injunctions and Blessing

10:1 And now, my child, listen to my words and attend to my commandments, and let not these words of mine depart from your heart all your days, for you are a holy priest of the Lord,
10:2 and all your seed will be priests. And command your sons thus, so that they may do according to this regulation as I have shown you.
10:3 For my father Abraham commanded me to do thus and to command my sons.
10:4 And now, child, I rejoice that you were elected for the holy priesthood, and to offer sacrifice to the Most High Lord, to do as is proper, according to that instruction.
10:5 Whenever you receive a sacrifice to carry out before the Lord from any flesh, accept in addition according to the reckoning of the wood thus, as I command you, and the salt and the fine flour and the wine and the frankincense accept in addition from their hands for all animals.
10:6 Each time whenever you go to the altar, wash your hands and feet; and whenever you come out of the sanctuary, let no blood touch your garment. Be not connected with it on that same day.
10:7 And wash your hands and feet thoroughly from all flesh.
10:8 and let not any blood or any soul be seen upon you, for blood is soul in the flesh.
10:9 And if in your house . . . yourself, to eat any flesh, hide its blood in the earth first, before you eat of the flesh so that you should no longer eat in the presence of blood.
10:10 For thus my father Abraham commanded me for thus he found in the writing of the book of Noah concerning the blood.
10:11 And now, beloved child, as I say to you, you are beloved of your father and holy to the Most High Lord. And you will be more beloved than all your brothers.
10:12 And blessing shall be pronounced by your seed upon the earth and your seed shall be entered in the book of the memorial of life for all eternity.
10:13 And your name and the name of your seed shall not be annihilated for eternity.
10:14 And now, child, Levi, your seed shall be blessed upon the earth for all generations of eternity.

Variants

10:4 τοῦτο—Charles, de Jonge τούτῳ manuscript

Parallels

Jubilees 21:17–18 resembling 10:6–10
21:17 No blood is to be visible on you or on your clothing. My son, be careful with blood, be very careful to cover it with dirt.
21:18 You are not, therefore, to consume any blood, because is the vital force. Do not consume any blood.

Jubilees 21:1 resembling 10:10
21:1 In the sixth year of the seventh week of this jubilee Abraham summoned his son Isaac and gave him orders as follows:

Parallels

Jubilees 21:17–18 resembling 10:6–10
21:17 No blood is to be visible on you or on your clothing. My son, be careful with blood, be very careful to cover it with dirt.
21:18 You are not, therefore, to consume any blood, because is the vital force. Do not consume any blood.

Jubilees 21:1 resembling 10:10
21:1 In the sixth year of the seventh week of this jubilee Abraham summoned his son Isaac and gave him orders as follows:

Chapter 11: Birth and Naming of Levi's Children

The Greek text continues until the middle of 11:8 (περὶ αὐτοῦ) where it ends. The Aramaic resumes in Cambridge c with some odd letters apparently belonging to 11:4 and then with continuous text from the middle of 11:5. Two lines are missing from Cambridge c before the surviving text. We return, therefore, in 11:5 to Aramaic as the dominant text. Cambridge d commences at the second-last word of this chapter, העלנ[א].

11:1–8 = Greek 62–69
11:5–11 = Cam c 66–72
11:8–11 = 4QLevi[e] frags. 2–3

11:1 καὶ ὅτε ἀνεπληρώθησάν μοι ἑβδομάδες τέσσαρες ἐν τοῖς ἔτεσιν τῆς ζωῆς μου, ἐν <ἔτει> ὀγδόῳ καὶ εἰκοστῷ ἔλαβον γυναῖκα ἐμαυτῷ ἐκ τῆς συγγενείας Ἀβραὰμ τοῦ πατρός μου, Μελχά, θυγατέρα Βαθουήλ, υἱοῦ Λαβάν, ἀδέλφου μητρός μου.
11:2 καὶ ἐν γαστρὶ λαβοῦσα ἐξ ἐμοῦ ἔτεκεν υἱὸν πρῶτον, καὶ ἐκάλεσα τὸ ὄνομα αὐτοῦ Γηρσάμ· εἶπα γὰρ ὅτι πάροικον ἔσται τὸ σπέρμα μου ἐν γῇ, ᾗ ἐγεννήθην· πάροικοί ἐσμεν ὡς τούτῳ ἐν τῇ γῇ ἡμετέρᾳ νομιζομένῃ.
11:3 καὶ ἐπὶ τοῦ παιδαρίου εἶδον ἐγὼ ἐν τῷ ὁράματί μου ὅτι ἐκβεβλημένος ἔσται αὐτὸς καὶ τὸ σπέρμα αὐτοῦ ἀπὸ τῆς ἀρχῆς ἱερωσύνης {ἔσται τὸ σπέρμα αὐτοῦ}.
11:4 λ ʹ ἐτῶν ἤμην ὅτε ἐγεννήθη ἐν τῇ ζωῇ μου, καὶ ἐν τῷ ι´ μηνὶ ἐγεννήθη ἐπὶ δυσμὰς ἡλίου.

11:5 ו[ה]רׄת עוד[ ]אׄחׄרׄןׄ | [וקרא]תי שמׄה קׄ[ה]ת

καὶ πάλιν συλλαβοῦσα ἔτεκεν ἐξ ἐμοῦ κατὰ τὸν καιρὸν τὸν καθήκοντα τῶν γυναικῶν, καὶ ἐκάλεσα τὸ ὄνομα αὐτοῦ Καάθ.

11:6 וחזי]תׄ די להן | [תהו]ה כנשת כל[עמא ו]די̇ לה תהוהׄ | כׄהׄנׄותא רבתא
לׄ[כל יש]ראל *vacat*

καὶ *ὅτε ἐγεννήθη*, ἑώρακα ὅτι ἐπ᾽ αὐτῷ ἔσται ἡ συναγωγὴ παντὸς τοῦ λαοῦ καὶ ὅτι <αὐτοῦ> ἔσται ἡ ἀρχιερωσύνη ἡ μεγάλη· *αὐτὸς καὶ τὸ σπέρμα αὐτοῦ ἔσονται ἀρχὴ βασιλέων, ἱεράτευμα τῷ Ἰσραήλ.*

11:7 *vacat* בשנת ארב[ע ותל]תין לחיי | יליד בירחא קמ[אה בה]ד
לירח[א] | עם מדנח שמש[א] *vacat*

ἐν τῷ <τετάρτῳ> καὶ λ´ ἔτει ἐγεννήθην ἐν τῷ πρώτῳ μηνὶ μιᾷ τοῦ μηνὸς ἐπ᾽ ἀνατολῆς ἡλίου.

11:8 ועוד | אׄוׄספת והוית ע̇[מ]הׄ וילידת לי בר | תליתי וקראתי שמה
מררי ארי | מר לי עלוהי לחדה ארי **כדי** יליד | **הוא** מית והווה מריר לי
עלוהי | סגיא מן די ימות ובעית והתחננת | עלוהי והיה בכל מרר *vacat*

καὶ πάλιν συνεγενόμην αὐτῇ *καὶ ἐν γαστρὶ ἔλαβεν*, καὶ ἔτεκέν μοι υἱὸν τρίτον, καὶ ἐκάλεσα τὸ ὄνομα αὐτοῦ Μεραρί· ἐλυπήθην γὰρ περὶ αὐτοῦ. *Greek ends.*

Chapter 11: Birth and Naming of Levi's Children

11:1 And when four weeks in the years of my life were completed for me, in the twenty-eighth year I took a wife for myself from the family of Abraham my father, Milka, daughter of Bethuel, son of Laban, my mother's brother.
11:2 She became pregnant by me and bore a first son, and I called his name Gershom, for I said, "My seed shall be sojourners in the land in which I was born. We are sojourners as now in the land which is reckoned ours."
11:3 And concerning the youth, I saw in my dream (*or*: vision) that he and his seed will be cast out of the highpriesthood.
11:4 I was thirty years old in the course of my life when he was born, and he was born in the tenth month towards sunset.
11:5 And she conceived again and she bore by me according to the proper time of women and I called his name Ko[hath.
another son (**Geniza**)
11:6 and] I [sa]w that to him [would] | be an assembly of all [the people and that] he would | have the high-priesthood; *he and his seed will be the beginning of kings, a priesthood* for [all Is]rael. |
11:7 In the th[irty-fou]rth year of my life | he was born in the [fi]rst month [on the fir]st of the mo[nth] | at the rising of [the] sun. |
11:8 And | I was w[i]th her once more and she bore me a third | son and I called his name Merari for | I was bitter on his account particularly, for when he was born | he was dying. And I was very bitter | on his account since he was about to die, and I implored and beseeched | on his account, and there was bitterness in everything.

11:9 בשנת ארבעין לחיי ילידת בירחה תלי֗ת֗[י] |
11:10 ועוד אוספת והויתי עמהא והרת | וילידת לי ברת**א** **ושויתי** שמהא |
$_{20}$יוכבד אמ֯ר֯ת֗ כדי ילידת לי ליקר | ילידת לי לכבוד לישראל
11:11 *vacat* **בשנת** שתין וארבע לי לחיי וילידת | בחד בחודשא **שביעיא** מן
בתר די | הע֯ל֯נ֯[א]$_{1}$ ל֯מצרים *vacat*

Variants

11:1 ἔτει—de Jonge ἔτεσιν manuscript **11:2** {τουτῷ}—appears to be corrupt **11:3** ἱερωσύνης—Charles and de Jonge consider the next four words ἔσται τὸ σπέρμα αὐτοῦ to be secondary, apparently by dittography **11:5** In Aramaic at the top of Cambridge c we observe the following: two lines missing except for the upper tag of a letter at the end of line 2, and then ה[ ]$_{3}$|[. . .כזמ֗[נא: see Commentary | ר֯ת עוד [וה]—ת[והר] Charles | וה[ר֯ת עוד] מני וילידת לי בר] א֗ה֗ר֯ן֯—Puech: Puech reconstructs the phrase א֗ה֗ר֯ן֯ | [הת]ק֯—Puech [קהת] Charles **11:6** ת֯[וחזי]—Puech י֗[וחזית] Greenfield Stone [וחזיתי] Charles | αὐτοῦ—eds. αὐτός manuscript | י[וד]—[ודי] Charles | רבתא—בבתא Charles | ל֯[כל]—Puech לכל Charles **11:7** אר[בע]—אר[בא] Charles | τετάρτῳ—Charles ἐνιαυτῷ manuscript **11:8** ע֗[מ]ה֯—Puech עמה Charles | תליתי—תליתוי Charles **11:9** תלי֗ת֗[י]—רב[יעא or שב[יעא 4QLevi[c] **11:10** עמהא—עמה Charles | ושויתי—ושוית 4QLevi[c] | אמ֯ר֯ת֗—אמ[רת] Charles **11:11** שביעיא—שב[י֯עא 4QLevi[c] | הע֯ל֯נ֯[א] למצרים—Puech ה[עלנא ל]מצרים Charles

Parallels

TPL 11:1–2 relating to 11:1–2
11:1 Ὅτε οὖν ἔλαβον γυναῖκα, ἤμην ἐτῶν εἰκοσιοκτώ, ᾗ ὄνομα Μελχά.
11:2 καὶ συλλαβοῦσα ἔτεκε, καὶ ἐκάλεσε τὸ ὄνομα αὐτοῦ Γερσάμ· ὅτι ἐν τῇ γῇ ἡμῶν πάροικοι ἦμεν· Γηρσὰμ γὰρ παροικία γράφεται.

TPL 11:4 relating to 11:4 and 11:7
11:4 καὶ ὁ Καὰθ ἐγεννήθη τριακοστῷ πέμπτῳ ἔτει, πρὸς ἀνατολὰς ἡλίου.

TPL 11:6a relating to 11:5
11:6 διὰ τοῦτο ἐκάλεσα τὸ ὄνομα αὐτοῦ Καάθ

TPL 11:5 relating to 11:6
11:5 πάσης τῆς συναγωγῆς

TPL 11:7 relating to 11:8
11:7 καὶ τρίτον ἔτεκέ μοι τὸν Μεραρί, τεσσαρακοστῷ ἔτει ζωῆς μου . . . ὅ ἐστι πικρία μου· ὅτι καίγε αὐτὸς ἀπέθανεν.

TPL 11:8 relating to 11:10
11:8 ἡ δὲ Ἰωχάβεδ ἑξηκοστῷ τετάρτῳ ἔτει ἐτέχθη ἐν Αἰγύπτῳ· ἔνδοξος γὰρ ἤμην τότε ἐν μέσῳ τῶν ἀδελφῶν μου.

11:9 In the fortieth | year of my life she gave birth in the thi[rd] month. |
11:10 And I was with her once more and she conceived | and bore me a daughter, and I named her | Jochebed. I said when she was born to me, "For glory | was she born to me, for glory for Israel." |
11:11 In the sixty-fourth year of my life she gave birth (*or*: she was born) | on the first of the seventh month, after we enter[ed] Egypt.

Parallels

TPL 11:1–2 relating to 11:1–2
11:1 When, therefore, I took a wife, I was twenty-eight years old, and her name was Melcha.
11:2 And she conceived and bore (a son) and she called his name Gersam; for we were sojourners in our land; for Gersam means sojourning.

TPL 11:4 relating to 11:4 and 11:7
11:4 And Kaath was born in the thirty-fifth year, towards sunrise.

TPL 11:6a relating to 11:5
11:6a therefore I called his name Kaath

TPL 11:5 relating to 11:6
11:5 of all the congregation

TPL 11:7 relating to 11:8
11:7 And as a third she bore me Merari in the fortieth year of my life . . . which is my bitterness; for also he died.

TPL 11:8 relating to 11:10
11:8 And Jochebed was born in the sixty-fourth year in Egypt; for I was renowned then in the midst of my brothers.

Chapter 12: Levi's Grandchildren and Great-Grandchildren

This chapter is preserved in Aramaic in Geniza Cambridge d and e. Column d ends with the word במצרים in 12:9.

12:1–9 = Cam d–e 73–81

12:1 בשנת שת | עש[רה ה]עלינה לארע מצרים ולבני [נסבת נשין מ]ן בנת
אחי לעדן אשויות | זמניהון ו[ילי]דו להון בנין *vacat*
12:2 שם בני | גרשון לבנ[י ו]שמעי *vacat* ושם בני | קהת עמרם ויצהר
וחברון ועוזיאל | [ו]שם בני מררי מחלי ומושי *vacat*
12:3 ונסב לה עמרם אנתא ליוכבד ברתי | עד די אנה חי בשנת תשעין
ואר[בע] | לחיי
12:4 וקריתי שמה די עמרם כדי | יליד עמרם ארי אמרת כדי יליד | דנה
ירים עמא מן ארע מצרים | *vacat* כדן יתקרא [שמה עמ]א ראמא
12:5 ביום חד ילי[ד ה]וא ויוכבד | ברתי
12:6 בר שנין תמנה עשרה העלת | לארע כנען ובר שנין תמנה עשרה |
כדי קטלית אנה לשכם ונמרת | לעבדי חמסא *vacat*
12:7 ובר שנין תשע | עשרה כהנית ובר שנין תמנה | ועסרין נסבת לי
אנתה *vacat*
12:8 ובר | שנין תמנה וארבעין הויתי כדי | העלנא לארע מצרים ושנין |
תמנין ותשע הויתי חי במצר[ים]
12:9 והוו כל יומי חיי שבע ותלתין [ו]מאה | שנין וחזיתי לי בנין
תל[יתאין] עד | די לא מיתת *vacat*

Variants

12:1 [ה]עלינה—[ה]עלינא Charles | נס[בת נשין מ]ן בנת—[נסבת נשין מ]ן בנת Puech . . . . בנת Charles | זמניהון—Puech זבניהון Charles | ו[ילי]דו להון—Puech [ ] להון Charles **12:2** ושם—שם Charles | לבנ[י]—[לבני] Charles | קהת עמרם—Puech ק[הת עמר]ם Charles | [ו]שם—[ושם] Charles **12:3** ונסב—[ונסב] Charles | ואר[בע—וא]רבע Charles **12:4** ירים—[יפיק] Charles יעיר Beyer | ארע מצרים—Puech א[רע מצ]רים Charles | כדן יתקרא—כדן [א]תקרא Charles | עמ]א ראמא—[י]ד ראמא Beyer **12:5** ילי[ד ה]וא—[ ]יא Charles **12:6** תמנה—Puech ת[מ]נה Charles | לארע—[לא]רע Charles | לשכם—[לש]כם Charles **12:8** במצר[ים]—במצרים Charles **12:9** ותלתין [ו]מאה—Puech ות[ל]י[ת]י[ן ומ]אה Charles

Parallels

TPL 12:1–4 relating to 12:1–3
12:1 Καὶ ἔλαβε Γηρσὰμ γυναῖκα, καὶ ἔτεκεν αὐτῷ τὸν Λομνὶ καὶ τὸν Σεμεΐ.
12:2 καὶ υἱοὶ Καὰθ' Ἀμβράμ, Ἰσαάρ, Χεβρών, Ὀζιήλ.
12:3 καὶ υἱοὶ Μεραρὶ Μοολὶ καὶ Ὀμουσί.

Chapter 12: Levi's Grandchildren and Great-Grandchildren

12:1 In the sixte[enth] year, we [en]tered into the land of Egypt and to my sons [I took wives] from the daughters of my brothers at the time of marriageability of their times and there were [born]sons to them.
12:2 The names of the sons of Gershon (were) Libn[i and] Shimei; and the names of the sons of Kohath (were) Amram and Izhar and Hebron and Uzziel; [and] the names of the sons of Merari (were) Mahli and Mushi.
12:3 And Amram married my daughter Jochebed while I was still alive, in the ninety-fo[urth] year of my life.
12:4 And I called Amram's name, when he was born, Amram; for I said when he was born, 'This one will raise up the people from the la[nd of Eg]ypt. Accordingly [his name] will be called the exalted pe[ople].'
12:5 On the same day he [was bo]rn, he and Jochebed my daughter.
12:6 I was eighteen years old when I entered the land of Canaan; and I was eighteen when I killed Shechem and destroyed the workers of violence.
12:7 I was nineteen when I became a priest and twenty-eight when I took a wife;
12:8 I was forty-eight when we entered the land of Egypt, and I lived eighty-nine years in Egy[pt].
12:9 And all the days of my life were one hundred [and thir]ty-seven years and I saw my thi[rd] generation before I died.

Parallels

TPL 12:1–4 relating to 12:1–3
12:1 And Gersam took a wife, and she bore him Lomni and Semei.
12:2 And the sons of Kaath (were) Ambram, Isaar, Hebron, Oziel.
12:3 And the sons of Merari (were) Mooli and Omousi.

12:4 καὶ ἐνενηκοστῷ τετάρτῳ ἔτει μου ἔλαβεν ὁ Ἀμβρὰμ τὴν Ἰωχάβεδ θυγατέρα μου αὐτῷ εἰς γυναῖκα· ὅτι ἐν μιᾷ ἡμέρᾳ ἐγεννήθησαν αὐτὸς καὶ ἡ θυγάτηρ μου.

TPL 12:5–6 relating to 12:6–7
12:5 ὀκτὼ ἐτῶν ἤμην ὅτε εἰσῆλθον εἰς γῆν Χανάαν· καὶ ὀκτωκαίδεκα ἐτῶν ὅτε ἀπέκτεινα τὸν Συχέμ· καὶ ἐννεακαίδεκα ἐτῶν ἱεράτευσα· καὶ εἰκοσιοκτὼ ἐτῶν ἔλαβον γυναῖκα· καὶ τεσσεράκοντα ἐτῶν εἰσῆλθον εἰς Αἴγυπτον.
12:6 καὶ ἰδού ἐστε, τέκνα μου, τρίτη γενεά.

Syriac fragment[1]
Numbers indicate corresponding verses of ALD

twb dkm' ḥy' lwy. šrk' dmḥw' mn dytq' dylh.
'mr lwy bdytq' dylh hkn.
12:6 br ḥ hwyt šnyn kd 'lt l'r'' dkn'n.
wbr y̅ḥ̅ šnyn hwyt kd qṭlt lškym w'wbdt lklhwn 'bdy 'wl'.
12:7 wbr y̅ṭ̅ šnyn khnt
wbr k̅ḥ̅ šnyn nsbt ly 'ntt'
12:8 wbr m̅. šnyn hwyt kd 'lt lmṣryn.
wṣ šnyn 'mrt bmṣryn.
12:9 klhyn šny q̅l̅d̅ šny'.

[1] Cited from Charles, 1908, 254. He cites it from Wright, 1871, 997, British Museum Add 17.193, fol. 71a, no. 80. Charles recollated the manuscript.

12:4 And in my ninety-fourth year Ambram took Jochebed my daughter to him as wife; for they were born on the same day, he and my daughter.

TPL 12:5–6 relating to 12:6–7
12:5 I was eight years old when I went to the land of Canaan, and eighteen years when I killed Shechem, and at nineteen years I became a priest, and at twenty-eight years I took a wife, and at forty years I went to Egypt.
12:6 And behold, my children, you are a third generation.

Syriac fragment
Numbers indicate corresponding verses of *ALD*

Again, how long did Levi live, the rest of what is told from his testament. Levi, in his testament, said as follows:

12:6 I was eight years old when I entered the land of Canaan.
And eighteen years old when I killed Shechem and destroyed all the wrongdoers.
12:7 And being nineteen years old, I became a priest,
and being twenty-eight years old I took myself a wife.
12:8 And I was forty years old when I went into Egypt,
and ninety years I sojourned in Egypt.
12:9 All my years are one hundred and thirty-four.

Chapter 13: Levi's Teaching—The Wisdom Poem

The material in the Cambridge Geniza manuscript concludes in 13:12. Chapter 13 is found in three Qumran manuscripts, as follows: 4QLevi[a] frag. 1, cols. 1–2 contains 13:1–12a and 13:12b–16; 4QLevi[c] frags. 2–3 overlap with 13:11–13, 15 and 4QLevi[f] frag. 8 contains 13:13. Cambridge e starts with verse 12:10 and ends with חכמה in 13:6. The first three lines of Cambridge f are missing and the next four lines (13:7) are fragmentary and have many lacunae. However these imperfections are partly compensated for by the Qumran fragments.

In 13:1–12a words in « » are in 4QLevi[a] frag. 1 and not in the Geniza manuscript and words in ≤ ≥ are in the Geniza manuscript and not in 4QLevi[a] frag. 1. In this section, lacunae marked with [ ] are in the Geniza manuscript. As always, where the Geniza text is extant, we follow its wording and orthography. 4QLevi[a] frag. 1 col. 1 concludes with the word ועם in 13:11. The Geniza fragment concludes with the words מטמוריה ואל in 13:12. From that point on the text is 4QLevi[a] frag. 1 col. 2 and we accept the join of that fragment with 4QLevi[a] frag. 2. In this part of the chapter, the text is 4QLevi[a], the overlined text is 4QLevi[c] and the underlined text is 4QLevi[f]. The change of base text naturally leads to a certain unevenness in orthography. In 13:16 we have abided by the lineation of 4QLevi[a].

Verse	*Dominant Text*	*Additional Text 1*	*Additional Text 2*
13:1–10	Cam e 82–95	4QLevi[a]	
13:11–13	4QLevi[a]	4QLevi[c] (overline)	4QLevi[f] (underline)
13:14–15	4QLevi[a]	4QLevi[c] (overline)	
13:16	4QLevi[a]		

13:1 ובשׁ[נת מאה ות]מֹני | עשרה לחיי היא שׁנׂ[תא] די **מית בה** | יוסף
אחי קריתי לבנׂ[י ו]לֿבניהון | ושריתי לפקדה **הנון** כל די̇ הווה | עם לבבי
13:2 עניֹת ואמרת **לבני̇**

[שמ]עֿ[ו] | למאמר לוי אבוכון   והציתו לפקודי | ידיד אל
אנה לכון מפקד בני   ואנה | קושטא לכון מהחוי חביבי
13:3 רא]ש | «**כל**» **עובדיכון**   ועד | עלמא̇ יהו̇ו̇י קאים
יהוי קושטא   עמכון
צדקה | **וקושט̇[א** הן]תֿזֿ[ר]עוֿן   ת<הנ>עלון | עללה **בריכה**
≥ו[טא]בֿא≤ *vacat*
די זרע | **טאב טאב מהנעל**   ודי זרע ביש עלוהי תאיב זרעה
| *vacat*

13:4 *vacat* **וכֿען** <בני>
ספר «ו»**מוסר** | «ו»**חוכמה** <אליפו> לבניכון
ותהוי | **חוכמתא** עמכון **ליקר עלם**
13:5 | **די אליף חוכמתא**   **ויקר** היא בה
ודי שאיט חוכמתא   **לבשרון** «**ולשיטו**» | **מתיהב**
13:6 **חזו** «**לכן**» **בני** ליוסף אחי

Chapter 13: Levi's Teaching—The Wisdom Poem

13:1 And in the [hundred and ei]ghteenth ye[ar] of my life, that is the ye[ar] in which my brother Joseph died, I called my child[ren and] their children and I began to instruct them concerning all that was on my mind.
13:2 I spoke up and said to my chil[dren,
'List]en to the word of your father Levi
and pay attention to the instructions of God's friend.
I instruct you, my sons,
and reveal the truth to you, my beloved.
13:3 May truth be the essence of all your acts
and it will be with you forever.
If you s[o]w righteousness and truth,
You will bring in a blessed and good harvest.
He who sows good brings in a goodly (harvest),
and he who sows evil, his sowing turns against him.
13:4 And now, my sons,
<teach> reading and writing and teaching <of> wisdom to your children
and may wisdom be eternal glory for you.
13:5 For he who learns wisdom
will (attain) glory through it,
but he who despises wisdom
will become an object of disdain and scorn.
13:6 Observe, my children, my brother Joseph
[who] taught reading and writing and the teaching of wisdom,
for glory and for majesty; and kings <he advised>.

[די] מאלפא ספר ומוסר **חכמה** «**ליקר ולרבו ולמלכין**» <יעט הוא>

vacat

13:7 [«ו]**אל תמחלו חכמתא למאלף**»

[ל]א̊ תשב[קון] לב̇[ ]

גבר די אלף חכמה

כל י]ומוהי א̊[ריכין] | וסנה ל̊[ה שמ]**עה**

13.8 לכל מא[ת] **ומדינה** «**די יהך**» **לה אחא** ו̊חב̇ר הוי בה

Geniza יא̊ז̊ל

≤[לא כוא]ת נכר הוא בה≥ |

ו̊**לא דמ**[ה **בה ל]נכרי** ולא דמה | בה לכילי̊ [ ]

13:9 מ̊ן די כולהון **יהבי̊ן לה בה** **[ב]די כולה צבין** | למאלף מן

יקר חוכמתה *vacat*

רחמוה̊[י] | **סניאין** **ושאלי שלמיה רברבין** |

13:10 ועל כורסי <ד>י יקר ≥בדיל≥**למשמע מילי חוכמתה**

מהותבין לה

עותר רב די יקר היא **וסימא טאבא** לכל קניהא

חוכמתה «[ל]**ידעיה**»

13:11 הן | יאתון מלכין **תקיפין ועם** רב |

וחיל ופרשין ורתיכין סניאין עמהון |

וינסבון נכ̊סי מא̇ת ומדינה ויבוזון כל די בהון

13:12 אוצרי חוכמתא לא יבוזון ולא̊ ישכחון **מטמוריה**

ולא| יעלון תרעיה̇ ולא[ ]טב[י]ה א̊[

ולא] ישכחון למכבש שוריה [ ] ולא[ ]

ולא]| יחזון שימ̇תה

13:13 שימ̇תה .[ ]ד.[|] [ולא א̊ית̊י [כ]ל̊ מחיר נגדה[|]

בעא חכמה[חכ]מתה י[|]

מטמרה מנה פ̇[

13:14]אל[[

ולא חס[י]ר̊[ ]ו כל בעי[ה

ו̊קשט [[

13:15 וכען בני ס̊פר ומוסר ח̊[כ]מה

˙אלפ[ת] חזית ת..חו[ ] ת̊רתון אנון

[.˙]רבה תתנון

] י]ק̊ר

13:16 *vacat* א̊.[ ]א̊ף בספריא

קר̊[ית]י̊ן ראשין ושפטין

ידע̊[ ]ב ועבדין

[ ]א̊ף כהנין ומלכין

ת[ ]ן̊ מלכותכן

תהוי̊[יק]ר̊ ולא איתי סוף

13:7 [. . .]
and]do not be lax in the study of wisdom,
[and do n]ot lea[ve *her paths*].
a man who studies wisdom,
All [h]is days are l[ong]
and hi[s reputa]tion grows great.
13:8 To every la[nd] and country to which he will go,
he has a brother and a friend therein,
He is [not a]s a stranger in it,
and he is not li[ke] a stranger therein,
and not like a scoundr[el] in it [. . .]
13:9 Since all of them wi]ll accord him honour (or: glory) because of it,
[si]nce all wish to learn from his wisdom.
[His] friends are many
and his well-wishers are numerous.
13:10 And they seat him on the seat <o>f honour
in order to hear his wise words.
Wisdom is a great wealth of honour (or: glory) for those familiar with it
and a fine treasure to all who acquire it.
13:11 If there will come mighty kings and a great army
and cavalry accompanied by many chariots—
and they will seize the possessions of land and country
and will plunder that which is in them,
13:12 (Yet) the treasure houses of wisdom they will not plunder,
And they will not find its hidden places
and they will not enter its gates,

Geniza ends and henceforth the text is 4QLevi[a]

and will not [ ] its go[o]d things [
and will not] be able to conquer its walls [ ]
and will not[
and will not] see its treasure.
13:13 Its treasure[
and it is priceless[
He who seeks wisdom, [
wis]dom [ ]
to hide it from him [
13:14 and not lack[in]g[ ] all who seek [it
and truth[ ]

לעׄ[לם ולא]תׄעבר מנכן עד כל
דׄ[ריה]. בׄיקר רב

Variants

13:1 ובשׁ[נת מאה ות]מׄני—Puech **. . .** וב[שנת] Charles | שׁנׄ[תא]—Puech ש[תא] Charles | לבנׄ[י ו]לׄבניהון—Puech לב[ני ו]לבניהון Charles | שנ[תא]—[שת]**א** Charles | הנון—**אנון** 4QLevi[a] | דׄי—Puech ד[י] Charles **13:2** לבנׄי—לב[ני Charles | [שמ]עׄ[ו]—Puech [שמעו] Charles | לכון—**לכן** 4QLevi[a] **13:3** עובדיכון—**עבדכן** 4QLevi[a] | עלמׄא יׄהׄוׄי—Puech עלמ[א] י[הו]י Charles | עמכון—**עמ[כׄן** 4QLevi[a] | צדקה—**צדקתא** 4QLevi[a] | וקושׁטׄ[א]—וקוש[טא] Charles **וקשטא** 4QLevi[a] | הן]תׄזׄ[ר]עׄוׄן—Puech מׄלׄכני עׄלון **. . . . .** Charles | תׄ<הׄנ>עלון—Puech תׄנהׄעלון manuscript | בריכה—**בריכא** Charles | ≤בׄ[טא]ו≥—Puech ≤ו[זר]עא≥ Charles | די זרע—**דזרע** 4QLevi[a] | טב—**טאב** 4QLevi[a] 1.8 *bis* | מהׄנעל—**מעל** 4QLevi[a] **13:4** «ו»חוכמה—**וחוכמה** 4QLevi[a] | <אליפו>—Pass, Charles **אפילו** manuscript **13:5** אליף חוכמתא—**חכמה אלף** 4QLevi[a] | ויקר—**יקר** 4QLevi[a] | לבשרון—**לב[סׄרון** 4QLevi[a]: emended to לבושרן Charles **13:6** חכמה—**חכמא** Charles | <יעט הוא>—eds. **13:7** [ולארחתה ל]אׄ תשב[קו]—Puech]תשב[Charles: restoration uncertain | [כל]—Puech **]את** Charles | ומוהי—]מוהו[Charles | אׄ[ריכין] וסנה לׄ[ה שמ]עׄה—Puech]וסנה[ ]עה Charles | שמ]עׄה—**שמעא** 4QLevi[a] **13:8** מאׄ[ת—**מת** 4QLevi[a] מ[אתא] Charles | יהך—so 4QLevi[a], יׄאׄזׄל Geniza, Charles reads only ל | אחא וׄחׄבׄר—**אחא]** Charles | לכילׄי—לכיל] Charles who emends to לדיר **13:9** [ב]די—**בדי** 4QLevi[a] | כולה—**כלא** 4QLevi[a] | סניאין—שנׄאין 4QLevi[a] | שלמיה—**שלמה** 4QLevi[a] **13:10** <ד>י יקר—eds. ייקר manuscript | מהותבין—if the ןׄ[preceding למשמע in 4QLevi[a] is from this word, then its text differs considerably from the Geniza | למשמע—דמשמע Charles | מילי חוכמתה—מלי חׄכׄמׄתׄהׄ 4QLevi[a] | חוכמתה 2°—חכמתה Charles | וסימא—ושימה 4QLevi[a] | טאבא—**טׄבׄא** 4QLevi[a] 1. 20 **13:11** עמהון—**עמהם** Charles | נׄכׄסׄי—**. . . .** Charles | ומדינה—**וׄמׄדׄיׄתׄאׄ** 4QLevi[c] **13:12** ולא 1°—**לא** 4QLevi[c] | ולא 2°—Geniza ends and dominant text is 4QLevi[a] **13:13** כׄוׄלׄ—[כ]ל 4QLevi[f] | מטמרה—**מטמרא** 4QLevi[f]

Parallels

TPL 12:7 relating to 13:1
12:7 Ἰωσὴφ ἑκατοστῷ ὀκτωκαιδεκάτῳ ἔτει ἀπέθανεν.

TPL 13:1a relating to 13:2
13:1 Καὶ νῦν, τέκνα μου, ἐντέλλομαι ὑμῖν
Psalm 119:160 relating to 13:3
ראש דברך אמת ולעולם כל משפט צדקך:

TPL 13:6 relating to 13:3
13:6 καὶ σπείρετε ἐν ταῖς ψυχαῖς ὑμῶν ἀγαθά, ἵνα εὕρητε αὐτὰ ἐν τῇ ζωῇ ὑμῶν. ἐὰν γὰρ σπείρητε κακά, πᾶσαν ταραχὴν καὶ θλῖψιν θερίσετε.

13:15 And now, my sons, reading and writing and the teaching of wi[sdo]m which I lea[rned[ ] I saw. . . .[ ] you will inherit them
[ ]great you will give
[gl]ory
13:16 *vacat* . . . [ ]even in books
I re[ad] heads and judges
knows[ ] and servants
[ ] even priests and kings
[ ] your kingdom
will be [gl]ory and there is no end
fo[r ever]will pass [not] from you until all
in[habitants]in great glory

Parallels

TPL 12:7 relating to 13:1
12:7 Joseph died in (my) hundred and eighteenth year.

TPL 13:1a relating to 13:2
13:1a And now, my children, I command you . . .
Psalm 119:160 relating to 13:3
The sum of your word is truth, and every one of your righteous ordinances endures for ever.

TPL 13:6 relating to 13:3
13:6 And sow good things in your souls that you may find them in your life. For when you sow evil things, you will reap every trouble and affliction.

TPL 13:2–3 relating to 13:4–5
13:2 And do you, too, teach your children letters that they may have understanding all their life, reading unceasingly in the law of God.
13:3 For everyone who knows the law of God will be honoured, and he will not be a stranger wherever he goes;

TPL 13:9b relating to 13:6
13:9b as was also Joseph our brother. (See also *TPL* 13:2 cited above.)

TPL 13:2–3 relating to 13:4–5
13:2 διδάξατε δὲ καὶ ὑμεῖς τὰ τέκνα ὑμῶν γράμματα, ἵνα ἔχωσι σύνεσιν ἐν πάσῃ τῇ ζωῇ αὐτῶν, ἀναγινώσκοντες ἀδιαλείπτως τὸν νόμον τοῦ θεοῦ.
13:3 ὅτι πᾶς ὃς γνώσεται νόμον θεοῦ, τιμηθήσεται, καὶ οὐκ ἔσται ξένος, ὅπου ὑπάγει.

TPL 13:9b relating to 13:6
13:9 ὡς καὶ Ἰωσὴφ ὁ ἀδελφὸς ἡμῶν and see 13:2 cited above.

TPL 13:3–4 relating to 13:7–9
13:3 ὅτι πᾶς ὃς γνώσεται νόμον θεοῦ, τιμηθήσεται, καὶ οὐκ ἔσται ξένος, ὅπου ὑπάγει.
13:4 καίγε πολλοὺς φίλους ὑπὲρ γονεῖς κτήσεται, καὶ ἐπιθυμήσουσι πολλοὶ τῶν ἀνθρώπων δουλεῦσαι αὐτῷ, καὶ ἀκοῦσαι νόμον ἐκ τοῦ στόματος αὐτοῦ.

TPL 13:7 relating to 13:11–12
13:7 σοφίαν κτήσασθε ἐν φόβῳ θεοῦ μετὰ σπουδῆς· ὅτι ἐὰν γένηται αἰχμαλωσία, καὶ πόλεις ὀλοθρευθῶσι καὶ χῶραι καὶ χρυσὸς καὶ ἄργυρος καὶ πᾶσα κτῆσις ἀπολεῖται, τοῦ σοφοῦ τὴν σοφίαν οὐδεὶς δύναται ἀφελέσθαι, εἰ μὴ τύφλωσις ἀσεβείας καὶ πήρωσις ἁμαρτίας·

TPL 13:3–4 relating to 13:7–9
13:3 For everyone who knows the law of God will be honoured, and he will not be a stranger wherever he goes.
13:4 yea, he will gain many friends, more than his parents and many men will desire to serve him and to hear the law from his mouth.

TPL 13:7 relating to 13:11–12
13:7 Get wisdom in the fear of God with diligence; for though there be a leading into captivity and cities and lands be destroyed and gold and silver and every possession perish, nobody can take away the wisdom of the wise man, save the blindness of ungodliness and the mutilation (that comes) of sin;

COMMENTARY

Chapter 1: The Story of Dinah

Commentary on 1:1

The narrative concerns the incident at Shechem which is related in Genesis 34. The Aramaic text seems to be independent of the biblical phraseology, however, except where observed in our notes. First, an episode is related touching on Levi, Reuben and Jacob, perhaps parallel to *TPL* 6:3 which, in this context, tells of Levi taking counsel with Reuben and Jacob. This is followed by a discussion between "us" and the Shechemites, concerning their circumcision. Neither of these elements occurs in Genesis and they are part of the apocryphal embroidery of the biblical narrative also to be found in *Jubilees* and in *TPL*. They seem to be attested earliest in *ALD*.

Attitudes in biblical and post-biblical literature to the Shechem incident and to Levi and Simeon's actions varied. Sources mentioning this incident include Judith 9:2, *Joseph and Aseneth* 23:14, Josephus, *Jewish Antiquities* 1:337–342, Pseudo-Philo, *Biblical Antiquities* 8:7, Philo, *De migratione Abrahami* 223; *De mutatione nominum* 193–95, 199–200, Theodotus, *Work on Shechem*, cited in Eusebius, *Præparatio evangelica* 9:22. Compare Jacob's disapproving words in Genesis 49:5–7, *Jubilees* 30, *TPL* and *ALD*.[1]

טׄמאת . . "defiled"—The reading with *ṭet* seems fairly certain. The letter preceding it cannot be read (*pace* Puech). It is a conjugated form of a verb meaning "to defile, render unclean". It is a homograph, however, and could be first or second person. Before reading the *ṭet*, we had taken מאת as a noun meaning either as "a hundred", or as "home, place, town, country, city".

לבנׄ[י "the so[ns of (?)"—So Puech. Note, however, that he marks the *nun* as very uncertain. We are left, therefore, with a definite *bet*

[1] For an overall discussion of this episode, see Kugel, 1992.

and a rather uncertain *nun*. Puech conjectures בנ֯]י, the plural construct of בר "son". We have added a question mark, because in fact numerous words can start with a *bet* and perhaps a *nun*.

ע֯ל] דברת די "ac]cording to the manner of"—See 11QtgJob 34:3–4 (Job 40:8): האף תעדא דינה ותחיבנני על דברת די תזכא "Would you even remove his judgment? And would you make me guilty so that you would be innocent?"[2] די should be understood as a conjunction, not as a preposition. The expression is also reconstructed in 11QtgJob 1:7 (Job 18:4), העל דב֯[רתך] "is it for [your] sake",[3] and על דברת די is found in Biblical Aramaic (Daniel 2:30) and is calqued in late Biblical Hebrew as: ...על דברת ש (Qohelet 7:14).

ע֯ל] | דברת די כל אנש֯[...] למעבד כדין בכל֯[...] "according to the manner of all people[...] to do according to the law in all [...]". Is it possible that the author is referring to some kind of customary marriage agreement or dowry, promised by Hamor in relation to the marriage of Dinah and Shechem? If so, a parallel can be found in Targum Neophiti to Genesis 34:12: "Make very great for me the dowry and the marriage contract (פרן וכתובה),[4] and I will give just as you say to me".[5]

למעבד כדין "to do according to the law in all [...]"—Compare 1QapGen 20:13: ובכול מלכי ארעא אנתה שליט למעבד בכולהון דין "...and (you) have power over all the kings of the earth to mete out justice to all of them". In 1985 Greenfield and Stone suggested reconstructing למעבד כדין בכו[רתא] "to do according to the law of

[2] Sokoloff, 1974, 94–95 and 158; DJD 23, 160–61.

[3] Sokoloff, 1974, 29. This phrase was translated by Fitzmyer and Harrington, 1978, 11 as: "Is it on accoun[t of you that" (see *ibid.*, 42–43, 106–07). We have left aside the controversial text Psalm 110:4, which is much debated and anyway does not read דברת ש- but דברתי.

[4] פרן is a Greek loan word φερνή, see Sperber, 1984, 161–63.

[5] The noun דין is found as part of the formula designating the relationship between marriage partners in marriage agreements of the second century CE; for example, P. Murabbaʿât 20, l. 3 reads: [ד]י תהוא לי לאנתה כדין מ֯[שה ויהודאי].; DJD 2, 109–114, Yardeni, 2000, 1.119 and see Kister, 2000. For a similar formula, "Give (her to) me according to the custom (*nomos*) of the daughters of [Edom ?]" (line 5), see the Edomite marriage contract of 176 BCE in Eshel and Kloner, 1996, 11–12.

birth[right]".[6] Reconsideration of the passage, however, has led us to pose two questions. First, if the context is that of the Dinah incident, and that seems certain, what sort of relevance could "the law of birthright" have? Second, even if some relevance is admitted, who could the speaker possibly be? Therefore, we have come to prefer the interpretation given above. A third interpretation might take the expression למעבד כדין בכ֯ל[as "to do so in all[".[7] *TPL* 6:3 refers to Levi taking counsel with Reuben and Jacob about the Shechem incident and might be related to *ALD* here.

יעקב אבי ורא֯[ובן אחי | "... *took counsel with*] | Jacob my father and Reu[ben my brother..."—The words in italics give what we hypothesize was the sense of the phrase. One might restore מלכת but this is hypothetical. The general sense is supported by *TPL* 6:3 ἐγὼ συνεβούλευσα τῷ πατρί μου καὶ Ῥουβὴμ τῷ ἀδελφῷ μου "I advised my father and Reuben my brother".

Commentary on 1:2

ואמרנן "and we said"—The subjects of this verb are probably Simeon and Levi.

<אנתון> "you"—The manuscript reads אינון, but we have emended this to אנתון for reasons of context. This is quite plausible on graphic grounds. The original reading is difficult since direct speech of the sons of Jacob commences in line 20 (1:2): "and we said to them, [ ]". The speech would then continue in the general sense of "If you wish to marry our sister, you must become circumcised ...". In such a context, the third person pronoun would be impossible, leading to the reading we propose.

בברתן "our daughter"—Note that *Exposition on the Patriarchs* (4Q464) 7:8 refers to "daughters (plur.) of Shechem". This presumably reflects a variant form of the story, though the text is very fragmentary.[8]

[6] Appendix III in Hollander and de Jonge, 1985, 461.
[7] Charles, 1913, 364 translates "right".
[8] Stone and Eshel, 1992, 257.

א[חין] וחברין—This phrase is translated here "brothers and friends". However since it is clear from Genesis chapter 34 that there was a commercial dimension to the relationship between the sons of Jacob and the Shechemites, it is possible that "brothers and partners" would be the proper translation.[9] The words should be compared with *ALD* 13:8 אחא וֹחבֹר הוי בה "he has a brother and a friend therein", which is another linguistic contact with chapter 13. Variation between חבר "a friend" and שותף "partner" occurs in ben Sira 41:18, where ms B in the suggested reconstruction reads: [מחב]ר [ו]רע, while the Masada scroll and the margin of ms B read משותף ורע. This tends to show that חבר may mean "partner". Contrast the phrase in the Bible (Genesis 34:16) וישבנו אתכם והיינו לעם אחד "and we will live among you and become one people". *ALD* makes this more explicit.

Commentary on 1:3

נזורו עורלת בשרכון והתחמיון כוֹאֹתֹֹן "circumcise your fleshly foreskin and look like us"—This is based on Genesis 34:15 "that you will become as we are and every male among you be circumcised". The basic meaning of נזר in both Biblical Hebrew[10] and Aramaic is "cut, divide" as in Daniel 2:45, the Sefire inscription I A line 40 and 11QtgJob 5:3 (Job 21:21). In later Aramaic נז"ר + ערלה seems to be a technical term, translating the Hebrew מול "circumcise". Thus Targum Neofiti and Targum Pseudo-Jonathan translate Genesis 17:23 וימל את בשר ערלתם as ונזר ית בישרא דעורלתהון "and he circumcised the flesh of their foreskin"; similarly in Genesis 18:1, 21:4, and 34:22. This is the expression here.[11]

The formulation "foreskin of your flesh" is rather unusual. In Biblical Hebrew we find בשר ערלתו "flesh of his foreskin", e.g., Genesis 17:14, etc. and the Targum corresponds to this. Thus, the phrase "foreskin of flesh" used in *ALD* reverses the common biblical term. The only occurrence of an expression apparently cognate to *ALD* is in Ezekiel 44:6–9:

[9] Greenfield and Stone, 1979, 217.

[10] ויגזרו העצים "they cut down trees" (2 Kings 6:4); or גזרו את הילד החי לשנים "[d]ivide the living boy in two" (1 Kings 3:25).

[11] See Sokoloff, 1990, 126. A metaphoric use is to be found in Deuteronomy 10:16 ערלת לבבכם in Targum Neofiti ערלת טפשות לבביכון, "the foreskin of the stupidity of your hearts".

> Too long, O house of Israel, have you committed all your abominations, admitting aliens, uncircumcised of spirit (ערלי לב) and uncircumcised of flesh (ערלי בשר), to be in My Sanctuary and profane My very Temple, . . . Thus said the Lord God: Let no alien, uncircumcised of spirit and flesh (ערל לב וערל בשר), enter My Sanctuary—no alien whatsoever among the people of Israel.[12]

The phrase in Ezekiel is surely an inversion of the common "flesh of foreskin" and forms a striking image, particularly when the flesh is then set in contrast with the heart. 1QpHab uses Ezekiel's expression when it says: "Its interpretation concerns the Priest whose disgrace exceeded his glory because he did not circumcise the foreskin of his heart and excessiveness to slake his thirst" (11:12–13).[13] It is clear from context why 1QpHab uses Ezekiel. Since this phrase only occurs in Ezekiel, it is possible that *ALD* has Ezekiel in mind when it uses "the foreskin of your flesh". Nonetheless, it is hard to see why *ALD* should evoke Ezekiel 44:6–9 in the context of the Dinah story. It is using the expression rather literally, and the question still stands why the term "foreskin of flesh" is used in connection with the circumcision of the Shechemites, rather than "the flesh of your foreskins". Which is it that which was to be circumcised? In addition, one should be aware of the semantic difference between the two construct forms: ערלת בשר "the foreskin of the flesh" and ערלי בשר "uncircumcised of flesh". Thus "uncircumcised" is used in the texts mentioned above and in others with a metaphorical meaning, parallel to uncircumcised of ears (Jeremiah 6:10) or of heart (Jeremiah 9:25); but even then, compare, ". . . he should circumcise in the Yaḥad the foreskin of his tendency" (ערלת יצר 1QS 5:5) and 1QpHab 11:13 cited above.[14]

There might be a theological point here, setting "circumcision of flesh" in contrast with "circumcision of heart". Then, the deception perpetrated by the sons of Jacob would include the fact that the Shechemites would have only a fleshly circumcision, not a spiritual one. This in turn might explain the odd התחמיו כוֹאתֹן "you will look like us", i.e. externally (see next note). In contrast to "you will look

[12] *JPS*, 1985.

[13] Cf. 2 Esdras 1:31, "for you have rejected your festal days, and new moons, and circumcisions of flesh" (variant reading: see Bergren, 1990, 357).

[14] "Spirit" and "flesh" are commonly contrasted in Qumran literature: see Flusser, 1958.

like us", the biblical text in Genesis 34:15 says "you will become like us".[15] In addition, the shift from the biblical phrase "one people" to "brothers and friends" might be a further indication in the same direction. This is far from certain, however, and the following term במילת [קש]ו̊ט "with the circumcision [of tru]th" might show the contrary.[16]

והתחמיון "and look"—*Hitpe'el* of חמ"י meaning "to be seen, visible".[17] The root חמ"י is parallel to חז"י. חז"י is attested in various Aramaic texts found at Qumran, e.g., 1QapGen 6:11, 13:9 and 20:9; 4QLevi^b 2:15–16; and later, in *Genesis rabba* 13:9.[18] The root חמ"י is found in all Aramaic dialects, including Christian Palestinian Aramaic. This root can be detected in the Fragmentary Targum (e.g., Genesis 19:3) while in the Aramaic of Targum Neophiti both roots occur. חמ"י seems to replace the earlier חז"י, and it might have been introduced into the Geniza manuscript by a medieval copyist.

כו̊א̊תן "like us"—From כוות "like", with additional *aleph* as *mater lectionis*;[19] see Fragmentary Targum to Genesis 34:15 (ms C).

חתימין "sealed"—The combination of חת"מ + בשר referring to circumcision is found in some Midrashic sources. In *Exodus rabba* 19 we read:

> THIS IS THE ORDINANCE OF THE PASSOVER . . . but he commanded: 'Unless the seal of Abraham is inscribed on your flesh, you cannot taste thereof.' Thereupon all those who had been born in Egypt were immediately circumcised, and concerning these is it said: *Gather My saints together unto Me; those that have made a covenant with Me by sacrifice* (Psalm 50:5).[20]

[15] Greenfield and Stone, 1979, 218.

[16] The word מילה "circumcision" occurs neither in Biblical nor in Qumran Hebrew.

[17] See Sokoloff, 1990, 205–06.

[18] Theodor-Albeck, 1965, 1.118; See Sokoloff, 1990, 194.

[19] For more examples, see Fitzmyer, 1971, 196–98 and 1999, 461, and note 42.

[20] Translation from Lehrman, 1983, 235. זאת חקת הפסח. . . אמר להם אם אין חותמו של אברהם בבשרכם לא תטעמו ממנו מיד כל הנולד במצרים נמולו לשעה קלה. עליהם נאמר אספו לי חסידי כרתי בדיתי עלי זבח (תהלים נ, ה).

Yalqut Shimʿoni, Song of Songs 993 runs: "'Set me as a seal' (Song 8:6): This refers to Abraham who observed circumcision as a seal."[21] In *Midrash Tanḥuma yelamdenu, wa-yera'*[22] we read "that the Holy One Blessed be He sealed the covenant of circumcision in his flesh".[23] Similar also are *j. Berakot*, 9 14a; *b. Shabbat* 137b.[24] The second paragraph of the Grace after Meals has: ועל בריתך שחתמת בבשרנו "and for your covenant which You have sealed in our flesh". Thus, the idea of circumcision as a sealing is broadly attested in Rabbinic texts, but *ALD* here is the first occurrence of this idea.[25] Sealing, of course, expresses ownership.[26]

א[חין] "br[others]"—The single letter א is to be observed on the line following the end of the text. This is, most probably, the first letter of the (now lost) next word. The manuscript does not have a *custos* elsewhere and, in this case, scribal oversight was at play. The scribe presumably stopped writing the word after he realized that he had exceeded the regular twenty-three lines per column. We conjecture that the word was א[חין] "br[others]", thus parallel to the same phrase in verse 1:2.

[21] שימני כחותם זה אברהם שקיים המילה כחותם.

[22] This appears in Wertheimer, 1950, 1.152.

[23] שחתם הקדוש ברוך הוא בבשרו ברית מילה.

[24] *J. Berakot* 9 14a: "sealed with the sign of the covenant"; *b. Shabbat* 137b "and he sealed his offspring with the sign of the holy covenant" (*Schottenstein Edition*, 1997).

[25] See TDNT, 6, 662; and the word σφραγίς in Christian sources as referring to being signed. It is also used as a term for baptism in *2 Clement* and *Hermas* (Theognis 1, 19); see Bauer, 1957, s.v. σφραγίς. See Greenfield and Stone, 1979, 218. For circumcision as sealing, see Vasiliev, 1893, 1.212, line 6.

[26] See Stone, 1990, 158.

Chapter 2: The Wars of the Sons of Jacob

This chapter is composed of Cambridge b followed by a lacuna. We then place 1QLevi 8 and that is followed by two lines from the Athos Greek and 4QLevi^{b} 1:5–7 = chapter 2:4–5. A lacuna of nearly three columns separates Cambridge b from Cambridge a.[27]

Commentary on 2:1

Cambridge col. b (chapter 2) deals with a different subject to col. a (chapter 1), though both refer to the sons of Jacob. No clear reference to the Dinah affair is to be found in chapter 2. Chapter 1 talks of a discussion of Reuben and Jacob with Hamor, while the mention of Reuben in 2:1 in the third person indicates that this is most probably part of another story. Moreover, since this fragment comes more than two columns after the end of col. a (chapter 1), it seems unlikely that it would still be discussing the Dinah incident.[28] The action is localized in the Shechem region.

Our interpretation differs radically from Puech's readings and overall view. In this small fragment, of which only parts of nine lines were preserved, he confidently reconstructs no less than 14 words (most of them completely; or else on the basis of the slightest surviving marks). Puech's reconstruction is based on the identification of the scene as that of Joseph's sale, to which event no reference whatsoever actually occurs in the surviving text. Having identified the scene, he proceeds to reconstruct in accordance with his identification. Thus, he reads a final *pē* in line 15, after which he himself puts a question-mark, saying "La trace à la cassure n'exclut pas la tête de *pē* final de préférence à *waw* ou *nun* final".[29] In the photograph only a very small sign can be seen which seems to differ from a final *pē* as it occurs in the name Joseph in 13:6.

He then reads Joseph's name a second time in an unclear part of the text where hardly any letters can be seen, in line 19. The

[27] Charles, 1908a, 245 states that three columns are missing, but this is presumably an approximation.

[28] *Pace* Kugler, 1996, 52–53, 63–64 who perceives no need to demonstrate that 2:1 is part of the Shechem incident but assumes it. So did Becker, 1970, 77 and Hultgård, 1982, 2.96–97.

[29] Puech, 2002, 519.

lost brother thus found, Puech then proceeds to reconstruct the whole text with no other question-marks or apparent doubts. His reconstruction, however, is marred by a number of strange Aramaic words and meanings, such as וחשיבו which cannot mean "they conspired"; שמעין on which see the commentary below; the construction ומה מית יוסף also discussed in the commentary and לההדה "rejoindre" which form, an *ʾafʿel*, is not attested. He then draws this newly-composed and reconstructed text, with no clear typographic distinction between original and reconstructed letters, producing a misleading feeling of certainty.[30]

On closer examination, one can see that the text that actually survived scarcely allows this reconstruction. Only the name Shechem has any connection with the story of Joseph's sale (see Genesis 37:12–14), while all the rest stands against it:

1. There is no reference to the brothers' plot to kill Joseph "whenever" (בכל עדן) he was sent to them. According to Genesis 37:14, 37:18 etc. this was a single incident.

2. We fail to see any biblical or other basis for "et Dan rapporta [les discu]ssions [*de ses frères*] à Sichem et comment est mort Jos[eph par la main des arti]sans de violence . . .".[31] Simeon and Levi's swords are indeed called "weapons of violence" in Jacob's blessings in Genesis 49, but Dan is not included in this statement. Nor is he included in any other particular incident relating to Joseph's "death" as related in the latter part of Genesis 37.

3. The incident in lines 20–22 is quite bizarre and makes little sense in the context of the brothers' actions against Joseph and their sequel. According to Puech's reconstruction Judah tells (his brothers) "que moi (probably Levi) et Siméon, mon frère, nous étions allés rejoindre Ruben, notre frère, qui était à l'orient d'Asher . . .". In the biblical story, the brothers are described as being together, and Judah and Reuben try to stop the others from killing Joseph. The story in *Jubilees* 34:10–11 is shorter and not very different. Moreover, Puech's reconstruction of Cambridge col. b leaves Judah's sudden departure and abandonment of the flock quite unexplained (line 23).

As a result of these considerations, we are led to reject Puech's overall reconstruction of the text. We are led, with a measure of

[30] Puech, 2002, 519, fig. 2.
[31] Puech, 2002, 520, lines 17–18.

hesitation, to adhere to the interpretation that relates it to the wars of the sons of Jacob. The exact story is unparalleled, therefore the lacunae are difficult to restore. As well as Reuben, other sons of Jacob are mentioned: Simeon, Judah, and possibly Dan (according to an alternative reading of line 17).

There are no known parallels to the incident relating to the sheep at the end of 2:1. It is not connected with anything in the biblical narrative. In post-biblical sources we have extensive descriptions of the wars of the sons of Jacob with the Amorites and with the sons of Esau.[32] Conceivably, 2:1 relates to these wars, even though there are no specific points of contact, but only some broad resemblances.[33]

עדן "time"—Alternatively, "set time": see 12:1. Compare Daniel 2:8ff., 11QtgJob 31:1 (Job 38:23) ל]עדׄן עׄ[קת]א "for] the time of tr[ouble" and 4QTobit[c] (4Q198) 1:9.

ואחוי דן "and he told this"—Alternatively read "and Dan told [. . .]": so already Charles, 1913. Compare the next line. Puech then reconstructs [שמ]עׄ[י]ןׄ on the basis of very tiny fragments of two letters that he considers not incompatible with *ayin* and final *nun*. But, the word produced does not mean "[les discu]ssions" in Aramaic, and certainly not in the plural. The singular is reconstructed by him, more plausibly, in 13:7 and he translates it there "[renom]mée".

ומה "and that"—Puech, 2002, translates "comment", a meaning not found in the dictionaries. It could mean "and what".

[32] See *TPJudah* 3–7, *Jubilees* 34:1–9, Targum Pseudo-Jonathan to Genesis 48:22 and at the end of *Genesis rabba* 97:6 (Theodor and Albeck, 1965, 3:1249). These wars are also the subject of *Midrash Wayissa'u* published by Jellinek, 1938, 3:1–5 (in Hebrew); Alexander and Dan, 1972, 67–76 (in Hebrew) and Hollander and de Jonge, 1985, 451–56 (translation). The possibility that this refers to the events related in *TPJudah* 5 was already raised by Pass and Arendzen, 1900, 653.

[33] Such broad points of resemblance are the following. First, the story is set near Shechem, probably during the sons' shepherding, compare *Jubilees* 34:1–2. Second, the activity of at least four brothers is recorded in Cambridge b and in the stories of the wars many brothers are involved. Third the reading "to the east of Asher" in line 22 parallels the mention of coming to a city, in this instance Asher, from the east in the various wars of the sons of Jacob: cf. *TPJudah* 5:1–2. Fourth, along the same lines, we might understand the last part of Cambridge b as expressing Judah's eagerness to help, thus leaving the flock. The word "jumped" (קפ"צ) is used of Judah's warlike zeal in a somewhat different context in *Midrash Wayissa'u* (Alexander and Dan, 1972, 73, 2, line 54).

עב]די חמסא "do]ers of violence"—חמסא "violence" is sometimes found in the plural form חמסין, see Targum Neofiti and the Vatican manuscript of the Fragmentary Targum to Genesis 6:11.[34] The phrase עבדי חמסא "doers of violence" is found elsewhere in *ALD* 12:6 (with a parallel in Syriac) and in 1QapGen 5:18 and 11:14.

ואחוי אינו̇ן יהוד̊ה די אנה ושמעון אחי אזלנא "and Judah told them that I and Simeon my brother had gone"—This says that Judah told "them", apparently his brothers, that Levi and Simeon had gone somewhere or to somebody.

לה̇[ ]ר̊ד—This is probably a verb and a number of possible reconstructions exist.[35]

די למדנ̊ח̊ א̊שר "to the east of Asher"—Puech has די למדנח אשר "which is east of Asher". This does not contradict the material reading, which is nonetheless not completely certain. The sense is not quite clear. It is conceivable that Asher is not the name of a son of Jacob but a place name. Eusebius identified Aser, mentioned in Joshua 17:7 ("The boundary of Manasseh ran from Asher to Michmethath, which lies near Shechem,") with Tayāsīr, 15 miles north-east of Shechem, on the road to Scythopolis. He says "A city of the tribe of Manasseh. And now a village on the fifteenth milestone from Shechem in the direction of Scythopolis."[36] The same place is later mentioned by the Bordeaux Pilgrim (333 CE).[37]

ושור יהודה קדמא [ל]מ̊שבק עאנא "and Judah leaped forward [to] leave the sheep"—The verb שור is found in 4QTobit[b] (4Q197 Tobit 7:6) 4 3:8, ושור רעואל נשקה ובכ[ה] "then Raguel jumped up, kissed him, and broke into tea[rs]."[38] The verb is attested once in *j. Gittin* 47b

[34] Similarly Fragmentary Targum ms Vatican to Genesis 49:12 and ms Paris to Numbers 6:27.

[35] Probably an *'af'el* form. The following reconstructions might be reconsidered: מרד, טרד or סרד ("terrify": see 11QtgJob 22:1 [Job 33:6]). The last letter might be read as final *kaph*, thus we can reconstruct: ארך ("to wait": see 1QapGen 3:2). None of these is particularly convincing. The word could be a toponym.

[36] *Onomastikon* 26:22, see Klostermann, 1904. See also Wilkinson, 1977, 29, 150, map 8 and coordinates 187 194; Thomsen, 1907, 27.

[37] "Aser, where was the house of Job", see Wilson, 1896, 18, 67–68; Wilkinson, 1981, 154.

[38] Fitzmyer, DJD 19, 51 (= 4QpapTob[a] 14 2:11). The same meaning is found

(35).[39] The reading [ל]מֹשֹבק עאנא "[to] leave the sheep" seems certain, although the plot is unclear.[40]

Commentary on 2:2–3

The occurrence of the word שלם in 2:2–3 led Milik to suggest connecting this fragment with the Shechem incident, which starts with the words: ויבא יעקב **שלם** עיר שכם אשר בארץ כנען "Jacob came safely (שלם) to the city of Shechem" (Genesis 33:18). Milik identified this name with Jerusalem, based on other occurrences of this name as referring to Jerusalem.[41] However, one can hardly support this identification in the biblical context. שלם in Genesis 33:18 was usually understood by ancient and modern interpreters as an adverb "in peace" or "safely".[42] On the other hand, the Septuagint translated it as εἰς Σαλέμ "to Salem". Finally, the author of *Jubilees* 30:1 incorporated both interpretations, saying: "he went up to *Salem*, to the east of Shechem, *in peace*".[43]

Yet, the word שלם in our text is not preceded by the preposition *lamed* in its two occurrences, and is supplemented with the words: וכל אנש[. .]—"and every man". A similar phrase can be found in 1QapGen 21:19 ואתית לי לביתי בשלם ואשכחת כול אנשי שלם "Then I returned (came) home safely, and found all my household safe and sound".[44] This may be related to the end of the war; cf. *TPJudah* 7:7 and *Jubilees* 34:9. Further, verse 2:6 preserves the first person singular pronoun אֹנה "I", thus probably indicating that this is Levi's story, not Jacob's. Accordingly, we might tentatively reconstruct some-

in the translations of Tobit: καὶ ἀνεπήδησεν Ῥαγουήλ and Latin, *et exsiliit Raguhel*. Compare Syriac Tobit 2:4 *šwrt* (Payne Smith, 1903, 568). M. Morgenstern graciously consulted with us about this phrase.

[39] Written שוור or שבר, see Sokoloff, 1990, 540. For the more frequent occurrence of this verb in Jewish Babylonian Aramaic, see Sokoloff, 2002, 1116. A similar incident of Judah leaping in war ahead of the other brothers is to be found in *Midrash wayissaʿu* ed. Alexander and Dan, 1972, 73, 2, line 54.

[40] See Greenfield and Stone, 1979, 218.

[41] Psalm 76:3 where it parallels Zion and Genesis 14:18 ומלכי-צדק מלך שלם "and Melchizedek king of Salem", interpreted by 1QapGen as: ואתה לשלם היא ירושלם "and he came to Salem, that is Jerusalem" (22:13).

[42] See the Samaritan Pentateuch, ויבוא יעקב שלום and modern English translations such as RSV, NRSV, JPS, Fox, 1995 and others.

[43] Salem has been identified with the village Sālīm, located ca. 5 kms. east of Tel Balatah (ancient Shechem): Astour, 1992. Translation from Wintermute, 1985.

[44] Fitzmyer, 1971, 68–69.

thing similar in *ALD*: "[. . .] and peace *vacat* And I [returned home safely, and found] all [my] people safe and sound [. . .] I [. . .]."

If we are correct, this fragment might fit somewhere after the Shechem episode, probably after additional wars of the sons of Jacob with the Amorites and with the sons of Esau, some of which might be alluded to in 2:1.

Commentary on 2:4

ἐν ὕδατι καθαρῷ "in pure water"—Levi here washes his clothes in pure water and himself ἐν ὕδατι ζῶντι "in living water". The expression מים טהורים "pure water" occurs in the Bible only in Ezekiel 36:25, in a context which is not directly cultic. In *Joseph and Aseneth* 18:8–9 Aseneth washes her face in "pure water" before she meets with Joseph. In *TPL* 8:5 Levi is washed ἐν ὕδατι καθαρῷ "in pure water" while Philo, *Vita Mosis* 2.143 says that the High Priest is washed ὕδατι πηγῆς καθαρωτάτῳ καὶ ζωτικωτάτῳ "in the water of a most pure and living spring": cf. *1 Enoch* 17:4. Hence, it is clear, despite Ezekiel 36:25, that these expressions are related to cultic, particularly priestly purification. On the position of 2:4–5 as a separate incident from 3:1, see Introduction, section on "The Original Order of *ALD*".[45]

[45] See also Greenfield and Stone, 1979, 249–250.

Chapter 3: Levi's Prayer

Commentary on 3:1

נטלת לשמיא "I lifted up to heaven"—נטל is used in the Targumim usually just of the eyes, e.g., in Targum Neofiti to Genesis 24:63.[46] Based on the Greek, however, we may infer that the object here is "my eyes and my countenance". The same collocation of terms occurs in 4QpapTobit[a] 6:8 (4Q196; Tobit 3:12) where we find וכען ע]ליך אנפי ועינ̇[י נ]טלת "And now to] you my face and my eye[s] I [have lif]ted up". Here Septuagint manuscript Sinaiticus reads καὶ νῦν ἐπί σε τὸ πρόσωπόν μου καὶ τοὺς ὀφθαλμούς μου ἀνέβλεψα "and now I raised up my countenance and my eyes towards you." In manuscripts Alexandrinus and Vaticanus the word order is even closer to *ALD* τοὺς ὀφθαλμούς μου καὶ τὸ πρόσωπόν μου εἰς σὲ δέδωκα "I have set my eyes and my countenance towards you".[47]

Lifting one's eyes to heaven as part of a prayer is mentioned in Psalm 123:1 אליך נשאתי את עיני הישבי בשמים "To you I lift up my eyes, O you who are enthroned in the heavens!", which is followed by the prayer: "Have mercy upon us, O Lord, have mercy upon us, for we have had more than enough of contempt" (verse 3).

ἐλάλησα "I spoke"—This seems somewhat, superfluous in light of the end of 3:2 ηὐξάμην καὶ εἶπα "I prayed and said".

Commentary on 3:2

ואצבעת כפי וידי "the fingers of my hands and my hands"—Aramaic כפי is literally "my palms".[48] There seems to be a doubling of the idea of lifting up the hands in prayer in the forms of text preserved both in Aramaic and in Greek. It might be compared with the preceding verse, which mentions both "eyes" and "my countenance" in Greek. This is a possible reconstruction in Aramaic.[49]

---

[46] See Sokoloff, 1990, 348.

[47] Fitzmyer, DJD 19, 13–14. For נטל + עין see 11QtgJob 35:3 (Job 40:24) במטל עינוהי יכלנה "Can one overpower him by covering his eyes".

[48] In the LXX χείρ sometimes renders כַּף, the Hebrew equivalent of the Aramaic here: see, e.g., Genesis 20:5, 31:29, 40:11, etc.

[49] In the translation by Greenfield and Stone in Hollander and de Jonge, 1985, 459, note a, they assumed that a verb was lost from the first colon. Now, however,

In the Bible one finds the construct form אצבעות יד "fingers of hand" (2 Samuel 21:20) and כפות יד "palms of hand" (1 Samuel 5:4 and 2 Kings 9:35). However, אצבעות כף "fingers of palm" is not found, though כף "palm" and יד "hand" are sometimes parallel, e.g., in Jeremiah 15:21 and Psalm 71:4. We have already noted that Hebrew כף and its Aramaic cognate כף, both meaning "palm", are sometimes rendered by Greek χείρ "hand" in the LXX. Thus, the phraseology here is not implausible.

נש"א + יד "raise up palm" as an act of a prayer is found in Psalm 28:2 שמע קול תחנוני בשועי אליך, בנשאי ידי אל דביר קדשך "Listen to my plea for mercy when I cry out to you, when I lift my hands toward your inner sanctuary" (JPS) and the common phrase כף + פר"ש "spread out palm" is often used in prayer contexts in sources like Exodus 9:29, Ezra 9:5 and Job 1:13. This stance is part of Levi's preparation for prayer. Compare *Joseph and Aseneth* 11:19.

In 11QPs[a] 24:3–4 = Syriac Psalm 3:2 (Psalm 154) we read: פרשתי כפי למעון קדשכה "I spread out my palms towards your holy dwelling"; cf. also *Sibylline Oracles* 4:152ff. This might be taken to imply that τῶν ἁγίων "the holy ones" at the end of this hemistych derives from a Semitic like קדישין or קודשין. Nonetheless, the exact sense of "holy ones" or "holy things" remains enigmatic.

Commentary on 3:3

ἐννοιῶν "thoughts"—This might have been Aramaic רעיוניא: see Daniel (Th) 2:29, 2:30, 4:16, etc. However, the Greek there differs and the reconstruction of the Aramaic word must be regarded as quite speculative.

א]נתה בלחודיך ידע "you alone understand"—A similar phrase is partly reconstructed in 4QEnGiants[a] (4Q203) 9:3: די כל רזיא ידע] אנתה "Because [you] kno[w] all the mysteries".[50]

based on the similarity to the preceding verse, where two nouns have one verb, we have concluded that this should be considered part of the author's style.

[50] Stuckenbruck, 1997, 94–95; see 4Q534 1 1:8.

Commentary on 3:4

καὶ νῦν τέκνα μου μετ' ἐμοῦ "And now my children are with me"—The mention of Levi's children at this point seems out of place, and the reason for their introduction is unclear. Such a mention might have been more appropriate in the context of 3:15. In any case, the text here remains difficult; the reconstructed קדמי "with me" is uncertain.

אֹרחת קשט "paths of truth"—ארחת is plural in both Aramaic and Greek. The equivalent Hebrew expression דרך אמת "way of truth" occurs in Genesis 24:48, admittedly in a different sense.[51] ארחת קשטא "ways of truth" are mentioned also in 4QLevi[a] 4:5 א]רֹחת קשטא תשבקוֻן וֹכל שֽבילין["w]ays of truth you will abandon and all the paths of [" (see Appendix "Unplaced Fragments"). The same phrase was reconstructed in 4Qpseudo-Daniel[a], in a broken context: כשדיא[הֹאֹ בֹני[. . .]אורחת ק]ושטא "]the Chaldeans, indeed the children of [. . .] the ways of t[ruth . . .] (4Q243 7:2–3);[52] see also 4Q246 (titled *Apocryphon of Daniel* or *Aramaic Apocalypse*) 2:5 וכל ארחתה בקשוט "and all his ways are truth".[53] However, in all these instances no contrasting negative way occurs.

In the present passage, however, the use of "ways" or "paths", combined with the two spirits ideas in it, might provide a background upon which *duo viae* ideas developed. An earlier reference to the two ways concept is found in *1 Enoch* in the words of Enoch to his son Methuselah (especially *1 Enoch* 91:4, 91:19 and 94:1–4), part of which was preserved in 4QEn[g] (4Q212) 1 2:17–21 (91:18–19).[54] This refers to ארחת קשט]א "ways of truth" and to קושטא למהך בהון [. . . (perhaps) "ways] of truth in which to walk".[55]

The concept of two ways also occurs in the Genesis Apocryphon

[51] Compare also Malachi 2:6 which implies the straight path along which the Levite goes.

[52] Collins and Flint, DJD 22, 102. See there, of the eschatological period, ש]בקוֹ אוֹרֹ]חת "they [le]ft the w[ays of" (4Q243 33:1, where one might reconstruct אוֹרֹ]חת קושטא "w[ays of truth" or the like).

[53] Puech, DJD 22, 167–69. Baumgarten, 2003, 398 translates "paths of righteousness" and compares 1QS 4:2.

[54] See Flusser, 1991. Compare also Audet, 1953, 41–82.

[55] See the reconstruction by Milik, 1976, 260. The same type of discourse also occurs in Enoch's words to Methuselah concerning Lamech and his son Noah, 1QapGen 5:16–19.

when, quoting from "[A copy of] the book of the words of Noah" (1QapGen 5:29),[56] it says . . . והוית מהלך בשבילי אֹמֹת עלמא . . . ". . . and I walked in the paths of eternal truth . . ." (1QapGen 6:2–3), which is contrasted there with: . . . ולאזהרותני מן נְתִיב שקר די אזל לחשוך כול שבילי חמס "and to warn me away from the path of falsehood that leads to darkness . . . all the ways of lawlessness" (lines 3 and 5). Neither *ALD* nor the Genesis Apocryphon is a product of the Qumran sect.[57]

Such ideas were later connected with the dualistic world-view of the Qumran sect. The sect developed a concept of two spirits, one of truth and the other of falsehood, that is detailed in the Manual of Discipline (1QS 3:13–4:26). In this document the same contrast is integrated into the description of the two spirits, and in it one finds terminology of the two ways.[58]

The belief in two spirits has been compared with R. Aqiba's saying concerning Adam:

> אמר ליה פפוס. ומה אתה מקיים הן האדם היה כאחד ממנו, אלא הקדוש ברוך הוא נותן לפניו שתי דרכים אחד של מות ואחד של חיים, ובחר לו דרך המות.
>
> Papos said to him: "And how do you interpret: 'Behold, the man has become as one of us (כאחד ממנו)?'" It means that God put before him two ways, the way of life and the way of death, and he chose for himself the way of death.[59]

Commentary on 3:5 and 3:10

ארחק [מני מרי רוח עויה ורעיונא ב]אישא וזנותא . . . וקרבני למהוא לכה [עבד "Make far from me, my Lord, the unrighteous spirit, and evil thought and fornication (3:5) . . . and bring me forward, to be your [servant] (3:10)"[60]—As shown by David Flusser, at this point the *Prayer of Levi*

[56] Morgenstern, Qimron and Sivan, 1996, 40–41. For a discussion of this book title, see: Steiner, 1995.

[57] See commentary on 4QLevi[a] frag. 4, below.

[58] I.e., ואלה דרכיהן בתבל להאיר בלבב איש ולישר לפניו כול דרכי צדק אמת "And these are their ways in the world: to illuminate the heart of man and to level before him all the ways of true righteousness" (4:2); ודרכי נדה בעבודת טמאה . . . ללכת בכול דרכי חושך "filthy ways in unclean worship . . . walking in all the ways of darkness" (4:10–11). For other instances of this idea and for some similar concepts in Greek literature, see Stone, 1990, 190–97, especially note 28. See the recent survey by Kraft, 2000.

[59] *Mekilta d'Rabbi Ishmael*, Bešalaḥ 6:14–16 (Horovitz and Rabin, 1931, 112).

[60] See Greenfield and Stone, 1990, 157–58.

shows striking similarities to, and indeed shares some elements with, other apotropaic prayers. Such elements are found in *Plea for Deliverance* (11QPs[a] col. 19) and in Psalm 155 (*ibid.*, col. 24). Moreover, similar expressions can be found in the later Jewish prayer recited before the morning service: "Keep us far (הרחיקנו) from a bad man and a bad companion. Cause us to cleave (דבקנו) to good inclination and to good works".[61] Other apotropaic prayers of the Second Temple period which include some of these elements are the prayers of Noah and Abraham in *Jubilees* 10:3–6 and 12:19–20, as well as some references in 1QSb 1:7–8.[62] Compare this verse with *TPL* 4:2.

Commentary on 3:5

ארחק "make far"—This verb is used of exorcism in an Aramaic amulet of the Byzantine period: משבעת רוחה... דתזוע ותנער ותרחק מן קלארא... אסיר את ומרחק ממנה "Adjured are you, spirit . . . that you may move away and expelled and keep far from Klara . . . May you be bound and kept away from her".[63]

רעיונא ב]אישא "evil thought"—The original of διαλογισμόν here is uncertain. Observe that the Aramaic manuscript has nothing corresponding to ὕβριν "pride" found in the Greek text, and we have omitted it from our reconstruction. Note somewhat similar phraseology in *TPDan* 5:6. See also LXX Hosea 7:15 ואלי יחשבו רע καὶ εἰς ἐμὲ ἐλογίσαντο πονηρά, "yet they plot evil against me". It is also possible to translate, as does Philonenko, "et la luxure et l'orgueil, détourne-les de moi".[64] We prefer our phrase-division which yields more balance between the phrases.

[61] Flusser, 1966, 200. He found further similarities in the following sentence, according to the Italian rite: "Keep me near (קרבני) to all what Thou lovest and keep me far (ורחקני) from all what Thou hatest." His theories on the Two Ways are set forth in Flusser, 1991. Compare also Audet, 1953, and recently van Sandt and Flusser, 2002.

[62] Psalm 91 became widely used as an apotropaic prayer, for the first time in 11QApocryphal Psalms (11Q11) 6:3–15, where it was copied following a collection of incantations. To these examples may be added four sectarian, apotropaic prayers (4Q510, 4Q511, 4Q444 and 6Q18). See Eshel, 1999 and Eshel, 2003.

[63] No. 18:1–4 in Naveh and Shaked, 1993, 57–58.

[64] Philonenko, 1987, 835.

Commentary on 3:6

אחזיני "let there be shown to me"—This reconstruction seems plausible on the grounds of Aramaic usage; the Greek translation has a third person singular passive imperative δειχθήτω "let there be shown to me".[65]

ח]כמה ומנדע וגבורה "wisdom and knowledge and strength"—These terms are presumably derived from Isaiah 11:2 which reads: ונחה עליו רוח יהוה רוח חכמה ובינה רוח עצה וגבורה רוח דעת ויראת יהוה "The spirit of the Lord shall alight upon him: a spirit of wisdom and insight, a spirit of counsel and valor, a spirit of devotion and reverence for the Lord"; compare *1 Enoch* 93:10: די שבעה פ[עמי]ן חכמה ומדע תתיה[ב להון] "sevenf[old] wisdom and knowledge shall be giv[en to them]" (4QEn^g 1 4:13).[66] Moreover, the preceding expression τὸ πνεῦμα τὸ ἅγιον in *ALD* 3:6 corresponds to רוח יהוה "the spirit of the Lord" in Isaiah.[67] All the positive terms found here are drawn from the longer list in Isaiah 11:2, and a similar accumulation of positive language may be observed in 1QS 4:2–8. The negative language here differs from that in 1QS and no clear instance of this particular type of contrasting language was found elsewhere. This section is composed in balanced prose like parts of 1QS, such as the "Discourse on the Two Spirits" (1QS 3:13–4:26). The idea of Levitical priestly instruction in "knowledge and teaching (Torah)" is to the fore in Malachi 2:6–7.

Commentary on 3:7

רחמי<ן> "favor"—The text of the Qumran fragment, רחמיך "your favor", here is emended according to the Greek.

Commentary on 3:8

καὶ αἰνεῖν τοὺς λόγους σου μετ᾽ ἐμοῦ, κύριε "and to praise your words with me, O Lord"—This phrase is not preserved in Aramaic. It can be compared with 11QPs^a *Plea for Deliverance* 19:16–17 where, following

[65] Stone and Greenfield, 1993, 261.
[66] Milik, 1976, 265. A somewhat similar list is to be observed in Daniel 5:14.
[67] Philonenko, 1987, 835 gives a list of occurrences of this expression in Qumran and other contemporary literature.

a passage on the two spirits, we read: כי אתה יהוה שבחי "For thou, O Lord, art my praise".[68] The expression μετ' ἐμοῦ "with me" is a little difficult here.

דׄשפיר ודטב קדמיך "[. . .] that which is pleasant and good before you"—Since the parallel Greek material shows nothing corresponding to these words, it seems likely that a whole stych has fallen out by homoeoteleuton either at the level of the Aramaic *Vorlage* of the Greek or of the Greek itself (קדמיך—קדמיך or Greek ἐνώπιόν σου—ἐνώπιόν σου).[69] Alternatively, considering the similarity of these two Aramaic phrases, a doublet may have arisen in the *Vorlage* of the Aramaic text preserved at Qumran.

Commentary on 3:9

At this point the prayer turns to a plea for divine protection. It involves a number of elements:

[ו]אׄל תשלט בי כל שטן "And] let not any satan have power over me"—This phrase may derive originally from Psalm 119:133b. It implies the idea that demons were a threat. The same view also follows, it seems, from 3:11, "so that the wall of your peace is around me, and let the shelter of your power shelter me from every evil", with which compare the prayer for protection in 11QPs[a] 24:12–13 (Syriac Psalm 3, Psalm 155). There is a close parallel between the Aramaic expression in 3:9 here and the Hebrew 11QPs[a] *Plea for Deliverance* אל תשלט בי שטן "[l]et not Satan[70] have power over me" (19:15). Here in *ALD* שטן "satan" is apparently the name of a type or class of evil spirit, and not of Satan. While *Plea for Deliverance* might be taken to be ambiguous in this respect, *ALD* seems quite unambiguous for, were שטן a proper noun, the expression כל שטן "any satan" would be impossible. This view is strengthened by other similar expressions in Qumran texts such as 1QH[a] 22:6 תגער בכול שטן משחית "you will rebuke every destructive satan". It follows from the phraseology in 1QH[a] and in *ALD* that the use of "satan" with the distributive implies

[68] DJD 4, 78.
[69] See Greenfield and Stone, 1985, 459.
[70] Less likely: "a satan": Greenfield, 1992, 309–312.

more than one satan, and thus in such instances "satan" is a category of evil spirit and not a proper name (see further, commentary on 3:11).

T.H. Gaster maintains that:

> the name [i.e. Satan] is applied in three [biblical] passages (all post-exilic) to a super-human being, but in each case it is simply an appellative, not a proper name—i.e., it merely defines the role which the being in question happens to play in a particular situation.[71]

The passages to which he refers are Job 1–2, Zechariah 3:1–2 and 1 Chronicles 21:1. It is notable that while in Job and Zechariah reference is made to השטן "the accuser" indicating that a role is implied, in 1 Chronicles 21:1, שטן without the definite article is to be found. This word corresponds to אף יהוה "anger of the Lord" in the parallel passage in 2 Samuel 24:1 and, as Gaster remarks, the term "is simply a common noun (i.e., 'a satan') denoting a spirit . . . who happened on that particular occasion to act with untoward effect." The same usage of "satan" is to be observed in *1 Enoch* 65:6: "for they have learned all the secrets of the angels, and all the wrongdoing of the satans, and all their secret power"[72] and another similar instance is also to be observed in *1 Enoch* 40:7. The use of "satan" as a class of demon is also to be observed on an Aramaic magical bowl, published by Shaked and Naveh which refers to "all evil spirits, demons, devils . . . satans (סטניין) . . .".[73] Therefore, it appears that this passage in *ALD* is the earliest occurrence of this meaning of the word "satan", which is already foreshadowed in 1 Chronicles 21:1. Moreover, the formulae remarked upon here clearly show this passage to be a very early stage of the development of Jewish apotropaic prayers.[74]

πλανῆσαί με ἀπὸ τῆς ὁδοῦ σου "to make me stray from your path"—Compare 3:4.[75]

[71] Gaster, *IDB*, 4.224. Philonenko, 1987, 835 gives "satan" without a capital letter.

[72] Knibb, 1978, 154.

[73] No. 15:4–5 in Naveh and Shaked, 1993, 115; see also bowl no. 22:4 מכל שטן ומכל פגע ". . . from every satan and every trouble", *ibid.*, 130–31.

[74] See Stone and Greenfield, 1993, 263–64.

[75] Baumgarten associates this expression with the worshipper's aspiration to maintain a formalized straight stance of worshippers in prayer, and with regulations about the position of the feet during the Amida (2003, 397–98). His sources are much later and it seems to us that the metaphor of the way that was discussed above, explains the textual data in a satisfactory way.

Commentary on 3:10

מׇרִי "My Lord"—The word is not found in Greek. The word לכה "your" is a Hebraism.

Commentary on 3:11–12

3:11–12 are found only in Greek, and were doubtless included in the lost lines of Aramaic at the beginning of col. 2 of 4QLevi[b]. The lines seem excessively long in view of the parallel structure of the rest of this prayer.

τεῖχος εἰρήνης σου "the wall of your peace"—The expression "wall of peace" in 3:11 should be compared with 1QH[a] 17:33 משמר שלומכה "your guarding of peace". A similar combination of expressions occurs in the Jewish evening prayer השכיבנו, from which we cite a number of phrases: ופרש עלינו סכת שלומך "and spread over us the tabernacle of your peace"; והגן בעדנו והסר מעלינו אויב . . . והסר שטן מלפנינו ומאחרינו "and protect us and remove from us enemies . . . and remove satan from before us and from behind us".

The similarity between 11QPs[a] *Plea for Deliverance* and *ALD* here was already pointed out by D. Flusser.[76] He regarded both *ALD* and *Plea for Deliverance* as reflecting a common interpretation of Psalm 119:133b. He notes similar expressions in the Jewish liturgy, ואל ישלט בנו יצר הרע "let the evil inclination not rule over us" (morning service); וישלט בי יצר טוב ואל ישלט בי יצר הרע "and let the good inclination rule over me, and let the evil inclination not rule over me" (prayer before retiring at night); שתצילני . . . מפגע רע מיצר רע ומשטן המשחית "deliver me . . . from mishap and from the evil inclination and from the destructive satan" (Rabbi Judah's prayer in the morning service). The similarity with the Qumran expressions is striking.

Levi continues to pray for purification (3:13) and divine favor (3:14). He invokes the blessing of Abraham and Sarah, which probably draws on Genesis 18:10, and then refers to a blessing which appears to be that in Genesis 22:17–18.

The point of the prayer is Levi's desire to be a "participant in your words" and "to do true judgment for all time" (3:17). This seems to be a reference to the Blessing of Moses, where it says of

[76] Flusser, 1966, 197.

the sons of Levi that "they shall teach Jacob thy ordinances and Israel thy law" (Deuteronomy 33:10). Thus a series of blessings of significant weight in the biblical narrative are associated with Levi.

σκεπασάτω "shelter me"—This might be a corruption in Semitic of יסובבני "surround me" to יסוככני "shelter me", but the root סכ"כ is also used as a verb in an apotropaic context: באברתו יסך לך "he will cover you with his pinions" (Psalm 91:4). The whole phrase probably originated in the apotropaic realm, to be compared with: אמר ליהוה מחסי ומצודתי "I will say to the Lord, 'My refuge and my fortress'" (Psalm 91:2; cf. 91:9). In *Paralipomena of Jeremiah* 1:2 Jeremiah's and Baruch's prayers are described as ὡς τεῖχος ἀδαμάντινον περικυλοῦν αὐτήν "as adamantine (steel) wall around it (i.e., Jerusalem)". The image of a wall as a protection is found on an incantation bowl in the collection published by Naveh and Shaked, ונחדרה שורא דאדמסא דכיא לחונא בר כופיתי "and a wall of pure steel shall surround Ḥuna son of Kupitay"[77] and in an incantation text from Nippur, ושורא רבה דנחשא אחדרית ליה "and I have surrounded it with a great wall of bronze".[78]

Commentary on 3:13

The fragmentary letters]לע which precede verse 13:14 in 4QLevi^b 1 2:5 do not seem to correspond to anything in Greek. Fitzmyer reconstructs the word as [לע]ינ[יך] "to [your] ey[es" but the basis for this is unclear.[79] We might suggest reconstructing: לע]בד "to do". The surviving Aramaic letters, although they cannot be translated, indicate that at least one hemistych was lost from the Greek text here.

καὶ προσάρωμαι πρός σε αὐτός. "and let me, myself, be raised to you"—The meaning of προσάρωμαι "be raised" is intriguing. Is it a metaphorical use, referring to Levi's rising to a level of righteousness? It might be taken to express a type of religious experience that Levi expected to undergo as a result of his repentance, purification and prayer. Indeed, following this prayer he receives a vision of the heavens on

[77] No. 1, 11–12; Naveh and Shaked, 1985, 124–25.
[78] Montgomery, 1913, 133–37, no. 4:6.
[79] Fitzmyer and Harrington, 1978, 90.

a height (see 4:4–6). It might also be taken with a middle sense, "je m'élèverai", as does Philonenko.[80]

Commentary on 3:14

καὶ μὴ ἀποστρέψῃς τὸ πρόσωπόν "And turn not your countenance aside"—The expression may be drawn from ולא יסיר פנים "and will not turn away his face" (2 Chronicles 30:9), which in Greek is almost identical with the phrase here, καὶ οὐκ ἀποστρέψει τὸν πρόσωπον αὐτοῦ.

[בר עבדך] "[son of your servant]"—Note the proximity of language of "servant" and that of "son" and the usage found in 3:16 and 3:18.[81]

Commentary on 3:16

צלות עב]דך "the prayer of [your ser]vant"—Here we read in Greek τῆς φωνῆς τοῦ παιδός σου "the voice of your servant". Since φωνῆς "voice" does not usually serve to translate צלות on its own, we should probably reconstruct צלות [קל "[voice of] the prayer" here in the original.

Commentary on 3:17

εἰς πάντα τὸν αἰῶνα "for all time"—Only the first two letters of the Aramaic text have survived. In view of the Greek, we have reconstructed the Aramaic as לכ[ל עלם, even though that is an unusual expression. This reconstructed Aramaic has influenced our English translation here.

Commentary on 3:18

בר עבדך "son of your servant"—This verse is probably related to *TPL* 4:2.[82]

καὶ ἐσιώπησα ἔτι δεόμενος "And I became silent still continuing to pray". Compare with 1QapGen 20:16 where, of Abraham after prayer, it says, בכית וחשית "I wept and I was silent". Presumably,

[80] Philonenko, 1987, 835.
[81] Stone, 1990, 207–08.
[82] Greenfield and Stone, 1990, 157–58; Stone and Greenfield, 1993, 251.

like Abraham, Levi continues in silent prayer. An older instance of silent prayer is described in 1 Samuel 1:13, but that is clearly exceptional. Philo refers to silent prayer in *De plantatione* 126, *De specialibus legibus* 1.272 and *De gigantibus* 52. A number of other Jewish sources of the period regard silent prayer as unusual.[83] It is still remarkable that *ALD* stresses the silent prayer that follows the voiced prayer here.[84] Contrast *ALD* and 1QapGen with Daniel 9:20–21 which emphasizes speech in prayer.

[83] *Biblical Antiquities* 50:5, Josephus, *Wars*, 3.353–54. The virtue of silent prayer is noted in Clement of Alexandria, *Stromateis* 7:7; *Acts of Peter* 39 and other sources.
[84] See the discussion on silent prayer by van der Horst, 1994.

Chapter 4: Travels and Vision of Levi

Commentary on 4:1

From this point on, the text of the Qumran fragment has no parallel in Greek. We regard these lines as the beginning of a new chapter. The incidents narrated in 4:1–6 are not found in *TPL*.

Commentary on 4:2

אבל מין "Abel Mayyin"—Levi leaves Abel Mayyin before receiving his vision (4:4) and no further information about Abel Mayyin is given in *ALD*. There, nonetheless, are a number of points to be made about this place name.[85]

(1) First, Abel Mayyin in Aramaic is equivalent Abel Mayyim in Hebrew.

(2) Second, the biblical hapaxlegomenon Abel Mayyim is Chronicles' identification of Abel-Beth-Maacah, as is evident from the parallel between 1 Kings 15:20 and 2 Chronicles 16:4. In 1 Kings Abel-Beth-Maacah is found while 2 Chronicles, relating the same incident, has Abel Mayyim (LXX Αβελμαιν).

(3) Third, the name Abel Mayyim does not occur in *TPL*. In *TPL* 2:3 and 2:5 the equivalent place is called Abelmaul, which most scholars identify as Abel Meholah and it is connected with a high mountain called Aspis, i.e., shield (*TPL* 5:3).[86] This mountain's name arises from a midrash on Mount Sirion as *širion* "armour, shield". Mount Sirion, also called Si'on and Senir, is identified by Deuteronomy 3:8–9 as Mount Hermon.[87]

(4) Fourth, *TPL* locates the high mountain, Mount Aspis/Sirion = Mount Hermon, in Abel-Meholah.[88] This provides a northern geographical context for this part of *TPL*. The inclusion of the high mountain called Aspis (i.e., shield) in *TPL* 2:5–6 shows that this

---

[85] See, on this matter, in further detail, Stone, 2003, 433–34.

[86] Milik, 1955, 403–05, says that Abel Maul of Greek *T̂PL* reflects geographical carelessness and the location Abel Mayyim was in the region of Abel-Beth-Maacah in the Persian period. They are facilely identified by Becker, 1970, 74–75.

[87] A different name midrash on Hermon may be observed in *1 Enoch* 6:6.

[88] Apparently, 'Αβιλά in 6:1 is also Abel Meholah as is clear from the context. The location of Mount Aspis and the confusion of names in *TPL* is discussed in some detail by Baarda, 1992, 22–24. He makes a number of acute observations, but does not illuminate *TPL*'s transformation of the geographical data of *ALD*.

tradition is deeply embedded in *TPL*. Yet, it sets Mount Aspis = Sirion = Hermon in Abel Meholah and sets that site, incorrectly, in the north. In fact, both in *ALD* and in *TPL* most of this patriarchal story takes place in and around Shechem and Hebron and, moreover, no other source hints at a northern geographical context for any of these events. It results, in our view, from the author/redactor of *TPL* confusing the geographical situation, which he may not have known at first hand.[89]

(5) In contrast, in *ALD* the only place name we have is Abel Mayyin. A high mountain is mentioned (though the actual word "mountain" is reconstructed in a lacuna) but it is part of a vision and not of real geography. Therefore, in *ALD*, Abel Mayyin is the only geographical indication and it is not related to an actual high mountain. The author/redactor of *TPL*, however, moved the mountain from the visionary to actual geography and identified it as Hermon/Sirion.

To conclude this matter, we may say that *TPL*'s identification of the rare Abel Mayyim as the more common Abel-Beth-Maacah in the North emerges from the parallel texts of Kings and Chronicles. *TPL*'s subsequent confusion of Abel-Beth-Maacah with Abel Meholah, created geographical chaos. The confusion in *TPL* is compounded by two further developments. First, the high mountain is moved from the vision into the description of the geography; it is identified with Sirion/Siʾon and thus with Hermon. Second, the rare place name Abel Mayyin is replaced, not by Abel-Beth-Maacah (which would have had a certain plausibility after the northern context had been introduced because Hermon was brought into the story) but with the much better known location, Abel Meholah, which is actually in the center of the country. Thus *TPL* can make such a geographically bizarre statement as "that mountain of the Shield [Aspis] in Abelmaul" (*TPL* 2:5). An "Abel" is a valley, and it is hard to see how a mountain the size of Hermon could be thought to be in a valley except by someone who did not know the geography of the country well. Moreover, the site of the eminently northern Mount Aspis/Sirion/Hermon is asserted to be in Abel Meholah, in the cen-

[89] On northern traditions in Second Temple Jewish writings, see Nickelsburg, 2001, 238–247; de Jonge, 1974; Milik, 1955, 403–05; 1976, 195–96 in reconstructed text.

ter of the country, in trans-Jordan. The completely secondary nature of the development in *TPL* is thus evident and more need not be added on this point here.[90]

In that case, Chronicles' equivalation of Abel Mayyim with Abel-Beth-Maacah should be regarded as irrelevant to *ALD*. It seems more than possible, therefore, that Abel Mayyim was not in the North and as far as *ALD* is concerned, a location might be sought for Abel Mayyim in the area around Samaria. Itzhak Ben-Zvi, an expert on modern Samaritan traditions, pointed out that Bet el-Maʾ (House of Water) is the name of a spring sacred to the Samaritans, 1.5 km. from Shechem. J.T. Milik identified it as Abel Mayyim.[91] Based on the Shechem setting of the wars and the phonetic similarity between Sirion and a place named Sarin documented in some Samaritan sources, E. Eshel and H. Eshel proposed identifying Sirion as Sarin mentioned three times in the Samaritan chronicle, *The Tulida*.[92] This, of course, remains in the realm of hypothesis.

Some points arise from this passage of *TPL* which cast light on *ALD*. First, in the vision in *TPL* 5:3 the angel commissions Levi to take vengeance and gives him a shield (ὅπλον) and a sword (ῥομφαίαν).[93] In some other sources Levi and Simeon either have their own swords (Genesis 34:25) or are given a sword by God (Simeon in Judith 9:2). Doubtless some of the moral issues raised by the Shechem story have influenced its different retellings.[94] In *TPL* 6:1 Levi finds the shield (here ἄσπις),[95] but not a sword. In *TPL* 5:3 and 6:1 the vision of receiving a sword must have been an adequate assertion of the acceptability of Levi and Simeon's conduct in Shechem. The Shechem incident was much longer in *ALD* than in *TPL*, as is evident from chapter 1. The vision, which occurs in a secondary position here in

[90] This matter is dealt with in some further detail in Stone, 2003, and by Eshel and Eshel, 2002.

[91] For the value of modern Palestinian Arabic place names for historical geography, see Aharoni, 1979, 105–130. The correctness of Milik's identification is secondary to our argument. Regardless, for *ALD*, Abel Mayyin is in the center of the country. See Milik, 1955, 403–05.

[92] Eshel and Eshel, 2002, 120–126.

[93] Concerning the angelic commissioning, see Kugel, 1992, 3–6. Milik suggested that in the original story, Levi found an axe (גרזן in Hebrew) and, therefore, the mountain is called Gerizim: see Milik, 1978, 97.

[94] On the moral problems of Shechem episode, see Kugel, 1992.

[95] The word ἄσπις (Greek for "shield") is mentioned in *1 Enoch* 8:1; *TPJudah* 3:4 and 9:5; *Joseph and Aseneth* 26:6, etc.

TPL, might have received its inspiration from text lost from *ALD* preceding chapter 1. That cannot be proved, of course, but such a text could have provided the divine sanction for the actions of Levi and Simeon, in contrast to Genesis 49:5. Despite all this, nonetheless the issue remains: why was the shield introduced, and why was it bronze?[96]

Commentary on 4:3

ויתבת "and I remained"—The sense could also be "sat up", i.e. after vision. Lacking context, a determination is difficult.

Commentary on 4:4

חזויא . . . חזיון "visions"—both forms are difficult in Aramaic. The correct forms are חזון and חזוא.

אחזית "I was shown"—Probably this verb should be taken as a passive *ʾafʿel* form of the root חז"י, see 4Q209 25:3 (*1 Enoch* 78:10) ח]שבון אחרן אחזית לה "I was shown another computation for it". It is not clear according to *ALD* whether Levi enters a trance state here or whether a dream vision is described. In *TPL* 2:5 clearly a dream vision is described. The words ואנה אתעירת מן שנתי "and I awoke from my sleep" in 4:13 might incline us to consider this to be a dream vision. In Zechariah 4:1 a waking in the midst of a vision experience is described "and wakened me (ויעירני), as one that is wakened (יעור) from his sleep". Both cases in Zechariah use עו"ר, the same verb used by *ALD* 4:13.

Milik reconstitutes 4QLevi[b] 1 2:16–18 as:

> וחזית שמ]יא פתיחין וחזית טורא] | תחותי רם עד דבק לשמ]יא והוית בה
> ואתפתחו] | לי תרעי שמיא ומלאך חד [אמר לי . . .
>
> And I saw the hea[vens opened and I saw a mountain] | beneath me, high until it reached the hea[vens. And I was in it, and there were opened | to me] the gates of heaven and an angel [said to me . . .[97]

This is of course highly speculative and is chiefly based on an extrapolation from the text of *TPL* 2:4–5. In Hollander and de Jonge's translation that passage reads:

[96] No reply to this second question has been found.
[97] Milik, 1955, 404.

> And I felt grief for the race of the sons of men and I prayed to the Lord that I might be saved. Then a sleep fell upon me and I beheld a high mountain (that was the mountain of the Shield in Abelmaul).[98]

Commentary on 4:5

רם "high"—We take this as an adjective, "high". It might also be a verb "reached up".

Commentary on 4:6

תרעי שמיא "gates of heaven"—For the expression "gates of heavens" compare *TPL* 5:1 which is one of the points of contact between *ALD* chapter 3 and *TPL*.[99]

Commentary on 4:7–8

As we have shown in the Introduction, one of the striking aspects of the thought of *ALD* is that Levi is regarded as combining both the priestly and the royal functions. Yet, Levi is told in *TPL* 8:11a: "And they said to me: Levi, your seed will be divided into three offices (ἄρχας)". Of the first office it says "And he who believes will be the first; no portion will be greater than he" (8:12), followed by "the second will be in the priesthood" (8:13).

Milik suggested that this context of the first office, superior to priesthood, was also related to 1QLevi frags. 1, 2 and 7.[100] He further maintained that 1QLevi frag. 1 also corresponds to *ALD* 4:9–11. Grelot does not challenge the affinity between 1QLevi frag. 1 and *ALD* 4:9a but argues that they are the end of a paragraph dealing with the priestly kingdom, while the kingdom of sword documented in *ALD* 4:9b–10 refers to the Levites who also had a military function.[101] One might add that there is a connection between Levi's

[98] Hollander and de Jonge, 1985, 132.

[99] Its function in *TPL* is discussed by Stone, 2003, 434–35.

[100] DJD 1, 88–89.

[101] Grelot, 1956, 395–96: but see Kugler, 1996, 85, note 91. This aspect of Grelot's thesis is not convincing as he presents it. His basic insight is repeated by Caquot, 1998, 7, and see already Lévi, 1907, 167. Of course, the Levites' zeal was praised in Exodus 32:28 and in Numbers 25:7–8, where it is cited as a reason for their election to the priesthood: see Exodus 32:29 and Numbers 25:11–13. Compare ben Sira 45:6–25 and especially 45:23. Contrast Becker, 1970, 78–79, but his own view is also problematic.

zealous action in Shechem and Phineas's actions in Numbers 25:12–13. In both cases, Levites took up the sword to protect purity, and in both instances the action was regarded positively and became viewed as a basis for the Levitical worthiness for priesthood.[102] We accept the placement proposed by these two scholars and, considering the relationship between the vision in *TPL* 8 and *ALD* 4:9–12, we place 1QLevi 1 and 7 close to *ALD* 4:9.[103] Therefore, 1QLevi frag. 1 was tentatively inserted at this point, close to the beginning of Bodleian a, i.e., *ALD* 4:9.

Milik suggested putting frag. 2 at the end of line 2, thus reconstructing מלכו]תא ל["king]dom to/for[", while Grelot prefers to reconstruct it as כהנו]תא ל[קרבה קרבניא . . . and to regard it as preceding line 3, [על כן יהוי לך ולזרעך מלכות כהנו]תא ל[קרבה קרבניא]ל[א]ל[עליון "Therefore you and your seed will have a kingdom of priest]hood to[offer sacrifices to the Most High God."[104] Both reconstructions are speculative and we regard the placement of 1QLevi frag. 2 as uncertain.[105] Moreover, both these interpretations would become doubtful if the alternate translation proposed in the commentary on 4:7 is accepted. The association of royal language with Levi and the priesthood is clear, though the exact import of the verse is not.

The expressions applied to Levi here are related ultimately, of course, to Exodus 19:6. Targum Neofiti translates ממלכת כהנים "a kingdom of priests" there as מלכין וכהנין "kings and priests".[106] The double messiah language of *Testaments of the Twelve Patriarch* is well known (see, e.g. *TPJudah* 21:2–4). What is consistently striking in *ALD* is the combination of royal and priestly qualities in the high priestly line. See Introduction, "Levi's Special Role".

[102] Of course, in the case of the Shechem incident, the positive interpretation was far from universal, as is evident from the views adduced above in commentary on 1:1. V. Hillel has drawn this connection to our attention. See also the remarks of de Jonge, 1999, 84.

[103] However, it is likely that *TPL* 8:11a is a reworking, probably Christian in character, of a prophecy attributing royal characteristics to Levi. Such a prophecy would have been very strange to Christian readers (or for that matter, to most Jewish readers as well).

[104] See Grelot, 1956, 396, note 4.

[105] See also our note on the text.

[106] The verse from Exodus has informed the language of *Jubilees* 32:20. Compare כהנין ומלכין "priests and kings" in *ALD* 13:16.

Commentary on 4:7

מלכות כהנותא רבא מן מלכות] "the kingdom of the priesthood is greater than the kingdom ["—The words כהנותא רבא might mean "high priesthood" though in 11:6 we have כֹּהֻנֹּתא רבתא. The language comparing the kingdom of priesthood with something else, apparently another sort of the kingdom, evokes *TPJudah* 4:3, though there the contrast is between priesthood and kingdom: cf. also *TPJudah* 21:4.[107]

The verse *TPL* 8:14 might be related to *ALD* 4:7. It reads,

> ὁ τρίτος, ἐπικληθήσεται αὐτῷ ὄνομα καινόν, ὅτι βασιλεὺς ἐκ τοῦ Ἰουδὰ ἀναστήσεται, καὶ ποιήσει ἱερατείαν νέαν, κατὰ τὸν τύπον τῶν ἐθνῶν, εἰς πάντα τὰ ἔθνη.
>
> The third will be called with a new name, because a king will arise from Judah and will establish a new priesthood after the fashion of the Gentiles for all the Gentiles.

See Introduction, "Levi's Special Role in *ALD*" for further discussion of this material.

Commentary on 4:9

We might reconstruct the very end of the preceding column as [. . . *and for the kingdom of peace there is*]. The first part of the text extant in Bodleian a from שלמא "peace" to למאכל "for food" deals with priesthood, which is evident because it mentions "first fruits". This is the end of a sentence, the first part of which has been lost and which apparently presented a list of good things that will be found in a good kingdom.[108] This description is to some extent parallel to *TPL* 8:16, where in the second investiture it mentions the privileges of priesthood, "Every desirable thing of Israel will be for you and your seed; and you will eat everything beautiful to see".

The second part of the verse, from ולמלכות חרבא "And for the kingdom of the sword" up to וכפנא "and hunger" is written in contrast

[107] J.C. Greenfield suggested orally that כהנותא רבא might be an abstract form of כהנא רבא. Contrastive language is notable in *TPJudah* 21:4, but there it is the superiority of "the priesthood of God" to "the kingdoms of the earth". In *ALD* the salient point is the combination of royal and priestly features in a single priestly line.

[108] Grelot, 1956, 393.

to the preceding sentence and describes the travails to be associated with the kingdom of the sword.[109]

It is clear from 4:11 that these sentences form part of an address to Levi by one or all of "those seven" (4:12) angels who appeared to him in a dream vision: cf. *TPL* 8:2. We might be tempted to speculate that the lost sentence praised the priesthood, which was contrasted with the kingship described in the second sentence. This is not certain, however, for the contrast could have been, for example, between "kingdom of peace" and "kingdom of the sword", or a different one.

שלמא "peace"—This word seems to be part of a construct expression.

חמדת "choice"—This is the construct state of the noun חמדה, attested nowhere else in the feminine. The masculine plural form חמדנין "desirous things" occurs in Targum Neofiti to Genesis 50:1; compare the phrase ארץ חמדה "a pleasant land" in Jeremiah 3:19, Zechariah 7:14 and Psalm 106:24. The phrase may be related to Numbers 18:13;[110] cf. *TPL* 8:16, πᾶν ἐπιθυμήτον.[111]

פנשא "fighting"—This verb, meaning "to strike, to fight someone", may modify חרב. Compare the noun פנשות "striking" in the Fragmentary Targum to Genesis 32:26.[112]

נחשירותא "chase"—This word comes from the Old Persian ancestor of Persian *naxčīr*, meaning "hunt, fight between wild beasts, fight between heroes, carnage".[113] The combination of קרב and נחשיר is

[109] Grelot, 1956, 394–96 explains מלכות חרבא "kingdom of the sword" as referring to the vision in *TPL* 5:2–3, where Levi is given a sword and shield and commanded to avenge Shechem. If any relationship exists, which we doubt, it might be in the reverse direction. On this passage see Stone, 2003, especially 435.

[110] בכורי כל אשר בארצם אשר יביאו ליהוה לך יהיה "The first-fruits of all that is in their land, which they bring to the Lord, shall be yours." This is translated by Targum Onqelos as: בכורי כל דבארעהון דייתון לקדם יהוה דילך יהי; cf. also ראשית בכורי אדמתך "the choicest of the first-fruits of your land", Targum Onqelos ריש בכורי ארעך in Exodus 23:19 and 34:26.

[111] See Grelot, 1956, 392 who notes that ἐπιθυμήτον translates חמדה in Jeremiah 12:10.

[112] Sokoloff, 1990, 425.

[113] See Brockelmann 1928, 424; de Menasce, 1956, 213–14; Asmussen, 1962.

found in 1QM 1:9–10: וביום נפול בו כתיים קרב ונחשיר חזק לפני אל ישראל "On the day when the Kittim fall there shall be mighty encounter and carnage before the God of Israel" (see also lines 10 and 13 there).[114] This word with the suffix ון- is attested in 4Q246 1:5: ונחשירון רב במׄדינתא (or: נחשירין) "and a great carnage in the provinces".[115]

נצפתא "conflict"—As noted by Charles and Grelot, the verb *nṣp* in Syriac means "to hiss, to rage".[116]

Commentary on 4:10

The angelic address continues with a prophecy about different periods, written as contrast of positive and negative times (זמנין . . . זמנין). In this, it resembles Qohelet 3 and is apparently parallel to *ALD* 4:9. The contrasts here are not particularly of priestly and royal characteristics. The verbs תאכול "it shall eat", etc. are taken as third person feminine singulars. Thus, the subject would be the feminine singular מלכות חרבא "kingdom of the sword". A more speculative reading would construe the verbs as second person singular, and forming part of the angel's address to Levi, "you shall eat, etc.".[117] Lacking any substantial supporting arguments, and none have been adduced, this interpretation is probably to be rejected. In the Geniza manuscript the verbs have a *plene* spelling, while תעמל, the one verb extant in 1QLevi frag. 3, is *defectiva*.

זמנין "sometimes"—In Targum Onqelos Genesis 33:3 etc., this plural of the word "time" translates the Hebrew פעמים.

[114] Yadin, 1962, 260–61; For the combination קרבא ונחשירותא see Ephrem, *Opp. Gr.* 403B *qrbtnʾ wnḥšyrtʾ* "warlike and hunter" *apud* Payne Smith, 1901, 2.2343.

[115] Puech, DJD 22, 167–169, 172. The word נחשיר is also known from the Syriac translation to Genesis 10:9. There נבור ציד "mighty hunter" is translate as *gnbrʾ nḥšyrtnʾ*, where *nḥšyrtnʾ* means "hunter". Compare: נחשירכן in Targum Pseudo-Jonathan to Genesis 25:27 (originating in Middle Persian: **naḥšīrakān*).

[116] Charles, 1908a, 246. Grelot, 1956, 396 note 2. Brockelmann 1928, 443. Another possibility is to assume a change of *bet* to *pē* of the root *nṣb* in *peʿal* or *ʾetpeʿal*, meaning: "gain victory, triumph, be glorified [see נצח]": see Goshen-Gottstein, 1970, 48.

[117] So Lévi, 1907, 175; Charles, 1913, 364.

תנוד שנת עינא "sometimes lie awake"—For this phrase see Targum Onqelos Genesis 31:40 and Daniel 6:19; cf. Esther 6:1.[118]

Commentary on 4:11

הכין רבינך מן כולה "how we made you greater than all"—The verb רבינך may also mean "anointed": compare רבות later in this verse. A variant text of part of 4:11 is preserved in 4QLevi[c] 1:1 ה[כה רעיתך מן כל בשר[א "h]ow I have preferred you to all flesh". Observe the following points.

(a) The difference between הכה and הכין is to be explained by Aramaic dialectal features.[119] Yet, the occurrence of both forms in the Geniza manuscript here exemplifies the scribe's inconsistent orthography.

(b) The root רע"י is very rare in Qumran Aramaic, except for the noun רעוא "acceptability" which is to be found, for example, in 1QLevi frag. 52.[120] The use here is a calque on Biblical Hebrew.

(c) It is possible that the Geniza text arose from a graphic variant,[121] yet the difference of number indicates that this is also a substantially variant text.

(d) In 4QLevi[c] we read מן כל בשׂר[א] "above (literally: from) all flesh", while Bodleian a has מן כולה "above all". מן כל בישרא recurs in 6:1 where the Greek reads ἀπὸ πάσης σαρκός. See further the commentary on 6:1. The text of 4QLevi[c] cannot be recovered here.

והיך יהבנא לך רבות שלם עלמא "and how we gave you the anointing (*or*: greatness) of eternal peace"—These lines form the conclusion of the angelic prophecy.

רבות "anointing"—The Aramaic root רב"י corresponds to מש"ח "anoint", known from the Targums, as well as meaning "greatness, dignity"; see 1QapGen 6:23 [ואש]כׄחׄת אׄנׄהׄ נוח חׄן רׄבׄוׄ וקׄוׄשׁׄטׄ, "[and I fou]nd, I,

[118] J.C. Greenfield suggested that this may be a medieval orthography of עינה "its (f.) eye" (oral communication).

[119] See Stone and Greenfield, DJD 22, 39–40 for a more detailed discussion. Contrast Grelot, 1956, 397–98.

[120] See Appendix "Unplaced Fragments".

[121] We might assume that רבינך was changed to רעינך and then to רעיתך. On previous translations of רבינך, see Grelot, 1956, 397–98.

Noah, grace, greatness and truth . . .".[122] However, רבות does also mean "anointing" and we prefer this translation here.

שלם עלמא "of eternal peace" This sentence seems to conclude the installation of Levi as High Priest, cf. *TPL* 8 and *Jubilees* 32:1. Yet, the expression here does not occur in either of those two sources. The mention of "eternal peace" harks back to "peace" in 4:9, both instances referring to the priesthood. With the whole phrase, compare the "anointing for an eternal priesthood" in Exodus 40:15, and also Numbers 25:12–13 where Phineas' descendants are promised "a covenant of peace" and "a covenant of eternal peace" (קיים רבות עלם in Targum Pseudo-Jonathan).[123] The same language lies behind Malachi 2:5. The priestly connection of these associated verses supports the meaning "anointing" above.[124] The term "eternal peace" is common among the Dead Sea Scrolls, so, e.g., 1QH[a] 19:27, 7:19, 1QS 2:4, etc. Compare ben Sira 45:24, "Therefore a covenant of peace was established with him, that he should be a leader of the sanctuary and of his people, and his descendants should have the dignity of the priesthood forever." It is intriguing that both Levi's violent action against Shechem and Phineas's violent action to protect Israel's purity were regarded as qualifying them for "eternal priesthood", the one in *ALD* and the other in Numbers. See above 4:9–10 commentary.

Commentary on 4:12

שבעתון "those seven"—Previous editors read שבעתין, but the reading with *waw* is sure, compare the *waw* in ולמלכות (4:9).[125] This reading,

[122] Morgenstern, Qimron and Sivan, 1996, 42–43. משחה is found in 1QLevi frag. 37, and see Appendix, "Unplaced Fragments".

[123] The expression רבות שלם עלמא may be a combination of Numbers 25:12 and 25:13.

[124] The alternative reading would take רבו simply as "greatness", i.e., of Levi. It might then refer back to the kingdom or covenant of peace at the beginning of the column; observe the pair המשל ופחד "dominion and fear" equivalent to ש[לטן ורבו "rule and greatness" in 11QtgJob 9:4 (Job 25:2): compare *TPL* 11:5ff. We prefer, however, the reading given in the translation, which is clearly an exegesis of Numbers 25 as we have noted.

[125] See Grelot, 1956, 395 as a speculation. The new material reading was published by Greenfield and Stone, 1979, 218–19 and resolves the issues addressed by Grelot.

a numeral with a pronominal suffix, implies clearly that Levi's installation in the priesthood was carried out by seven angels (or visionary men), as in *TPL* 8.[126]

Commentary on 4:13

אדין אמרת חזוא הוא דן וכדן אנה מתמה די יהוי <לי> כל חזוה "Then I said, 'This is a vision and like this vision, I am amazed that <I> should have any vision at all'."—There are a number of difficulties in the text. For one, the manuscript has the word לה "to him", producing "he should have" which makes no sense here. We emend the לה of the text to לי, "I should have". It is possible that a scribe, scrupulous to avoid a homograph of the *Tetragrammaton*, transposed an original *hē* at the end of the verb and the *yod* of לי.[127] Grelot entertained a number of possibilities, but eventually decided for מה די יהוי לה כל חזוה.[128] This seems impossible in context, for the preceding phrase that he accepts, "Alors je dis, 'Cette vision-ci est comme l'autre'" is problematic since it transgresses the canons of Aramaic syntax, even if the *waw* of וכדן is dropped.[129] We would translate the whole phrase simply as above, with the single emendation.[130]

אף דן "this too"—This seems to imply that the vision with the seven angels is a second vision. This cannot be stated categorically, however, due to the lacuna preceding 4:9.[131] Kugler translates, improbably, "this very thing" rather than "this too".[132]

[126] The full argumentation is given in Greenfield and Stone, 1979, 218–19. Previous views are summarized there.

[127] Though a homograph of the *Tetragrammaton* does occur a few lines later in the word די הוה in 5:2, making this explanation less likely. R. Buth suggested translating the unemended text as, "that there would be any vision of it". Context inclines us to the emendation.

[128] Grelot, 1956, 400.

[129] For other suggested translations of the phrase, see Grelot, 1956, 399–400.

[130] Greenfield and Stone, 1979, 219.

[131] On this see Haupt, 1969, 31.

[132] Kugler, 1996, 49–50, 78, 82, note 79, 206. This, of course, bears on his argument about whether "Levi-Apocryphon" (his term) had one or two visions. It is crucial for him, so a more exhaustive grammatical analysis should have been made. The Aramaic dictionaries do not give this meaning for אף.

Chapter 5: Levi's Priesthood and Blessing and Instruction

Commentary on 5:1

ועֲלנא על אבי יצחק ואף הוא כדן [ברכ]ני "and we went[133] to my father Isaac and he thus[134] [blessed] me"—A number of phrases in this pericope are close to *TPL* 9, which relates the same events, i.e., those ensuing on Levi's vision of consecration. We reproduce them above following the text. In *TPL* 9:1 we find, "I and Judah went up with our father to Isaac". Judah's name does not appear in *ALD*, and who "we" are is not made explicit there. The reference might be to the whole family. Often, in other instances, Judah and Levi appear together in *TPL*, but in the older *ALD*, Judah plays no role at this juncture.[135]

Commentary on 5:2

אדין כדי הוה יעקב [אבי]מְעַשר כל מה די הוה לה כנדרה "Then, when Jacob [my father] tithed everything which he possessed in accordance with his vow"—The first הוה has, in the past, been emended to חזה by Charles following *TPL* 9:3,[136] a view accepted by Greenfield and Stone in 1979. However, in light of 4QLevi[c], Greenfield and Stone subsequently abandoned the emendation and read as above.[137] There is a lacuna in the Geniza manuscript, Cambridge col. a, line 16. While Charles did not propose any conjecture, Grelot did and his conjecture exactly corresponds to the text published subsequently from the Qumran fragment.[138] The word order in 1QLevi 4 varies somewhat from that in the Geniza text.

---

133 Charles, 1913, 374 has "I went".

134 I.e., "according to this".

135 For a discussion of the application of royal, i.e., Judahite, terminology to Levi in *ALD*, along with the absence of Judah in *ALD* from contexts in which he is found in *TPL*, see Introduction, "Levi's Special Role in *ALD*". Judah is mentioned in 2:1, but in a quite different context.

136 That verse reads, εἶδεν ὁ πατήρ μου Ἰακὼβ ἐν ὁράματι περὶ ἐμοῦ, ὅτι ἔσομαι αὐτοῖς εἰς ἱερέα πρὸς τὸν θεόν. καὶ ἀναστὰς τὸ πρωὶ ἀπεδεκάτωσε πάντα δι ᾿ ἐμοῦ τῷ κυρίῳ. "My father Jacob saw in a vision concerning me, that I should be a priest for them to God. And arising in the morning, he tithed everything to the Lord through me".

137 See Stone and Greenfield, DJD 22, 40–41. See Grelot, 1983, 105–06 who also rejects this emendation.

138 Grelot, 1956, 404.

כנדרה "in accordance with his vow"—This word is unexplained in *ALD*: no vow has been mentioned, at least in the surviving text: see Introduction, pp. 15–16, 40. In *TPL* 9:3–4 we read "And when we came to Bethel, my father Jacob saw in a vision concerning me that I should be a priest for them to God. And after having risen early in the morning he paid tithes of all to the Lord through me".[139] Observe that no hint of a vow occurs in *TPL* either, but there is a vision of Levi's destined priesthood, as a result of which Jacob pays him tithes. It is not unreasonable to speculate that *ALD* also originally had a dream vouchsafed to Jacob before this point in the story, and that this was the context of the missing vow.[140]

Commentary on 5:3

[באדין] אנה הוית קדמי בראש [כהנו]תׄה "[Then] I was first at the head of the priesthood"—M. Morgenstern proposed reconstructing באדין "then", comparing Daniel 6:12, 6:13 and 6:14.[141] The word קדמי has caused problems and Charles took it as the ordinal "first" which we accept here.[142] In the following we read מׄעׄשׄ[ר] based on the remains of the letters surviving in the Geniza manuscript. This reading is confirmed by both 4QLevi^{c} and 1QLevi.

Commentary on 5:4

ואלבשי לבוש כהונתא ומלי ידי והוית כהין לאל עלמיא "and he invested me in the priestly garb and consecrated me and I became a priest of the God of eternity"—This sentence marks the end of Levi's investiture.[143]

[139] Hollander and de Jonge, 1985.

[140] It would be unwise to build much on the word אדין which, though often translated "then", frequently just marks the next stage of the narrative.

[141] Greenfield and Stone, 1979, 219 proposed וכען "and now". Grelot accepted כען but had difficulties with the reading: see 1983, 105.

[142] Stone and Greenfield, DJD 22, 41. In Greenfield and Stone, 1979, 219 we emended, on the basis of *Jubilees* 32:9, to קדמה "before him (i.e., Jacob)". For the reverse corruption, see 4:13. This emendation would produce the idiom הוה קדם which would correspond to Hebrew היה לפני "served". However, in light of the 4QLevi^{c} manuscript, the emendation now seems superfluous: see further Stone and Greenfield, DJD 22, 40 and see the earlier remarks by Grelot, 1983, 106.

[143] Greenfield and Stone, 1979, 220 have, incorrectly לביש.

ואלבשׁי "and he invested me"—The form in the Geniza manuscript is best understood as an *ʾafʿel* with 1 person sing. suffix, known from Palestinian Aramaic. Dalman quoted ארכבי from *Genesis rabba* 65:22,[144] cf. קפחי "he smote me" *Leviticus rabba* section 30:6[145] and שלחי לנבך "he sent me to you" (with 1 sing. suffix) in the poem אזל משה.[146] It is also known in Samaritan Aramaic as noted by Z. Ben-Ḥayyim.[147] The usual form in Qumran Aramaic would be אלבשני.

ומלי ידי "and he consecrated me"—The *waw* and the *mem* of ומלי are bracketed by Charles, but they may both be discerned in the manuscript. The phrase ומלי ידי literally "he filled my hands" is the technical term for priestly consecration as in Exodus 28:41 where dressing Aaron and his sons precedes their consecration; cf. also Exodus 29:4. This expression is misunderstood by the author/redactor of *TPL* who translates it καὶ ἐπλήρωσαν τὰς χεῖράς μου θυμιάματος "and they filled my hands *with incense*" (*TPL* 8:10). This misprisal is an indication that a Semitic text lies ultimately behind this section of *TPL* and that the Semitic idiom was misunderstood.

לאל עלמיא "of the God of eternity"—Examination of the Geniza manuscript shows that in the word עלמיא "eternity" the letters *ʿayin, mem* and *ʾalef* are written over other letters, but the identity of these letters is not clear. Grelot has suggested that the original was עליון. In favour of this is the phrase כהן לאל עליון in Genesis 14:18, where Melchizedek received the tithe, as Levi does in our text. The same term is found in *ALD* 5:8 כהין לאל עליון למארי שמיא "priest of the Most High God, the Lord of heaven" and *ALD* 8:6 and see commentary on 5:8. Note, however, the reading of 4QLevi[c] here which is עלמיא.[148] The expression אל עולם occurs in Genesis 21:33.[149]

[144] See Dalman, 1905, 362; Theodor and Albeck, 1965, 2.743.

[145] Margulies, 1993, 4.703.

[146] 2:25 in Oxford Geniza ms, in a poem for Passover, see Sokoloff and Yahalom, 1999, 84–85 and see 3 sing. fem. suffix (דחקתי, דחפתי, סאבתי) in a poem for Purim, *idem*, 192–93, 31, lines 8–9.

[147] Ben-Ḥayyim, 1967, vol. 3.2, 242–43.

[148] Although the text of the Qumran fragment is somewhat damaged, the decipherment appears certain.

[149] Brooke, 1994, 171 conjectures that this title may have existed in 4Q252, his pericope f.

וברכת לאבי בחיוהי וברכת לאחי "and I blessed my father during his lifetime and I blessed my[150] brothers"—The correct reading is בחיוהי "during his lifetime"; Cowley's initial misreading בחיותי was not corrected by Charles and is still reflected by Grelot in 1956.[151] Levi's pronouncing a blessing on his father is a use of priestly prerogative. The patriarchal custom was for fathers to bless their children (see *ALD* 5:5). Here, in *ALD*, Levi has been blessed by his grandfather before he was invested as priest by Jacob (5:1), "All of us" (5:7) are blessed by Isaac later on. Therefore, Levi's act of blessing here, following as it does on his offering of sacrifices on behalf of his father and brothers, serves to assert and confirm his priestly status. See Numbers 6:22–27 and ben Sira 45:15. It also shows that while Isaac had priestly status, Jacob did not.[152]

Commentary on 5:5

אבא "my father"—Grelot points out that this form is not standard Aramaic and compares it with Abba as an address to God in Mark 14:36, Galatians 4:6 and Romans 8:15.[153]

ואשלמית להקרבה קורבנוהי בבית אל "and I finished bringing his sacrifices in Bethel"—This somewhat allusive verse refers to an incident not preserved in the surviving text of *ALD*. In *Jubilees* 31:3 and 31:26 Jacob is said to have built an altar and prepared sacrifices. He did not complete the sacrifices because Isaac declined to participate due to his old age. Following Levi's vision of investiture at Bethel (32:1), Jacob gives a tithe. Levi then performed the Sukkot sacrifices and celebration at Bethel.[154] It is possible that this incident, perhaps in a different form, is what is implied by ואשלמית "and I finished" here in *ALD*. The expression "and I offered all of his sacrifices" in 5:4 is doubtlessly a general one referring to Levi's overall function after his consecration, while here the text refers to a specific incident.

[150] Charles, 1913, 364 has "all my brethren". The word "all" is not in the Aramaic text.
[151] Grelot, 1956, 405.
[152] A problem with Jacob's role was discussed, but not explained by Becker, 1970, 85.
[153] Grelot, 1983, 107–08. This seems to be the first occurrence of this form.
[154] VanderKam, 2000, 548–551.

Commentary on 5:6

The events related in *ALD* 4:9–5:8 are paralleled in *TPL* 8:1, 9:1–6 and in *Jubilees* 31–32. They are set forth in the following table.

Jubilees	*TPL*	*ALD*
31:1 Start off in Shechem		
31:3 Jacob goes to Bethel and invites Isaac and Rebecca to come to Bethel		
31:4–5 Isaac refuses, invites Jacob, Levi and Judah to go to Isaac to the residence (= *birah*) of Abraham (cf. 31:6)		
31:32 Isaac sends Rebecca and Jacob to Bethel		
32:1 Levi dreams at Bethel	**8:1** Levi dreams at Bethel and investiture	**4:9–12** Levi's vision of investiture
	9:1 Judah and Levi and Jacob go to Isaac	**5:1** "We" go to Isaac
	9:3 Isaac will not come to Bethel; Isaac blesses Levi	
32:2 Tithe to Levi **32:3** Jacob invests Levi	**9:4** Levi and Judah return to Bethel, Jacob sees vision of Levi there & Jacob gives tithe	**5:2** Jacob gives tithe Jacob invests Levi
		5:3–5 Levi offers sacrifices and blesses his father and brothers in Bethel
	9:5 "We" went to Hebron	**5:6** Go from Bethel and encamp at the residence of Abraham with Isaac
	9:6 Isaac instructs Jacob (in Hebron??)	**5:7–8ff.** Isaac blesses his sons and instructs Jacob

From the table above, which shows the chief locations and movements of the heroes of the tale, it is clear that the story in *Jubilees* is much abbreviated where the texts run parallel and that certain incidents, occurring in *ALD* and *TPL* at the present juncture, are found earlier on in the story in *Jubilees*. The most striking is that Levi and Judah, or the brothers, travel with Isaac to the residence or fortress (בירה) of Abraham in different contexts in *ALD* 5:6 and in *Jubilees* 31:5. This incident is succinctly presented in *TPL* 9:5 as their going to Hebron. None of the incidents found in *TPL* but not in *ALD* occur in *Jubilees*, while *Jubilees*' very brief narrative in 32:3, not found in *TPL*, does occur in *ALD*. This makes the additional incidents of *TPL* suspect.

Because *ALD* starts in *medias res*, it is not clear where, according to this document, Levi receives his vision of investiture. In the two other sources he receives it in Bethel. "We" go to Isaac (*ALD* 5:1) who blesses Levi, but Isaac's location is not specified. From *Jubilees* 31:5, he appears to be in Hebron at Abraham's residence. They return to Bethel, where Jacob recognizes Levi's priesthood and gives him tithes, while Levi blesses him and his brothers and offers sacrifices. Then they go to Isaac, who blesses Levi and instructs him in the laws of priesthood.

אבונן . . . אבונה "our father . . . our father"—Note the orthographic variation: first we have אבונן, then later in the verse we have אבונה. The first form is the older (see, e.g., Targum Neofiti to Genesis 28:10; *Genesis rabba* 65:16).[155] In *ALD* 5:7 the orthographic variant אבונא occurs.

ואזלנא מבית אל "and we went from Bethel"—Bethel also may have played a special role in the Second Temple period. Comparing *Jubilees*, *ALD* and the *TPL*, J. Schwartz showed the uniqueness of *Jubilees*' account of Jacob's attempted construction of a temple or a sanctuary in Bethel. Accepting VanderKam's dating of *Jubilees*,[156] Schwartz proposes attributing *Jubilees* 31–32 to the period of Judas Maccabeus's military campaigns, more particularly to the time immediately after the second campaign of 163 BCE, when Judas was forced to retreat to the mountains of Gophna. At that time, Schwartz surmises, when it was impossible to carry out the cult in the Jerusalem temple, the inhabitants of Bethel tried to reclaim their ancient cultic primacy, but were unsuccessful.[157] In *Jubilees* 31 this incident also is attributed to Levi and Judah.

[155] Theodor and Albeck, 1965, 729, line 4.

[156] VanderKam, 1977, 217–238.

[157] Schwartz, 1985, 72–74. Nevertheless, as he himself noted, "There has been no shortage of hypotheses regarding the dating of *Jubilees* and the nature of its author" (p. 71) and thus his claim for *Jubilees*' exact date is not conclusive.

שריגא—Contrast the orthographies שארי in 5:8 and מארי in 5:8.

בירת אברהם "the residence of Abraham" This term is parallel to Greek αὐλὴ Ἀβραάμ. בירה occurs ten times in Esther, once in Daniel, thrice in Ezra, twice in Nehemiah and four times in Chronicles. Of these nineteen biblical occurrences, none is translated αὐλή. In 2 Chronicles 17:12 and 27:4 the plural is translated οἰκήσεις. Abraham also has an αὐλή in *Testament of Abraham* 1 3:5, see chapter 4.[158] According to LSJ αὐλή is a house around a courtyard. In the parallel account in *Jubilees* 31:5, Levi came to his grandfather's house in Hebron, which is called in Latin *bari(s)*, a transliteration of the Greek βᾶρις. The word βᾶρις is also mentioned in Syncellus to *Jubilees*.[159] We hear more details about the house of Abraham from *Jubilees* 22:24, where Abraham says to Jacob: "This house I have built for myself to put my name on it upon the earth. It has been given to you and your descendants forever. It will be called Abraham's house."[160] Isaac and his family lived in this house (29:16–19). Jacob goes there to visit his father with Levi and Simeon (31:5–6), and settles there with his family (33:21). According to *Jubilees* 31:6 and 36:12 it is called a tower (cf. 36:20). Finally, it is mentioned in the story of the war between the sons of Esau and Jacob (36:20, 37:14–17 and 38:4–9). "Tower" is used in this general context in *Jubilees* 37:14, 37:16–17 and 38:4–8.

An account parallel to the last-mentioned story is found in *Midrash Wayissaʿu* where the term בירה also occurs: בא עליהם בחיל גדול... והקיפו לבירה אחת שהיו חונים שם יעקב ובניו "He came upon them with a great force ... and they surrounded a *birah* where Jacob and his sons were encamped."[161]

P. Mandel discussed the occurrences of the word בירה in Hebrew and בירתא in Aramaic in the rabbinic corpus, as well as its Syriac counterpart (*byrtʾ*).[162] He came to the conclusion that *Birah* II (בירה/בירתא) in the Second Temple period sources is "a large building

[158] In *Testament of Abraham* 1 5:1 he has an οἶκος and in Recension 2, chapter 3 he lives in an οἶκος.

[159] Mosshammer, 1984, 124.

[160] Charles, 1913, 364 translates "castle".

[161] Alexander and Dan, 1972, 74, 3, lines 5–7; Hollander and de Jonge, 1985, 454.

[162] Mandel, 1992, 195–217; Mandel, 1994, 275; see also Lemaire and Lozachmeur, 1987, 261–66.

in which people lived in private apartments. It often surrounded an inner courtyard, was adjacent to a main thoroughfare, and had shops along its ground floor".[163] This description, according to Mandel, fits exactly with the Roman *insula*. As for the Greek term βᾶρις, according to Mandel it "originally corresponds to a structure closely similar to *Birah* II (and in particular denoting a manor house)".[164] From the material in *Jubilees*, however, we may infer that it had the aspect of a fortress as well.

In *ALD* 5:6 Isaac is living at Abraham's residence. Does 5:1 imply that Isaac usually lived somewhere else? If we compare with *TPL* 9:6 (see Table above) we might be tempted to believe this was in Hebron; compare *Jubilees* chapter 31.

Commentary on 5:7

<וחזא> "<and he saw>"—The clear reading והזא of the Geniza manuscript is probably a scribal error of *hē* instead of *ḥet* and a *waw* instead of *zayin*. The corrupt reading arose through graphic errors that can occur in most forms of the square Hebrew script. The emendation to וחזא was proposed by Charles, in accordance with Greek καὶ ἴδεν and *Jubilees* 31:9.[165]

Commentary on 5:8

כהין "a priest"—The Greek takes this as a participle and therefore translates it as a verb ἱεράτευσα, but Aramaic has only the noun, though Hebrew has a verb as well.

אל עליון "Most High God"—The Greek has simply κυρίῳ "Lord". The epithet אל עליון "Most High God" is mentioned particularly in the story of Melchizedek (Genesis 14:22), and its parallel in 1QapGen (22:15, 22:16 and 22:22; see below), as well as in Abram's prayer, earlier in 1QapGen (22:12 and also 22:17) and his sacrifice (21:2 and 21:20). In LXX Genesis 14:22 אל עליון is translated κύριος ὕψιστος. Here Greek of *ALD* has τῷ κυρίῳ δεσπότῃ.

These expressions bear some resemblance to Genesis 14:19 and

[163] Mandel, 1994, 275.
[164] Mandel, 1992, VIII.
[165] Charles, 1908a, 247; see commentary on 6:3.

14:22 אל עליון קנה שמים וארץ "God Most High, maker (possessor) of heaven and earth" and compare בריך אנתה אל עליון מרי לכול עלמים "Blessed (are) you, O God Most High, my Lord, for all ages!" (1QapGen 20:12–13). Note Psalm 110:4 כהן לעולם "priest forever" which also refers to Melchizedek. It is interesting to observe that in Hebrews 7 the argument is made for the superiority of the priesthood of Melchizedek over that of Levi. Is the attribution to Levi of a title used of Melchizedek intentional, just as the Judah language was deliberately used of Levi?

(ל)מארי שמיא "Lord of heaven"—The expression occurs in the more or less contemporary text in Daniel 5:23, ועל מרא שמיא התרוממת "You exalted yourself against the Lord of heaven", and it is reminiscent of קנה שמים וארץ "maker (possessor) of heaven and earth" in Genesis 14:19 and 14:22 (see preceding note); the Targums of Genesis are not the same as Aramaic *ALD* here. The same expression occurs several times in 1QapGen. Thus we find "I rejoiced at the words of the Lord of heaven" (מרה שמיא 7:7; see 12:17) and "Blessed be Abram by the Most High God, the Lord of heaven and earth" (מרה שמיא וארעא; 22:16 and 22:21); see *TPBenjamin*, κύριον τὸν θεὸν τοῦ οὐρανοῦ (3:1; compare *1 Enoch* 106:11). It is also comparable with the title found in "Request for a Letter of Recommendation" from Elephantine (Cowley no. 30) as the epithet of God, אלה שמיא "the God of Heaven" (line 2).[166]

Later it is found in an Aramaic dedicatory inscription from a synagogue at ʾUmm el-ʿAmud in the Galilee, dated to the fourth century CE, which mentions הדן תקא דמרי שומיא "this ark (?) of the Lord of heaven".[167] It might be a Judaization of the Phoenician title *bʿl šmyn* which was current in Aramaic throughout the first millennium BCE and into the first millennium CE.[168]

לפקדה יתי "to instruct me"—Missing from the Greek. *TPL* 9:6 says, referring to the same event: "And Isaac called me continually to put

[166] Dated to 407 BCE, see Cowley, 1923, 108–114; Porten and Yardeni, 1986, 68–71.

[167] Naveh, 1978, 40–41, no. 20. The same epithet was also reconstructed in another synagogue inscription from Dura Europos, dated to the third century CE, which reads: [דכי]ר לטב קדם [מרי ש]מיא "[rememb]ered for good before the [Lord of He]aven" (*ibid.*, 139, no. 104); see Sokoloff, 1990, 331.

[168] See Fitzmyer, 1971, 88.

me in remembrance of the law of the Lord, as the angel of God has shown to me." One of the meanings of פקד in *qal* in Hebrew is "to recall, to remember",[169] e.g., Genesis 21:1 and Jeremiah 15:15 זכרני ופקדני "remember me and visit me",[170] a meaning which does not occur in Aramaic: compare *TPL* 9:6 τοῦ ὑπομνῆσαι. It seems probable that *TPL* 9:6 is based on *ALD* 5:8, which the author/redactor elaborated and to which he added his own exegesis.

דין "the law"—The Greek translates this as κρίσιν "legal decision, judgment, punishment", which is to take it in the wrong way. The word דין occurs in different senses in *ALD* 5:8, 6:1 and 6:2. In all instances it is translated by Greek κρίσις, although that translation does not really fit the context in 5:8 and 6:1. In *TPL* 9:7 in corresponding text we find νόμον: compare also 10:8 and commentary there. This is, therefore, a stereotypical translation practice of the Greek of *ALD*; compare in general Deuteronomy 33:10. In *Jubilees* 31:15 Levi is blessed as the giver of righteous judgments.

כהונתא "priesthood"—This spelling also occurs in 1QLevi, frag. 1: see commentary on 11:6–7. In *ALD* 5:4 the Hebraising כהונתא is to be found, which is the regular spelling in Targum Neofiti. Compare the phrase with Hebrew expression משפט הכהנים (Deuteronomy 18:3 "the priests' due" and 1 Samuel 2:13 "the custom of the priests").[171] The phrase דין כהונה is mentioned only later, in *Yalqut Shimʿoni* (Pinḥas, 772) but in a different context. It is also to be compared with הלכות כהונה, known from *Genesis rabbah* 43:6 concerning Melchizedek:[172]

> Brought forth bread and wine: R. Samuel b. Naḥman said: He instructed him in the laws of priesthood (הלכות כהונה מסר לו), "bread" alluding to the shewbread, and "wine" to libation.[173]

[169] Köhler and Baumgartner, 1996, 3.955; Scharbert, 1960, 209–226.
[170] JPS has "remember me and take thought of me".
[171] Probably because of this, Charles, 1913, 364 translates the present expression "rights of the priesthood". He also translates thus in 6:1.
[172] Theodor and Albeck, 1965, 420–21.
[173] Freedman and Simon, 1951, 1.356.

Chapter 6: Priestly Teaching—Purity

General Observations on Chapters 6–10

This section of *ALD* contains cultic teaching. It includes a number of lists—of trees for sacrificial use, of the prescriptions for animal sacrifice, of sacrificial ordinances and of metrological equivalents. This material is of considerable interest because, despite some points of contact with later sacrificial practice as reported by Rabbinic literature, for the most part it is unique. The list of sacrifices is particularly interesting since it is not related to the fixed daily, Sabbath, New Moon or festival liturgical sacrifices already prescribed in the Pentateuch. There are no parallels to *ALD*'s sacrificial ordinances in other sources. This material seems to be evidence for cultic lists and handbooks that existed in the third century BCE and provides a unique insight into the priestly practice of that time. We cannot even guess at its exact origin.

The whole is set inside a repetition of Isaac's exhortation, that starts in 5:7–6:4. Chapter 10:1–2 resembles that passage which is at the start of Isaac's speech, thus forming a kind of *inclusio*.

Commentary on 6:1

לי לוי "to me, Levi"—In Greek we find τέκνον Λευί without Aramaic לי "to me". Perhaps a haplography/dittography was at play in Aramaic. In the next phrase, τέκνον in Greek corresponds to ברי "my son".

ברי "my son"—The Geniza text has two occurrences of this word here, the second of which is dittographic and is not found in Greek. Compare 6:2 and 6:3 below when the same word is omitted.

ומן כל חטא "of all sin"—Missing in the Greek.

דינך "your judgment"—This word could be translated either as "your liability", i.e. judgment which might be given against you, or as "your judgment". Charles translates "rights";[174] see 5:8 and 6:2. In *ALD* 5:8 Levi has learned דין כהונתא "law of the priesthood"; later

[174] Charles, 1913, 364.

in 6:2 he teaches his son דין קושטא "the true law"; in *Jubilees* 31:15 Levi is blessed as dispenser of righteous judgment, an idea deriving, of course, from Deuteronomy 33:10. This might then support the second of the two possible interpretations indicated above, although the first of these seems more likely on intrinsic grounds.[175] Another association of laws with Levi are the extensive cultic injunctions which are inculcated in 6:3–10:13.

דינך רב הוא מן כל בישרא "your judgment is greater than that of all flesh"—The Greek reads ἡ κρίσις σου μεγάλη ἀπὸ πάσης σαρκός: see the preceding note on דין. Part of this phrase was apparently preserved in 4QLevi[f] frag. 7 which has מן כֹוֹל בֹשׂר]א, "than that of all flesh".[176] However, that fragment might equally derive from elsewhere in *ALD*, just happening to be unattested in any of the surviving sources. Indeed, in 10:5 we read ἀπὸ πάσης σαρκός in text surviving only in Greek. That presumably goes back to a similar Aramaic. In 4QLevi[c] 3 we read: ה[כה רעיתך מן כל בשר]א "h]ow I loved you more than all flesh[". This is in 4:11 of *ALD* where the Geniza manuscript has מן כולה "of all".

Commentary on 6:2

ברי "my son"—Missing from the Greek.

דין קושטא "the true law"—Righteousness in legal matters is called קושטא "truth"; see, e.g., Genesis 24:49, 47:29 and Exodus 34:6.

אחוינך "I will show you"—חו"י in the *ʾafʿel* means "to show": see Targum Neofiti to Deuteronomy 5:24 and *ALD* ἀναγγελῶ σοι here. This verb normally translates רא"ה, and only in Isaiah 30:10 does it render חז"י.

דין כהנותא "the law of the priesthood"—These words are omitted from the Greek, perhaps because the phrase seems to be a duplication of the same words in 5:8.

[175] Lévi, 1907, 176 translates "ton privilège". See also commentary on 5:8.
[176] Stone and Greenfield, DJD 22, 69–70.
[177] Puech, 2002, 527.

Commentary on 6:3

לקדמין "first of all"—This word is not translated into Greek. There may have been a parablepsis in Aramaic לקדמין/דין (or in Greek **πρῶτον**—**προσέχε**). See, however, 6:4.

הי<ז>הרו "be<w>are"—Puech justly remarks that the Geniza manuscript's error of *waw* instead of *zayin* here is also found in והוא for וחזא in 5:7.[177]

פחז "fornication"—In the Greek, this word is translated συνουσιασμός "sexual intercourse, fornication, lewd behaviour", and it is listed here with טמאה "impurity" and זנות "harlotry". All three words have the appearance of Hebrew words. The word פחז is used extensively in Hebrew and Aramaic, while זנות is clearly Hebrew.[178]

ἀκαθαρσία "impurity"—This noun usually translates טמאה in the Septuagint, but three times it translates נדה (Leviticus 20:21, Ezekiel 7:20 and 2 Chronicles 29:5). Thus, in *1 Enoch* 10:11 which reads: μιανθῆναι ἐν αὐταῖς ἐν ἀκαθαρσίᾳ αὐτῶν "to be polluted with them in their impurity", the words ἀκαθαρσίᾳ αὐτῶν can also be understood in the same way as here.[179] It should be noted that *TPL* 9:9 reads ἀπὸ τοῦ πνεύματος τῆς πορνείας "from the spirit of fornication".

Commentary on 6:4

πρῶτος—This word is not found in the Aramaic. Note the lack of a Greek equivalent to the same word in 6:3. A causal relationship between these two instances is not apparent.[180]

---

[178] The word פחז was studied in detail by Greenfield, 1978. He observed that all the terms "have the appearance of Hebrew loan words" (36).

[179] Compare also *Jubilees* 7:21:

> For it was on account of these three things that the flood was on the earth, since (it was) due to fornication that the Watchers had illicit intercourse . . . with women. When they married of them whomever they chose they committed the first (acts) of uncleanness (VanderKam, 1989, 47).

The same exegesis of the fallen angels is found in *Genesis rabba* 26:5 (Theodor and Albeck, 1965, 248) "Hence it is written *For they were fair* which refers to virgins, *And they took them wives* refers to married women; *Whomsoever they chose*: that means males and beasts" (tr. Freedman and Simon, 1951, 213). This was already noted by Jung, 1926, 95, note 152.

[180] Lévi, 1907, 168 points to the parallel in Tobit 4:12.

ואנת אנתתא מן משפחתי סב לך "And marry a woman from my family"—The Greek text, apparently due to an Aramaic corruption (perhaps haplography of אנת and אנתתא), reads simply (and incomprehensibly) σὺ ἀπὸ τοῦ σπέρματος λάβε σεαυτῷ. With no word for "woman", the word μου "my" was presumably lost; we have restored it in the text. *TPL* 9:10 correctly interprets this as "and is not of a race of strangers and or Gentiles".

משפחתי "my family"—The Greek has σπέρμα which might go back to זרע. The view encouraging endogamy may be observed in other texts of the time: see Tobit 4:1 and 4QNaph as well as the endogamous marriages recorded on the Genealogical Table. In *Jubilees* we find a "shift from sibling unions to cousin unions in the antediluvian genealogies".[181] In *Visions of Amram* (4Q545) 1 a 1:5–6 Uzziel, Amram's younger brother, married Amram's daughter Miriam when she was thirty years old.[182] This shows both the endogamous marriage and the idea that thirty was an ideal age. Much more might be added on this issue, which is most significant in this period. The actual text found in Aramaic might then be a Hebraism. Nowhere in the LXX does σπέρμα translate משפחה.

זניאן "harlots"—Greek has πολλῶν which is graphically corrupt for πορνῶν. We have so emended.

זרע קדיש אנת וקדיש זרעך היך קודשא "you are a holy seed, and sanctify your seed like the holy place"—Greek reads καὶ τὸ σπέρμα τοῦ ἁγιασμοῦ σου ἐστίν, "yours is the seed of the holy place". The idea of "holy seed" may be observed in Isaiah 6:13 and Ezra 9:2; cf. *Jubilees* 31:14. We take קדיש as a verb, cf. Greek ἁγίασον. Charles, 1913 translates "holy is thy seed", taking it as an adjective. Both are possible.

לכל—Greek omits this word; compare 6:5.

[181] Halpern-Amaru, 1999, 19–31.
[182] Puech, DJD 31, 334.

Commentary on 6:5

קריב "near to"—Compare *Jubilees* 31:16b. Note that there "the sons of Jacob" occurs in the second hemistych, and not "holy ones" (angels?). We reserve judgment as to whether קדישוהי "his holy ones" means "angels" or, perhaps, "holy, sacred things".[183] Kugler speaks of "holy ones" and thinks it evokes Zechariah 3:1–10.[184] Baumgarten goes even further and talks of Joshua the high priest standing "in the company of angels".[185] 11QPs[a] 24:3–4 reads פרשתי כפי למעון קודשכה "I spread out my palms toward your holy dwelling".[186] See commentary on 7:1.

לכל "to all"—Greek omits this word; compare 6:4.

כען "now"—Greek omits this word.

[183] Stone and Greenfield, 1993, 261.
[184] Kugler, 1996, 73.
[185] Baumgarten, 2003, 398.
[186] See further Stone and Greenfield, 1993, 261.

Chapter 7: Priestly Teaching—Wood Offering

Commentary on 7:1

וכדי תהוי קאים למיעל "and when you are about to enter"—Thus this construction should be translated. It contrasts with the construction הוי סחי and תהוי לביש which mean "wash" (imperative) and "are (will be) robed".[187]

בית אל "the Sanctuary"—Literally, "the house of God". Greek translates correctly ἐν τοῖς ἁγίοις while in the corresponding text in *TPL* 9:11, we read εἰς τὰ ἅγια "to the holy place".[188] In Ezra 5:2 and other places, we find Aramaic בית אלהא which is sometimes translated literally as τὸν οἶκον τοῦ θεοῦ "the house of God". In fact, here אל in בית אל is Hebrew, not Aramaic. This reading may be influenced by the place name Bethel, which has already been mentioned in the text (5:5–6).[189]

הוי סחי במיא "wash in water"—See J.C. Greenfield's remarks on such periphrastic imperatives.[190] At this point, Greek adds πρῶτον "first". Oddly Greek also adds the same word elsewhere, twice in 6:4. The first occurrence is probably secondary by dittography from 6:3 and the second occurrence in 6:4 is a graphic corruption in Greek. The word is also added following הסק אינון "offer it up" in 7:4, and note לקדמין in 6:3.

Commentary on 7:2

רחיע "lave"—See *ALD* 8:2 ועוד רחע ידיך ורגליך מן דמא and Athos Greek ms e καὶ πάλιν νίψαι σου τὰς χεῖρας καὶ τοὺς πόδας ἀπὸ τοῦ αἵματος, "and once more wash (lave) your hands and feet of the blood". The language of these verses is very close, and compare also

[187] See Morgenstern, in his review of Kugler, 1999, 137. Kugler, 1996, 96, translates this expression as "When you rise to enter" (compare Charles, 1913, 364), but Morgenstern justly comments that it is more idiomatic to translate, "when you are ready to enter", taking the meaning as we did here. He compares later Aramaic as well as Amoraic Hebrew עומד ל-. See Greenfield, 1969.

[188] This might be an indication of the dependence of *TPL* on the Greek of *ALD*. Note that the disputed τῶν ἁγίων in 6:5 might also be from τὰ ἅγια. There seem to be no further instances of the translation of בית אל as τὰ ἅγια.

[189] See discussion in Schwartz, 1985, 63–85, especially 67–68.

[190] Greenfield, 1969.

7:1. The word רחע is used *ALD* 8:4 concerning the sacrifice: רגלין רחיען, "the hindquarters washed"; see also *New Jerusalem* (11Q18) 13:2 ר]חׄע רגלוהי "he wa]shed his legs". The word סחי "wash" is used in 7:1. Perhaps the contrast between the two words רחע and סחי is that expressed by the Greek here, which renders רחע by νίζω, properly "to wash part of the body" and סחי by λούω "to bathe". The root רח"ע occurs in the Imperial Aramaic used at Elephantine, while סח"י is found in the *peʿal* in the Aramaic Targumim, meaning either "to wash" or "to bathe" (in general, with reference to public baths).[191] The form רחיע with a *yod* is an orthographic vagary of the scribe.

תקרב "you approach"—The *peʿal* of this verb means "to approach, come near", while the *ʾafʿel* is "to bring near". In 7:4 we have a Hebrew *hifʿil* ומהקריב.

כל דנה "at all"—Greek here takes תקרב as transitive προσενέγκαι. It then has ὁλοκάρπωσιν "burnt offering" where the Geniza has כל דנה "at all". Two speculative explanations of this variation may be offered: first, that it arises from an Aramaic corruption of דנה to the graphically similar זבח "sacrifice". This, however, does not explain the word כל "all". Second, in the LXX ὁλοκάρπωσις is equivalent to עולה "whole burnt offering", Aramaic עלתה. So, we might suggest a graphic confusion in which ת of עלתה was corrupted into דנ producing *עלדנה which was then corrected into כל דנה. Reading the verb as transitive, one might then translate "before you offer a burnt offering on the altar". That would agree largely with the Greek, though it has two reflexes of different forms of קרב, ἐγγίσαι and προσενέγκαι. This suggests yet further textual complications.

Commentary on 7:3

תהוי נסב "you are about to sacrifice"—Greek has μέλλῃς προσφέρειν, compare the commentary on 7:1.

עוד תאב "once again"—עוד is Hebraizing for Aramaic תוב. Compare 7:2 which has תאיב תוב, to which expression that here almost completely corresponds, except that it uses the Hebraism עוד.

[191] Sokoloff, 1990, 372.

Commentary on 7:4

ומהקריב "And offer"—On the *hif'il* here, see above, commentary on 7:2. In any case, this form with the מ is bizarre, as is the following מהצלחין.

πρῶτον1°—This word in the Greek text is secondary and nothing corresponds to it in Aramaic. The same word is added in 7:1. It is conceivable that this reflects a special concern of the Greek translator or his *Vorlage* for the correct sequence of priestly actions.

ובקר "And examine"—This is regularly equivalent to Greek forms like ἐπισκόπων, as it is here.[192] Licht suggested that the term מבקר used by the Qumran sect lies behind the Christian usage of ἐπίσκοπος.[193] This does not seem very relevant to the usage here. Regardless, the term serves in Rabbinic literature for the examination of sacrificial animals. Compare also its uses in Ezra 4:15, 4:19, etc.; 1QapGen 22:29 וכען בקר ומני כול די איתי לך "and now examine and count all that you have" and 4Q541 24 2:4 בקר ובעי ודע "examine, and seek and know".[194] The examination of wood destined for the altar is recorded in *m. Middot* 2:5 using the verb מתלעים (see below).

מן תולעא "for worms"—Note that Greek reads here ἀπὸ πάντος μολυσμοῦ "from all impurity" and has nothing corresponding to the words ובאדין . . . מיזדהר "and then . . . acting with care". The word πάντος corresponds to nothing in Aramaic. Interestingly, in the next verse Aramaic has מן כל "from all" which words do not appear there in Greek. It is reasonable to view these two readings as connected. Moreover, the words מן כל "of any of all" at the beginning of 7:5 should be taken with מיזדהר "acting with care" at the end of 7:4. If so, it seems likely that the word תולעא "worm" has been lost and we should restore "thus I saw my father Abraham being beware of any worms". Then the textual development lying behind the Greek

[192] See Greenfield and Stone, 1990, 158–161, where the root בק"ר in *ALD* and Qumran sectarian works is discussed.

[193] See the comments of Licht, 1965, 116 and Nauck, 1957, 200–209, especially 201–07. He discussed the use in the Damascus Document in comparison with that in early Christianity.

[194] Puech, DJD 31, 252.

is clear. There was a homoeoteleuton leading to the loss of all words between מן1° and מן2° which produced the present text of Greek. The addition of *waw* in Aramaic is a subsequent secondary correction, following on the loss of תולעא in Aramaic. The wood used for sacrificial purposes was to be wormless and free of rot, see *Jubilees* 21:13 and *m. Middot* 2:5 discussed below.

כדנה "thus"—4QLevi[f] has כדן. This form is older than כדנה, but is more familiar than it in the Middle Ages.[195]

Commentary on 7:5

תריעשר "twelve"—So also Greek, although only eleven trees are mentioned in the Greek text.

די חזין "which are fitting"—Greek omits; note similar omission in 7:3.

להסקה "to offer up"—Aramaic also has מינהון "of them", which is not readily translated into English. Greek has πρόσφερε, which de Jonge emends, convincingly, to προσφέρειν.

Commentary on 7:6

The list of trees in the Aramaic texts of *ALD*, both from the Geniza and from Qumran, may be compared with that in the Greek translation and a similar list in *Jubilees* 21:12. These are set forth in the following table.

ALD Aram	4Q	*ALD* Greek	*ALD* Translation	*Jubilees*[196]
ארזא	—	κέδρον	cedar	cypress
דפרנא	דפרנא	ουεδεφωνα	juniper (bay)	silver fir (*defrana*)
סנדא	סינדא	σχῖνον	almond (Ar.), mastik (Gr.)	almond
אטולא	—	στρόβιλον	fir	fir
שוחא	—	πίτυν	pine	pine
אדונה	—	ολδινα	ash	cedar

[195] Stone and Greenfield, DJD 22, 69.
[196] The translation of the Ethiopic is that of VanderKam, 1989, 123–25.

Table (*cont.*)

ALD Aram	4Q	*ALD* Greek	*ALD* Translation	*Jubilees*
ברותא	ברותא	βερωθα	cypress	juniper
תאנתא	תככה̊	θεχακ	fig/*tkkh*	date
אע משחא	—	κυπάρισσον	oleaster (Ar.), cypress (Gk)	olive wood
ערא	ע]רא	δάφνην	laurel	myrtle
הדסה	אדסה	μυρσίνην	myrtle	laurel wood = cedar juniper bush
אעי דקתא	]עעי	ἀσφάλαθον	asphalathos	balsam

The lists are basically the same and, when we bear in mind certain difficulties in the identification of the trees, and also a measure of indefiniteness about some of the Ethiopian terms in the passage from *Jubilees*, they may be even more similar than they seem. Nothing like this list is known from Rabbinic halachah.

A number of specific remarks may be made about the list.

1. A number of Aramaic tree names were transliterated into Greek, rather than translated: ουεδεφωνα (דפנא\דפרנא), ολδινα (אדונה: on this corrupt name, see below), βερωθα (ברותא) and θεχακ (תככה: the form in the Qumran manuscript).
2. It was Charles who suggested that ουεδεφωνα is a corrupt transliteration of דפרנא. A cognate instance will be noted below.
3. ארזא—This designates the cedar in Jewish Palestinian Aramaic,[197] and also the pine in Jewish Babylonian Aramaic.[198]
4. דפרנא "juniper (bay)"—The related word in Syriac is *dfrn*ʾ; likewise דפנא in Jewish Palestinian Aramaic means "laurel or bay tree"; from Greek δάφνη. Note however, that below, ערא is translated by Athos Greek as δάφνη.[199]
5. סנדא "mastik" or "almond"—In Jewish Babylonian Aramaic סנידדתא means "almond".[200]

[197] Sokoloff, 1990, 94.
[198] Sokoloff, 2002, 165.
[199] Löw, 1881, 62 suggest identifying it with אשכרוע. Our thanks are expressed to M. Kislev for counsel on the identification of the trees.
[200] See Sokoloff, 2002, 1108.

6. אטולא "fir"—Given in Greek as στρόβιλον. This form is corrupt for אצטרובלא, which in turn derives from στρόβιλος as suggested by Löw.[201]
7. שוחא—Probably אשוחא "fir tree" in Jewish Babylonian Aramaic, which is also *šwḥ* in Arabic.[202]
8. Charles suggested that ολδινα is a "corrupt transliteration of אורנא". We accept Charles' emendation, which is reflected in our translation "ash".[203] Observe, however, that ΟΛΔΙΝΑ > *ΟΔΙΝΑ > אדינה which is exactly the reading of the Geniza manuscript. This reading is, nonetheless, apparently corrupt for אורנא.[204]
9. Charles thought the name θεχακ found in the Athos Greek manuscript to be a corrupt transliteration of תאנתה "fig", found in the Geniza manuscript. Here, however, 4QLevi[f] preserves the form תככה which is the original from which θεχακ was transliterated. A reflex of it may also be preserved in the Ethiopic of *Jubilees* 21:12.[205] The type of tree designated by תככה remains unknown.
10. עא משחא "oleaster" This is not an olive tree, although that is the tree mentioned in this position in the list in *Jubilees*.[206] It is translated as κυπάρισσον by the Greek, but that is also not accurate either. In fact, it is an oleaster. *M. Tamid* 2:3 specifically forbids the use of olive wood on the altar (see below).[207]
11. הדסה "myrtle"—אדסא in 4QLevi[f] 5–6 1:5; Biblical Hebrew הדס.
12. אעי דקתא "asphalathos"—The translation is based on the Greek, which is presumably a variation of ἀσπάλαθος "spinous shrub".[208]

---

[201] Löw, 1967, 3.15, see Sokoloff, 2002, 125 meaning "pine nut": see Syriac *'sṭrwbly'* Brockelmann, 1928, 34.

[202] VanderKam, 1989, 124 suggests correcting it to שיטא. See further Stone and Greenfield, DJD 22, 69; Löw, 1881, 264 identifies it with צלף.

[203] Löw, 1881, 39 suggests identifying it with ערבה.

[204] Various emendations of the text are bruited by Löw, 1967, 3.16. Another possibility is that אדונה is a mistake for אדרה which is a type of tree, see Sokoloff, 2002, 82. See *j. Ketubot* 7, 31d where אדרה is identified as תדהר "plane tree": see, e.g., *BDB*, 187, *s.v.*

[205] Perhaps, then, VanderKam's comment on 1989, 128 (*Jubilees* 21:12) should be modified and Ethiopic *tanāka* should be regarded as another corruption of this unknown tree name.

[206] Grelot, 1991, 256 translates "olivier". See note 214 below.

[207] See also *t. Menaḥot* 9:14. Löw, 1881, 138 identifies it with אלה.

[208] Discorides 1.19, see Gunther, 1959, 20.

The tree intended by the Aramaic words cannot be determined. The reading with ד is confirmed by Targum Pseudo-Jonathan to Genesis 22:3 קיסין דקיתא.[209]

Commentary on 7:7

ἅ σε ἀναφέρειν—Perhaps corrupt for ἃ δεῖ ἀναφέρειν "which it is necessary to offer" reflecting חזין. This word caused problems already in Greek, see commentary on 8:7.

Here it seems appropriate to add some notes on lists of trees in the Bible and in Rabbinic literature. The Bible does not give any specific laws regarding the wood to be used on the altar for burning the sacrifices. Thus, Leviticus 1:7, which deals with placing the wood on the altar, says nothing about a requirement that the wood be split or without worms. *M. Middot* 2:5 (cited above) says that there was a chamber in the northwest corner of the women's courtyard which was known as the chamber of the wood (לשכת דיר העצים) where "the priests that were blemished examine the wood for worms since any wood wherein was found a worm was invalid (and could not be burnt) upon the altar".[210]

After *ALD*, the examination of the wood is next known from *Jubilees* 21:12–15, in Abraham's testament to his son Isaac.

> 21:12 Be careful about the (kinds of) woods (that are used for) sacrifice so that you bring no (kinds of) woods onto the altar except these only: cypress, silver-fir, almond, fir, pine, cedar, juniper, date, olive wood, myrtle, laurel wood, the cedar whose name is the juniper bush, and balsam.
> 21:13 Of these (kinds of) woods place beneath the sacrifice on the altar ones that have been tested for their appearance. Do not place (beneath it) any split or dark wood; (place there) strong (kinds of) woods and firm ones without any defect—a perfect and new growth. Do not place (there) old wood, for its aroma has left—because there is no longer an aroma upon it as at first.
> 21:14 Apart from these (kinds of) woods there is no other which you are to place (beneath the sacrifice) because their aroma is distinctive and the smell of their aroma goes up to heaven.

[209] דקתא does not seem to be connected with the word דקתא cited by Sokoloff, 2002, 1094 (*b. Qiddushin* 9a) which means "alluvial ground".

[210] That rule is limited, according to the Babylonian Talmud, "only [if found] in damp wood, but in dry wood it can be scraped away and [the wood] is valid" (*b. Menaḥot* 85b; translation from Epstein, 1989).

> 21:15 Pay attention to this commandment and do it, my son, so that you may behave properly in all your actions.[211]

This paragraph includes the names of thirteen kinds of wood suitable for sacrifice, some of which parallel the list in *ALD*. It is included above in the comparative table. The passage also specifies that they must be examined and explains why. The wood should not be split, dark, or old, but strong and firm, without any defect. Thus it should be "a perfect and new growth".

These trees with these particular characteristics are chosen, "because their aroma is distinctive and the smell of their aroma goes up to heaven". Thus, old wood is to be avoided, "for its aroma has left—because there is no longer an aroma upon it as at first" (*Jubilees* 21:13). This idea is already found in *ALD* 7:5 די ריח תננהון בשים סליק "whose smoke rises up with a pleasant odor". *M. Tamid* 2:3 says that all kinds of wood are fit for the fire on the altar except the olive and the grapevine:[212]

> וכי כל העצים כשרים למערכה? הין, כל העצים כשרים למערכה חוץ משלזית ומשלנפן, אבל באילו רגלים: במורביות שלתאינה ושלאגוז ושלעץ שמן.
>
> Were all kinds of wood valid for use in the Altar fire? Yea, all kinds of wood were valid for the use in the Altar fire save only olive-wood and the wood of the vine; but their custom was to use only boughs of the fig-tree or the walnut-tree or of oleaster-wood.[213]

The Mishnah offers no reason for prohibiting these trees, but later, the Babylonian *amoraim* explain it as intended either to avoid the destruction of fruit trees, or by the fact that these trees do not burn well and cause excessive smoke (*b. Tamid* 29b). The concern with the smoke fits the older lists in *ALD* and *Jubilees*. In *t. Menaḥot* 9:14, where the same issue is discussed, five additional trees are enumerated by Rabbi Eliezer: sycamore, carob, palm, mayish (celtis), and oak. The Tosefta also notes that the use of wood from dismantled

---

[211] VanderKam, 1989, 123-25. Small parts of this text were preserved at Qumran in 4Q219, 2:7–12 (*Jubilees*). However, part of only one tree name survived: א]רעיבו[ת "juniper, cedar" (line 7): see VanderKam and Milik who suggest reconstructing א]רעיבו[ת אשר שמו ארז] (DJD 13, 46, 50–51).

[212] See Kugler, 1996, 104, note 152. We also consulted a lecture by Schiffman, 2002.

[213] Danby, 1933, 583.

construction is forbidden in any case. The Mishnah's oleaster, עץ שמן, is in all likelihood *pinus halepersis*, which is עא משחא here.[214]

There are a number of lists enumerating four, ten and even fourteen kinds of cedars (*b. Rosh Hashanah* 23a and parallels and *j. Ketubot* 7 31d).[215] Intriguingly, a list of fourteen evergreen trees is known from *Geoponica* XI:1, which shares six names with our list.[216] Yet, it is not related to their aroma or their use in the sacrificial cult. Moreover, in *TPL* 9:12 the twelve trees permitted for the altar are characterized as ἀεὶ ἐχόντα φύλλα "evergreens", which is surely a conflation of the two traditions.

Much earlier, and in a quite different context, Hesiod in *Works and Days*, as part of his agricultural advice about those things to be done during the month of October, says:

> When the piercing power and sultry heat of the sun abate, and almighty Zeus sends the autumn rains . . . then, when it showers its leaves to the ground and stops sprouting, the wood you cut with your axe is least liable to worm. Then remember to hew your timber: it is the season for that work . . . (§§415–22). . . . Poles of laurel or elm are most free from worms and a share-beam of oak and a plough-tree of holm oak (§§435–436).[217]

Worm-free wood was a most desirable commodity and it was essential for the offering of sacrifices.

[214] See Greenfield and Stone, 1979, 221, note 3. Charles' translation "olive" (1913, 2.365) is wrong. Albeck, 1930, 23 dealt with this passage in detail and has made the plausible suggestion that "olive" in *Jubilees* 21:12 is also a mistranslation of עץ שמן. See also VanderKam, 1989, 124–25.

[215] For a discussion of these lists with other such lists in rabbinic literature, see: Löw, 1881, 59–60; Löw, 1967, 15–16. Albeck, 1930, 23 had noted a connection between the list of trees in *Jubilees*, *TPL* 9, *ALD* 7:6 and those found in the Mishnaic sources. Lévi, 1907, 170–71 observes that the trees enumerated in these lists of cedars are mostly not cedars. They are all evergreens and see the next note.

[216] See the edition of Beckh, 1895, 326. The *Geoponica* mentions Φοῖνιξ, Κίτριον, Στρόβιλος, Δάφνη, Ἐλαία, Κυπάρισσος, Κερατέα, Πίτυς, Πρῖνος, Πύξος, Μυρσίνη, Κέδρος, Ἰτέα, καὶ Ἄρκευθος. This list is titled as: Δένδρα ἀειθαλῆ ἐστι, μηδέποτε φυλλοροοῦντα ἐν τῷ χειμῶνι, ιδ΄. *1 Enoch* 3 refers to a list of fourteen evergreen trees, though it does not specify them. Charles discussed the text of *Jubilees* with its parallels in *TPL* and *Geoponica* (see Charles, 1902, 134–35) as did VanderKam, 1989, 124–25.

[217] Evelyn-White, 1914, 32–35.

Chapter 8: Priestly Teaching—Sacrifices

Commentary on 8:1

When the length of the book and the fragmentary nature of its preservation are considered, it is remarkable that this passage occurs in three copies at Qumran. Perhaps its position towards the middle of the work played a role. Yet, there are no Qumran fragments of the long passage 9:1–11:8 which follows it immediately.

על מדבחא "upon the altar"—Greek omits all the words between על מדבחא "upon the altar" in 7:7 and על מדבחא "upon the altar" in 8:1 by homoeoteleuton.[218]

כותלי מדבחה "the sides of the altar"—Compare Leviticus 5:9 קיר המזבח "side of the altar". Targum Neofiti to Leviticus has כתלא דמדבחא.

Commentary on 8:2

מליחי<ן> "salted"—Reading with the text of 4QLevi^{d}, cf. 4QLevi^{f}. Puech would correct "the salted portions" to "les parties (qui ont été/une fois) salées". We fail to see the distinction.[219]

Commentary on 8:3

<ראשא> "its head"—The Geniza reads ואשה, emended by Charles to ראשא. The meaning of the final ה is ambiguous. It might be the third person singular possessive, as we have translated. However it could equally be the definite article, compare 4QLevi^{d} 2:3, 4QLevi^{f} 2–3:8 and 1QLevi 45 ראשא. This would agree with the Greek τὴν κεφαλήν and compare the orthography of אבריה in 8:2.[220]

---

[218] Charles says "Aram[aic] adds . . ." (1908a, 249, note 13).

[219] This is what the English past participle means here: see Puech, 2002, 532. In this note, Puech implies a criticism of Greenfield and Stone for not knowing, in 1979, the then unpublished Qumran manuscripts.

[220] Charles's emendation of ו to ר was accepted by Greenfield and Stone, 1979, 222. His emendation of the final ה to א was not accepted. It remains doubtful today, despite the Qumran manuscripts.

הוי מהנסק לקדמין "burn . . . first"—4QLevi^{d} 2:3 must have read [ל]ק̊[דמין] הוי מהנסק.[221] If we can depend on Greek word order, which is not certain, τὴν κεφαλὴν ἀνάφερε πρῶτον might reflect the Geniza text.

מהנסק "burn"—Aramaic סלק could mean "offer up" or "burn". We have chosen the translation "burn" in view of the preceding line. Greek is the similar ἀνάφερε.[222]

תרבא "fat"—See 1QapGen 10:14 ותרבא על נורא אקטרת "I burned the fat on the fire":[223] compare Targum Onqelos to Leviticus 3:3.

ולא "and . . . not"—So the Geniza; 4QLevi^{d} 2:4 has ואל. Qumran Aramaic usually employs אל with the jussive.

לה—Greek has not understood this word, which is an ethical dative. It has omitted the next two words "the sacrifice of the ox" and paraphrased לה as "upon its head".

נ<כס>ת תורא "of the slaughtered bull"—The reading נסבת of the Geniza manuscript is clearly corrupt.[224] Compare Targum Onqelos Leviticus 3:9 and 4:10. This differs from the Greek which has καὶ μὴ ὀπτανέσθω τὸ αἷμα ἐπὶ τῆς κεφαλῆς αὐτῆς· "And let the blood not be seen on its head". Similar reformulations are to be found in the Greek throughout this section. See, however, the preceding note on this instance.

Commentary on 8:4

ובתר צוארה ידוהי "and after its neck, its forequarters"—4QLevi^{d} 2:5 has ובתרהן ידוהי "and after them, its forequarters". Similar differences of formulation may be seen in the following lines in like phrases. This variant formulation is almost identical with καὶ μετὰ τοῦτο τὸν τράχηλον found in the Greek translation. The relationship of the texts is set forth in the following table.

221 See Stone and Greenfield, DJD 22, 49.
222 Stone and Greenfield, DJD 22, 48.
223 Morgenstern, Qimron and Sivan, 1996, 44–45.
224 Greenfield and Stone, 1979, 222. This emendation was already proposed by Lévi, 1907, 170, note 1. Might the corruption be due to some sort of contamination with the following words, i.e., נכסת תורא with בתרוהי?

Geniza	Qumran	Greek
ובתרוהי	ובתרוהי	καὶ μετὰ τοῦτο
צוארה	[צור]א̇	τὸν τράχηλον
ובתר צוארה	ו̇בתרהן	καὶ μετὰ τοῦτο
ידוהי	ידיא	τοὺς ὤμους
ובתר ידוהי	[ובתרהן]	καὶ μετὰ ταῦτα
ניעא עם כן דפנה	[ניעא עם כן דפנה]	τὸ στῆθος μετὰ τῶν πλευρῶν
ובתר ידיא	ובת[ר̊הן	καὶ μετὰ ταῦτα
ירכאתא עם שדרת חרצא	ירכתא ושדרת̊[חרצא]	τὴν ὀσφὺν σὺν τῷ νώτῳ
ובתר ירכאתא	[ובתר ירכתא]	καὶ μετὰ ταῦτα
רגלין רחיען עם קרביא	[רגלין רחי]ע̊ן עם קרביא	τοὺς πόδας πεπλυμένους σὺν τοῖς ἐνδοσθίοις

It will be readily observed that there is variation between ובתר with the part of the beast and ובתר with the pronominal suffix. The Geniza text always has the former, while in all but one instance the Qumran and Greek texts agree in having the latter. In the last instance Geniza and Qumran agree against the Greek. Thus, to return to the instance of ובתר ידיא "and after the forequarters", we may observe that no word corresponds to "forequarters" in either the Greek or the Geniza text. In all instances but this, the "and after NN" clause refers to the immediately preceding body part. Here, however, it refers to the one preceding that. Yet, the plural ending on ובת[ר̊הן and the ταῦτα of Greek suggest that the Geniza text should be sustained. This seems to be the case, even if the formulation in this instance departs from the regularity of the list.

Another description of the slaughtering of a bull is to be found in 11Q*New Jerusalem* (11Q18) frag. 13. It reads as follows:

1.]בארבע רגלוהי ונשט תורא ·[
2. ר[ח̊ע רגלוהי וקרבוהי ומלח כולה]
3. ן[ש̊ויה על נורא ואיתי קמח סולת]
4. ר[ו̊ב̇ע סתא ואסקה למדבחא כולה]
5. רו[ב̇ע סתא ונסך לנוא מורכי̊]ותא
6.]א ובשרא מתערב בחדא[
7.] ר̇יחא [*vacat*

Translation
[1][. . .] by its four legs, and stripped the bull [. . . [2]he wa]shed its legs and its intestines, and salted all of it [[3]. . . and] placed it on the fire, and brought fine sifted flour [[4]. . . a fo]urth of a seah, and he brought all of it to the altar [[5]. . . a fou]rth of a seah, and he poured it into [the] troughs [[6]. . .] the [ ] and the flesh were mixed together [[7]. . .] the smell. *vacat*[225]

The editors of this text noted that the same terminology is used in 4QLevi^{d}.[226] They also referred to Josephus, *Antiquities* 3. 9. 1 (§227), which reads:

> The beasts being slaughtered, the priest drench with the blood the circuit of the altar, and then, after cleansing them, dismember them, sprinkle them with salt, and lay them upon the altar, already laden with wood and alight. The feet and the inwards of the victims (τοὺς δὲ πόδας τῶν ἱερείων καὶ τὰ κατὰ νηδύν) are carefully cleansed before being placed with the other portions for consecration in the flames.[227]

As noted by Thackeray, according to Leviticus 1:13 only the inwards and the legs are required to be washed.[228] This rule is followed by *ALD*: "(and after the haunches) the hindquarters washed, with the entrails". Nevertheless, as Feldman adds, "Josephus' view is that the whole animal is to be washed, but that the feet and the inwards are to be cleaned with particular care".[229] The animal as a whole is cleansed as substitute for flaying. The complete animal is to be cleansed also according to 2 Chronicles 4:6, Ezekiel 40:38 and *m. Tamid* 4:2.

The order in which the parts of a sacrificial animal should be offered is described in Leviticus 1:8–9 and 1:12–13 as follows: the head, the fat, the innards and the legs. Other parts are not mentioned. In *m. Tamid* 3:1 and *m. Yoma* 2:3 the order of offering the limbs is as follows: הראש והרגל ושתי היידים, העוקץ והרגל, החזה והגרה ושתי הדפנות והקרבים "the head and [right] hind leg, the two forelegs, the rump and the [left] hind leg, the breast, and the neck, and the two flanks and the inwards."[230]

[225] DJD 23, 325–26. Cited by permission of Oxford University Press.
[226] DJD 23, 326.
[227] Thackeray, 1930, 424–27.
[228] Thackeray, 1930, 425, note h.
[229] Feldman 2000, 293, note 599.
[230] Danby, 1933, 163.

Some commentators explained this order as starting with the head which follows the biblical rule, and then the remaining parts are offered in order of size, from the largest to the smallest. This differs from the order found in *ALD*. An alternative order is given in the name of Rabbi Joshua, in *m. Yoma* 2:3 בדרך הילוכו היה קרב "It was offered in the order in which it had walked",[231] which means that the parts of the animal should be put on the altar in the same order in which they would have been encountered looking at the animal from head to tail. This order, as noted by Schiffman, reflects the same view as in *ALD*. On this order, a baraita in *b. Yoma* 25b states:

> BEN AZZAI SAID BEFORE R. AKIBA, ETC.: Our Rabbis taught: what is "THE WAY OF ITS WALKING"? The head, right hind-leg, breast and neck, the two fore-legs, the two flanks, the tail and the left hind-leg. R. Jose says: It was offered up in the order in which it is flayed . . . R. Akiba says: It was offered up in the order in which it was dissected . . . R. Jose the Galilean says: It was offered up in the order of its best parts.[232]

The view of Rabbi Akiba that the animal is offered in the same way in which it is butchered is, as noted by Schiffman,

> in complete agreement with the order set out in our text. According to a baraita in *b. Yoma*, because of respect for the divine service, the fat was arranged so as to cover over the parts of the neck which had been cut by the slaughterer. In this way, the blood of the wound would not have been visible. This very same procedure was expected by our text.

Thus, as he concludes,

> the Aramaic Levi Document was totally in accord with the second view regarding the order in which the parts of the animal were to be offered, and agrees also with rabbinic tradition regarding the manner in which the fat was to be put on the head.[233]

ניעא "breast of an animal"—For the term, see Targum Neofiti to Leviticus 7:30 and compare Syriac *nʿʾ*.

כן דפנא "side"—כן seems to be related Syriac *knʾ* meaning "base, stalk".[234] דפנא means "rib": see, for example, או דדפנא או דאטמא

[231] Danby, 1933, 163.
[232] Epstein, 1974, Yoma 25b.
[233] Schiffman, 2002.
[234] Brockelmann, 1928, 333.

"(meat) either of the rib or of the thigh" (*b. Baba Meṣia* 23b). This reading and not Charles's בן was confirmed by autopsy examination of the manuscript.

ובתר ידיא "and after its forequarters"—The reading of 4QLevi[d] 2:6 is ובתרהן "and after them". See commentary on 8:4.

שדרא "spine"—A word found only in Jewish Babylonian Aramaic.[235]

חרצא "loin"—This word occurs in Jewish Palestinian Aramaic as related to humans, mainly in a metaphoric sense, e.g., אסר חרציה "he girded his loins",[236] while in Jewish Babylonian Aramaic it also relates to the physical human or animal loins.[237]

Commentary on 8:5

ἐν ἅλατι "with salt"—The word ἐν is an Aramaism in Greek, cf. במלח.

Commentary on 8:6

נישפא "fine meal"—See נשף or נשיף "fine flour" in the Aramaic dockets of the fourth century BCE from Idumaea.[238]

והקטיר עליהון לבונה "and burn the frankincense over them"—The phrase is deeply Hebraised, under the influence of such biblical language as Leviticus 2:15–16.

בסרך "due order"—J. Licht commented on the similar semantic fields of the word סרך in Qumran Hebrew and of Greek τάξις, which is found in the Greek translation here. He also compares the Greek word τάγμα.[239]

Commentary on 8:7

[במדה] ובמתקל "[by measure] and weight"—Compare Leviticus 19:35 במדה במשקל ובמשורה "(in measuring) length, weight or quantity".

---

[235] Sokoloff, 2002, 1113.
[236] Sokoloff, 1990, 215.
[237] Sokoloff, 2002, 484.
[238] Eph'al and Naveh, 1996, 11.
[239] Licht, 1965, 66. See on the issue here, Greenfield and Stone, 1979, 222.

חזתא̊—This word is corrupt in the Geniza manuscript and the Greek is also corrupt, reading τῷ καθήκι τῶν. The corrupt word חזתא is presumably related to חזי meaning "fitting", and doubtless καθηκι derives from Greek καθήκων or some cognate, with the same meaning. The material reading of the Aramaic is certain.

Chapter 9: The Measures of Wood, Salt, Fine Flour, Oil, Wine and Frankincense

Commentary on 9:1

ליה "for it"—Greek correctly precedes this with καθήκει which is lost in Aramaic. Observe the corruption involving this word in 8:7.

פר <תרין> "if it is the second bull"—Greek has τῷ ταυρῷ τῷ δευτέρῳ, reading an Aramaic text פר תרין* "second bull" and not פר תורין "bull of oxen" and we have emended the Geniza text accordingly.[240]

Commentary on 9:6

{αποδεδεικτω}—Greek is corrupt. It should probably be some form of a verb in the second person.

Commentary on 9:7

δίμοιρον "two thirds"—Charles has "half".[241]

Commentary on 9:10

τῷ μεγάλῳ "the great"—Charles observes that what is apparently a reference to the same creature in 9:1 designates it τῷ τελείῳ and that in Aramaic there we find רבא "large".

Commentary on 9:13

καὶ ἀμνοῦ "and of a lamb"—This word, in the genitive case, is not easily construed in context.

Commentary on 9:17

καὶ τὸ τρίτον τοῦ σάτου "and a third of a saton"—Σάτον is the usual Greek word for a seah. In fact, a seah is one third of an ephah, so perhaps we should read καὶ τὸ σάτον τὸ τρίτον τοῦ ὑφή ἐστιν "and the saton is a third of an ephah": see Introduction, section on "Sacrificial Ordinances and Measures".

[240] Lévi, 1907, 169–170 discusses this reading at some length, but proposes an emendation based on a Hebrew original.
[241] Charles, 1913, 365.

Commentary on 9:18

ὁλκῆς1° . . . ὁλκῆς2° "of the weight . . . of . . . weight"—In neither of the occurrences of this word in the present section is the reason for the genitive case easily understood.

θερμῶν "*thermoi*"—The identification of this term, a monetary value, is discussed in the Introduction, section on "Sacrificial Ordinances and Measures".

καὶ ὁλκῆς μιᾶς "and of one weight"—This phrase is either corrupt or incomplete.

Chapter 10: Concluding Injunctions and Blessing

Commentary on 10:1

Note the resemblance to Exodus 15:26 ויאמר אם שמוע תשמע לקול יהוה אלהיך והישר בעיניו תעשה והאזנת למצותיו "He said, 'If you will heed the Lord your God diligently, doing what is upright in His sight giving ear to His commandments'." *ALD*'s hortatory language is based on Pentateuchal phraseology.

Commentary on 10:2

τὴν κρίσιν ταυτήν "this regulation"—As we have seen in 5:8–6:2, κρίσις may also translate דין; see also commentary on 5:8. Note that "for you are a holy priest" resembles the Aramaic expression ארו כהין קדיש אנת מתקרי "since you are called a holy priest" in 6:4.

Commentary on 10:9

ουσης—This Greek is apparently corrupt.

Commentary on 10:10

τῆς βίβλου τοῦ Νῶε περὶ τοῦ αἵματος "of the book of Noah concerning the blood"—Is the book called "The Book of Noah about the Blood", or is this phrase to be translated "the 'Book of Noah' concerning the blood"? It is connected with the commandment about blood in Genesis 9:4–6: cf. Leviticus 17:13.[242] Noah made the first animal sacrifice under the new, post-diluvian order, and he also received the commandment about blood. With the title compare 1QapGen 5:29 [פרשגן] כתב מלי נ֯ו֯ח "[A copy] of the book of the words of Noah",[243] and the expression פרשגן כתב מלי חזות ע֯מרם "copy of the words of the vision of Amram" in 4Q543 1 a–c:1.[244]

[242] Stone, 1999, 138.
[243] Morgenstern, Qimron and Sivan, 1996, 40–41.
[244] DJD 31, 292; Steiner, 1995, 66–71. See also, Stone, 1999, 137–141 on the "Book of Noah".

Chapter 11: Birth and Naming of Levi's Children

Commentary on 11:1

To the information known from other sources, *ALD* adds the fact that Melka was "daughter of Bathuel, son of Laban, my mother's brother".[245] Melka is also mentioned in *Jubilees* 34:20 (and in the Syriac version including the wives of the patriarchs based on it), but there she is "one of the daughters of Aram—one of the descendants of Terah's sons".[246] The chapter opens with the double date of Levi's marriage to Melka, formulated by week (i.e., of years): "[w]hen four weeks of my life were completed for me". This has no parallel in other sources.

Commentary on 11:2

καὶ ἐκάλεσα τὸ ὄνομα αὐτοῦ Γηρσάμ· εἶπα γὰρ ὅτι πάροικον ἔσται τὸ σπέρμα μου ἐν γῇ ᾗ ἐγεννήθην· πάροικοί ἐσμεν ὡς τούτῳ ἐν τῇ γῇ ἡμετέρᾳ νομιζομένῃ "and I called his name Gershom, for I said, 'My seed shall be sojourners in the land in which I was born. We are sojourners as now in the land which is reckoned ours'."—To this onomastic midrash, *TPL* 11:3 adds that in a vision Levi saw that Gershom and his seed will be expelled from the high-priesthood. In *ALD* Levi names Gershom, while in *TPL* 11:2 it is Melka who does so.

Similarly to *TPL* 11:3, in the name midrash of Kohath in *TPL* 11:5 the actual name explanation is followed by a vision, which confirms the onomastic etymology. *TPL* may have picked up this literary structure from *ALD*'s midrash on Gershom or that on Kohath (11:6).

The actual expression here resembles Genesis 15:13. That verse is not just a folk etymology, but a prediction, "for your seed will be a sojourner in a land which is not theirs". Gershom son of Levi is mentioned in Genesis 46:11, but there the word play with גר שם "sojourner there" does not occur. The two elements are combined in the name midrash of another Gershom, the son of Moses, mentioned

[245] For the name of Levi's wife in other ancient sources, see Ilan, 1993, 6 and Table 1. In *Sefer ha-yashar* she is called עדינה "'Adina".

[246] Moreover, as noted by B. Halpern-Amaru, "Of the wives of the sons, only she, like the four matriarchs, descends from the house of Terah": see Halpern-Amaru, 1999, 118.

GENEALOGY DOWN TO TERAH

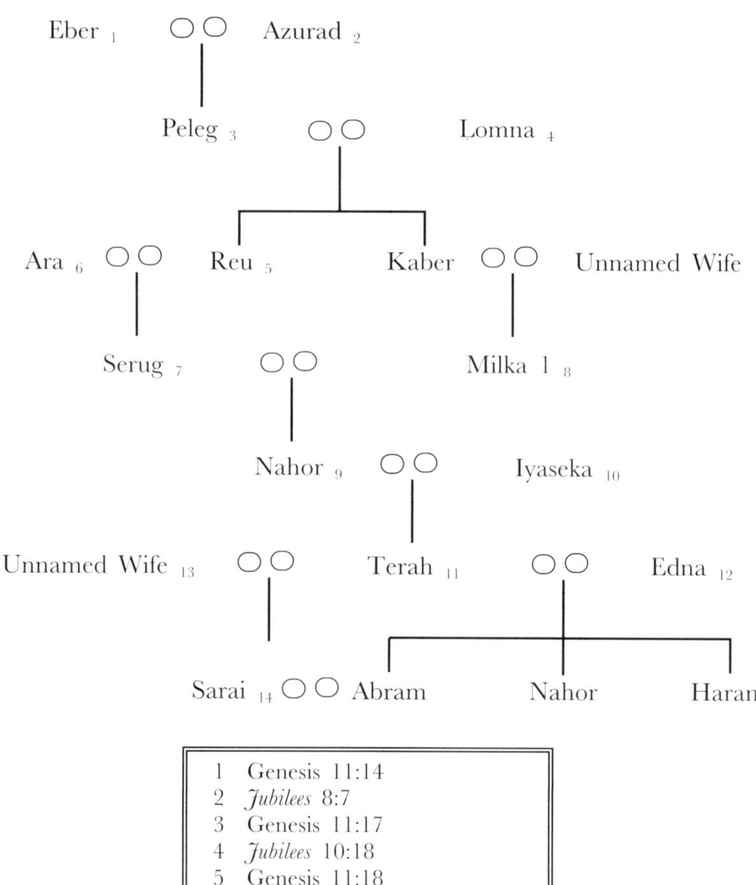

1	Genesis 11:14	
2	*Jubilees* 8:7	
3	Genesis 11:17	
4	*Jubilees* 10:18	
5	Genesis 11:18	
6	*Jubilees* 11:1	
7	Genesis 11:20	
8	*Jubilees* 11:7	
9	Genesis 11:22	
10	*Jubilees* 11:9	
11	Genesis 11:24	*Jubilees* 11:10
12	Genesis 11:26	*Jubilees* 11:14
13	Genesis 20:12	*Jubilees* 12:9
14	Genesis 11:29 31	

FROM NAHOR TO AMRAM

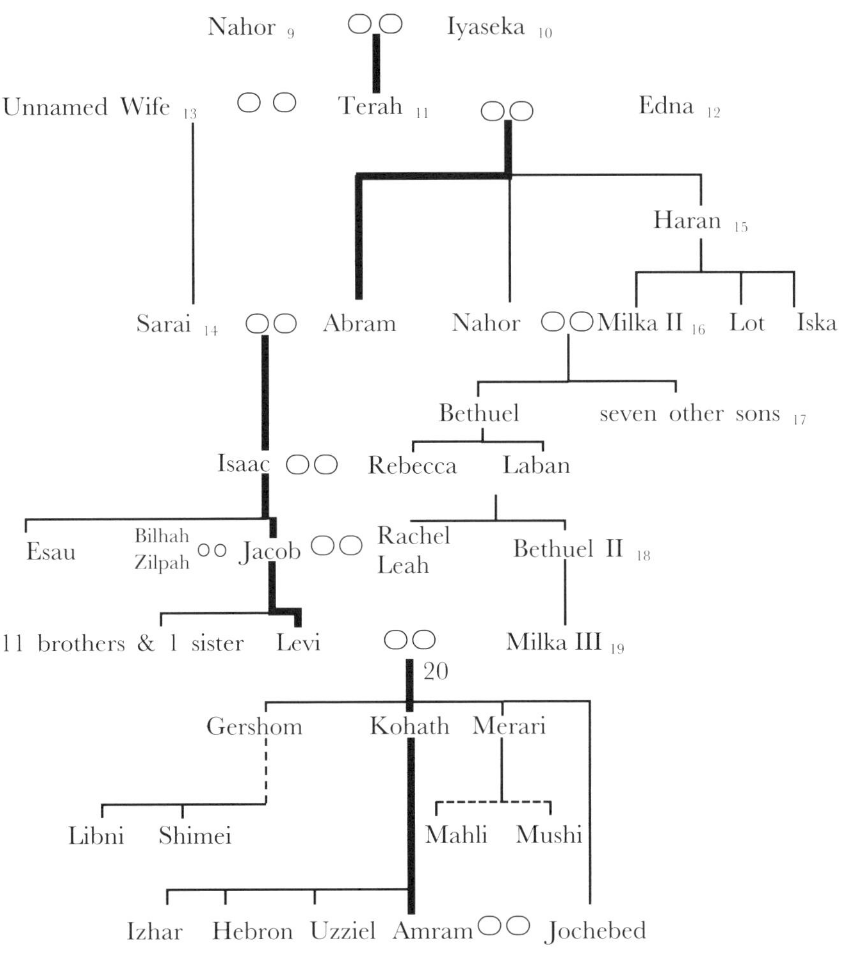

9	Genesis 11:22
10	*Jubilees* 11:9
11	Genesis 11:24 *Jubilees* 11:10
12	Genesis 11:26 *Jubilees* 11:14
13	Genesis 20:12 *Jubilees* 12:9
14	Genesis 11:29 31
15	Genesis 11:27 *Jubilees* 12:10
16	Genesis 11:29 *Jubilees* 12:10
17	Genesis 22:20–22
18	*ALD* 11:1
19	*ALD* 11:1
19	*ALD* 11:1 *Jubilees* 34:20
20	Genesis 46:11

in Exodus 2:22 and 18:3. There we read, כי אמר גר הייתי בארץ נכריה "for he said, 'I have been a stranger in a foreign land'." *ALD*, therefore, drew the etymology from Gershom son of Moses and applied it to Gershom son of Levi. To make this transition, the verb tense was changed from the past to the prediction's future. The word πάροικος for גר is to be found in the LXX of both texts in Exodus, in *ALD* here, and in the LXX of Genesis 15:13. Indeed, this is a common translation of גר in the LXX. The etymology is probably made from the Hebrew גר and not from Aramaic, for in Exodus גר is rendered דייר by Targum Onqelos and דייר ותותב by Targum Neofiti. Below, in the study of the etymologies of Kohath, Merari and Jochebed, we will note the doubling of some etymologies and their further repetition in a Hebraized form at the end of the Aramaic etymology proper.

We have translated the unclear words ὡς τούτῳ as "now", following LSJ οὗτος VIII.7. The sense seems to be that Levi and his family are sojourners in the land which is to be theirs. It was understood thus in *TPL* 11:2 ὅτι ἐν τῇ γῇ ἡμῶν πάροικοι ἦμεν· Γηρσὰμ γὰρ παροικία γράφεται "for we were sojourners in our land; for Gershom means sojourning".

Commentary on 11:3

καὶ ἐπὶ τοῦ παιδαρίου εἶδον ἐγὼ ἐν τῷ ὁράματί μου ὅτι ἐκβεβλημένος ἔσται αὐτὸς καὶ τὸ σπέρμα αὐτοῦ ἀπὸ τῆς ἀρχῆς ἱερωσύνης {ἔσται τὸ σπέρμα αὐτοῦ} "And concerning the youth, I saw in my dream that he and his seed will be cast out of the highpriesthood."—This might be regarded as another explanation of the name, in a dream form and not as an etymology, yet it is difficult to see quite how. The function of the verse is to explain (or justify) the selection of the descendants of Levi's second son, Kohath, as the high-priestly line rather than those of his eldest son, Gershom. This explanation was taken up by *TPL* 11:2, which says, "And I saw concerning him that he would not be in the first rank".[247]

The difficult reference to the removal of the Gershomites from the high-priesthood might refer to the story in Judges 18:30 about

[247] Hollander and de Jonge, 1985, 163 think this is more relevant to Kohath, Levi's second son.

Jonathan son of Gerson (Gershom) son of Manasseh who set up idols for the Danites and whose family were priests to the Danites until the captivity of the land. In the text of Judges,[248] Gerson the father of Jonathan is said to be son of Manasseh (ויהונתן בן גרשם בן מנשה). Gerson son of Manasseh might have been confused with Gershom son of Moses and again with Gershom son of Levi, or else have been assumed to be a descendant of Gershom son of Levi because of his name and his family's priestly function. The removal of the Manassid Gersonites (Gershomites) from the High Priesthood might then have been the result of the Babylonian exile and the post-exilic dominance of the Kohathites.

Commentary on 11:4

כזמ̇[נא—There were some words following this conjecture, presumably corresponding to ἐπὶ δυσμάς ἡλίου (see variants to 11:5). It is tempting to relate כזמ̇[נא to κατὰ τὸν καιρόν in 11:5, but that would imply a very different word order from the one reflected by the Greek and the surviving Aramaic. That, of course, is possible.

Commentary on 11:5–7

There are a number of small lacunae in the Aramaic manuscript in these verses. In the lacuna in line 7 (11:6) the Greek has a longer text than could have fitted into the Aramaic manuscript. It reads αὐτὸς καὶ τὸ σπέρμα αὐτοῦ ἔσονται ἀρχὴ βασιλέων, ἱεράτευμα τῷ Ἰσραήλ "he and his seed will be a beginning (*or*: source, etc.) of kings, a priesthood for Israel." This may have been lost by parablepsis in Aramaic.

Commentary on 11:5

Puech reconstrusts the lacunose first part of the Geniza line together with the following, using a different word order to those of the extant Aramaic and Greek. As we have remarked in the commentary on 11:4 and 11:5–7, as far as can be told, the extant Aramaic and the Greek texts differ in this section. Puech's reconstruction is:

---

[248] The reading "Moses" is witnessed by the LXX as well as in some other ancient versions: see Moore, 1895, 401–402. The rabbinic explanation for it can be found in *b. Baba Bathra* 109b. For another explanation see Weitzman, 1999.

3 [והו]ה כזמ[נא חזה לנשין והות]ע̊[מ]ה̊
4 [וה]ר̊ת עוד[מני וילידת לי בר] א̊ח̊ר̊ן̊

3 [And it] was at the t[ime fitting for women, and I was] w[ith] her
4 [And she] conceived again[from me and bore me] another [son].

His reading [בר] א̊ח̊ר̊ן̊ is uncertain, but attractive, and these words do not occur at all in the Greek text.[249] Despite that, with some reservations we have taken the reading א̊ח̊ר̊ן̊ "another" into the text here. Not a single letter of the word is unmistakably preserved. Puech may have divined the overall sense of the phrase, but his actual restoration of the lost text is quite hypothetical.[250]

κατὰ τὸν καιρὸν τὸν καθήκοντα τῶν γυναικῶν "according to the proper time of women"—These words stress the absolute properness and regularity of Kohath's birth.[251]

Commentary on 11:6–7

The name midrash of Kohath offers two explanations of his name:

1. That to him would be "an assembly of all [the people and that]" he would have the high priesthood. It should be observed that Aramaic לה תהוה could be translated "he would have". The Greek translation is ἐπ' αὐτῷ.
2. He and his seed will be the beginning of kings, a priesthood for Israel. This explanation survives in Greek only, but is probably original. It may or may not have been a Hebrew gloss, as is found in the onomastic midrashim of Merari and Jochebed. The antiquity of this double explanation is confirmed by *TPL* 11:5–6 as is explained below.[252]

Why was Kohath called "assembly of all [the people]?" Greenfield and Stone observed that *ALD* is exegeting the name Kohath using

[249] Puech, 2002, 535.

[250] See Puech, 2002, 536 who speaks with more confidence than the actual textual remains warrant.

[251] See 2 Kings 4:16 למועד הזה כעת חיה "[a]t this season, in due time", translated by Targum Jonathan as לזמנא הדין כעדן דאתון קיימין "At this time, about the time that you are living". The expression recurs in Genesis 18:10, 18:14 and 2 Kings 4:16–17, all of divinely ordained births, and in no other biblical context.

[252] Note the double explanation of Benjamin in Genesis 35:18 and perhaps also Genesis 49:8 and 49:19. Hultgård's discussion of this passage is unclear (1982, 2.103).

the verb יקהת from Genesis 49:10, where it occurs in Jacob's blessing of Judah: "The scepter shall not depart from Judah, nor the ruler's staff from between his feet, until tribute (שילה) comes to him; and the obedience of the peoples is his (לו יקהת עמים)."[253] The Hebrew of the last phrase has been taken differently in the past and many sources understand יקהת as a verb, meaning "gather, assemble" or a noun meaning "gathering" or "assembly". So Aquila to Genesis 49:10 who translates σύστημα λαῶν "assembly of nations": cf. 4QCommGen A (4Q252) 5:6 which reads:]כנסת אנשי "assembly of men[".[254] In *Genesis rabba* 99:8 we read: מי שאומות העולם מתקהלין עליו "the one to whom the nations of the world (i.e., the Gentiles) assemble".[255] This interpretation of יקהת depends on a popular etymology deriving from the roots קו״י or קה״ל.[256] It should be observed that in Genesis 35:11 the words קהל גוים יהיה ממך "a company of nations shall come from you" are translated by Targum Onqelos as וכנשת שבטין יהון מנך "and an assembly of tribes shall come from you" and in Deuteronomy 33:5 בהתאסף ראשי עם "when the leaders of the people assemble (RSV)" is translated by Onqelos as באתכנשות רישי עמא, using the same terminology. Thus the expressions in *ALD* and in 4Q252 resound in the language used by the Targum for an assembly of peoples.[257] A person to whom the nations assembled had royal connections, as is already explicit in the Genesis 35:11b "and kings shall spring from you". Since *ALD* attributes to Kohath exactly the same etymological tradition that other sources attribute to יקהת in Genesis 49:10, we may infer that the author of *ALD* saw a relationship between the two words. This etymological tradition was ancient, since it is witnessed not only by Aquila, but by *ALD* which is of the third century BCE.

In addition, the Geniza manuscript has a lacuna following כנשת כל "an assembly of all". Charles restored [עמא ודי] "[the people and]" and observes that παντὸς τοῦ λαοῦ in the Greek supports his

[253] Greenfield and Stone, 1979, 223–24.

[254] Brooke, DJD 22, 205.

[255] Theodor and Albeck, 1965, 3.1280. This interpretation is derived from לישנא אחרינא, probably an addition to *Genesis rabba* taken mainly from the *Tanḥuma*, see *Tanḥuma wayeḥi* 10 and parallels.

[256] Greenfield and Stone, 1979, 237; Stone, 1999, 134.

[257] Schorch, 1997, 78–81 points to a Samaritan Targum manuscript that translates יקהת as כנש. He proposes that behind these interpretations is a Hebrew word קהת "gather" that is preserved in Samaritan Hebrew. This word is the background of the Kohath etymology.

restoration. In the corresponding place in *TPL* 11:5 we read ἐν ὑψηλοῖς ἵστατο πάσης τῆς συναγωγῆς "he was standing on high in the midst of all the congregation". We may thus conclude that *ALD* not only connects the two words Kohath and יקהת, but relates the whole of Genesis 49:10 to Kohath.

Genesis 49:10 was understood eschatologically in the Second Temple period, and taken to refer to the Judahite or Israelite messiah. Thus, the very transfer of the etymology together with the latter part of the verse shows that *ALD* attributed to Levi the messianic prophecy which was originally pronounced about Judah.[258]

The ensuing words in *ALD* are וד]י לה תהוה כהנותא רבתא "and that] he would have the high-priesthood" which are in Greek ἐπ 'αὐτοῦ ἔσται ἡ ἀρχιερωσύνη ἡ μεγάλη.[259] Here in the Greek translation we read the following words which are not found in the Aramaic of *ALD*: αὐτὸς καὶ τὸ σπέρμα αὐτοῦ ἔσονται ἀρχὴ βασιλέων ἱεράτευμα τῷ Ἰσραήλ "he and his seed will be the beginning (*or*: authority) of kings, priesthood (*or*: sanctity) for Israel."[260] We suggest that these words are not an addition by the Greek translator, but existed originally in Aramaic and are missing from the Geniza manuscript. This is clear when we compare them with *TPL* 11:5–6, "and I saw in a vision that he was standing on high in the midst of the congregation; therefore I called his name Kaath, which is the first place of greatness and instruction".[261] The comparison of the phrase preserved only in the Greek translation of *ALD* with *TPL* 11:5–6 leads to the following conclusions:

1. *ALD* simply reads "and I saw" while in *TPL* the vision is more developed. It is unclear whether the expression in *ALD* refers to a symbolic vision (not preserved), or serves simply to add authority to what follows: compare 11:3. The editor of *TPL* thought that a symbolic vision was being described, yet he could find none such in his source. Therefore, he himself composed a suitable vision and added an interpretation to it, as is usual in apocalyptic visions.

[258] In 4Q252 5:5 (Brooke, DJD 22, 205) we have the unambiguous exegesis of the first part of Genesis 49:10 of a Davidic messiah.

[259] Observe the inconsistency of spelling of כהנותא here and כהונתא in 5:4.

[260] The word ἱεράτευμα serves in the LXX to translate כהנים "priests" in ממלכת כהנים "a kingdom of priests" in Exodus 19:6. It does not occur in *TPL*. On ἀρχή see Stone, 1999, 134. One might also translate ἀρχή here as "the chief".

[261] Hollander and de Jonge, 1985, 161.

2. According to *TPL*, in a vision Kohath stood on a height, which is explained as "the first place of greatness and instruction". This expression does not occur in *ALD* and it was derived from ἀρχή in the Greek translation of *ALD*,[262] which was supplied with a visual realization by the editor of *TPL*, as a high place upon which Kohath was standing. Equally, the "assembly of peoples" was transferred from the name midrash in *ALD* and made part of the content of the vision in *TPL*.

3. The word ἀρχή in the Greek translation of *ALD* is reflected twice in *TPL*. First, in the high place, as we have just explained, and for a second time in the interpretation of the dream, where the height is said to mean that Kohath is ἀρχὴ μεγαλείου καὶ συμβιβασμός "the first place of greatness and instruction". The idea of instruction comes from Deuteronomy 33:10 and is probably a reference to the Levitical teaching function.[263]

This analysis shows that the expression that survives only in the Greek of *ALD* was most probably original, and was certainly in the Greek text that served the editor/author of *TPL*.

In the Greek translation of *ALD*, we find βασιλέων "of kings", corresponding to which *TPL* has the word μεγαλείου. This Hollander and de Jonge translate "majesty", but we prefer the more literal "greatness". Perhaps their translation is influenced by *ALD*. Indeed, we should understand "greatness" to be an expression softening "of kings" found in *ALD*. "Of kings" in *ALD* results from the author's view which attached royal messianic attributes to the house of Levi. This seemed odd to the editor/author of *TPL* who did not understand the relationship between Levi and the royal messiah.[264]

From the use of Genesis 49:10 in Kohath's name midrash, it emerges very clearly that *ALD* applied Israelite messianic language

[262] The word μεγαλείου may go back to an Aramaic derived from רב"י which can also mean "anointing". This is, however, purely speculative. The text of *TPL*, therefore, shows that its author/redactor had ἀρχή before him.

[263] It is possible that elevation was part of the installation of a king, see 2 Kings 11:14 (Athaliah upon a pillar) and 2 Kings 9:13 (Jehu goes up steps where he is proclaimed king). The evidence is not strong enough to establish that such a custom existed, but merely to suggest the possibility; compare steps up to thrones in 1 Kings 10:19 || 2 Chronicles 9:18.

[264] They are also held apart in Jacob's blessing according to *Jubilees* 31:13–20. The royal role of Judah is represented (see v. 20); however, in v. 15 it does say of Levi, "And they shall be judges and princes and chief of all the descendants of Jacob's sons". See VanderKam, 1999, 507–09.

to the Priestly-Levitical messiah. This is particularly striking in view of the frequent references to the dual figures, Judah and Levi, in *Testaments of the Twelve Patriarchs*. Thus, *ALD* takes an extreme and unusual position in this matter and tends to attribute to Levi language drawn from the royal context (see our remarks above concerning Genesis 35:11 and Deuteronomy 33:5). This is further discussed in the Introduction, "Levi's Special Role in *ALD*".

Other examples expressing this view may be found in *ALD*. Thus in the 1QLevi frag. 1 we read: לב[ניך מלכות כהנותא רבא מן מלכותׄ] "to your so]ns kingdom of high-priesthood is greater than the kingdom[". Similarly in *ALD* 13:16 (4QLevi[a] 1–2 2:15–16) we find:]אׄף כהנין ומלכין [. . .]ןׄ מלכותכן "]even priests and kings [. . .] your kingdom".

Commentary on 11:6

At the beginning of this verse the Greek translation reads ὅτε ἐγεννήθη, following the initial καί. The *waw* is reconstructed in Aramaic.

Charles contrasts the verse with *Jubilees* 21:2, where Abraham conveys the commandments to Isaac, while in *TPL* 9:6 Isaac passes them on to Levi. Here the stress is on the transmission of the priestly teaching, and this is highlighted even more in the form of text preserved in Greek.[265]

כל[עמא וד]י "of all [the people and that]"—This is in accordance with the Greek.

Commentary on 11:7

לחיי "of my life"—This word is omitted from Greek.

קמ]אה "first"—This form, reconstructed in the Geniza manuscript, has a late orthography. See *Jubilees* 28:14 where the date of Levi's birth is given thus: "Jacob again went in to Leah. She became pregnant and gave birth to a third son for him. He named him Levi on the first of the first month during the sixth year of this week". So *Jubilees* sets Levi's naming, and perhaps his birth, on the same date that *ALD* assigns to Kohath's birth.

[265] See Stone, 1999, 133–149.

THE DATES OF THE BIRTH OF THE CHILDREN OF LEVI

Verse	Name	Month	Day	Hour
11:4	Gershom	10	–	evening
11:7	Kohath	1	1	morning
11:9	Merari	3	–	–
11:11	Jochebed	7	1	–

The dates *ALD* gives for the birth of Levi's children are far more detailed than in *TPL*.[266] Although they are not consistently full, as may be observed in the above Table, it seems likely that they were reckoned by a calendar resembling 364–day calendar found in *Jubilees* (6:32), and *1 Enoch* 74:12, 11QPs[a] 27:4–6 and 4QMMT (4Q394 3–7 1:2–3). First, as typical of that calendar, the months are numbered, not named. Second, three of the four children were born at exact three-monthly intervals; Gershom in the tenth, Kohath in the first and Jochebed in the seventh. By the 364–day calendar, the months are identical in the coincidence of dates and days of the week in a three-month cycle. Moreover, in the two cases in which dates are given, they are the first of the month—Wednesday. Some decades ago, Jaubert pointed out that in works written according to this calendar, a predominant number of important events occur on Wednesday.[267] It is noteworthy, finally, that the most important of Levi's sons, Kohath, from whom the high-priestly line sprang, was born (and perhaps named) on the first day of the first month of the year. It is surely no coincidence that according to *Jubilees* 28:14 Levi himself was born on the same date, the first day of the first month.[268] Since the cycle starts with Kohath, perhaps it ends with Gershom who was born in the evening of the first day of the tenth month.[269] The only problematic date is that of Merari, the first day of the third month. Nevertheless, the parallel text 4QLevi[c] reads יעא[, which

[266] See *Yalqut Shimʿoni* Shemot, 162 on the dates of birth of the sons of Jacob.

[267] Jaubert, 1953.

[268] The same birth date for Levi is given in *Midrash Tadšē* viii (ed. Epstein, 1957, 151). An examination of *Jubilees* shows that many portentous events took place on this date: see 6:25 (Noah's ark), 13:8 (altar built by Abraham), 24:22 (Isaac's vision and altar built) and 27:19 (Jacob's vision).

[269] This paragraph is based on Greenfield and Stone, 1979, 224–25. On the start of the day at Qumran, see Talmon and Ben-Dov, DJD 21, 1–36, 46–48; Albani, 1992, 3–47.

might be reconstructed as רב]יעא, "fourth". If this reconstruction is accepted, the Qumran manuscript may preserve all four dates at exact three monthly intervals. It is worth noting that Joseph was born, according to *Jubilees* 38:24 "on the first of the fourth month".[270]

Commentary on 11:8

ועוד—This word is a Hebraism and it is not reflected separately in the translation: see 8:2.

καὶ ἐν γαστρὶ ἔλαβεν "and she conceived"—These words are missing from the Aramaic text. Grelot thinks we should restore them, cf. 11:10.[271]

תליתי "third"—There is a small hole in the parchment at this point. The crack above it suggests that the parchment has shrunk somewhat. Charles proposes restoring a *waw* in the hole and then regarding it as secondary. We cannot see any sign of the *waw* and so read as above.[272]

מררי "Merari"—A triple onomastic midrash is offered for this name:

> a. For I was bitter on his account particularly, for when he was born he was dying.
> b. And I was very bitter on his account since he was about to die, and I implored and beseeched on his account.
> c. And there was bitterness in everything.

P. Grelot was of the opinion that *ALD* is translated from Hebrew.[273] As one of his proofs he uses the fact that here one finds the word מר which is Hebraism, based on Ruth 1:13 כי מר לי "for . . . bitter for me", where the Targum reads ארום מריר לי. Biblical scholars usually explain the name Merari as meaning "strong".[274] *ALD*, however, relates מררי to the root מר״ר "bitter". Thus in Hebrew the *peʿal*

[270] Joseph was also born on the same date as Levi here, according to *Midrash Tadšē* viii (ed. Epstein, 1957, 151): "Joseph was born on the first of the first month . . ."; see Charles, 1902, 170–72.

[271] Compare Grelot, 1955, 92.

[272] Charles, 1908a, 253.

[273] Grelot, 1955.

[274] Köhler and Baumgartner, 1995, 1.639. In Ugaritic *mrr* means "strengthen, bless".

means "to be bitter" and the *pi'el* means "to make bitter".[275] The meaning "bitterness" for the noun or "bitter" for the adjective, is found in Royal Aramaic (Aḥiqar line 89).[276] Thus the name midrash of Merari in *ALD* could have originated either in Hebrew or in Aramaic and was presumably equally understood by speakers of both languages. However, the first etymology מר לי "I was bitter" is a Hebraism, perhaps dependent on Ruth,[277] while the second והווה מריר לי is Aramaic. Moreover, the first two name midrashim on Merari are different formulations of the same etymology. An equivalent midrash on the same name is found in *TPL* 11:7 "and since his mother gave birth with difficulty, she called him Merari, which is my bitterness, for also he died". Note that in *TPL* the possessive suffix is exegeted explicitly ("my bitterness"), while in *ALD* its exegesis is only implicit.

עלוהי "on his account"—Greek breaks off here. In the Aramaic, two back slashes occur to fill a short line, as may be seen elsewhere in the manuscript.

לחדה "particularly"—Grelot was of the opinion that this is a Jewish Aramaic form, as can be found in the Targum to Genesis 1:31, 17:20 and Psalm 119:8[278] and Kutscher also observed that it is found in various Targums.[279] It occurs three times in the Genesis Apocryphon (13:15; 20:33 and 22:32), as well as in other Aramaic texts from Qumran (e.g. 4QTob[b] [4Q197] 4 2:1, 4Q544 1:2, as both לחדא and לחדה). It also occurs in Christian Palestinian Aramaic.[280] The corresponding form סגיא is equally found in Palestinian Aramaic and occurs in the second, almost synonymous etymology in this verse.

הוא מית "about to die"—Compare Genesis 35:18.[281]

[275] Compare the derivative nouns מרור (grapes) and מרורים (bitter herb and bitter drinks).

[276] The verb "to make bitter" and the noun "bitterness" are known also later in Palestinian Aramaic: Sokoloff, 1990, 332.

[277] Grelot, 1955, 93.

[278] Lévi, 1907, 178, note 1 states that A.E. Cowley was of the opinion that this word originates in Syriac, while its parallel in the next name midrash, סגיא is Aramaic. This is also Grelot's view, 1955, 93.

[279] Kutscher, 1958, 12, note 54.

[280] See Sokoloff, 1990, 280.

[281] Grelot, 1955, 93–94.

התחננת "beseeched"—An *ʾitpeʿal* form.[282] The same expression occurs in 1QapGen 20:12 (אתחננת).

והיה בכל מרר "and there was bitterness in everything"—This third etymology is a Hebrew gloss following the two basically Aramaic name midrashim. It changes the subject from Levi to the general situation and its exact meaning is unclear. A similar Hebrew gloss is found in the midrash of the name "Jochebed" below.[283]

Commentary on 11:10

הויתי "I was"—Compare this orthography with הוית in *ALD* 11:8 and with שוית in the continuation of this verse.

עמהא "with her"—With this orthography, compare שמהא later in this verse and קניהא in 13:10.

ושויתי שמהא "I named her"—Grelot says that this is a Hebraism going back to ושמתי שמה (see Judges 8:31, Nehemiah 9:7 and Daniel 1:7) and he points to uniqueness of ושויתי שמהא in 11:10.[284] Here the expression has some support in Greek ἐκάλεσα. Note that in 12:4 we have וקריתי "I called" with the same meaning.

וילידת "and bore"—This could be translated as "and has borne".

כדי ילידת לי ליקר ילידת לי לכבוד לישראל "when she was born to me, 'For glory was she born to me, for glory for Israel'."—Here we have a repetition of the same phrase, once in Aramaic and once in Hebrew, the latter with an addition "for Israel" (see below). It is worth noting that the Hebrew comes at the end of this double etymology and the Aramaic at the beginning. We propose that the Hebrew was a gloss that was included in the etymology, and we have already observed similar glosses occurred with Merari and apparently with Gershom.

The actual midrash involves a Hebrew word, כבוד and not an Aramaic one. This served Grelot to support his view that *ALD* was

[282] Sokoloff 1990, 209.
[283] See Milik, 1976, 214–15, on triple etymologies.
[284] Grelot, 1955, 95.

originally composed in Hebrew and he suggests the following development in Aramaic. The original text read:

<ארי> אמרת כדי ילידת לי (. . .) ילידת (. . .) לכבוד לישראל

He thinks that (a) ליקר, a marginal gloss, translating לכבוד, was intruded at the wrong place; (b) לי then entered the text after the second occurrence of ילידת.[285]

We propose that the midrash was either drawn from an earlier source, or that a literate Jew of the third century BCE could have written יקר for Hebrew כבוד.[286] We also observe that the glossator read לי as an abbreviation for לישראל "for Israel" which shows that the Hebrew phrase is a secondary gloss. In *TPL* 11:8 the second etymology is not represented and the first one is paraphrased as "For I was renowned then in the midst of my brothers".

In the Bible, Jochebed is mentioned as the mother of Moses and Aaron (Exodus 6:20), thus being Amram's aunt. Only later is she referred to as בת לוי אשר ילדה אתה ללוי במצרים "a daughter of Levi who was born to Levi in Egypt" (Numbers 26:59). The tradition adduced here in *ALD*, that Levi was 64 when she was born, that is sixteen years after they came to Egypt, contradicts the rabbinic view, first found in *Genesis rabba* 94:9: יוכבד עיבורה בארץ כנען ולידתה בארץ מצרים . . . על פילי שלמצרים נולדה, "Jochebed was conceived in the land of Canaan and born in the land of Egypt. . . . She was born in the gates of Egypt."[287] The same calculation is the basis of *4QVisions of Amram* (4Q543 1 a–c:2–4). That text reads: ודי פקד̇ א̇נון ב]יום מותה (?) בשנת מאה] ו̊תלתין ושת היא ש̊נ̇ת̇א די[. . . בשנת מאה] וחמישין ו̊ת̊רתין לנ̊]לות י]ש̊[ר]אל למ̊[צרי]ן̊. . . "which he commanded them on [the day of his death (?) in the one hundred] and thirty-sixth year, that is the the year that [. . . in the hundred] and fifty-second year of the ex[ile of I]s[ra]el to E[gyp]t . . ." Therefore, Amram died at the age of 136, which is 152 years of the Egyptian exile. In other words, he was born sixteen years after they entered Egypt.[288]

In rabbinic literature, the only onomastic midrash relating to Levi's three sons is in the late collection שכל טוב (*Sekel Tob*), compiled in

[285] Grelot, 1955, 95.

[286] Milik, 1976, 214 thinks that the use of Hebrew etymologies here, as well as some that he discerns in *1 Enoch*, is deliberate. He also opposes Grelot's view.

[287] Theodor and Albeck, 1965, 3.1180.

[288] DJD 31, 292–93; Wise, 1997, 23–24.

Rome at the end of the twelve century. This work includes aggadic traditions on the books of Genesis and Exodus, mainly based on earlier rabbinic sources. The author gives etymologies for Jacob's grandsons. For Levi's sons the text reads:[289]

> בני לוי גרשון. מתגורר זרעו בעבודת בית אלוהיו ושינה בהלכותיהן. קהת. הנקווה ומצוי לעבודת הקודש, ודומה לו ולו יקהת עמים (בראשית מט י). ומררי. על שם מרות וגדולה.
>
> The sons of Levi. Gershon: his seed dwells (מתגורר) in the service of the house of his God and changed (שינה) their halachot. Kohath: the one who is gathered in (נקווה) and present for the holy service, and ולו יקהת עמים (Genesis 49:10) resembles it. And Merari: because of lordship (מרות) and greatness.

It is intriguing that there is a negative element in the Gershom etymology, which is comparable to our comments on 11:2–3. As for Kohath, *Sekel Tob* observed the similarity to יקהת, but made nothing of it. Merari is derived from a different but graphically similar root.

Commentary on 11:11

In this verse the birth of Jochebed is set in Levi's sixty-fourth year, on the first day of the seventh month, after Levi's descent into Egypt. According to 12:8, Levi entered Egypt at the age of 48.[290] According to 12:3 Amram married Jochebed in Levi's 94th year, that is, when she was thirty years old. In 12:5 the text adds that Amram and Jochebed were born on the same day, the first day of the seventh month (11:11), so we may infer that they were both exactly 30 when they were married. In many sources, it is stated that Adam and Eve were 30 years old when they first had intercourse and begat a child.[291] In *Visions of Amram* (4Q545) 1a:5–6 when Miriam was thirty she married Uzziel, her uncle (and see 6:4 commentary). Thus, it is possible that 30 was considered an ideal age. The chronological calculation of *ALD* resembles that of *Biblical Chronology* (4Q559) 2:5–9, even though that text is largely restored.[292]

[289] Buber, 1964, 290.

[290] *TPL* 12:5 says that Levi was 40 when he entered Egypt: compare *Jubilees* 45:1 and see Table below.

[291] See Stone, 1996, 92 and many references there.

[292] ". . . And Jacob was] sixty-five y[ears old when he fathered Levi.] . . . And Levi was thirty-f]ive when he fa[thered Kohath. And Kohath was twenty-ni]ne

ALD 11:11 says that Levi was 64 at the birth of Jochebed. Because Jochebed and Amram were born on the same day, Levi was 64 when Amram was born. According to 4Q559 Levi was 35 when Kohath was born and Kohath was 29 when Amram was born, i.e., Levi was 64 when Amram was born.

חודשא "month"—This word occurs twice in Qumran Aramaic texts (see 1QapGen 12:14 and 4Q558 63:2), but it is probably Hebraism.[293]

when he fathered Am[r]am. And Amr[am was one hundred and twenty-three when he fathered Aaron. And Aaro[n] left Egy[pt . . ." Translation from Wise, 1997, 11. See Nebe, 1997, 86.

[293] That is the view of Grelot, 1955, 96.

Chapter 12: Levi's Grandchildren and Great-Grandchildren

Commentary on 12:1

After the story of the birth and naming of Levi's children, *ALD* and in its footsteps *TPL*, continue with the story of Levi's grandchildren and great-grandchildren. The first verse of *ALD* in this chapter is only partially preserved in the Geniza manuscript. The list of Levi's grandchildren includes the offspring of Gershom, Kohath and Merari. Note that according to it, Merari was not dead, apparently contradicting the phrase in his name midrash in *ALD* 11:8, "he was dying".[294]

ALD 12:1 refers to the fact that Levi's sons Gershom, Kohath and Merari married his brothers' daughters. Moreover, Levi himself married the granddaughter of his maternal uncle while his daughter Jochebed married her fraternal nephew. Thus endogamy is rife in the priestly genealogy.

[ה]עֲלינה "we [en]tered"—We have chosen to translate thus, cf. 11:11 (though reconstructed), 12:6 and 12:8. Alternatively, take it as "He (God) brought us in". However, in *ALD* we do not have any such cases and the verb's intransitive meaning is well established in the verses we cited. In content, this verse corresponds to Genesis 46:28 where we read ויבאו ארצה גשן "so when they came to the land of Goshen": so also the Targums.[295]

[נסבת נשין מ]ן̊ "[I took wives] from"—This reconstruction and reading of Puech is attractive although, of course, נסבת נשין "I took wives" is pure conjecture.[296]

לעדן "at the time of"—The expressions לעידן or בעידן mean "at the time of".[297]

[294] This is taken somewhat differently in *TPL* 11:7, which reads, "for he also died".

[295] This phrase is omitted by the LXX and a number of daughter versions, and it is singular in *Jubilees* 45:1 (with rather different phraseology) and in Origenic Greek witnesses, as also Syrohexapla, Armenian, Vulgate, Syriac, etc.

[296] Puech, 2002, 538.

[297] The form עידן is found in Christian Palestinian Aramaic as well as in Samaritan Aramaic, see Sokoloff, 1990, 402–403.

אשויות "marriageability"—This word is obscure. From the context it does not seem to be related to Biblical Aramaic אשיא from אוש, meaning "foundation" (Ezra 4:12),[298] which also occurs in other dialects.[299] On the basis of the context, it means something like "at the time of the sexual maturity/marriageability of their sons", but it is nowhere attested except here. We relate it to the root שו"י "to put, place" or "to agree"[300] in the *ʾafʿel* and propose that the form here is corrupt.[301] The *ʾafʿel* occurs in a document of apportionment of slaves from Elephantine reading אנחנה אשתוין כחדה ופלגן עלין "we were equal as one (owned jointly) and divided (between) us" (lines 2–3).[302]

In his study of the Hebrew form שווה in the Piyyut and Midrash, Yalon describes one of its meanings as "proximity, connection".[303] We view this evidence, therefore, as supporting the contextual interpretation of לעידן אשויות to mean "to the proper time for marriage" proposed above.[304]

זׄמניהון "of their times"—Puech, following Charles, reads the first sign as ז. This is possible but not completely certain. Our initial tendency was to read בׄניהון "of their sons".[305] Neither reading makes any

[298] This is a Sumerian loan word in Akkadian: Kaufman, 1974, 100.

[299] See Sokoloff, 1990, 78; Sokoloff, 2000, 84. Even less probably, might it be a corrupted form of אשון, found in Proverbs 20:20 באישון חשך (*qrē* באשון) meaning "time, season", another loan-word from Akkadian-Sumerian, known also from Jewish Aramaic. Yet, this does not yield a satisfactory sense either.

[300] Sokoloff, 1990, 540; Sokoloff, 2002, 1118.

[301] See *j. Demai* 2:1 (22c). We would like to express our thanks to M. Kister and S. Fassberg, whom we consulted concerning this form.

[302] Cowley no. 28; Porten and Yardeni, 1989, 48–51. The legal use of שו"י in the *ʾafʿel* also occurs in an eleventh century marriage contract found in Egypt, ואשוון ואתקנון בינהון בתנאי בית דינא "And they agreed and fixed between themselves the court stipulations". See Friedman, 1981, vol. 2, The *Ketubba* Texts, no. 1 line 21, pp. 8, 13, 25. See further *j. Ketuboth* 1:2 (25b); *j. Qiddushin* 3:4 (64a).

[303] לשון קרבה וחיבור: Yalon, 1971, 212–18.

[304] The phrase עדן אשויות is analogous to the biblical phrase עת דדים (Ezekiel 16:8) which signifies marriageable age as a criterion. Note that דדים is an abstract form, as probably is אשויות. Most ancient commentators interpret this as "time of redemption", but the Syriac has *zbnʾ dʿzrtʾ*. The word *ʿzrtʾ* means 'marriageable, of marriageable age' (Payne Smith, 1903, 409; cf. Qimḥi's commentary there.) Different explanations of this phrase are offered by Grelot, 1955, 98–99. They are not convincing.

[305] We abandon the reading מבניהון that was proposed in Greenfield and Stone, 1979, 225.

particular sense. זמן is close in meaning to the preceding עדן, but from the sentence structure this does not appear to be a doublet.[306]

Commentary on 12:2

The list of Levi's grandchildren originates in Exodus 6:16–19 and compare 1 Chronicles 6:2–4. The list is repeated in *TPL* 12:1–3, with some differences.[307]

Commentary on 12:3

In *ALD* and in *TPL* (12:4) the list of Levi's grandchildren is followed by the marriage between Amram and Jochebed, a sequence drawn from Exodus 6:19 and Numbers 26:59.[308] *ALD* gives Levi's age as 94 at the time of Amram's marriage. Moreover, it notes that Amram and Jochebed were born on the same day (see above).

Commentary on 12:4

עמרם2° "Amram"2°—The preceding words די עמרם "of Amram" seem otiose and have no structural parallel in the preceding onomastic midrashim (11:2, 11:5, 11:8 and 11:10). It is significant that it is Levi who named Amram, and not his father Kohath. This, together with the fact that Amram is the only grandson of Levi provided with an onomastic midrash, highlights the significance attached to his position in the priestly line. In fact, it is not Amram who will raise the people up from Egypt, but Amram's son Moses. This transfer is no different, however, than that in the prophecy delivered to Kohath in 11:6. That prophecy says that Kohath will receive the high priesthood, when actually his grandson Aaron received it. The position of the onomastic midrash, after Amram's marriage and not after his birth, is unparalleled in *ALD* or *TPL*.

ירים "will raise up"—This new reading explains the onomastic midrash. *Zohar*, Exodus 19a gives a similar name midrash for Amram, "Why was he called Amram? Because a people, higher than all the high ones, descended from him" (שיצא ממנו עם רם על כל רמים).[309]

[306] Puech, 2002, 538.

[307] Hollander and de Jonge, 1985, 164, observe that *TPL* uses the Septuagint forms of these names where they differ from the Semitic.

[308] So also Hollander and de Jonge, 1985, 164.

[309] Translation by Sperling, Simon and Levertoff, 1949, 3.61.

Commentary on 12:6–9

These verses summarize the chronology of events of Levi's life and supplement the dates given in the preceding chapter for the birth of Kohath (11:7), Jochebed (11:11) and in 13:1 for Levi's age at the time of Joseph's death. As we can see in the following table, these dates have some parallels.

CHRONOLOGY OF EVENTS OF LEVI'S LIFE

Event	*ALD*	*TPL*	Syriac
Entered Canaan	18 (12:6)	8 (12:5)[310]	8 (12:6)
Killed Shechem	18 (12:6)	18 (12:5)[311]	18 (12:6)
Became Priest	19 (12:7)	19 (12:5)	19 (12:7)
Married	28 (12:7)	28 (11:1)	28 (12:7)
Birth Gershom	30 (11:4)[312]		
Birth Kohath	34 (11:7)	35 (11:4)[313]	
Birth Merari	40 (11:9)	40 (11:7)	
Entered Egypt	48 (12:8)	40 (12:5)[314]	40 (12:8)
Birth Jochebed	64 (11:11)	64 (11:8)[315]	
Amram married Jochebed	94 (12:3)	94 (12:4)	
Joseph died	118 (13:1)	118 (12:7)	
Levi died	137 (12:9)	137 (19:4)	134 (12:8)
Sojourn in Egypt	89 (12:8)	97 (12:5)	90 (12:8)

From this table we can deduce the following:

1. With minor exceptions, the chronology of *ALD* and *TPL* are identical. The Syriac fragment is a paraphrase but is most likely based

[310] According to Demetrius the Chronographer, as quoted by Polyhistor, Levi was "ten years and six months" old (21:8): see Holladay, 1983, 73.

[311] According to Demetrius, Levi was "twenty years and six months old" (21:9).

[312] Survives only in Athos Greek: the Geniza is missing here.

[313] So also 4Q559, see above: on the reconstruction of these dates, see above, p. 189; Demetrius "sixty".

[314] According to Demetrius, Levi was fourty-three years old (21:7).

[315] So also 4Q559 2:7, see above: on the reconstruction of these dates, see above, p. 194.

on *TPL*, with some differences. While *TPL* and Syriac both set Levi's descent into Egypt when he was 40 (not 48, as *ALD*), *TPL* compensates for it by setting his sojourn in Egypt to 97 years, while Syriac has 90. Instead of extending Levi's sojourn in Egypt, it reduces Levi's age at his death to 134, against the biblical witness of 137 (Exodus 6:16).[316] *ALD* and *TPL* are clearly based on 137, though the figures are not quite accurate. In *Seder ʿolam* we read that Levi was 44 when they entered Egypt, "Joseph was 39 years old when our forefathers descended into Egypt and Levi was 44 years old" (2:35).[317]

2. *TPL* gives two dates for the Shechem incident. In 2:2 it says that Levi was "a young man of about twenty years of age". However, since this is an approximate date, it does not contradict the age of 18 in the chronological list in 12:6.

3. *TPL* and Syriac both set the date of Levi's entry into the land of Canaan at the age of 8, which seems to be a better reading than 18 of *ALD* 12:6.

4. Pierre Grelot, in a somewhat speculative article, argues that *ALD* and *TPL* here preserve part of an ancient priestly chronology and a genealogy which are both also partly preserved in priestly material in the Pentateuch. (See Exodus 12:40–41 and also Exodus 6:18–20, Numbers 3:19 and 26:57–59.) This is possible, of course, and the correlations he shows in the table on p. 389 are rather striking.[318] Yet his argument, as he himself admits, is not completely conclusive.[319]

בנין תל̊[יתאין] "third generation"—Literally "third sons", perhaps modelled on Joseph in Genesis 50:23: וירא יוסף לאפרים בני שלשים, translated by Targum Onqelos as: וחזא יוסף לאפרים בנין תליתאין "And Joseph saw children of the third generation of Ephraim", while Targum Neofiti reads: וחמא יוסף לאפרים בנין דר תליתאי, "and Joseph saw the sons of Ephraim, the third generation".

[316] Even then, the figures are not reconciled.
[317] Guggenheimer, 1998, 30–31.
[318] Grelot, 1971.
[319] Grelot, 1971, 392.

Chapter 13: Levi's Teaching—The Wisdom Poem

Technical Notes

Chapter 13 contains the Wisdom Poem and some subsequent parenetic text. The Geniza text comes to an end with the words מטמוריה ולא "hidden places and not . . ." in 13:12. 4QLevi[a] frag. 1 cols. 1–2 and frag. 2 overlap with part of the surviving Geniza text and continue with material which is not in the Geniza manuscript. Fragments of this passage also occur in 4QLevi[c] and 4QLevi[f], in some instances adding a few letters or words to the material surviving in 4QLevi[a].[320] Where Geniza and another witness survive, plain text is the Geniza manuscript and bold text is the other witness. After the end of the Geniza manuscript, plain text is 4QLevi[a], and text with an overbar or underlining is extant in one of the other two witnesses. Square brackets indicate lacunae in 4QLevi[a].

In the text following 13:11, we accept the reconstruction of Greenfield and Stone.[321] However, it should be noted that the text on the right, after line 6 of 4QLevi[a] frag. 1 col. 2, is not joined physically with the preceding. The best consecutive join is frag. 2 line 5 with frag. 1, col. 2, line 9.

In the Geniza manuscript, the top five lines of the column containing material belonging to the end of 13:6 and the beginning of 13:7 are lost except for a few letters. Some of this text is extant in 4QLevi[a], though some of the letters surviving in the Geniza manuscript seem to bear no obvious direct relationship with what survives in the Qumran manuscript and belong to the material missing from the end of 13:6 of the Geniza.

Finally, the text of the Qumran fragment seems to have been longer than that of the Geniza manuscript at this point and various possible reconstructions are discussed by Stone and Greenfield.[322] They showed that the text of 4QLevi[c] is a shorter recension than the other witnesses, and we may conclude that there were at least two recensions of *ALD*.[323]

[320] See Stone and Greenfield, DJD 22, 71.
[321] Stone and Greenfield, DJD 22, 13.
[322] Stone and Greenfield, DJD 22, 60.
[323] DJD 22, 60.

General Notes

Chapter 13 includes a long summons given by Levi to his children when his brother Joseph died, 19 years before he himself died. The last part, which is very fragmentary, resembles Isaac's blessing of Levi found in *Jubilees* 31:13–17. It is worth noting that the conjunction of ספר ומוסר חכמה "reading and writing and the teaching of wisdom" with the verb אלף "teach" occurs no less than three times in this chapter. It serves to distinguish between sections, in this respect functioning like וכען "and now" (13:4 and 13:15).

The Wisdom Poem 13:4–14

The poetic section in *ALD* is almost without parallel in Aramaic sources. The following chief parts may be distinguished in chapter 13:

13:2 Levi's summons to his children
13:3 The importance of righteousness and truth
13:4–14 Wisdom poem
13:15–16 A vision of the glorious future of Levi's descendants

The author was not a skilled poet and, although the passage is essentially poetic in form, at times the line between poetry and prose is unclear. However, he uses paired words and parallel phrases, devices known from earlier Aramaic poetry.[324] This is typical of poetry in the early Semitic languages, such as Akkadian, Ugaritic, and Hebrew. The latter part of 13:10 is less poetic in character. In general, we should observe the following main poetic pairs, those followed by (G) surviving only in the Geniza manuscript:

אוצר – מטמור
לבשרון – לשיטו
יקר – רבו
מוסר – חכמה
מת – מדינה
נכרי – כילי (G)
צדקתא – קשטא
ראשין – שפטין
שאלי שלמה – רחמוהי (G)

[324] Greenfield, 1979, 49–51.

שניאין – רברבין (G)
שמעו – אציתו (G)

There are a number of rare or unique lexemes in this text, mainly in the part preserved in 4QLevi[a]. Thus note שיטו (13:5), כילי (Geniza 13:8), בס"ר (13:5), מטמור (13:13) and מח"ל (תמחלו 13:7).

The collocation of elements in this poem, as far as it can be discerned from the fragments, resembles that in the first part of Proverbs 8. Thus the value of wisdom is stressed (cf. Proverbs 8:18–19); its relationship with kings and princes (Proverbs 8:15–16) and its treasures (Proverbs 8:21). 4Q525 titled *Beatitudes* also shares some features with this poem, e.g., in 2–3 2:9 it refers to the relationship with kings, saying:[325] ועטרת פז ז]הב [תשית על ראו]שו ועם מלכים תוש]יבהו "[and places a crown of g]old [upon] his he[ad], and with kings it shall se[at him]".[326]

A dominant image in this passage is wisdom as a city, particularly as a city that cannot be conquered or plundered. This image is rather unusual. Later in the text, wisdom is described as priceless: see 13:13 and commentary there.

In 13:15–16 the author returns to parenesis. This is clear from the second person suffixes in 13:16 (מלכותכן.. מנכן) and from the words כען בני (13:4 and 13:15).[327] This combination of elements is familiar. There is a reading in books (13:16) which is comparable to the numerous eschatological prophecies drawn in the *Testaments of the Twelve Patriarchs* from a putative "Book of Enoch". Such prophecies may be found in *TPL* at 10:5, 14:1 and 16:1. The third of these references introduces an eschatological prophecy which extends through *TPL* chapters 16–18.[328] The eschatological character of the Aramaic document is clear from 13:16 which read: ... ולא איתי סוף לע]למ ... ולא] תעבר מנכן עד כל ד]ריה ...]. ביקר רב "... and there is no end fo[r ever ...] will pass [not] from you until all in[habitants ...]. In great glory".

In addition to these features, in the same verse the combination

[325] As reconstructed by Puech, DJD 25, 122, 127.

[326] One should also compare this description with Wisdom of Solomon 6–11 describing wisdom, as well as with ben Sira 51. This description evokes those in 13:6 and 13:10.

[327] An comparable opening phrase, חזו לכן בני occurs in 13:6.

[328] Yet, no particular points of connection emerge between this eschatological prophecy and the fragmentary words surviving in the Aramaic document.

of "priests and kings" is to be noted, as well as the word מלכותכן "your (plural) kingdom". This important word is apparently addressed by Levi to his (priestly) offspring. This combination is to be found elsewhere, and is discussed in the Introduction above.[329]

A comparison between *ALD* 12:9–13:13 and *TPL* 12:6–13:7 reveals the relation between them. *TPL* is clearly based on *ALD*, but changes and modifies it. Of special interest is the change from "wisdom" in *ALD* 13:4–5 to "the law of God" in *TPL* 13:2–3.[330] This occurs several times in this passage, and arouses some surprise. If *TPL* is a Christian reworking of Jewish material, it remains difficult to understand why a Christian author/redactor would have replaced "wisdom" with "the law".[331]

In the wisdom poems in Baruch 3:36–4:1 and in ben Sira 24:23 the identification of wisdom with the Torah is a point strongly made, and it is implied in the earlier 11QPs[a] 18:12–15. Similarly, when we compare the text of 11QPs[a] 21–22 with the Syriac and Greek versions of ben Sira 51, in the praise of wisdom, we observe the same shift as between *ALD* and *TPL*. There the change from erotic love song to wisdom and then to Torah learning can be seen.[332] Hollander sets forth clearly that in *TPL* 13 Joseph is presented as a wise man, who gained his wisdom by obeying the Law, comparing also ben Sira 15:1–6, and particularly 15:1.[333] Despite this, there is no case in ben Sira where חוכמה is translated νόμος. In *ALD* 13:4–5 Aramaic חוכמה occurs and is rendered, as we noted, "law of God"

[329] See Introduction, section on "Levi's Special Role in *ALD*". See Greenfield and Stone, 1979, 223–24 and also the observation there concerning 5:2 (§9) on pp. 219–222. It is conceivable that some such statement, combining priesthood and royalty, stood behind *TPL* 8:14.

[330] See in detail below, commentary on 13:4.

[331] This observation was already made by Stone and Greenfield, DJD 22, 3; cf. de Jonge, 1999, 88–89. Although Christ is sometimes identified as wisdom in early Christian writing, this does not provide an explanation. V. Hillel points out that in *ALD* chapter 5 Levi learns the law of the priesthood, but in *TPL* 9:5–6 he first learns the law of the Lord (νόμος κυρίου) and then the law of the priesthood (9:7). The change in *TPL* from *ALD* fits with *TPatriarchs*' overall concern for the Law of God. See, for example, *TPNaphtali* 3:2, 8:7, *TPGad* 3:2, 4:7 and often elsewhere (oral communication). The way *TPatriarchs* understands the idea of Law demands separate discussion. It seems, however, that V. Hillel's point, based partly on de Jonge, 1999, 87–88, is well taken, and the shift from "wisdom" in *ALD* to "Law" in *TPL* is in line with the overall outlook of the author/redactor of *TPatriarchs*. In addition, see de Jonge, 1981, 513–523, and especially 516–18.

[332] Eshel, 2003, 44–50.

[333] Hollander, 1981, 60–61.

by *TPL* 13:2–3.[334] Moreover, Law is nowhere mentioned in *ALD*. Hollander makes the same point in his analysis of Joseph's role in the two works when he says

> in the Greek T. Levi 13 this connection between Joseph and wisdom has not been taken over from the original source. In contrast to ArLevi vv. 83–95, a passage which centres round truth and wisdom, the Greek T. Levi 13 emphasizes the role of God and makes wisdom evidently subordinate to it. Wisdom in itself is no longer the main theme, but the law of God, which should be read, taught and obeyed by Levi's sons. Thus Joseph's exemplary role as teacher 'of the writings and discipline of wisdom' was no longer appropriate to the new context of the Greek T. Levi 13, which stresses the function of the 'Levites' as teachers of the law. Hence, the author of the (Greek) Testaments has remodeled the example of Joseph that he found in his source, which repeated the traditional motif of the connection between Joseph and wisdom, and has rather put him forward as the great example of the one who received δόξα after a period of distress and humiliation by being 'enthroned with kings', a reward given to every Levite who reads, teaches, and keeps the law, thereby gaining wisdom from it.[335]

He offers no explanation of this change. That shift is made by the author/redactor of *TPL* and he was Christian. It is not explained by the earlier Jewish identification of wisdom as Torah or of Torah as the means by which wisdom is to be gained.

The relations between *ALD* and *TPL* in this section can be summarized as follows:

ALD	*TPL*
12:9–13:2	12:6–7
13:2–3	13:1
13:3	13:5–6
13:4–5a	13:2–3a
13:5b	–
13:6	13:9
13:7–10	13:3b–4
13:10–11	13:7–8

[334] See also commentary on 13:4 below. Hollander 1981, 61 observed that in *ALD* Joseph is a wisdom figure. On ancient wisdom in the biblical presentation of the Joseph figure, see Müller, 1972, 272–280.

[335] Hollander, 1981, 62. Cited by permission.

Moreover, the latter part of *ALD* 13:1 and 13:2a are implied by the setting in *TPL* 13:1.[336] The statement about Levi's age at the time of Joseph's death forms the superscription of the exhortation in *ALD* 13:1 and has been turned into the last of the dates in *TPL* 12. It will be readily observed, therefore, that *TPL* has shortened, expanded and re-arranged the textual material available to it from *ALD*. Yet, other than the "wisdom/Torah" alternation observed above, there is little indication of systematic editorial direction in *TPL*'s use of its source.

Commentary on 13:1

ובשׂ]נת מאה ות[מׂני עשרה לחיי היא שׂנ[תא] די מית בה יוסף אחי "And in the [hundred and ei]ghteenth ye[ar] of my life, that is the ye[ar] in which my brother Joseph died"—The same date is given in *TPL* 12:7. Joseph died at the age of a hundred and ten years (Genesis 50:26; for the date see *Jubilees* 46:8). The *Testament of Simeon* says: "A copy of the words of Simeon, the things which he said to his sons before he died, in the hundred and twentieth year of his life, in which year Joseph died" (1:1);[337] while Zebulun gave his testament "in the hundred and fourteenth year of his life, two years after the death of Joseph" (1:1).[338] It is intriguing to read in *Seder ʿolam rabba*, chapter 3 "you do not find among all the tribes (i.e., sons of Jacob) one whose life was shorter than that of Joseph, and you do not find among all the tribes one who lived longer than Levi".[339] Joseph's death was regarded as a significant turning point in Patriarchal history from Exodus 1:6 and 1:8 on.[340] Joseph, as is well known, is a central figure in *TPatriarchs*.[341] What is significant in *ALD*'s mention of Joseph's exemplary conduct, and particularly in a sapiential

[336] On these parallels, see Stone and Greenfield, DJD 22, 3.

[337] Hollander and de Jonge, 1985, 110.

[338] Hollander and de Jonge, 1985, 256.

[339] Guggenheimer, 1998, 40. See also *Yalqut Shimʿoni*, Shemot, 162 and compare *Jubilees* 46:3 and 46:8.

[340] Compare *Jubilees* 34:15, *TPSimeon* 1:1, Hebrews 11:22 and Augustine, *City of God* 7.

[341] Hollander, 1981. Compare, for example, *TPL* 13:1 (material not in *ALD*) with *TPBenjamin* 3:1, etc. The comparison of these two sources, of course, opens up the issue of the double "Golden Rule" in *TPatriarchs*, on which see: de Jonge, 1999, 87–88; de Jonge, 2002; Hollander and de Jonge, 1985, 418. For further bibliography see Hollander, 1981, 7–9, 100–01 and notes 22–30.

connection, is that in *ALD* his role is already paradigmatic. Thus, views that see the key to Joseph's central role in *TPatriarchs* to be that he was regarded in Christian sources as a forerunner of Christ, do not provide an adequate explanation of this phenomenon. Von Rad pointed out long ago that Daniel's mantic role in the Book of Daniel is fashioned on that of Joseph.[342] It is far from clear that the wisdom here attributed to Joseph is thought of as mantic, and it seems much more likely to be that of the wise courtier, but Joseph's early paradigmatic function in both courtly and mantic wisdom may lie in the background of his role in *ALD*. To the basis of this complex understanding of Joseph, the Christian redactor/author of *TPatriarchs* may subsequently have added the Joseph—Christ typology.

Commentary on 13:2

In a number of points, *TPL* 12–13 has drawn on *ALD* and the setting of *TPL* 13:1 implies ALD 13:1–2.[343]

שמ[עֹ]ו[למאמר לוי אבוכון והציתו לפקודי ידיד אל "List]en to the word of your father Levi and pay attention to the instructions of God's friend"—An almost similar opening of a testament is reconstructed in 4Q539 2–3:2, titled *Testament of Joseph*, וכען ש]מעו בני[למאמר יוסף אבוכון ואצי]תו לי חביבי "And now li]sten my sons [to the words of Joseph your father, and pay] attention to me my beloved." Of course, since the reconstruction of the substantial lacuna in 4Q539 is inspired by *ALD* 13:2, perhaps the phrases were originally less similar. Other examples of the parallelism צו"ת || שמ"ע may be observed, such as Targum Onqelos to Genesis 4:23 and to Numbers 23:18.

Commentary on 13:3

צדקה וקושׂ]א "righteousness and truth"—Compare Levi's prayer in chapter 3 where קושטא is frequently used and see *Testament of Qahat* (4Q542) 1:12 and *4QApocryphon of Levi*[b] (4Q541) 13:3 קֹושׂ[ו]צֹ[דק(ה) "truth and justice" which have this expression.[344] Against Charles,

[342] See von Rad,1976, 439–447 and von Rad, 1965, 2.306–07. The issue of divinatory wisdom has been to the fore in discussions of apocalyptic origins in recent decades. See the works of Müller, 1972; *idem*. 1969. A recent summary is found in the first pages of VanderKam, 1997, especially p. 337.

[343] See above "General Notes".

[344] DJD 31, 247.

we have moved the word צדקה (צדקתא Qumran) from the end of the preceding verse to the beginning of this verse.[345]

די זרע טאב טאב מהֿנעל "He who sows good brings in a goodly (harvest)"—The idea that wisdom has a good harvest is prominent in ben Sira 6:19–20, "Come to her like one who plows and sows, and wait for her good harvest. For when you cultivate her you will toil but little, and soon you will eat of her produce."

Commentary on 13:4

ספר ומוסר וחוכמה <אליפו> לבניכון "<teach> reading and writing, and teaching <of> wisdom to your children" See below 13:6 and 13:15: compare *4QBirth of Noah*[a] (4Q534) 7:1 (= 4Q536 2,2 10–11).[346]

ספר "reading and writing"—So already Isaiah 29:11f. This word may also be translated simply as "letters" or even just "reading".[347] It is equivalent to Greek γράμματα as in *TPL* 13:2 διδάξατε δὲ καὶ ὑμεῖς τὰ τέκνα ὑμῶν γράμματα "And do you, too, teach your children letters".[348] The expression מוסר חוכמה "instruction in wisdom" occurs in Proverbs 15:33. The tradition that attributes learning and wisdom to Levi derived in part, doubtlessly, from the priestly function of instruction and judgment: see, e.g., Deuteronomy 33:10, Malachi 2:7 and ben Sira 45:17. The similar phrase *ʾlptw sprʾ wḥkmtʾ* in Aḥiqar (ms66v §10) should be noted.[349] The whole is somewhat analogous to the branches of learning known to Enoch according to *Jubilees* 4:17, "writing and knowledge and wisdom".

חוכמה "wisdom"—The word חוכמה "wisdom" in ALD has been replaced by νόμος "Law" here in 13:4b = *TPL* 13:2b, in 13:5a =

[345] See Stone and Greenfield, DJD 22, 10, note on line 8.
[346] DJD 31, 151, 167–68.
[347] As in Stone and Greenfield, DJD 22, 11.
[348] Translation from Hollander and de Jonge, 1985, 164. For ספר as "letters" see Greenfield, 1993. Hollander and de Jonge, 1985, 166 compare with Daniel 1:4 וללמדם ספר ולשון כשדים translated in NRSV "they were to be taught the literature and language of the Chaldeans", but it surely means "reading and writing", i.e., they were to be made literate. They also mention Greek *Gospel of Thomas* 15:1, Plutarch *Vitae decem oratorum* VI Aeschines (*Mor.* 840 B). Compare also 13:6 below.
[349] Conybeare, Harris and Lewis, 1913 [38].

TPL 13:2, in 13:7a[350] = *TPL* 13:3a, in 13:9 = *TPL* 13:4c and in 13:10 = *TPL* 13:4b. In 13:4 חוכמה = σύνεσιν *TPL* 13:2. This phenomenon may be indicative of the editorial tendencies in *TPL* and was already noted by Küchler.[351] "Wisdom" is read in both documents in some instances.[352]

In *TPL* 13:2 we read ἀναγινώσκοντες ἀδιαλείπτως τὸν νόμον τοῦ θεοῦ "reading unceasingly the Law of God" corresponding to ותהוי חוכמתא עמכון ליקר עלם "and may wisdom be eternal glory for you".[353] We have noted above that *TPL* introduces "the Law" where *ALD* has different words. On the one hand, this is notably anachronistic, and on the other, one is led to wonder why a Christian reworker would replace "wisdom" with "Law". This matter is discussed in further detail in "General Notes" at the start of the commentary on this chapter.

Commentary on 13:5

Wisdom brings honour, many friends and social position to those who have it. This idea is already found in biblical wisdom literature, e.g., Proverbs 3:35, "the wise shall obtain honor, but dullards get disgrace as their portion" and cf. ben Sira 10:30, 11:1 and 39:4: compare also Proverbs 8:11, Wisdom 8:10, etc.[354] Very striking is the parallel in ben Sira 39:4, referring to the wise man:

> He serves among the great
> and appears before rulers;
> he travels in foreign lands
> and learns what is good and evil in the human lot.

לבשרון "disdain"—4QLevi[a] 1 1:11 reads לב̇[סרון. The usual Aramaic form is בוסרון as in Palestinian Targum of Ezekiel 7:19 and also in Jewish Palestinian Aramaic in general. The form with *sin* is strange in Aramaic of the time, but it does occur.[355] It is also known in

[350] Compare *ALD* 13:5a.

[351] Küchler, 1979, 498. See p. 204 and note 331 above.

[352] See 13:11b corresponding to *TPL* 13:7c. It is not certain whether *ALD* 13:10 indeed corresponds to *TPL* 13:7a. If it does, this is a second instance of "wisdom" in both texts. See "General Notes" above.

[353] Compare 1QS 6:6 איש דורש בתורה יומם ולילה "someone . . . engaged in the study of the Law, day and night".

[354] On the social role of the sage see Stone, 1987, 577.

[355] Sokoloff, 1990, 87. Charles considered this to be a Hebraism. The spelling with *sin* is a hypercorrection, the root being בס"ר. Note ויבסרון 4Q542 (*Testament of*

Syriac.[356] The *qṭlwn* form is common in Aramaic of this period,[357] as well as the root בס"ר, cf. *4QTestament of Qahat* (4Q542) 1 1:6.

ולשיטו "and (to) scorn"—In 4QLevi[a] 1 1:11 the word שיטו "scorn" is found following "disdain". It does not occur in the Geniza manuscript, but is probably original. The actual nominal form שיטו is unknown, but the root שו"ט is common in Targumic Aramaic and in other dialects.[358] The roots בס"ר and שו"ט are a fixed pair: see Syriac Aḥiqar, ms68r §28.[359]

Commentary on 13:6

ליוסף אחי [די] מאלפא "to my brother Joseph [who] taught"—It was observed that from context the verb would make better sense taken intransitively, something like אלף הוה "had studied".[360] Even the present form could be taken intransitively.[361] Joseph's learning did lead to his reaching high places, and see further commentary on 13:1.

ולמלכין "and to kings"—It is plausible that this word begins a new sentence, something like ולמלכין יעט הוה "and he did advise kings".[362] We have, indeed, restored <יעט הוא>; compare Aḥiqar line 12: [ס]פרא חכימא יעט אתור כלה "the wise [sc]ribe, counselor of Assyria, all of it".[363]

Commentary on 13:7

אל תמחלו "do not be lax"—This verb is unknown in Biblical Hebrew. In Mishnaic Hebrew it is a synonym of סלח "to forgive (sin), to

Qahat) 1 1:6. In Murabaʿât 42:67 the spelling with *sin* is found: see Milik, DJD 2, 156. The form in *-ōn* may be matched by חשבון three times in the Qumran Enoch texts, cf. Milik, 1976, 203 and elsewhere. Note also דכרנה in Ezra 6:2.

356 Brockelmann, 1928, 81 *s.v. bsrwtʾ*.

357 Greenfield and Stone, 1979, 227.

358 For further details, see Stone and Greenfield, DJD 22, 8.

359 Conybeare, Harris and Lewis, 1913, 105.

360 See our comment in Stone and Greenfield, DJD 22, 10.

361 Some Rabbinic texts refer to Joseph as a teacher, see *b. Sota* 52–53, but in a quite different context.

362 VanderKam has proposed reading "counsel".

363 Porten and Yardeni, 1993, 26–27. This is in contrast with Sokoloff who says: "The root יעט is attested in JA (i.e., Jewish Aramaic) only in LJLA" (i.e., late Jewish Literary Aramaic). Sokoloff, 2000a, 92.

remit (a debt)". It has the same meaning in Jewish Aramaic dialects.[364] Perhaps one may translate "do not be weary/negligent of teaching wisdom". Another occurrence is 4QLevi[a] 4:6 and see commentary there.

[ל]אׄ תשב[קין]] "[do n]ot lea[ve]"—Puech reconstructs ולארחתה "and her paths" in the lacuna.[365] This is a conjecture and may be regarded as reasonable but not necessary. In any case, the negative אל usually serves with prohibitions, see 3:9, 13:17 and in the first half of the present verse. לא seems to be used in this sense in 8:3 and 8:7, though they are debatable. It could be translated "you will not leave . . .".

Commentary on 13:8

יהך "he will go"—As elsewhere in the Aramaic texts from Qumran, the archaic root הו"ך "to go" is used rather than אז"ל. The Geniza text is damaged at this point, with only a *lamed* surviving. We have reconstructed the verb אזל, thus having a parallel expression here.

אחא וׄחׄבׄרׄ "brother and a friend"—See *ALD* 1:2: נהוי כולן א[חין] וחברין "that we all become broth[ers] and friends".[366]

נכרי "a stranger"—For the term, see Aḥiqar נכריא "strangers" in line 139.[367] For the pair כילי/נכרי, see *4QTestament of Qahat* (4Q542) 1 1:4–6.[368] כילי is a rare word, see Isaiah 32:5 and 32:7.[369] Joseph retained wisdom, even in adverse circumstances. This is set forth strikingly in Wisdom 10:13–14 and compare also *TPL* 13:9. The passage from Wisdom reads (referring to Joseph):

> When a righteous man was sold, wisdom did not desert him,
> but delivered him from sin.
> She descended with him into the dungeon,
> and when he was in prison she did not leave him,

[364] Sokoloff, 1990, 300. Syriac *mḥl* is 'debilis factus est': see Brockelmann, 1928, 381.
[365] Puech, 2002, 545.
[366] On the wise man's foreign travel, see ben Sira 39:4.
[367] Porten and Yardeni, 1993, 42–43.
[368] DJD 31, 268.
[369] See further Stone and Greenfield, DJD 22, 10–11.

until she brought him the scepter of a kingdom
and authority over his masters.

Commentary on 13:9

ושאלי שלמיה "his well-wishers"—See 4QTobit^b (4Q197) 4 3:3 (Tobit 7:1) for the same expression.

רברבין "numerous"—This word could also be translated "great ones" but the meaning we have chosen is favoured by the parallelism.

Commentary on 13:10

כורסי <ד>י יקר "seat <o>f honour"—In Literary Aramaic we usually find the form כרסא, while in Jewish Palestinian Aramaic we have כרסי. Sitting on "your seat of honour" refers to God in 4QEnoch^b (4Q202) 1 3:15 (*1 Enoch* 9:4) וכורס]אׄ יקרך "Thy glorious throne". See as well in the Paris manuscript of the Fragmentary Targum to Exodus 17:16 (P) where כס יה is translated כורסי איקריה; see the parallel Hebrew expression כסא כבוד, translated כורסי יקרא and referring both to God (Jeremiah 14:21) and to a human being (1 Samuel 2:8 and Isaiah 22:23).

סימא טאבא "a fine treasure"—On wisdom as a treasure see "General Notes" at the start of the commentary on this chapter.

Commentary on 13:11

עם "army"—The word עם also means "army" in the Bible, cf. Ezekiel 17:15 and 26:7.

רתיכין "chariots"—This is a word of Iranian origin found frequently in the Targums.[370]

Commentary on 13:12

אוצרי חוכמתה לא יבוזון ולא ישכחון מׄטמוריה "the treasure houses of wisdom they will not plunder, And they will not find its hidden places" See *2 Baruch* 44:13 "These are they who acquired for themselves

[370] Sokoloff, 1990, 78.

treasures of wisdom, And with them are found stores of understanding." See also the description of wisdom in Wisdom 6–11.

מטמוריה "hidden places"—The plural of the noun מטמור. The nouns טמור "secret" and טמירה "hidden thing" are known in Jewish Palestinian Aramaic.[371] The form in *ALD* 13:13 is מטמרה in the Geniza, while in 4QLevi[f] 8:2 it is מטמריא.

Commentary on 13:12–13

שׂימ̊תה "treasure"[bis]—This word is found in the various dialects of Palestinian Aramaic.[372] In these dialects, as in the Geniza text, it is written with a *samek* rather than a *sin* as it is here.[373] "Treasure" is often used of the fruit of wisdom or of righteous action: see Wisdom 7:14, ben Sira 29:11 and 29:12; compare *2 Enoch* 50:5.[374] Wisdom is also described as a treasure in 13:10 as in Isaiah 33:6 and Wisdom 7:14 (θησαυρός). As priceless, wisdom here is to be compared with 4Q525 (Beatitudes) 2 3:2–3: לוא תלקח בזהב א[ו בכסף . . .] עם כול אבני חפץ[. . .] "it will not be acquired with gold o[r with silver . . .]with all precious stones".[375] In biblical wisdom literature, wisdom is often compared to gold, said to be better than gold, but it is not said to be gold. In many other passages it is compared with precious metals and jewels: see Job 28:18, Proverbs 8:11 and 16:16.

Commentary on 13:13

ולא א̊ית̊י [כ]ל̊ מחיר נגדה "and it is priceless"—The verb נגד "to draw, acquire" translates Hebrew משך in various contexts.[376] The expression here is to be compared with Job 28:18 ומשך חכמה מפנינים "and the price of wisdom is above pearls" which is rendered by the late Targum there as ונגדא דחכמתא מן מרגליין.[377]

[371] Sokoloff, 1990, 226.

[372] Sokoloff, 1990, 375.

[373] In Syriac, one of the uses of the verb *sm* is "deposit a treasure" and the noun *symtʾ* is in frequent use: see Brockelmann, 1928, 469–70. In Mandaic both *simta* "treasure" and *simat hiia* "Treasure of Life" are used: Drower and Macuch, 1963, 327.

[374] See Stone, 1990, 239–40.

[375] Puech, DJD 25, 129.

[376] Levy, 1868, 2.88.

[377] Stec, 1994, 188.

חכ[מתה י] בעא חכמה֯[“He who seeks wisdom, [. . . wis]dom [. . .]"—Perhaps this was בעא חכמה֯[. . . חכ]מתה י[השכח] or the like: cf. 4QLevi[a] 1 1:9.

Commentary on 13:15

וכען בני “And now, my sons”—This opening, together with the second person plural, shows that the author here shifts to parenesis.

ס֯פר ומוסר ח֯[כ]מה “reading and writing and the teaching of wi[sdo]m”—The same expression also occurs in the exhortation with which the wisdom poem opens, in 13:6, where Joseph is said to teach his children ספר ומוסר חוכמה “reading and writing (= ספר) and the teaching of wisdom.”[378]

Commentary on 13:16

The preceding verse ends with a *vacat*, and this verse is a beginning of a new section, signalled by the marginal paragraph mark. The following broken lines have no exact parallel in the other sources, but from their remains they seem to deal with a positive prophecy about Levi’s descendants. Starting with a reference to books he has read (“. . . even in books I re[ad . . .”), the text mentions “heads and judges”, and later “even priest and kings”, and finally kingdom and “endless glory”.

ראשין ושפטין “heads and judges”—The word שפטין “judges” is extremely rare in Aramaic, and is in all likelihood a Hebraism.[379] The phrase has an antique flavour and is surely based on a Hebrew *Vorlage*; cf. Joshua 23:2, 24:1 לראשיו ולשפטיו “their heads and their judges”; cf. also Micah 3:11.[380]

ועבדין “and servants”—This could be taken to mean “servants” or “making.”

[378] See “General Notes” above and discussion on 13:4–6.

[379] The only known instances are from Elephantine: see Cowley, 1923. There are sure examples in the Aḥiqar proverbs and in text no. 52, line 5; this enigmatic text has other Hebraisms.

[380] Moshe Greenberg notes Deuteronomy 29:9 ראשיכם שבטיכם perhaps meaning “your heads, your judges” (oral communication).

כהנין ומלכין "priests and kings"—See discussion in Introduction above. Even though "and kings" here might be the beginning of a new sentence, the second person plural ending in the next line again points to the relationship between royal language and the Levitical line, since it reflects Levi's address to his sons.[381]

מלכותכן "your kingdom"—*Or*: "your rule".

Following the words ולא]תׄעבר מנכן עד כל, perhaps something like [דׄ]ר[יה] "generations" can be hypothesized to have existed. See General Notes above for a discussion of the eschatological character of this prophecy.

[381] The corresponding passage in *TPL* 8:14–15 is clearly Christian, combining royal, priestly and prophetic characteristics: see further Hollander and de Jonge, 154.

UNPLACED FRAGMENTS

Fragments That Cannot be Placed in the Sequence of *ALD*

4QLevi[a] *Frag. 3*

1. ל[ ]א כל עממיא
2. ש]ה̊רא ו̊כ̊וכביא
3.]מן
4.]ל[ש]הרה

1.] all the peoples
2. m]oon and stars
3.]from
4. to the [m]oon

General Observations

There may be some merit in Milik's proposal to connect this fragment with *TPL* 14:3. The phrase ש]ה̊רא ו̊כ̊וכביא might be related to οἱ φωστῆρες τοῦ οὐρανοῦ, ὡς ὁ ἥλιος καὶ ἡ σελήνη and, for that matter, כל עממיא of line 1 might be connected with πᾶσι τοῖς ἔθνεσι of *TPL* 14:1. The texts are, however, far from identical, though *TPL* 14 might have been based on this passage. For the combination of שהרא וכוכביא in a visionary context, see 1QapGen 7:2.[1]

Notes

line 2: ש]ה̊רא m]oon—The *hē* is represented only by the end of the top line. We chose this word because of the following כ̊וכביא 'stars' and because it occurs in the next line. Milik proposes to read שמשא.[2]

4QLevi[a] *Frag. 4*

1.]כ̊ן תחשכ̊ון[
2.]א הלא קבל [ ]..ך .[
3.]נח ועל מן תהוא חובתא[

[1] Morgenstern, Qimron and Sivan, 1996, 42.
[2] Milik, 1976, 23.

4. [ ]ה֯לא עלי ועליכן בנ֯י ארו ידעונה
5. א]ר֯חת קש֯א תשבק֯ו֯ן וכל שבילי
6.]ת֯מחלון ותהכון בה בחשו֯כ֯א֯ [ ]
7. [ ].ד֯י ח[ש]וכה תתא עליכו֯[ן] ותה֯כ֯ון
8. [ז.. [ ]כ֯ע֯ן זמ[נין] תהוון לשפלין

1.] your [ ] you/they will darken [
2.] did [ ] not receive [
3.] and upon whom will be the guilt [
4.]is it not upon me and you, my sons, for they will know it.
5. w]ays of truth you will abandon and all the paths of
6.]you will be lax and you will walk in it in darkness[
7.] of d[ar]kness will come upon you and you will walk
8.] now, at ti[mes] you will be lowly

General Observations

There are no parallels to this fragment in the surviving Greek and Aramaic texts of *ALD*.[3] It is clearly parenetic in function and lines 5–8 are predictory.

From what has survived we may infer that this fragment was part of a father's speech to his sons, including a prophecy about their future sins and abandonment of the paths of truth. This will bring upon them a period of darkness and humiliation. Its context as well as some of the phrases found in it, especially the leaving the paths of truth (line 5) recall the Prayer of Levi (chapter 3). The "Two Ways" idea was dealt with at length in the commentary on 3:4 and is probably being evoked here, even though the surviving text mentions only one way.

The present fragment presumably foresees the wandering of the Levites from righteousness. This is a major topic in *TPL*, see chapters 10, 14 and 16–17. The language of darkening is used, though in a different context, in *TPL* 14:4.

4Q537, tentatively identified by Milik as *Testament of Jacob*,[4] also combines testamentary and apocalyptic elements. It refers both to priestly sacrifices in frag. 12:1–2 etc., and to walking in the path of error in frag. 5:2.

[3] This fragment was partly published by Milik, 1976, 23.
[4] See DJD 31, 171–190.

Notes

Commentary on line 1
תחשכוׄן—"they will darken"—Observe the same word in lines 6 and 7: compare 1QapGen 6:3 ולאזהרותני מן נתיב שקר די אזל לחשוך עלמא "and to warn me away from the path of falsehood that leads to everlasting darkness". This is related, of course, to contrastive light-dark dualism.

Commentary on line 2
] הלא קבל "did [ ] not receive"—Milik reads: הלא קבל חנוך "did not Enoch accuse [. . .]" which is possible, but not necessary. The verb ending is lost and enables Milik's speculative reading of ך. .[at the end of this line as חנוך "Enoch". The verb could be singular or plural.

Commentary on line 3
נח at the start could be read more plausibly as "Noah" than the final *kap* preceding as חנוך "Enoch".

Commentary on line 4
ארו ידעונה "for they will know it"—The *waw* is not completely clear. If we read ידעונה, it is third person plural verb with a third person singular accusative suffix. We might expect the verb here to be in the second person plural.[5]

Commentary on line 5
שבילי "paths of"—See 1QapGen 6:2, 5 and 11QtgJob 8:4 (Job 24:13) and 34:3 (Job 34:27). We suggest reconstructing these lines in light of the similar language in Noah's words in 1QapGen 6:1–2 וכדי נפקת מן מעי אמי לקושט נציבת וקושטא כול יומי דברת והוית מהלך בשבילי אמת עלמא "And when I emerged from my mother's womb, I was planted for truth and all my days I conducted in truth, and I walked in the paths of eternal truth."[6] Thus we may suggest reconstructing frag. 4:4–6 as follows:

בני ארו ידעונה
[. . . א]ורחת קשטא תשבקון
וכל שבילי [אמת עלמא] תמהלון

[5] One might speculate that this is some form derived from ידע אנה "I know".
[6] Morgenstern, Qimron and Sivan, 1996, 40–41.

My sons, behold they will know it
.... w]ays of truth you will abandon
and with regard to all the paths of [eternal truth] you will be lax

Commentary on line 6
תׄמחלון "you will be lax"—See *ALD* 13:7 [. . .]]אל תמחלו חכמתא למאלף "do not lax in the study of wisdom". The verb מחל, meaning "remit a debt", is found in Mishnaic Hebrew.[7] שב"ק "abandon" seems to parallel מח"ל "be lax", both drawn from the legal realm.[8]

Commentary on line 8
תהוון לשפלין "you will be lowly"—The idea is not unique, see Malachi 2:9 "And I, in turn, have made you despicable and vile (נבזים ושפלים) in the eyes of all the people, because you disregard My ways and show partiality in your rulings", see *Testament of Qahat* (4Q542) 1 1:6 ותהון לשפלו{ת} ולנבלו בעיניהון "and you will be lowly and vile in their eyes".

4QLevi[a] *Frag. 5*

2.]בׄאיכן אדין ידין[ ]בכן
3.]שנון בכן מן כל מׄ[ ].

2.] your [ ]then[ ]in you
3.] in you than all [

4QLevi[b] *Frags. 3–4*

2.]אׄשבען ו֯[ ].מס .[ ].ׄר גבריא
3.]אׄנתה֯ ותח֯ל֯ל שמה ושם אבוה
4. [ ]. .ׄרח֯ ע֯ם֯ .[ ]ב֯ה֯ [ ]י֯דה ק֯.[ ]ז֯. ב֯ה֯תא וכל
5.]לׄה זי חבלת שמה ושם֯ אׄבהתה ואׄבהתת לכל אחיה
6.]אבוה. ולא מתמחא שם חׄסיׄה מן כל עמהׄא לעלם
7.]ל֯ .שׄ לכל דרי עלמׄא וכׄ[ ]תׄ. קדישין מן עמא
8.]ל֯ וה֯ת֯[ ]מׄעשר קודש קרבן לאלפן

[7] See *j. Gittin* 43d (55) || *j. Qiddushin* 64a (38): see Sokoloff, 1990, 300, Moreshet, 1980, 209, note 8. See above, commentary on 13:7.
[8] See Greenfield, 2000, 113–115 on שבק in *BMAP* 5:4–5 and in 1QapGen 22:19–20: ונכסיא כולהין שביקון לך "and all the possessions are left for you".

2.]he beswore us and [ ] [ ] men
3.]a wife and she desecrated her name and the name of her father
4.]with [ ] shame and every
5.] who profaned her name and the name of her ancestors, and shamed all her brothers.
6.] her father; and the name of the righteous will not be wiped out from all her people for ever.
7.] for all the generations of eternity and [ ] the holy ones from the people
8.]holy tithe a sacrifice for teaching (?)

General Observations

These fragments might be different from the rest of the manuscript or from a different manuscript altogether, since they appear to vary somewhat, both in layout and perhaps in script. Yet, the deterioration of the parchment due to the ravages of time make a definite paleographic or codicological determination impossible. So, we have preferred to leave them here, but regard them with a measure of doubt. As for content, lines 1–5 of these two fragments, which join together, seem at first glance to deal with the Dinah story, but on further examination this is doubtful. Just how Dinah's rape could be related to the statements made here and how they can be related to the Dinah material in chapter 1, is quite obscure. Although the Dinah incident is prominent in *TPL*, there is no textual or conceptual correspondence between these two fragments of *ALD* and *Testament of Levi*.[9] In line 6, the subject shifts to positive prophecy related to the Levitical line. This is indicated both by the prediction of the eternal existence of "the pious" and by the mention of tithing (line 8).[10] However, as far as we can tell, once again there is no textual parallel to this material in the surviving *ALD* fragments. Perhaps then, not Dinah but a wayward priestly daughter is discussed in the first lines. The same conclusion, that the fragment is not about the Dinah incident, is reached by Baumgarten. He also regards the

[9] Dinah is discussed in *Jubilees* 30:5–7, again without textual correspondence with the present fragments. See chapter 1 above on attitudes to the Dinah incident.

[10] On the role of tithing in Levi's priestly function, see Kugel, 1993, especially pages 2–11. It should be observed that in 5:2–4 the subject of Jacob's tithe occurs again.

subject to be the promiscuous daughter of a priest who, by later Qumran law, permanently stained her family's priestly status.[11]

Notes

Commentary on line 3
אנתה[—"Wife" or "woman."
ותחלל "she desecrated"—The verb is used in Hebrew for the desecration of one's parent, so Leviticus 21:9 where it is translated "It is her father she defiles". There Targum Onqelos uses the passive מתחלא "she is profaned". In Mishnaic Hebrew and Jewish Aramaic dialects, חלל שם is used for desecrating the divine name, but not in contexts like this one, which refers to desecrating a human's name.

Commentary on line 4
בהתא "shame"—Both the noun בהתא here in the verb בהת in the *ʾApʿel* (אבהתת) in line 5 are well known in Aramaic.

Commentary on line 5
Observe the form זי in this line rather than the form די which is usual in Aramaic at Qumran. This isolated occurrence of זי adds some weight to the idea that this fragment may not belong to *ALD* (see General Remarks, above). The sentiment expressed in this line is parallel with that in Leviticus 21:9 which says of the daughter of a priest את אביה היא מחללת "she profanes her father". Compare the Dinah story in *Jubilees* which reads "because she has dishonoured the name of the house of her father" (30:7).[12]
חבלת "profaned"—The *paʿel* of this verb is used in the Targumim for corrupt and perverse acts, usually translating Hebrew השחית; see, e.g., Genesis 6:12. The expression חבל שם is otherwise unknown.

Commentary on line 6
חסיה "righteous"—The etymology of the name "Essene" from חסיה was suggested many years ago.[13] The main objection in the past to this

[11] Baumgarten, 2003, 400–401.
[12] But, compare Baumgarten's view cited above.
[13] See Schürer, 1909, 654–56; Schürer, 1979, 2.559–560; Cross, 1995, 54. This view was already presented by him in 1961. A comprehensive survey is given by Vermes, 1975, 9–19.

etymology was that this word is attested only in Syriac. In Syriac, it may serve as a translation of ὅσιος.[14] It should be observed, however, that it is found in Old Aramaic, in the Carpentras Stele (*KAI*, no. 269), line 4. Its occurrence in the present text shows that is was also used in the literary Aramaic attested at Qumran.

Commentary on line 7
לכל דרי עלמ̇א "for all the generations of eternity"—Possibly translate, "for all the inhabitants of the world".[15]

4QLevi^b Frag. 5 col. 1

.2].[עם . [
.3]כ̊הנות עלמא

2.] with [
3.] eternal priesthood.

General Notes

The expression כהנות עלמא "eternal priesthood" confirms the fragment's Levitical character; see Exodus 40:15, while in Numbers 25:13 we find ברית כהונת עלם "covenant of eternal priesthood". Column 2 of frag. 5 consists of only two letters, which do not make a whole word.

4QLevi^b Frag. 6

אמרת מא

This could be translated "I said" or "you said", masculine or feminine. The next word could mean "what".

[14] Brockelmann, 1928, 245–46.
[15] In the commentary to this fragment, we are much indebted to Stone and Greenfield, DJD 22, 34–35.

4QLevi[d] *Frag. 3*

1. ארו מן יקר בא.]
2. אנה די תמרין לי {די} .]
3. יקירין מן נשיא]

1. Behold from honour [
2. I, that you will say to me that [
3. more honoured than women[

General Observations

This small fragment contains text that, like the next fragment, cannot be identified with any other material from *ALD*, nor does it resemble anything in *TPL*. The only observation that can be made is that it is part of an address in the first person.

The word יקר "honour" is used in Jochebed's onomastic midrash (11:10) and frequently in the Wisdom Poem (13:4, 13:4–6, 13:9–10 and 13:15–16).

4QLevi[d] *Frag. 4*

2.]ונברין[
3.]ה דנה .[
4. מ̊ר̇י̇ה̇ כ.[

2.]and men[
3.] this [
4.] the Lord [

General Observations

Nothing can be said about the content and context of this tiny fragment. In line 4 we might read *aleph* instead of *mem*, thus: א̊ר̇י̇ ה̇..

4QLevi[f] *Frag. 1*

1.]מין מן כי[1.
2.]כ̊ול לביך[2.
3.].ד̊י.. כ̊ול..[3.

1.] from [
2.]all your hearts [
3.] that . . . all . . . [

General Observations

This fragment relates to no other part of *ALD*, nor does it show any obvious connection to *TPL*. It contains part of a second-person address.

1QLevi[a] *(= 1Q21)*

General Remarks

1QLevi was published by Milik in 1955,[16] again by Fitzmyer and Harrington in 1978 and reedited by Puech in 2003.[17] The manuscript is extremely fragmentary. We have placed certain of its fragments in the running text above. Frag. 1 = 4:7 was set above preceding the beginning of Bodleian a and Milik joins it with frag. 2. Milik also recognized that frag. 3 contains parts of Bodleian a, lines 1–9 (4:9–11). He placed fragment 4 in Bodleian a, lines 15–16 (5:2) and he suggests that frag. 7 is connected with frag. 1, and we have placed it following that fragment (4:8). He further suggests that frag. 26 overlaps with two words in Bodleian col. a, l. 1 (4:9). We observe that frag. 45 has the last word of 8:2 and the first word of 8:3. These fragments are published at the relevant points in the preceding sequential text.

The other fragments belong to the unknown sections of *ALD* or are so small as to resist identification. Consequently they are given here with such comments as are possible. The readings and reconstructions follow Milik's suggestions, with some further proposals by the present authors. We have not given lines that have no identifiable letters on them and we have not translated lines that have no identifiable words on them.

Frag. 5

]יׄצחק[

]Isaac[

Milik suggests placing this below frag. 4, see *ALD* 5:1. This is possible but far from completely persuasive.

[16] In DJD 1, 87–91.

[17] Fitzmyer and Harrington, 1978, 80–88; Puech 2003. Our text is based on Milik and incorporates a number of Puech's ameliorations.

Frag. 6

]וכדי[

] and when [

Milik suggests that is is perhaps from *ALD* 5:1. However, this word could occur in many places, including text not attested in any surviving Aramaic.

Frag. 7 ii

3. לא̇[

3. not [

Frag. 9

1. ש[ניא̇]ן
2. ל[הו̊ין ש[
3.]ד̊ לי עד .[
4.]ש̊א̊[

1.] many [
2.] will be [
3.] to me until [

Frag. 10

1.]די להוין̊[
2.]ל[

1.]for they will be[

Frag. 11

1.]ב̊ה אדין יח̊ז̊א̊[
2.]ן̇ בעא[

1.] in him/it then he/it will see [
2.] seeks [

Frag. 12

1.]לֿהֿוֿאֿ לֿלֿוט
2.]ל[

1.] will be to curse

Frag. 13

1.]יֿן משלֿ[
2.]לֿ[

Frag. 14

1.]◦ וֿאֿנֿתֿ[
2.]תֿםֿ ומ.[

Frag. 15

כ]הֿנא קר[ב

]the priest approa[ches

Frag. 16

]די לאֿ[

Frag. 17

]כתא[

Frag. 18

]שֿגיא[

] many [

Frag. 19

י]עקׂב[

Ja]cob[

Frag. 20

1.]מׂמלל אׂ[
2.]לׂ[

]speaking[

Frag. 21

]מיׂך[

Frag. 22

1.]ןׂ רברבׂ[ין
2.]הוו מתׂ[

1.] great[

Frag. 23

1.]ארי שׂ[
2.]חׂהא[

1.] behold [

Frag. 24

1.]לׂהדרה א[ל עליון
2. ק]שט

1.]to glorify Go[d Most High
2. tr]uth[

Frag. 25

1.]ם̊ [ל̇]ה[
2. ע]בד בהון די ◦[
3.]ין̊ בחי̊ר̊[ין

2. d]id in them that [
3.] .. elec[t (plur.)

בחיר "elec[t (plur.)"—..בה Milik;

Frag. 27

]אדין[

Frag. 28

]ר/ד מן זרע̊[

] . from seed[

Frag. 29

1. יעק]ב̊ א̇בי[
2.]ע̊שׂי̇ר̇י ה]וא

1. Jac]ob my father [
2. wa]s tenth [

Commentary on line 2

ע̊שׂי̇ר̇י ה]וא "wa]s tenth"—Milik reads שׂי̇ר̇י̇ה .[This fragment may be related to the material in *Jubilees* 32:2–3 concerning the counting of Jacob's sons up to Levi who was the tenth. He also gave a tithe. The giving of the tithe was an important matter also for *ALD*, see 5:2. The text does not coincide with *Jubilees* or with *ALD* and the fragment may equally have come from another juncture in the narrative.

Frag. 30

2.]לֿא לזנו.[
3.].י להֿ בעא צ[
4.]לֿ[

] to fornication [
] to her, asked [

General Notes

Milik connects this fragment with *ALD* 6:3 (Isaac's blessing), and the citation in *CD* 4:17.[18] All this is dependent on reading זנות in line 2, which is possible. זנות "fornication" is also mentioned in *ALD* 3:5 (Levi's prayer) and in *Testament of Qahat* (4Q542) 3 2:13 מן זנותא שגי—"will multiply because of fornication".

Frag. 31

]י טעותא

] of error

General Notes

Fitzmyer and Harrington propose reading: רוח]י טעותא, "spirit]s of error";[19] compare 4QpsDan[b] (4Q244), reading: לֿ]שידי טעותא "demons of error" (frag. 12:2).[20] This fragment might express a sentiment similar to Levi's prayer in 3:9, "Make far from me, O Lord, the unrighteous spirit".

Frag. 32

]רֿ שמיא לֿ[

]heavens [

See discussion on frag. 37 below.

[18] On this see Greenfield, 1988, 319–322 and see above, Introduction, pp. 4–5.
[19] Fitzmyer and Harrington, 1978, 84–85.
[20] Collins and Flint, DJD 22, 129.

Frag. 33

]תׄה או הןׄ[

Frag. 34

.2]יהיב .[

2.] given [

Frag. 35

.1]יׄתׄ[
.2]. יׄשׁׄ[

Frag. 36

]דן תׄ[

Frag. 37

.1]מׄין תלׄיׄתׄ[י
.2]כׄל משחה לׄ[
.3 מ]ן שמיא וׄ[

1.]thir[d
2.]any oil [
3. fro]m heaven and[

General Remarks

Milik connected this fragment, together with frag. 32, with *TPL* 2–3 and the description of the heavens "dont quelqes ff. se trouvent dans le 4QLévi".[21] שמיא "heaven" is mentioned several times in *ALD* (3:1, 4:6 and 5:8), but nowhere משחה "oil" mentioned in the same context. Another possibility is explain משחה as "measure",[22] see (cf. 2Q24

[21] Milik, DJD 1, 90.
[22] Sokoloff, 1990, 333–34.

1:3). The fragment might tentatively be connected with one of Levi's visions.

Frag. 38

]אלֹן[

Frag. 39

]. כל תל..[

Milik reads: כל תלא, but the head of the surviving letter cannot be that of an *ʾalef.*

Frag. 40

]י֯ן בקר֯[23]

Frag. 41

]קשט֯ .[

]truth[

Frag. 42

]למ֯נ֯ע֯ל .[

Frag. 43

]בא֯ש֯.[

This might be related to 13:3 זרע ביש; "sows evil" or 3:5 ב]אישא וזנותא דחא "turn away evil and fornication," or neither.

[23] See *ALD* 7:4, The fragment possibly can be reconstructed אעין מהצלח]ין בקר[אנון.

Frag. 44

]עׄלׄ[

Frag. 46

1.]עׄד .[
2.]לׄ[

Frag. 47

]וׄצׄדׄק[

Frag. 49

1.] .שׄ..ן[
2.]ה באדין קד[

2.]then[

Frag. 50

]·ין ברךׄ[

]blessed[

Frag. 51

1.].מן קרבא[

] from the war [

קרבא "war"—This word occurs in *ALD* 4:9 but the preceeding word מן in this fragment does not fit that context.

Frag. 52

1.]מרי חׄזׄ..[
2. ר]עותא[

The first line might be the word "my lord" and the second line means "acceptability." No context was found for these words in *ALD*.

Frag. 53

1.]דין .[
2.]י .אר בה[

Frag. 54

1.]חזה להין לבֿ[
2.]שריא ..[
3.]ל[

1.] fitting for them [

We might reconstruct: לבֿ]נוהי "for his sons", or the like in line 1. See *ALD* 12:9.

Frag. 55

1.]הֿויתֿ[
2.]שת די הואֿ[

Line 1 is a form of the verb "to be"

Frag. 56

]הוו כדן מן .[

Frag. 57

1.]. וֿימת[
2.]הוה רחם[

1.] and he died [
2.] he was loving [

Frag. 58

י]שׂראל ב[

] Israel in [

Israel is mentioned in the name midrash of Jochebed: לכבוד לישראל, "for glory for Israel" (11:10).

Frag. 59

1.]ין ..[
2.]כדנהֿ[

2.] like this [

Frag. 60

]כֿיומי.[

] as days of [

ARAMAIC CONCORDANCE

Abbreviations

adj.	adjective
adv.	adverb
conj.	conjugation, conjunction
constr.	construct state
f.	feminine
GN	geographical name
H	Hebraism
interj.	interjection
m.	masculine
n.	noun
num.	numbers
part.	particle
pl.	plural
PN	personal name
prep.	preposition
pron.	pronoun
vb.	verb

אב n.m.	father	1.1, 4.1, 5.1, 5.4, 5.5, 5.6, 5.6, 5.7, 7.4, 13.2
אבר n.m.	portion, limb	8.2
אדון n.m.	ash (tree)	7.6
אדין adv.	then	4.1, 4.3, 4.4, 4.13, 5.2, 5.5, 7.1, 7.4, 8.1
אוצר n.m.	treasure house	13.12
אורח n.f.	path	3.4
אזל vb.	to go	2.1, 5.6, 13.8 (Qumran)
אח n.m.	brother	2.1, 2.1, 2.1, 2.1, 5.4, 12.1, 13.1, 13.6, 13.8
אחרן adj.	another	11.5
אטולה n.f.	fir	7.6
איתי particle of existence	there is	13.13, 13:16
אכל vb	to eat	4.9, 4.10
אל n.m.	God	5.3, 5.4, 5.8, 6.5, 8.6, 13.2

אל adv.	not	3.9, 13.7
אלף vb.	to teach, learn	5.8, 6.2, 13.4, 13.5, 13.6, 13.7, 13.7, 13.9, 13.15
אם conj. (H)	if	9.1, 9.1
אמר vb.	to say	1.2, 3.2, 4.13, 6.1, 7.5, 7.7, 11.10, 12.4, 13.2
אנה pron.	I	2.1, 2.3, 2.3, 2.4, 4.3, 4.13, 4.13, 5.3, 5.8, 12.3, 12.6, 13.2, 13.2
אנש n.m.	man	1.1, 2.3, 4.13
אנתה n.f.	woman, wife	6.4, 12.3, 12.7
אנת pron.	you (m.)	6.4, 6.4, 6.4, 6.5
אנתון pron.	you pl. (m.)	1.2
אע n.m.	wood	7.4, 7.5, 8.1, 8.7, 9.1
אע-דקה n.f.	asphalthos (?)	7.6
אע-משחה n.m.	oleaster	7.6
אף conj.	also	4.13, 5.1, 5.5, 13.16, 13.16
אצבע n.m.	finger	3.2
ארבע num.	four	11.7, 11.11, 12.3
ארבעין num.	forty	11.9, 12.8
ארו/ארי conj.	since, behold	6.4, 6.4, 7.4, 11.8, 11.8, 12.4, 13.9
ארז n.m.	cedar	7.6
ארע n.f.	land	4.9, 12.1, 12.4, 12.6, 12.8
אשויות see שוי		
אתי vb.	to come	13.11
ב prep.	in, at within	1.2, 1.3, 2.1, 2.1, 2.1, 3.9, 4.13, 5.3, 5.4, 5.5, 5.6, 6.5, 7.1, 8.1, 8.5, 8.6, 8.6, 8.7, 9.1, 11.7, 11.7, 11.8, 11.9, 11.9, 11.11, 11.11, 11.11, 12.1, 12.3, 12.5, 12.8, 13.1, 13.1, 13.5, 13.8, 13.8, 13.8, 13.9, 13.11, 13.16
באיש/ביש adj.	evil	3.5, 13.3
בדיל conj.	in order that	13.10
בזז vb.	to despoil, plunder	13.11

בירה n.f.	residence	5.6
בכורין n.m.pl.	first fruits	4.9
בלחוד prep.	by . . . self	3.3, 9.1
בלל vb.	to mix	8.6
בסרון see בשרון		
בעי vb.	to ask, wish, etc.	11.8, 13.13, 13.14
בקר vb.	examine	7.4
בר n.m.	son	1.1, 3.18, 5.3, 6.1, 6.2, 6.3, 11.8, 12.1, 12.1, 12.2, 12.2, 12.2, 12.2, 12.6, 12.6, 12.7, 12.7, 12.8, 12.9, 13.1, 13.1, 13.2, 13.2, 13.4, 13.4, 13.6, 13.15
ברה n.f.	daughter	1.2, 11.10, 12.1, 12.3, 12.5
ברות n.m.	cypress	7.6
ברך vb.	to bless	5.4, 5.4, 5.5, 5.5, 5.7, 13.3
בשים adj.	having pleasant odour, fragrant	7.5
בשר n.m.	flesh	1.3, 4.11 (Qumran), 6.1, 6.5
בשרון n.m.	disdain	13.5
בתר prep.	after	8.4, 8.4, 8.4, 8.4, 8.4, 8.6, 8.6, 11.11
גבורה n.f.	might	3.6
גבר n.m.	man, person	6.5, 13.7
גזר vb.	to cut, circumcise	1.3
גלי vb.	to reveal	4.13
גמר vb.	to complete	12.6
דבק vb.	to attach, join	4.5
דחי vb.	to repel	3.5
-ד, די, זי conj.	that, because, who, which, of	1.1, 1.2, 2.1, 2.1, 2.1, 3.8, 3.8, 3.15, 4.7, 4.13, 5.2, 5.8, 7.2, 7.3, 7.5, 7.5, 7.7, 7.7, 8.7, 8.7, 9.1, 11.6, 11.8, 11.11, 12.3, 12.4, 12.9, 13.1, 13.1, 13.3, 13.3, 13.5, 13.5, 13.7, 13.8, 13.9, 13.10, 13.11, 13.15

דין n.m.	law	1.1, 3.17, 5.8, 6.1, 6.2, 6.2
דלק vb.	to burn, light, kindle	8.1
דם n.m.	blood	8.1, 8.2, 8.3
דמי vb.	to resemble, be like	13.8, 13.8
דמך vb.	to sleep	4.10
דן pl. אלין pron.	this, that	2.1, 4.13, 4.13, 7.6, 7.7, 8.1
דנה pron.	this	7.2, 7.4, 8.6, 12.4
דפנא n.f.	rib, side	8.4
דפרן n.m.	juniper (bay)	7.6
הא interj.	behold, here is, but	8.1
הדס n.m.	myrtle	7.6
הוא pron.	he, it	4.13, 5.1, 6.1, 9.1, 11.8
הוי vb.	to be, exist, happen	1.2, 1.3, 1.3, 2.1, 3.10, 4.7, 4.13, 5.2, 5.2, 5.3, 5.4, 7.1, 7.1, 7.1, 7.2, 7.2, 7.3, 7.3, 8.3, 8.6, 8.7, 8.7, 11.6, 11.8, 11.8, 11.10, 12.8, 12.8, 12.9, 13.1, 13.3, 13.3, 13.4, 13.5, 13.8, 13.16
הוך vb.	to walk, move toward	13.8 (Qumran)
היא pron.	she	13.1, 13.10
היה vb. (H)	to be	11:8
היך adv.	as if, as	4.11, 6.4
הינון/אינון pron.	they (m.), those	2.1, 7.4, 7.4, 7.6, 7.7, 13.1, 13.15
הכה adv.	how	4.11 (Qumran)
הכין adv.	how	4.11
הן conj.	if	1.2, 13.11
הרי vb.	to conceive	11.5, 11.10
זהר vb.	to warn, be careful	6.1, 6.3, 7.4
זכי vb.	to be pure	6.5
זמן n.m.	time	4.10, 4.10, 4.10, 4.10, 4.10, 4.10, 12.1
זנו n.f.	fornication	3.5, 6.4
זנות n.f. (H)	fornication	6.3

זרע n.m.	seed, offspring	3.15, 6.4, 6.4, 6.4, 13.3
זרע vb.	to sow, plant	13.3, 13.3, 13.3
זרק vb.	to sprinkle	8.1
חביב adj.	beloved, dear	13.2
חבר n.m.	friend	1.2, 13.8
חד num.	one	4.6, 11.7, 11.11, 12.5
חדי vb.	to be happy, rejoice	5.7
חודש n.m. (H)	month	11.11
חוי vb.	to tell	2.1, 2.1, 13.2
חוכמה n.f.	wisdom	3.6, 13.4, 13.4, 13.5, 13.5, 13.6, 13.7, 13.7, 13.9, 13.10, 13.10, 13.12, 13.13, 13.13, 13.15
חושבן n.m.	calculation, amount	8.7
חזי vb.	to see	5.7, 6.2, 7.3, 7.4, 7.5, 7.7, 8.3, 8.5, 8.7, 12.9, 13.6, 13.12, 13.15
$_2$חזי vb.	to see a vision	4.4, 4.5, 4.11
חזיו n.m.	vision	4.4, 4.4, 4.13, 4.13
חטא n.m.	sin	6.1
חיי vb.	to live	12.3, 12.8
חיין n.m.	life, lifetime	5.4, 11.7, 11.9, 11.11, 12.3, 12.9, 13.1
חיל n.m.	strength, army	13.11
חלל vb.	to desecrate	6.4
חמדה n.f.	choice, desire	4.9
חמי vb.	to see	1.3
חמס n.m.	violence	2.1, 12.6
חמר n.m.	wine	8.6
חנן vb.	supplicate	11.8
חסר vb.	to lack	8.7, 13.14
חפי vb.	to cover	8.3
חרב n.m.	sword	4.9
חרץ n.m.	loin	8.4

חתם vb.	to seal, sign	1.3
טב adj.	good, precious	3.8, 13.3, 13.3, 13.10, 13.12
טומאה n.f.	uncleanliness	6.1, 6.3, 6.5
טמא vb.	to defile	1.1
טמר vb.	to hide, conceal	4.13, 6.2
יד n.f.	hand, forequarter (of an animal)	3.2, 5.4, 7.2, 7.3, 8.2, 8.4, 8.4, 8.4
ידיד n.m. (H)	friend	13.2
ידע vb.	to know	3.3, 5.8, 13.10, 13.16
יהב vb.	to give	4.11, 5.3, 13.5, 13.9
יום n.m.	day	12.5, 12.9, 13.7
ילד vb.	to give birth, bear	11.7, 11.8, 11.8, 11.9, 11.10, 11.10, 11.10, 11.11, 12.4, 12.4, 12.5
יסף vb.	to add, increase	11.10
יקר n.m.	glory	11.10, 13.4, 13.5, 13.6, 13.9, 13.10, 13.10, 13.15, 13.16
ירח n.m.	month	11.7, 11.9
ירך n.f.	thigh	8.4, 8.4
ירת vb.	to inherit	13.15
ית part.	accusative marker	5.8, 5.8
יתב vb.	to sit	4.3, 13.10
יתר vb.	to add	8.7
(-)כ prep.	as, like, according to	1.1, 5.2
כבוד n.m. (H)	glory	11.10
כבש vb.	to conquer	13.12
כדי adv.	when	4.2, 5.2, 5.8, 7.1, 7.2, 7.3, 8.1, 8.5, 11.8, 11.10, 12.4, 12.4, 12.6, 12.8
כדן adv.	so, thus	4.13, 5.1, 12.4
כהונה/כהנו n.f.	priesthood	4.7, 5.4, 5.8, 6.2, 7.1, 11.6,
כהין n.m.	priest	5.4, 5.8, 6.4, 13.16
כהן vb.	to serve as a priest	12.7

כוות(-) prep.	like	1.3, 1.3
כורסי n.m.	chair, throne	13.10
כותל n.m.	wall	8.1
כילי n.m.	scoundrel	13.8
ככר n.m.	talent	9.1
כל pron.	everything, all, each	1.1, 1.1, 1.2, 2.3, 3.9, 4.9, 4.9, 4.11, 4.13, 4.13, 5.2, 5.3, 5.4, 5.7, 6.1, 6.1, 6.1, 6.2, 6.3, 6.3, 6.4, 6.5, 6.5, 6.5, 7.2, 7.3, 7.5, 8.5, 8.6, 8.6, 8.7, 11.6, 12.9, 13.1, 13.3, 13.8, 13.9, 13.9, 13.10, 13.11, 13.14, 13.16
כמיסת adj.	adequate, worthy	8.5
כן n.m.	base, stalk	8.4
כן adv.	thus	8.6
כנשה n.f.	assembly	11.6
כען adj.	now	4.11, 6.2, 6.5, 13.4, 13.15
כף n.m.	palm	3.2
כפן n.m.	hunger	4.9
כפן vb.	to be hungry, starve	4.10
ל(-) prep.	to, towards, for	1.1, 1.2, 1.3, 2.1, 2.1, 3.1, 3.10, 3.17, 3.18, 4.6, 4.7, 4.9, 4.11, 4.11, 4.13, 4.13, 5.2, 5.3, 5.3, 5.4, 5.4, 5.4, 5.7, 5.8, 5.8, 6.1, 6.1, 6.3, 6.4, 6.4, 6.4, 6.5, 6.5, 7.1, 7.2, 7.3, 7.4, 7.5, 7.5, 7.7, 8.3, 8.5, 8.6, 8.7, 8.7, 9.1, 9.1, 11.6, 11.6, 11.7, 11.7, 11.8, 11.8, 11.8, 11.8, 11.9, 11.10, 11.10, 11.10, 11.10, 11.10, 11.10, 11.11, 11.11, 11.11, 12.1, 12.1, 12.1, 12.1, 12.2, 12.3, 12.3, 12.3, 12.6, 12.6, 12.6, 12.7, 12.8, 12.9, 13.1, 13.1, 13.1, 13.2, 13.2, 13.2, 13.2, 13.2, 13.4, 13.4, 13.5, 13.5, 13.6, 13.6, 13.6, 13.6, 13.6, 13.7, 13.8, 13.8, 13.8, 13.9, 13.10, 13.10, 13.10, 13.16
לא adv.	no	4.13, 6.2, 6.4, 7.2, 8.3, 8.7, 8.7, 8.7, 12.9, 13.8, 13.8, 13.12, 13.12, 13.12, 13.12, 13.12, 13.13, 13.14, 13.16
לב n.m.	heart	4.13

לבונה n.f. (H)	frankincense	8.6
לבוש n.m.	garment	5.4, 7.1
לבש vb.	to dress	5.4, 7.1, 7.2
לות prep.	to, toward, with	4.12, 5.6
לחדה adv.	particularly	11.8
לקדמין prep.	first of all	6.3, 8.3
מאה num.	hundred	12.9
מאמר n.m.	word, command	13.2
מארי/מרי n.m.	lord	3.3, 3.10, 3.14, 5.8
מאת n.f.	land	13:8, 13:11
מדבח n.m.	altar	7.2, 7.3, 7.5, 7.7, 8.1, 8.1, 8.7
מדינה n.f.	country	13.8, 13.11
מדנח n.m.	east	2.1, 11.7
מה pron.	what, which	2.1, 5.2
מוסר n.m.	instruction	13.4, 13.6, 13.15
מות vb.	to die	11.8, 11.8, 12.9, 13.1
מחיר n.m.	price	13.13
מחל vb.	to be lax	13.7
מטמור n.m.	hidden place	13.12, 13.13
מיין n.m.pl.	water	7.1
מילה n.f.	word	13.10
מילה n.f. (H)	circumcision	1.3
מין n.m.	kind	7.5
מלאך n.m.	angel	4.6
מלח n.m.	salt	5.4
מלח vb.	to salt	8.2, 8.5
מלי vb.	to be full, fill	5.4
מלך n.m.	king	4.8, 13.6, 13.11, 13.16
מלכו n.f.	kingdom	4.7, 4.7, 4.9, 13.16
מן prep.	from	3.18, 4.2, 4.7, 4.11 (Qumran), 4.12, 4.13, 5.3, 5.6, 6.1, 6.1, 6.2, 6.3, 6.3, 6.4, 6.5,

		7.4, 7.5, 7.5, 7.5, 7.7, 8.1, 8.2, 8.7, 11.8, 11.11, 12.1, 12.4, 13.9, 13.9, 13.13, 13.16
מנדע n.m.	knowledge	3.6
מנה n.m.	mina (coin)	9.1
מעשר n.m.	tithe	5.3
מר adj. (H)	bitter	11.8
מריר adj.	bitter	11.8
מרר n.m.	bitterness	11.8
משח n.m.	oil	8.6
משפחה n.f. (H)	family	6.4
מתקל n.m.	weight	8.7, 9.1
נגד n.m.	value	13.13
נגד vb.	to depart	4.1, 4.12
נדד vb.	to be restless	4.10
נדר n.m.	to make a vow	5.2
נוח vb.	to rest	4.10
נור n.m.	fire	8.1
נחשיר n.m.	chase	4.9
נטל vb.	to lift up	3.1
ניחח n.m.	pleasantness	8.6
ניע n.m.	breast of an animal	8.4
נישף n.m.	fine meal	8.6
נכס n.m.	possession	13.11
נכסה n.f.	sacrifice	8.3
נכרי/נכר n.m.	stranger	13.8, 13.8
נסב vb.	to take	6.4, 6.4, 7.3, 12.3, 12.7, 13.11
נסך vb.	to libate	8.6
נצפה n.f.	conflict	4.9
נתן vb.	to give	13.15, see יהב
סנדה n.m.	mastik, almond	7.6

סגי adj.	much, many	11.8, 13.9, 13.11
סגי vb.	to increase	13.7
סוף n.m.	end	13.16
סחי vb.	to wash, bathe	7.1
שימה/סימה n.f.	treasure	13.10, 13.12, 13.13
סלק vb.	to go up, come up, rise	7.3, 7.4, 7.5, 7.5, 7.7, 8.1, 8.2, 8.3, 8.7, 9.1, 9.1
ספר n.m.	reading and writing	13.4, 13.6, 13.15, 13.16
סרך n.m.	due order	8.6, 8.7
עאן n.f.	sheep	2.1
עבד vb.	to do	1.1, 8.7, 8.7
עבד n.m.	slave	3.16, 3.18, 12.6, 13.16
עבר vb.	to pass	13.16
עד prep.	while, until	4.5, 7.2, 12.3, 12.9, 13.3, 13.16
עדן n.m.	time	2.1, 12.1
עובד n.m.	deed, act	8.6, 13.3
עוד prep. (H)	more, again	7.3, 8.2, 11.5, 11.8, 11.10
עור vb.	to awake	4.12
עורלה n.m. (H)	foreskin	1.3
עותר n.m.	wealth	13.10
עין n.m.	eye	4.10
על prep.	on, about, to, concerning, against	4.1, 5.1, 7.7, 8.1, 8.1, 8.3, 8.6, 11.8, 11.8, 11.8, 13.3, 13.10
על-דברת prep.	according to the manner	1.1
עלה n.f.	burnt offering	7.7
עליון adj.	high	4.7, 5.8, 8.6
עלל vb.	to enter, bring in	5.1, 7.1, 11.11, 12.1, 12.6, 12.8, 13.3, 13.3, 13.12
עללה n.f.	harvest	13.3
עלם n.m.	eternity, world	4.11, 13.3, 13.4, 13.16

עם n.m.	people, army	12.4, 13.11
עם prep.	with	4.8, 6.4, 8.4, 8.4, 8.4, 11.7, 11.8, 11.10, 13.1, 13.3, 13.4, 13.11
עמל n.m.	work	4.9
עמל vb.	to work	4.10
עני vb.	to answer, begin to speak	13.2
עסרין num.	twenty	12.7
עע see אע		
ער n.m.	laurel	7.6
עשר vb.	to tithe	5.2
פגשה n.f.	fighting	4.9
פחז n.m.	fornication	6.3
פקד vb.	to command, instruct	5.8, 13.1, 13.2
פקוד n.m.	instruction	13.2
פר n.m. (H)	bull	9.1
פרש n.m.	rider	13.11
פתגם n.m.	word, thing	6.2
צבי vb.	to want, desire	1.2, 13.9
צדקה n.f.	righteousness	13.3
צואר n.m.	neck	8.4, 8.4
צות vb.	to listen, pay attention	13.2
צלו n.f.	prayer	3.16
צלח vb.	to split	7.4
קדיש adj.	holy	6.4, 6.4, 6.5
קדם adv.	forward, before	2.1
קדש vb.	to sanctify	6.4
קודם prep.	before	3.7, 3.8, 5.3, 7.4, 8.6
קודש n.m.	holy place	6.4
קום vb.	to rise, stand	7.1, 13.3
קורבן n.m.	sacrifice	5.4, 5.5, 8.6,

קמאה prep.	first	11.7
קושט/קשוט n.m.	truth	1.3, 3.2, 3.4, 3.17, 6.2, 13.2, 13.3, 13.3, 13.14
קטל vb.	to kill, murder	12.6
קטל n.m.	killing	4.9
קטר vb. (H)	to burn, offer incense, cense	8.6
קני vb.	to acquire	13.10
קרא vb. (H)	to read	11.8, see קרי
קרב n.m.	war, battle	4.9, 7.2
קרב n.m.	entrails	8.4
קרב vb.	to come near, sacrifice	3.10, 5.4, 5.5, 7.2, 7.3, 7.4, 8.7
קרי vb.	to read, call	6.4, 12.4, 12.4, 13.1
קריב adj.	near	6.5, 6.5
ראש n.m.	head, chief	5.3, 8.3, 13.16
רב adj.	great, large	4.7, 6.1, 9.1, 11.6, 13.9, 13.10, 13.11, 13.15, 13.16
רבו n.f. (from רב״י)	anointment	4.11
רבו$_2$ n.f. (from רב״ב)	greatness	13.6
רגל n.f.	foot, leg	7.2, 7.3, 8.2, 8.4
רום vb.	to rise up, exalt	12.4
רחם n.m.	friend	13.9
רחמין n.m.pl.	mercy, compassion	3.7
רחע vb.	to lave	7.2, 7.3, 8.2, 8.4
רחק vb.	to be distant	3.5
ריח n.m.	smell	7.5, 8.6
רם adj.	high, elevated	4.5, 12.4
רעי vb.	to desire, want	4.11 (Qumran)
רתיך n.m.	chariot	3.11
שאל vb.	to ask, inquire	13.9

שביעי num.	seventh	11.11
שבע num.	seven	4.12, 12.9
שבק vb.	to leave	2.1, 13.7
שדרה n.f.	spine	8.4
שוח n.m.	pine	7.6
שוט vb.	to despise	13.5
שוי vb.	to put in place, agree	11.10, 12.1
שור vb.	to jump	2.1
שור n.m.	wall	13.12
שיטו n.f.	scorn	13.5
שכב vb.	to lie down	4.3
שכח vb.	to find, be able	3.7, 13.12, 13.12
שלט vb.	to rule	3.9
שלם n.m.	peace, well-being	2.2, 2.3, 4.9, 4.11, 5.5, 13.9
שלם vb.	to come to an end, complete	5.5
שם n.m.	name	7.6, 11.5, 11.8, 11.10, 12.2, 12.2, 12.2, 12.4
שמין n.m.pl.	sky, heaven	3.1, 4.5, 4.5, 4.6, 5.8
שמע vb.	to hear, understand	13.10
שמש n.f./m.	sun	11.7
שנה n.f.	sleep	4.10, 4.13
שנה n.f.	year	11.7, 11.9, 11.11, 12.1, 12.3, 12.6, 12.6, 12.7, 12.7, 12.8, 12.8, 12.9, 13.1, 13.1
שפט n.m. (H)	judge	13.16
שפיר adj.	beautiful	3.8
שרי vb.	to dwell	5.6, 5.8, 8.1, 8.1, 8.2, 13.1
שת num.	six	9.1
שתין num.	sixty	11.11
שת-עשרה num.	sixteen	12.1
שׂטן n.m.	a satan (type of evil spirit)	3.9

תאנה n.f.	fig-tree	7.6
תוב vb.	to return	7.2, 7.3, 13.3
תוב adv.	again, more	7.2
תולעה n.f.	worm	7.4
תור n.m.	ox	8.3, 9.1
תחות prep.	under	4.5, 7.7
תככה n.f.	unknown tree	7.6 (Quman)
תליתי num.	third	4.7, 11.8, 11.9, 12.9
תלתין num.	thirty	11.7, 12.9
תמה vb.	to wonder, be astonished	4.13
תמני num.	eight	12.7, 12.8
תמנין num.	eighty	12.8
תמני-עשר num.	eighteen	12.6, 12.6, 13.1
תנן n.m.	smoke	7.5
תקף adj.	to be strong	13.11
תרב n.m.	fat	8.3, 9.1
תרי-עשר num.	twelve	7.5
תרין num.	second	9.1
תרע n.m.	entrance	4.6, 13.12
תשע num.	nine	12.8
תשעין num.	ninety	12.3
תשע-עשרה num.	nineteen	12.7

Names of Persons and Places

אבל מין GN	4.2
אברהם PN	5.6, 6.4, 7.4
אשר GN	2.1
בית-אל GN	5.5, 5.6, 7.1
גרשון PN	12.2
חברון GN	12.2
יהודה PN	2.1, 2.1

יוכבד PN	11.10, 12.3, 12.5
יוסף PN	13.1, 13.6
יעקב PN	1.1, 4.1, 5.2
יצהר PN	12.2
יצחק PN	5.1, 5.6, 5.7
ישראל GN	11.6, 11.10
כנען GN	12.6
לוי PN	6.1, 13.2
מושי PN	12.2
מחלי PN	12.2
מררי PN	11.8, 12.2
מצרים GN	11.11, 12.1, 12.4, 12.8, 12.8
עוזיאל PN	12.2
עמרם PN	12.2, 12.3, 12.4, 12.4
קהת PN	11.5, 12.2
ראובן PN	1.1, 2.1
שכם GN	2.1, 2.1, 12.6
שמעון PN	13.3
שמעי PN	12.2

GREEK CONCORDANCE

Ἀβραάμ	3.14, 6.4, 10.3, 10.10
ἀγαπάω	10.11, 10.11
ἀγαπητός	10.11
ἅγιάζω	6.4
ἅγιασμός	6.4
ἅγιος	3.2, 3.6, 6.4, 6.5, 10.4, 10.6, 10.11
ἄδικος	3.5
ἀείρω	3.1
αἷμα	8.2, 8.3, 10.6, 10.8, 10.8, 10.10
αἰνέω	3.7
αἰών	3.15, 3.17, 3.17, 3.18, 10.12
ἀκαθαρσία	3.11, 6.1, 6.3, 6.5
ἀκούω	10.1
ἀλήθεια	3.2, 3.4, 6.2
ἀληθινός	3.17
ἅλίζω	8.5, 9.5, 9.6
ἅλς	8.5, 9.5, 9.6
ἀμνός	9.5
ἄν	8.7, 9.6, 9.16
ἀναγγέλλω	6.2
ἀναπετάννυμι	3.2
ἀναποιέω	8.6, 9.12, 9.15
ἀνάπτω	10.6
ἀναφέρω	7.3, 7.4, 8.3, 8.7, 9.1, 9.5
ἄνθρωπος	6.5
ἀνοίγνυμι	3.1
ἀνομία	3.11, 3.11

ἀπό 3.5, 3.9, 3.11, 3.11, 3.11, 3.14, 3.18, 6.1, 6.1, 6.2, 6.3, 6.3, 6.3, 6.4, 6.5, 7.4, 8.2, 9.7, 10.7, 10.9

ἀποδείκνυμι 9.6

ἀποστρέφω 3.5, 3.14

ἅπτω 10.6

ἀρέσκω 3.7

ἀρήν 9.4

ἀρνίον 9.9, 9.11, 9.13

ἄρχω 8.1, 8.2

ἀσφάλαθος 7.6

αὐθημερόν 10.6

αὐτάρκως 8.5

αὐτός 3.11, 3.15, 6.5, 7.4, 7.6, 8.3, 8.3, 8.5, 9.1, 9.1, 9.5, 9.6, 9.9, 9.15, 9.15, 9.16, 10.6, 11.6, 11.8

ἀφίστημι 3.18

β΄ 9.1

βάτος 9.18

βεβηλόω 6.4

βερωθα 7.6

βιβλίον 10.12

βίβλος 10.1

βουλή 3.6

βωμός 7.2, 7.3, 8.7, 9.5

γάρ 6.4, 10.3, 10.8, 10.10

γαστήρ 11.8

γενεά 3.17

γεννάω 11.6

γῆ 3.11, 10.12

γίνομαι 3.11, 3.16, 6.5, 9.18

γινώσκω 3.3, 5.8

γνῶσις 3.6

γραφή	10.1
δ´	9.18
δάκτυλος	3.2
δάφνη	7.6
δέ	3.16
δεῖ	7.3
δείκνυμι	3.6
δέρμα	9.9
δεσπότης	3.6, 3.11
δεύτερος	9.1, 9.7
δή	3.11
διά	10.7
διαλογισμός	3.3
διδάσκω	6.2
δίδωμι	3.4, 3.6, 3.15
δίκαιος	3.15
δίμοιρος	9.7
διό	3.11
δοῦλος	3.1
δυναστεία	3.11
δύο	9.11, 9.16, 9.18
ἐάν	10.9
ἐγγίζω	7.2
ἐγγύς	3.16, 6.5, 6.5
ἐγώ	2.4, 3.1, 3.1, 3.1, 3.2, 3.2, 3.4, 3.4, 3.4, 3.5, 3.6, 3.6, 3.7, 3.9, 3.9, 3.10, 3.10, 3.11, 3.11, 3.11, 3.14, 3.14, 3.17, 3.17, 6.4, 10.1, 10.3, 10.3, 10.10, 10.10, 10.11
εἰ	9.3, 9.4, 9.5
εἰμί	3.1, 6.4, 6.5, 9.17, 9.18, 9.18, 10.2, 10.8, 10.9, 10.11, 10.14, 11.6
εἰρήνη	3.11
εἰς	3.2, 3.15, 3.17, 3.17, 9.1, 9.1, 9.2, 10.4

εἰσακούω 3.16

ἐκ 6.4, 9.1, 9.3, 9.3, 9.7, 9.11, 9.15, 10.6

ἐκπορεύω 10.6

ἔκτος 9.13

ἔλαιον 8.6, 9.11, 9.14

ἐλεέω 3.1

ἐμφέρω 10.12

ἐν 6.5, 8.5, 8.6, 8.7, 8.7, 9.1, 9.10, 9.12, 10.8, 10.9, 10.10, 10.12, 10.12, 11.7, 11.8

ἔναντι 10.5

ἐνδιδύσκω 7.2

ἐνιαύσιος 9.5

ἔννοια 3.3

ἐντέλλω 10.3, 10.3, 10.10

ἐνώπιον 3.7

ἐξαλείφω 3.11, 10.13

ἐξελέγχω 10.4

ἐπάνω 8.6

ἐπί 7.3, 8.3, 8.7, 9.5, 9.16, 9.16, 10.6, 10.8, 11.6

ἐπισκοπέω 7.4

ἔργον 8.6

ἔριφος 9.4, 9.5, 9.9, 9.11, 9.14, 9.15

ἔτι 3.18

ἔτος 11.7

εὐθύς 2.5

εὐλογέω 3.14, 3.15, 10.12, 10.14

εὑρίσκω 3.7, 10.1

εὔχομαι 3.2

ἐφίστημι 3.3

ἕως 10.12

ζάω 2.5

ζωή	10.12
ἤ	9.3
ἡμέρα	3.18
ἥμισυς	9.8, 9.15
θερμός	9.18, 9.18
θεχακ	7.6
θυμιάζω	8.6
θυσία	10.4, 10.5
θυσιαστήριον	10.6
Ἰακώβ	3.14
ι´	9.18
ιβ´	7.5
ἱερεύς	6.4, 10.2
ἱερωσύνη	10.4
ἴσος	9.8
ἰσχύς	3.6
καθαρίζω	3.11
καθαρός	6.5
καθήκω	8.5, 8.7, 8.7, 9.1, 9.5, 9.9, 10.4
κακός	3.11
καλύπτω	8.3
καλῶς	3.1, 3.3, 3.11
κατά	9.14, 10.4
κατασπένδω	9.14
κατέναντι	3.2
κατισχύω	3.9
κέδρος	7.6
κεφαλή	8.3, 8.3
κλείω	6.4
κρέας	9.5, 10.9
κριός	9.3, 9.8, 9.11, 9.13, 9.14, 9.15

κρίσις	3.17, 6.1, 6.2
κρύπτω	6.2
κύκλος	3.11
κυπάρισσος	7.6
κύριος	3.3, 3.5, 3.7, 3.14, 6.5, 10.4, 10.11
λ´	9.3, 11.7
λαμβάνω	6.4, 11.8
λατρεύω	3.1
λέγω	3.2, 3.15, 6.1, 7.5, 7.8, 10.11
Λευί	3.16, 6.1, 10.14
λίβανος	8.6, 9.16
λιβανωτός	9.15
λόγος	3.7, 3.17
λούω	2.5
μ´	9.2
μακρύνω	3.5
μέγας	6.1, 9.5, 9.10
μέλλω	7.3
μέρος	9.7, 9.7, 9.11, 9.18
μετά	3.4, 3.7, 6.4, 8.4, 8.4, 8.6, 8.6
μέτοχος	3.17
μέτρον	8.7, 9.14
μή	3.9, 3.14, 3.18, 6.2, 6.4, 8.3, 8.7, 10.6, 10.8
μηθείς	8.7
μήτηρ	3.14
μνᾶ	9.1, 9.1, 9.1, 9.2, 9.3, 9.3, 9.18
μνημοσύνη	10.12
μολυσμός	7.4
μόνος	3.3, 9.1, 9.1, 9.16
μοσχάριον	9.1
μόσχος	9.2, 9.7

μυρσίνη 7.6
ν΄ 9.18
νίπτω (νίζω) 7.2, 7.3, 8.2, 10.6, 10.7
νῦν 3.4, 6.2, 10.1, 10.4, 10.11, 10.14
Νῶε 10.1
ξύλον 7.4, 7.5, 8.7, 9.1
ὄγδοος 9.13
ὁδός 2.5, 3.4, 3.9
οἶκος 10.9
οἶνος 8.6, 9.14
ολδινα 7.6
ὁλκή 9.16, 9.18, 9.18, 9.18
ὁλοκάρπωσις 7.2
ὅλος 2.5
ὄνομα 7.6, 10.13
ὀπταζόμαι 8.3
ὁράω 10.8, 11.6
ὅσος 7.3, 8.7, 8.7
ὅταν 7.1, 7.2, 7.3, 10.5, 10.6, 10.6
ὅτε 5.8, 11.6
ὅτι 10.4, 10.10, 11.6
οὐ 6.2, 9.16, 10.6, 10.13
ουεδεφωνα 7.6
οὐκέτι 10.9
οὐρανός 3.1, 3.11
οὗτος 7.6, 7.8, 8.6, 9.12
οὕτως 8.7, 10.3, 10.10, 10.10
ὀφθαλμός 3.1
παῖς 3.14, 3.16, 3.18
πάλιν 7.2, 7.3, 8.2, 11.5, 11.8
παραδίδωμι 3.11

παραλαμβάνω	10.5
πᾶς	2.5, 3.3, 3.3, 3.4, 3.9, 3.11, 3.17, 3.17, 3.18, 6.1, 6.2, 6.3, 6.3, 6.5, 7.4, 8.5, 9.15, 10.6, 10.6, 10.7, 10.8, 10.8, 10.12
πατήρ	3.14, 10.3, 10.10, 10.11
πέντε	9.1, 9.7
πεντήκοντα	9.1
περί	10.1
περισσεύω	8.7, 9.9
πίτυς	7.6
πλανάω	3.9
πλύνω	2.4
πνεῦμα	3.5, 3.6
ποιέω	2.5, 3.7, 3.17, 3.17, 8.7, 8.7, 8.7, 10.3, 10.4, 10.5
πορεύω	10.6
πορνεία	6.3
πόρνος	6.4
πούς	7.2, 7.3, 8.2, 10.6, 10.7
πρό	7.2
πρόβατον	9.3
πρός	3.1, 3.11, 7.2, 10.6
προσάγω	3.1, 9.16
προσαίρω	3.11
προσέχω	6.1, 6.3
προστάσσω	10.4
προσφέρω	7.2, 7.3, 9.3, 10.4
προσχόω	9.16
πρόσωπον	3.1, 3.11, 3.14, 3.18
πρῶτος	6.4, 7.4, 7.4, 8.3
πῦρ	8.1
ῥῆμα	6.2
σάρξ	6.1, 10.7, 10.8

Σάρρα 3.14

σατανᾶς 3.9

σάτον 9.5, 9.7, 9.7, 9.8, 9.9, 9.10, 9.11, 9.11, 9.12, 9.13, 9.17

σεαυτός 6.1, 6.3, 6.4

σεμίδαλις 8.6, 9.9, 9.10, 9.12, 9.15

σικλίον 9.18

σίκλος 9.15, 9.16, 9.18, 9.18

σιωπάω 3.18

σκεπάω 3.11

σκέπη 3.11

σοφία 3.6

σπένδω 8.6

σπέρμα 3.15, 6.4, 6.4, 6.4, 6.4, 6.4, 6.4, 10.12, 10.12

σπονδή 9.14

σταθμόν 8.7, 9.1

στέαρ 8.3, 9.1, 9.1, 9.3, 9.16

στολή 10.6

στόμα 3.1

στρόβιλος 7.6

σύ 3.3, 3.7, 3.7, 3.7, 3.9, 3.10, 3.10, 3.11, 3.11, 3.11, 3.14, 3.14, 3.14, 3.16, 3.16, 3.17, 3.18, 3.18, 6.1, 6.2, 6.2, 6.2, 6.4, 6.4, 6.4, 6.4, 6.5, 6.5, 7.2, 7.2, 7.3, 7.3, 8.2, 10.6, 10.8, 10.9, 10.11, 10.11, 10.11, 10.12, 10.12

συγγίγνομαι 11.8

συλλαμβάνω 10.11

συνουσιασμός 6.3

συντελέω 3.11

σχίζω 7.4

σχῖνος 7.6

σῶμα 6.5

τάλαντον 9.1

τάξις 8.7

ταῦρος	9.1, 9.1, 9.5, 9.5, 9.7, 9.10, 9.10, 9.12, 9.14, 9.15
τεῖχος	3.11
τέκνον	3.4, 6.1, 10.1, 10.4, 10.11, 10.14
τέλειος	9.1, 9.2, 9.5
τέταρτος	9.12, 9.18, 11.7
τίκτω	10.11
τότε	2.4, 3.1, 8.1
τράγος	9.3, 9.8, 9.11
τράχηλος	8.4
τρεῖς	9.3
τρίτος	9.9, 9.11, 9.15, 9.17, 9.17
ὕδωρ	2.5
υἱός	3.14, 3.17, 3.18, 10.3
ὑποκάτωθεν	3.11
ὑφή	9.17
ὕψιστος	10.4, 10.11
φάγω	10.9
φωνή	3.16
χαίρω	10.4
χάρις	3.7
χείρ	3.2, 3.2, 7.2, 7.3, 8.2, 10.6, 10.7
ψυχή	10.8, 10.8
ὦμος	8.4
ὥρα	10.6
ὡς	8.5, 10.4, 10.11
ὡσεί	9.18

BIBLIOGRAPHY

Aharoni, Y.
1979 *The Land of the Bible: A Historical Geography* (2nd ed., rev.). trans. and ed. A.F. Rainey. London.

Albani, M.
1992 "Die lunaren Zyklen im 364-Tage-Festkalender von 4QMischmerot/4QS[e]". *Forschungsstelle Judentum: Mitteilungen und Beiträge* 4:3–47.

Albeck, Ch.
1930 *Das Buch der Jubiläen und die Halacha* (Bericht der Hochschule für die Wissenschaft des Judentums 47). Berlin.

Alexander, T. and Dan, Y.
1972 "The Complete '*Midrash Vayisa'u*'". *Folklore Research Center Studies*. 3:67–76 (in Hebrew).

Asmussen, J.P.
1962 "Das iranische Lehnwort naḫšīr in der Kriegsrolle von Qumrān (1QM)". *ActaOr* 26:3–20.

Astour, M.C.
1992 "Salem". *The Anchor Bible Dictionary*. ed. D.N. Freedman. New York: 5.905.

Audet, J.-P.
1953 "Affinités littéraires et doctrinales du 'Manuel de Discipline'". *RB* 60: 41–82. Translated and reprinted in *The 'Didache' in Modern Research*. ed. J. Draper. Leiden: 1996, 129–147.

Baarda, T.
1992 "The Shechem Episode in the Testament of Levi: A Comparison with Other Traditions". *Sacred History and Sacred Texts in Early Judaism. A Symposium in Honour of A.S. van der Woude* (CBET 5). eds. J.N. Bremmer and F. García Martínez. Kampen: 11–73.

Bauer, W.
1957 *A Greek-English Lexicon of the New Testament* (4th ed.). Revised and edited by W.F. Arndt and F.W. Gingrich. Chicago.

Baumgarten, J.
2003 "Some 'Qumranic' Observations on the Aramaic Levi Document". *Sefer Moshe: The Moshe Weinfeld Jubilee Volume*. eds. C. Cohen, A. Hurvitz and S.M. Paul. Winona Lake: 393–401.

Becker, J.
1970 *Untersuchungen zur Entstehungsgeschichte der Testamente der zwölf Patriarchen* (AGAJU 8). Leiden.

Beckh, H.
1895 *Geoponica sive Cassiani Bassi Scholastici De re rustica eclogae*. Leipzig.

Beit-Arié, M.
1993 *The Makings of the Medieval Hebrew Book: Studies in Palaeography and Codicology*. Jerusalem.

Ben-Dov, J. and Horowitz, W.
2003 "The 364-Day Year in Mesopotamia and Qumran". *Meghillot* 1.3–26 (in Hebrew).

Ben-Ḥayyim, Z.
1967 *The Literary and Oral Tradition of Hebrew and Aramaic Amongst the Samaritans*. Jerusalem vol. III, Part II: The Recitation of Prayers and Hymns (in Hebrew).

Bergren, T.A.
1990 *Fifth Ezra: The Text, Origin and Early History* (SCS 25). Atlanta.
Brockelmann, C.
1928 *Lexicon Syriacum* (2nd ed., rev.). Halle.
1895 *Lexicum Syriacum*. Berlin.
Brooke, George J.
1994 "The Genre of 4Q252: From Poetry to Pesher". *DSD* 1:160–179.
Buber, S.
1965 *Midrash Proverbs*. repr. Jerusalem (in Hebrew).
1964 *Midrash Sekel Tov*. repr. Jerusalem (in Hebrew).
Caquot, A.
1998 "Les Testaments qoumrâniens des pères du sacerdoce". *Revue d'histoire et de philosophie religieuses* 78/2:3–26.
Charles, R.H.
1913 *The Apocrypha and Pseudepigrapha of the Old Testament*. Oxford.
1908a *The Greek Versions of the Testaments of the Twelve Patriarchs*. Oxford.
1908b *The Testaments of the Twelve Patriarchs*. London.
1902 *The Book of Jubilees or The Little Genesis*. London.
Charles, R.H. and Cowley, A.
1907 "An Early Source of the Testaments of the Twelve Patriarchs". *JQR* 19:566–583.
Collins, J.J.
1990 "The Sage in the Apocalyptic and Pseudepigraphic Literature". *The Sage in Israel and the Ancient Near East*. eds. J.J. Gammie and L.G. Perdue. Winona Lake: 343–354. Reprinted in *Seers, Sybils and Sages in Hellenistic-Roman Judaism*. Leiden: 1997, 339–350.
Clarke, E.G.
1984 *Targum Pseudo-Jonathan of the Pentateuch: Text and Concordance*. New Jersey.
Conybeare, F.C., Harris, J.R. and Lewis A.S.
1913 *The Story of Aḥikar from the Aramaic, Syriac, Arabic, Armenian, Ethiopic, Old Turkish, Greek and Slavonic Versions*. Cambridge.
Cook, E.M.
1998 "The Aramaic of the Dead Sea Scrolls". *The Dead Sea Scrolls after Fifty Years: A Comprehensive Assessment*. eds. P.W. Flint and J.C. VanderKam. Leiden: 1.359–378.
Cowley, A.
1923 *Aramaic Papyri of the Fifth Century B.C.* Oxford.
Cross, F.M.
1995 *The Ancient Library of Qumran* (3rd ed.). Sheffield.
Dalman, G.
1905 *Grammatik des jüdisch-palästinischen Aramäisch*. Leipzig.
Danby, H.
1933 *The Mishnah*. London.
Denis, A.-M. and Haelewyck, J.-C.
2000 *Introduction à la littérature religieuse judéo-hellénistique*. Turnhout.
DiTommaso, L.
2001 *A Bibliography of Pseudepigrapha Research 1850–1999* (JSPSup 39). Sheffield.
Drower, E.S. and Macuch, R.
1963 *A Mandaic Dictionary*. Oxford.
Eph'al, I. and Naveh, J.
1996 *Aramaic Ostraca of the Fourth Century BC from Idumaea*. Jerusalem.
Epstein, A.
1957 *Mi-kadmoniyyot Ha-Yehudim*. ed. A.M. Habermann. Jerusalem: 2.144–171 (in Hebrew).

Epstein, I.
1974–1989 *Hebrew-English Edition of the Babylonian Talmud*. London.
Eshel, E.
2003 "Apotropaic Prayers in the Second Temple Period". *Liturgical Perspectives: Prayer and Poetry in Light of the Dead Sea Scrolls* (STDJ 48). Leiden: 69–88.
1999 "Demonology in Palestine During the Second Temple Period". (Ph.D. dissertation). Hebrew University, Jerusalem.
Eshel, E. and Eshel, H.
2002 "Toponymic Midrash in 1 Enoch and in Other Second Temple Jewish Literature". *Henoch* 24:115–130.
Eshel, E. and Kloner, A.
1996 "An Aramaic Ostracon of an Edomite Marriage Contract from Maresha, Dated 176 B.C.E.". *IEJ* 46:1–22.
Eshel, H.
2003 "Four Alphabetical Hymns from Qumran". *Studies in the History of Eretz Israel: Presented to Yehuda Ben Porat*. eds. Y. Ben-Arieh and E. Reiner. Jerusalem: 39–56.
Evans, C.A.
2000 "Messiahs". *Encyclopedia of the Dead Sea Scrolls*. eds. L.H. Schiffman and J.C. VanderKam. Oxford: 1.537–542.
Evelyn-White, H.G., trans.
1914 "Hesiod's Works and Days". *Hesiod, the Homeric Hymns and Homerica* (LCL). ed. G. Hugh. London: 2–63.
Fassberg. S.E.
2002 "Qumran Aramaic". *Maarav* 9:19–31.
Feldman, L.H.
2000 *Flavius Josephus; Volume 3: Judean Antiquities 1–4*. Leiden.
Fitzmyer, J.A.
2000 "Aramaic". *Encyclopedia of the Dead Sea Scrolls*. eds. L.H. Schiffman and J.C. VanderKam. Oxford: 1:48–51.
1999 "The Aramaic Levi Document". *The Provo International Conference on the Dead Sea Scrolls. Technological Innovations, New Texts and Reformulated Issues* (STDJ 30). eds. D.W. Parry and E. Ulrich. Leiden: 453–464. Reprinted in *Dead Sea Scrolls and Christian Origins*. Grand Rapids: 2000, 237–248.
1971 *The Genesis Apocryphon of Qumran Cave 1*. Rome.
Fitzmyer, J.A. and Harrington, D.J.
1978 *A Manual of Palestinian Aramaic Texts* (Biblica et Orientalia 34). Rome.
Flusser, D.
1991 "'Which is the Right Way that a Man should Choose for Himself?' (Sayings of the Fathers 2:1)". *Tarbiz* 60:163–178 (in Hebrew).
1966 "Qumran and Jewish Apotropaic Prayers". *IEJ* 16:194–205.
1958 "The Dead Sea Sect and Pre-Pauline Christianity". *Scripta Hierosolymitana* 4:215–266.
Fox, E., trans.
1995 *The Five Books of Moses*. London.
Freedman, H. and Simon, M.
1951 *Midrash Rabbah: Genesis I*. London and Bournemouth.
Friedman, M.A.
1981 *Jewish Marriage in Palestine: A Cairo Geniza Study*. Tel Aviv.
Fuller, R.
1993 "The Blessing of Levi in Dtn 33, Mal 2, and Qumran". *Konsequente Traditionsgeschichte, Festschrift für Klaus Baltzer zum 65. Geburtstag*. eds. R. Bartelmus, T. Krüger and H. Utzschneider. Göttingen: 31–44.

García Martínez, F. and Tigchelaar, E.J.C.
1997–98 *The Dead Sea Scrolls Study Edition*. Leiden.

Gaster, T.H.
1962 "Satan". *Interpreters Dictionary of the Bible*, ed. G.A. Butterick, *et al.* New York: 3.224–28.

Goshen-Gottstein, M.H.
1970 *A Syriac-English Glossary with Etymological Notes*. Wiesbaden.

Greenfield, J.C.
1993 "'Because He/She Did Not Know Letters': Remarks on a First Millennium C.E. Legal Expression". *JANESCU* 22:39–44. Reprinted in *'Al Kanfei Yonah*. eds. S.M. Paul, M.E. Stone and A. Pinnick. Leiden: 2001, 2.939–944.
1992 "Two Notes on the Apocryphal Psalms". *"Sha'arei Talmon", Studies in the Bible, Qumran, and the Ancient Near East Presented to Shemaryahu Talmon*. eds. M. Fishbane and E. Tov. Winona Lake: 309–314. Reprinted in *'Al Kanfei Yonah*. eds. S.M. Paul, M.E. Stone and A. Pinnick. Leiden: 2001, 2.640–45.
1988 "The Words of Levi son of Jacob in Damascus Document IV.15–19". *RQ* 13:319–322.
1979 "Early Aramaic Poetry". *JANESCU* 11:45–51. Reprinted in *'Al Kanfei Yonah*. eds. S.M. Paul, M.E. Stone and A. Pinnick. Leiden: 2001, 1.167–173.
1978 "The Meaning of פחז". *Studies in the Bible and the Ancient Near East, Presented to S.E. Loewenstamm on his Seventieth Birthday*. eds. Y. Avishur and J. Blau. Jerusalem: 35–40. Reprinted in *'Al Kanfei Yonah*. eds. S.M. Paul, M.E. Stone and A. Pinnick. Leiden: 2001, 2.725–730.
1977 "On Some Iranian Terms in Elephantine Papyri: Aspects of Continuity". *Acta Antiqua Academiae Scientiarum Hungaricae* 25:113–118. Reprinted in *'Al Kanfei Yonah*. eds. S.M. Paul, M.E. Stone and A. Pinnick. Leiden: 2001, 2:148–153.
1969 "The 'Periphrastic Imperative' in Aramaic and Hebrew". *IEJ* 19:199–210. Reprinted in *'Al Kanfei Yonah*. eds. S.M. Paul, M.E. Stone and A. Pinnick. Leiden: 2001, 1.56–67.

Greenfield, J.C. and Stone, M.E.
1990 "Two Notes on the Aramaic Levi Document". *Of Scribes and Scrolls: Studies on the Hebrew Bible, Intertestamental Judaism, and Christian Origins Presented to John Strugnell on the Occasion of his Sixtieth Birthday*. ed. H.W. Attridge, *et al.* Lanham: 153–161.
1985 "The Aramaic and Greek Fragments of a Levi Document". *The Testaments of the Twelve Patriarchs: a Commentary* (SVTP 8) by H.W. Hollander and M. de Jonge. Leiden: 457–469.
1979 "Remarks on the Aramaic Testament of Levi from the Geniza". *RB* 86: 214–230. Reprinted in M.E. Stone, *Selected Studies in Pseudepigrapha and Apocrypha* (SVTP 9). Leiden, 1991, 228–246.

Grelot, P.
1991 "Le coutumier sacerdotal ancien dans le *Testament araméen de Lévi*". *RQ* 15:253–263.
1983 "Une mention inaperçue de 'Abba' dans le *Testament araméen de Lévi*". *Semitica* 33:101–108.
1971 "Quatre cents trente ans (Ex XII,34): du Pentateuque au Testament araméen de Lévi". *Hommage a André Dupont-Sommer*. eds. A. Caquot and M. Philonenko. Paris: 383–394.
1956 "Notes sur le Testament araméen de Lévi". *RB* 63:391–406.
1955 "Notes et mélanges: le Testament araméen de Lévi: est-il traduit de l'hébreu?" *RÉJ*, n.s. 14:91–99.

Grintz, Y.M.
1957 *The Book of Judith*. Jerusalem (in Hebrew).
Guggenheimer, H.W.
1998 *Seder Olam*. Northvale and Jerusalem.
Gunther, R.T.
1959 *The Greek Herbal of Dioscorides*. New York.
Halpern-Amaru, B.
1999 *The Empowerment of Women in the Book of Jubilees*. Leiden.
Haupt, D.
1969 "Das Testament des Levi: Untersuchungen zu seiner Entstehung und Überlieferungsgeschichte" (Th.D. dissertation). Halle-Wittenberg.
Hirshfeld, Y.
1993 "Ḥamat Gader". *The New Encyclopedia of Archaeological Excavations in the Holy Land*. ed. E. Stern. Jerusalem: 2.565–566.
Holladay, Carl R.
1983 "Demetrius". *Fragments from Hellenistic Jewish Authors, Volume I: Historians*. Chico: 51–91.
Hollander, H.W.
1981 *Joseph as an Ethical Model in the Testaments of the Twelve Patriarchs* (SVTP 6). Leiden.
Hollander, H.W. and Jonge, M. de
1985 *The Testaments of the Twelve Patriarchs: a Commentary* (SVTP 8). Leiden.
Horovitz, S. and Rabin, I.
1931 *Mekhilta d'Rabbi Ishmael* (Corpus tannaiticum 3, 3). Frankfurt.
Horst, P.W. van der
1994 "Silent Prayer in Antiquity". *Hellenism-Judaism-Christianity: Essays on their Interaction*. Kampen: 252–277. Also printed in *Numen* 41:1–25.
Hultgård, A.
1982 *L'eschatologie des Testaments des Douze Patriarches*. Uppsala.
Ilan, T.
1993 "Biblical Women's Names in the Apocryphal Traditions". *JSP* 11:3–67.
Jaubert, A.
1953 "Le calendrier des Jubilés et la Secte de Qumrân: ses origines bibliques". *VT* 3:250–264.
Jellinek, A.
1938 *Bet ha-Midrasch*. Jerusalem (in Hebrew).
Jonge, M. de
2002 "The Two Great Commandments in the Testaments of the Twelve Patriarchs". *NT* 44:371–392.
1999 "Levi in Aramaic Levi and the Testament of Levi". *Pseudepigraphic Perspectives: The Apocrypha and Pseudepigrapha in Light of the Dead Sea Scrolls*. eds. E.G. Chazon and M.E. Stone (STDJ 31). Leiden: 71–89.
1988 "'The Testament of Levi and 'Aramaic Levi'". *RQ* 13:367–385. Reprinted in *Jewish Eschatology, Early Christian Christology and the Testaments of the Twelve Patriarchs* (NovTsup 63). Leiden: 1991, 244–262.
1981 "Levi, the Sons of Levi and the Law, in *Testament Levi* X, XIV–XV and XVI". *De la Tôrah au Messie. Mélanges H. Cazelles*. eds. J. Doré, P. Grelot and M. Carrez. Tournai: 513–523. Reprinted in *Jewish Eschatology, Early Christian Christology and the Testaments of the Twelve Patriarchs* (NovTsup 63). Leiden: 1991, 180–190.
1974 "Notes on Testament of Levi II–VII". *Travels in the World of the Old Testament: Studies Presented to Professor M.A. Beek on the Occasion of His 65th Birthday*. eds. H. van Voss *et al.* Assen: 132–145. Reprinted in *Studies on the Testaments of the Twelve Patriarchs* (SVTP 3). Leiden: 1975, 247–260.
1960 "Christian Influence in the Testaments of the Twelve Patriarchs". *NT* 4:182–235.

1953 *The Testaments of the Twelve Patriarchs. A Study of their Text, Composition and Origin.* Assen.

Jonge M. de in cooperation with H.W. Hollander, H.J. de Jonge and Th. Korteweg
1978 *The Testaments of the Twelve Patriarchs: a Critical Edition of the Greek Text* (PVTG 1, 2). Leiden.

Jonge, M. de and Tromp, J.
1998 "Jacob's Son Levi in the Old Testament Pseudepigrapha and Related Literature". *Biblical Figures Outside the Old Testament Pseudepigrapha.* eds. M.E. Stone and T.A. Bergren. Harrisburg: 203–235.

Jung, L.
1926 *Fallen Angels in Jewish, Christian and Mohammedan Literature.* Philadelphia.

Kaufman, S.A.
1974 *The Akkadian Influences on Aramaic.* Chicago.

Kister, M.
2000 "'כדת משה ויהודא' The History of a Legal-Religious Formula". *ATARA L'HAIM: Studies in the Talmud and Medieval Rabbinic Literature in Honor of Professor Haim Zalman Dimitrovsky.* eds. D. Boyarin, S. Friedman, M. Hirshman, M. Schmelzer and I.M. Tashma. Jerusalem: 202–208 (in Hebrew).

Klein, M.L.
1980 *The Fragment-Targums of the Pentateuch According to their Extant Sources.* Rome.

Kloner, A.
1990 "Lead Weights of Bar Kokhba's Administration". *IEJ* 40:58–67

Kloner, A. and Mindel, T.
1981 "Two Byzantine Hoards from the Ancient Synagogue of Ḥorvat Rimmon". *INJ* 5:60–68.

Klostermann, E.
1904 *Eusebius Onomastikon.* Leipzig.

Knibb, M.A.
1995 "Messianism in the Pseudepigrapha in the Light of the Scrolls". *DSD* 2:165–184.
1978 *The Ethiopic Book of Enoch.* Oxford.

Köhler, L. and Baumgartner, W.
1994–2000 *The Hebrew and Aramaic Lexicon of the Old Testament.* Leiden.

Kraft, R.A.
2000 "Early Developments of the 'Two-Ways Tradition(s),' in Retrospect". *For a Later Generation: The Transformation of Tradition in Israel, Early Judaism and Early Christianity.* eds. R.A. Argall, B.A. Bow and R.A. Werline. Harrisburg: 136–143.

Küchler, M.
1979 *Frühjüdische Weisheitstraditionen* (Orbis Biblicus et Orientalis 26). Freiburg.

Kugel, J.
1993 "Levi's Elevation to the Priesthood in Second Temple Writings". *HTR* 86:1–64.
1992 "The Story of Dinah in the *Testament of Levi*". *HTR* 85:1–34.

Kugler, R.A.
2001 *The Testaments of the Twelve Patriarchs.* Sheffield.
1999 "The Priesthood at Qumran: The Evidence of References to Levi and the Levites". *The Provo International Conference on the Dead Sea Scrolls. Technological Innovations, New Texts and Reformulated Issues.* eds. D.W. Parry and E. Ulrich. Leiden: 465–479.
1996 *From Patriarch to Priest: The Levi-Priestly Tradition from Aramaic Levi to Testament of Levi* (SBLEJL 9). Atlanta.

Kutscher, E.Y.
1958 "The Language of the Genesis Apocryphon: a Preliminary Study". *Scripta Hierosolymitana* 4. Jerusalem: 1–35.
Lehrman, S.M.
1983 *Midrash Rabbah: Exodus*. London.
Lemaire, A. and Lozachmeur, H.
1987 "*Birah/Birta'* en araméen". *Syria* 64:261–66.
Lévi, I.
1908 "Encore un mot sur le texte araméen du Testament de Lévi". *RÉJ* 55:285–87.
1907 "Notes sur le texte araméen du Testament de Lévi récemment découvert". *RÉJ* 54:166–180.
Levy, J.
1867–68 *Chaldäisches Wörterbuch über die Targumim*. Leipzig.
Lieberman, S.
1988a *The Tosefta*. New York.
1988b *Tosephta Ki-Fshuṭah*. New York.
Licht, J.S.
1965 *The Rule Scroll: A Scroll from the Wilderness of Judaea. 1QS, 1QSa, 1QSb*. Jerusalem (in Hebrew).
Löw, I.
1967 *Die Flora der Juden*. Hildesheim.
1881 *Aramäische Pflanzennamen*. Leipzig.
Mandel, P.
1994 "The Call of Abraham: A Midrash Revisited". *Prooftexts* 14:267–284.
1992 "'Birah' as an Architectural Term in Rabbinic Literature". *Tarbiz* 61:195–217 (in Hebrew).
Mandelbaum, B.
1987 *Pesikta de Rav Kahana According to an Oxford Manuscript*. New York.
Margulies, M., ed.
1993 *Midrash Wayyikra Rabbah*. New York and Jerusalem (in Hebrew).
Menasce, J.P. de
1956 "Iranian naxčīr". *VT* 6:213–14.
Milik, J.T.
1978 "Écrits préesséniens de Qumrân: d'Hénoch à Amram". *Qumrân: Sa piété, sa théologie et son milieu* (BETL 46). ed. M. Delcor. Louvain: 91–106.
1976 *The Books of Enoch: Aramaic Fragments of Qumrân Cave 4*. Oxford.
1972 "4Q Visions de 'Amram et une citation d'Origène". *RB* 79:77–97.
1955 "Le Testament de Lévi en araméen: Fragment de la Grotte 4 de Qumrân". *RB* 62:398–406.
Montgomery, J.A.
1913 *Aramaic Incantation Texts from Nippur*. (University of Pennsylvania Museum, Publications of the Babylonian Section 3.) Philadelphia.
Moore, G.F.
1895 *Judges* (ICC). Edinburgh.
Moreshet, M.
1980 *A Lexicon of the New Verbs in Tannaitic Hebrew*. Jerusalem (in Hebrew).
Morgan, M.A.
1983 *Sefer ha-Razim: The Book of Mysteries* (SBL Texts and Translations 25, Pseudepigrapha Series 11). Chico.
Morgenstern, M.
1999 Review of R.A. Kugler, *From Patriarch to Priest* (SBLEJL 9), Atlanta: 1996, in *JSS* 44:135–37.

Morgenstern, M., Qimron, E. and Sivan, D.
1996 "The Hitherto Unpublished Columns of the Genesis Apocryphon". *AbrN* 33:30–54.
Mosshammer, A.A.
1984 *Georgii Syncelli Ecloga Chronographica.* Leipzig.
Müller, H.P.
1972 "Mantische Weisheit und Apokalyptik". *Congress Volume, Uppsala 1971.* (VTSupp 22). Leiden: 268–293.
1969 "Magisch-mantische Weisheit und die Gestalt Daniels". *UF* 1:79–94.
Nau, F.
1915 *Ammonas, Successeur de Saint Antoine: Textes grecs et syriaques* (Patrologia Orientalis 11.4). Paris.
Nauck, W.
1957 "Probleme des frühchristlichen Amtsverständnisses (I Ptr 5 2f.)". *ZNW* 48:200–220.
Naveh, J.
1978 *On Stone and Mosaic: The Aramaic and Hebrew Inscriptions from Ancient Synagogues.* Jerusalem (in Hebrew).
Naveh, J. and Shaked, S.
1993 *Magic Spells and Formulae.* Jerusalem.
1985 *Amulets and Magical Bowls.* Jerusalem.
Nebe, W.
1997 "4Q559 'Biblical Chronology'". *ZAH* 10:85–88.
Nickelsburg, G.W.E.
2001 *1 Enoch 1: A Commentary on the Book of Enoch, Chapters 1–36; 81–108 (Hermeneia).* Minneapolis.
1984 "The Bible Rewritten and Expanded". *Jewish Writings of the Second Temple Period* (CRINT 2, 2) ed. M.E. Stone. Assen and Philadelphia: 89–156.
1981 *Jewish Literature Between the Bible and the Mishnah.* Philadelphia.
Pass, H.L. and Arendzen, J.
1900 "Fragment of an Aramaic Text of the Testament of Levi". *JQR* 12:651–661.
Payne Smith, R.
1903 *A Compendious Syriac Dictionary.* Oxford.
1879–1901 *Thesaurus Syriacus.* Oxford.
Philonenko, M.
1987 "Testament de Lévi, troisième fils de Jacob et de Léa". *La Bible: Écrits Intertestamentaires.* eds. A. Dupont-Summer and M. Philonenko. Paris: 833–857.
Porten, B. and Yardeni, A.
1993 *Textbook of Aramaic Documents from Ancient Egypt, 3: Literature, Accounts, Lists.* Jerusalem.
1989 *Textbook of Aramaic Documents from Ancient Egypt, 2: Contracts.* Jerusalem.
1986 *Textbook of Aramaic Documents from Ancient Egypt, 1: Letters.* Jerusalem.
Powell, M.A.
1992 "Weights and Measures". *The Anchor Bible Dictionary.* ed. D.N. Freedman. New York: 6.897–908.
Puech, E.
2003 "Notes sur le *Testament de Lévi* de la grotte 1 (1Q21)". *RQ* 21:297–310.
2002 "Le Testament de Lévi en araméen de la geniza du Caire". *RQ* 20:511–556.
1999 "Une nouvelle copie du Livre des Jubilés: 4Q484 = pap4QJubilés[j]". *RQ* 19:261–64.

1992 "Fragments d'un apocryphe de Lévi et le personnage eschatologique, 4QTestLévi[c–d] et 4QAJa". *The Madrid Qumran Congress: Proceedings of the International Congress on the Dead Sea Scrolls, Madrid 18–21 March, 1991.* eds. J. Trebolle Barrera and L. Vegas Montaner. Madrid and Leiden: 2.449–501.
1991 "Le testament de Qahat en araméen de la Grotte 4 (4QTQah)". *RQ* 15:23–54.

Pummer R.
1982 "Genesis 34 in Jewish Writings of the Hellenistic and Roman Periods". *HTR* 75:177–188.

Rad, G. von
1976 "The Joseph Narrative and Ancient Wisdom". *Studies in Ancient Israelite Wisdom.* ed. J.L. Crenshaw. New York: 439–477.
1965 *Old Testament Theology.* Edinburgh and London.

Ringgren, H.
1963 *The Faith of Qumran: Theology of the Dead Sea Scrolls.* New York.

Sandt, H. van de, and Flusser, D.
2002 *The Didache: Its Jewish Sources and Its Place in Early Judaism and Christianity* (CRINT 3, 5). Minneapolis and Assen.

Scharbert, J.
1960 "Das Verbum PQD in der Theologie des Alten Testaments". *BZ, NF* 4:209–226.

Schiffman, L.H.
2002 "Sacrificial Halakhah in the Fragments of the Aramaic Levi Document from Qumran, the Cairo Genizah and Mt. Athos Monastery". Delivered at the Seventh Orion International Symposium, 15–17 January 2002, *Reworking the Bible at Qumran in the Context of Second Temple Judaism.*

Schorch, S.
1997 "Die hebräische Wurzel *QHT*". *ZAH* 10:76–84.

Schürer, E.
1979 *The History of the Jewish People in the Age of Jesus Christ (175 B.C.–A.D. 135)*, vol. 2. Revised and edited by G. Vermes and F. Millar. Edinburgh.
1909 *Geschichte des jüdischen Volkes im Zeitalter Jesu Christi* (4th ed.). Leipzig.

Schwartz, J.
1985 "Jubilees, Bethel and the Temple of Jacob". *HUCA* 56:63–85.

Sear, D.R.
1988 *Roman Coins and Their Values* (rev.). London.

Slotki, J.J.
1939 *Midrash Rabbah.* London.

Smith, M.
1959 "What is Implied by the Variety of Messianic Figures?" *JBL* 78:66–72.

Sokoloff, M.
2002 *A Dictionary of Jewish Babylonian Aramaic of the Talmudic and Geonic Periods.* Ramat Gan.
2000a Review of *Hebräisches und aramäisches Lexikon zum Alten Testament*, by L. Köhler and W. Baumgartner in *DSD* 7:74–109.
2000b "Qumran Aramaic in Relation to the Aramaic Dialects". *The Dead Sea Scrolls: Fifty Years after Their Discovery.* eds. L.H. Schiffman, E. Tov and J.C. VanderKam. Jerusalem: 746–754.
1990 *A Dictionary of Jewish Palestinian Aramaic of the Byzantine Period.* Ramat-Gan.
1974 *The Targum to Job from Qumran Cave XI.* Ramat Gan.

Sokoloff, M. and Yahalom, J.
1999 *Jewish Palestinian Aramaic Poetry from Late Antiquity.* Jerusalem (in Hebrew).

Sperber, D.
1984 *A Dictionary of Greek and Latin Legal Terms in Rabbinic Literature.* Ramat Gan.

Sperling, H., Simon, M. and Levertoff, P.P.
1949 *The Zohar*. London and Bournemouth.
Starcky, J.
1963 "Les quatre étapes du messianisme à Qumran". *RB* 70:481–505.
Stec, D.M.
1994 *The Text of the Targum of Job*. Leiden.
Steiner, R.C.
1995 "The Heading of the *Book of the Words of Noah* on a Fragment of the Genesis Apocryphon: New Light on a 'Lost' Work". *DSD* 2:66–71.
Stone, M.E.
2003 "Levi, Aramaic" Document and Greek Testament of Levi". *Emanuel: Studies in Hebrew Bible, Septuagint and Dead Sea Scrolls in Honor of Emanuel Tov*, eds. S.M. Paul, R.A. Kraft, L.H. Schiffman and W.W. Fields. Leiden: 429–437.
2002 "Aramaic Levi in Its Contexts". *JSQ* 9:307–326.
2000a "Amram". *Encyclopedia of the Dead Sea Scrolls*. eds. L.H. Schiffman and J.C. VanderKam. Oxford: 1.23–24.
2000b "Levi, Aramaic". *Encyclopedia of the Dead Sea Scrolls*. eds. L.H. Schiffman and J.C. VanderKam. Oxford: 1.486–488.
2000c "Qahat". *Encyclopedia of the Dead Sea Scrolls*. eds. L.H. Schiffman and J.C. VanderKam. Oxford: 2.731–32.
1999 "The Axis of History at Qumran". *Pseudepigraphic Perspectives: The Apocrypha and Pseudepigrapha in Light of the Dead Sea Scrolls*. eds. E.G. Chazon and M.E. Stone (STDJ 31). Leiden: 133–149.
1998 "Warum Naphthali? Eine Diskussion im Internet." *Judaica: Beiträge zum Verständnis des Judentums* 54:188–191.
1996a *Armenian Apocrypha: Relating to Adam and Eve* (SVTP 14). Leiden.
1996b "The Testament of Naphtali". *JJS* 47:311–321.
1990 *Fourth Ezra: A Commentary on the Book of Fourth Ezra* (Hermeneia). Minneapolis.
1988 "Enoch, Aramaic Levi and Sectarian Origins". *JSJ* 19:159–170. Reprinted in *Selected Studies in Pseudepigrapha and Apocrypha* (SVTP 9). Leiden: 1991, 247–258.
1987 "Ideal Figures and Social Context: Priest and Sage in the Early Second Temple Age". *Ancient Israelite Religion: Essays in Honor of Frank Moore Cross*. eds. P.D. Miller, P.D. Hanson and S.D. McBride. Philadelphia: 575–86. Reprinted in *Selected Studies in Pseudepigrapha and Apocrypha* (SVTP 9). Leiden: 1991, 259–270.
Stone, M.E. and Eshel, E.
1992 An Exposition on the Patriarchs (4Q464) and Two Other Documents (4Q464^{a} and 4Q464^{b}). *Le Muséon* 105:243–264.
Stone, M.E. and Greenfield, J.C.
1997 "The Fifth and Sixth Manuscripts of *Aramaic Levi Document* from Cave 4 at Qumran (4QLevi^{e} aram and 4QLevi^{f} aram)". *Le Muséon* 110:271–292.
1996a "The Second Manuscript of *Aramaic Levi Document* from Cave 4 at Qumran (4QLevi^{b} aram)". *Le Muséon* 109:1–15.
1996b "The Third and Fourth Manuscripts of *Aramaic Levi Document* from Cave 4 at Qumran (4QLevi^{c} aram and 4QLevi^{d} aram)". *Le Muséon* 109:245–259.
1994 "The First Manuscript of *Aramaic Levi Document* from Cave 4 at Qumran (4QLevi^{a} aram)". *Le Muséon* 107:257–281.
1993 "The Prayer of Levi". *JBL* 112:247–266.
Stuckenbruck, L.T.
1997 *The Book of Giants from Qumran*. Tübingen.
Sukenik, E.L.
1935 "The Ancient Synagogue of El-Ḥammeh". *JPOS* 15:101–180.
Thackeray, H.St.J.
1930 *Josephus IV: Jewish Antiquities, Books I–IV* (LCL). London.

Theodor, J. and Albeck, Ch.
1965 *Midrash Bereshit Rabbah.* Jerusalem (in Hebrew).
Thomsen, R.
1907 *Loca Sancta.* Halle.
Tromp, J.
1997 "Two References to a Levi Document in an Epistle of Ammonas". *NT* 39:235–247.
VanderKam, J.C.
2000 *From Revelation to Canon: Studies in the Hebrew Bible and Second Temple Literature.* Leiden.
1999 "Isaac's Blessing of Levi and his Descendants in *Jubilees* 31". *The Provo International Conference on the Dead Sea Scrolls. Technological Innovations, New Texts and Reformulated Issues.* eds. D.W. Parry and E. Ulrich. Leiden: 497–519.
1997 "Mantic Wisdom in the Dead Sea Scrolls". *DSD* 4:336–353.
1989 *The Book of Jubilees.* (CSCO 510–511, ScrAeth 87–88). Louvain.
1977 *Textual and Historical Studies in the Book of Jubilees* (Harvard Semitic Monographs 14). Missoula.
Vasiliev, A.
1893 "Palaea Historica". *Anecdota Graeco-byzantina.* Moscow.
Vermes, G.
1975 *Post-Biblical Jewish Studies.* Leiden.
Wacholder, B.Z.
1990 "The Ancient Judeo-Aramaic Literature (500–164 B.C.E.): A Classification of Pre-Qumranic Texts". *Archaeology and History of the Dead Sea Scrolls* (JSPS 8). ed. L.H. Schiffman. Sheffield: 257–281.
Weitzman, S.
1999 "Reopening the Case of the Suspiciously Suspended Nun in Judges 18:30". *CBQ* 61:448–460.
Wertheimer, S.A.
1950 *Batei Midrashot.* Enlarged and amended by A.J. Wertheimer. Jerusalem.
Wilkinson, J.
1981 *Egeria's Travels to the Holy Land.* (rev. ed.). Jerusalem.
1977 *Jerusalem Pilgrims Before the Crusades.* Jerusalem.
Wilson, C.W.
1896 "Bordeaux Pilgrim". *Palestine Pilgrims' Text Society* 1:2. London.
Wise, M.O.
1997 "To Know the Times and the Seasons: A Study of the Aramaic Chronograph 4Q559". *JSP* 15:3–51.
Wright, W.
1871 *Catalogue of Syriac Manuscripts in the British Museum.* London.
Yadin, Y.
1962 *The Scroll of the War of the Sons of Light Against the Sons of Darkness.* trans. B. and Ch. Rabin. Oxford.
Yalon, H.
1971 *Studies in the Hebrew Language.* Jerusalem (in Hebrew).
Yardeni, A.
2000 *Textbook of Aramaic, Hebrew and Nabataean Documentary Texts from the Judaean Desert and Related Material. I: The Documents.* Jerusalem (in Hebrew).
Yeivin, Z.
1993 "Eshtemoa". *New Encyclopedia of Archaeological Excavations in the Holy Land.* ed. E. Stern. Jerusalem: 2.423–26.

INDEX OF ANCIENT AND MODERN PERSONS AND PLACES

Aaron 21, 31, 149, 193, 195, 198
Abel Mayyim 135–137
Abel Mayyin 12, 67, 135, 136, 137
Abel Meholah 135, 136
Abel-Beth-Maacah 135–137
Abelmaul 135, 136, 139
Abraham (patriarch) 21, 30, 36, 38–42, 63, 71, 75, 79, 81, 91, 93, 95, 115, 116, 127, 131, 133, 134, 151, 152, 153, 154, 164, 168, 188, 189
Abram (patriarch) 154
Adam 30, 36, 126, 194
Adina, Levi's wife 181
Aharoni, Y. 137
Akiba see Aqiba
Albani, M. 189
Albeck, Ch. 115, 119, 149, 152, 156, 159, 170, 185, 193
Alexander, T. 119, 121, 153
Ammonas 5, 6
Amorites 119, 122
Amram (Ambram) 25, 29–31, 99, 101, 160, 180, 193–195, 198, 199
Aqiba, Rabbi 126, 175
Aram (person) 181
Arendzen, J. 1, 2, 119
Asher (Aser) (place) 59, 118–120
Asmussen, J. 142
Aspis (mountain) 135, 136
Assyria 210
Astour 121
Athaliah 187
Audet, J.-P. 125, 127

Baarda, T. 135
Baillet, M. 25–27
Bar Asher, M. 1
Barag, D. 44
Baruch 132
Bauer, W. 116
Baumgarten, J. 12, 13, 125, 130, 156, 161, 190, 220, 221
Becker, J. 19, 117, 135, 139, 150
Beckh, H. 170
Beer-Zaith 28
Beit-Arié, M. 2
Ben Azzai (rabbi) 175
Ben-Dov, J. 35, 189
Ben-Ḥayyim, Z. 149
Benjamin (patriarch) 27, 184
Benjamin, tribe of 29
Ben-Zvi, I. 137
Bergren, T.A. 114
Bet el-Ma' 137
Bethel 15, 28, 40, 71, 148, 150–152, 162
Bilhah 21, 26
Book of Noah 1, 21, 36, 38, 91, 180
Bordeaux Pilgrim 120
Brockelmann, C. 142, 143, 167, 175, 210, 211, 213, 222
Brooke, G.J. 149, 185, 186
Buber, S. 194
Buth, R. 5, 146

Canaan 99, 101, 193, 199, 200
Caquot, A. 6, 38, 139
Charles, R.H. 2, 3, 6, 14, 45, 112, 117, 119, 143, 147–149, 150, 153, 154, 156, 157, 160, 162, 167, 170, 171, 176, 178, 185, 188, 190, 197, 207, 209
Chazon, E. 26
Christ 22, 204, 207
Collins, J.J. 35, 38, 125, 229
Constantine 43
Conybeare, F.C. 208, 210
Cook, E.M. 23
Cowley, A.E. 2, 3, 14, 150, 155, 191, 197, 214
Cross, F.M. 21, 221

Dalman, G. 149
Dan (patriarch) 26, 118, 119
Dan, J. 119, 121, 153
Danby, H. 169, 174, 175
Danites 183
Demetrius the Chronographer 199
Denis, A.-M. 5
Di Tommaso, L. 1

Dinah 17, 18, 111, 112, 114, 117, 220, 221
Drower, E.S. 213
Dura Europos 155

Edom 111
Egypt 27, 28, 97, 99, 101, 193–195, 197–199, 200
Elephantine 155, 163, 197, 214
Eliezer, Rabbi 169
Enoch 125, 218
Eph'al, I. 176
Epstein, A. 189, 190
Epstein, I. 168, 175
Esau, sons of 119, 122
Eshel, E. xi, 21, 111, 112, 127, 137, 204
Eshel, H. 137
Eshtemoa 43
Evans, C.A. 21
Eve 194

Fassberg, S.E. 23, 197
Feldman, L.H. 174
Fitzmyer, J.A. 23, 31, 111, 115, 120, 121, 123, 132, 155, 224, 229
Flint, P. 39, 125, 229
Flusser, D. 21, 114, 125–127, 131
Fox, E. 121
Freedman, H. 156, 159
Friedman, M.A. 197
Fuller, R. 34, 36

Galilee 155
García-Martínez, F. 30
Gaster, T.H. 130
George Syncellus 153
Gerizim, Mount 137
Gersam 97, 99
Gershom 35, 95, 99, 181, 182, 183, 189, 192, 194, 196, 199
– son of Manasseh 183
– son of Moses 182, 183
Gershomites 182, 183
Gershon (Gerson) see Gershom
Gophna 152
Goshen, land of 196
Goshen-Gottstein, M.H. 143
Great Sea 31
Greenberg, M. 214
Greenfield, J.C. xi, 2–5, 8, 12, 14, 17–25, 33–35, 37, 45, 111, 113, 115, 116, 121–123, 126, 128–130, 133, 141, 144–148, 158, 159, 161–162, 164–165, 167, 170–172, 176, 185, 189, 197, 201, 202, 204, 206, 208, 210, 211, 219, 222, 229
Grelot, P. 3, 19, 20, 42, 139, 140–150, 167, 190, 191–193, 195, 197, 200
Grintz, Y.M 12
Guggenheimer, H.W. 200, 206
Gunther, R.T. 167

Haelewyck, J.-C. 5
Halpern-Amaru, B. 21, 160, 181
Hamat Gader 43
Hamor 5, 111, 117
Hannah, Bilhah's mother 26
Harrington, D.J. 111, 132, 225, 229
Harris, J.R. 208, 210
Haupt, D. 146
Hebron, son of Kohath 99
Hebron (place) 136, 151–153
Hermon, Mount 135, 136
Hesiod 170
Hillel, V. xi, 140, 204
Hirschfeld, Y. 43
Holladay, C.R. 199
Hollander, H.W. 17, 26, 32, 39, 112, 119, 123, 138, 139, 148, 153, 182, 186, 187, 198, 204–206, 208, 215
Horovitz, S. 126
Horst, P.W. van der 134
Horowitz, W. 35
Evelyn-White, H.G. 170
Hultgård, A. 13, 14, 117, 184
Huna, son of Kupitay 132

Idumea 176
Ilan, T. 181
Isaac (patriarch) 15, 16, 17, 21, 30, 38–42, 71, 73, 93, 147, 150–155, 157, 168, 188, 189, 202, 224, 229
Ishmael 28
Israel 36, 37, 57, 69, 95, 97, 114, 132, 141, 143, 183, 184, 186, 192, 193, 234
Issachar 26
Izhar 99

Jacob 4, 12, 15, 16, 18, 26, 28, 30, 36–41, 57, 63, 67, 71, 110, 112, 117, 118, 121, 132, 147, 148, 150–153, 185, 187–189, 194, 220, 226, 228
Jacob, grandsons of 194

Jacob, sons of 12, 18, 112–114, 117, 119, 120, 122, 153, 161, 206
Jaubert, A. 189
Jehu 187
Jellinek, A. 119
Jeremiah 132
Jerusalem 121, 132, 152
Job 120
Jochabed 97, 99, 101, 182, 184, 189, 192–196, 198, 199, 223, 224
Jonathan, son of Gerson 183
Jonge, M. de 5, 6, 10, 13, 14, 17, 19, 22, 26, 32, 34, 35, 37–39, 112, 119, 123, 136, 138–140, 148, 153, 182, 186, 187, 198, 204, 206, 208, 215
Jose the Galilean, Rabbi 175
Joseph (patriarch) 21, 22, 27, 34, 37, 103, 107, 117, 118, 190, 199, 200, 202, 204–207, 210, 211, 214
Josephus (historian) 174
Joshua, high priest 161
Joshua, Rabbi 175
Judah (patriarch) 17, 20, 27, 35, 37, 39, 40, 59, 73, 118–120, 141, 147, 151, 152, 155, 185–188
Judah, Rabbi 131
Judas Maccabeus 152
Jung, L. 159

Kaath see Kohath
Kaufman, S.A. 197
Khirbet Rimmon 43
Kislev, M. 166
Kister, M. 111, 197
Kittim 143
Klein, M.L. 37
Kloner, A. 42, 43, 111
Klostermann, E. 120
Knibb, M.A. 34, 130
Kohath 25, 29–31, 35, 37, 38, 95, 97, 99, 181, 182, 184–189, 194–199
Köhler, L. 156, 190
Kraft, R.A. 126
Küchler, M. 209
Kugel, J. 15, 20, 41, 110, 137, 220
Kugler, R.A. 2, 7, 13, 14, 17–20, 34, 36, 39, 117, 139, 146, 161, 168
Kutscher, E.Y. 191

Laban 26, 95, 181
Lamech 125
Leah 188
Lehrman, S.M. 115
Lemaire, A. 153
Levertoff, P.P. 198
Levi (patriarch) 4–6, 11–13, 15–17, 20, 21, 26, 29, 30, 31, 32, 33, 34–41, 63, 75, 91, 101, 103, 110, 112, 118, 120–122, 124, 125, 131, 132, 134, 135, 137–140, 142, 143, 145–153, 155–158, 181, 182, 186–190, 192–195, 198–200, 202, 204, 206–208, 214, 215, 220, 228–230
Levi, children of 125, 196
Levi, grandchildren of 19, 196, 198
Levi, great-grandchildren of 19, 196
Levi, sons of 132, 181, 193, 194, 205
Lévi, I. 139, 143, 158, 159, 170, 172, 178, 191, 172
Levites 139, 140, 205
Levy, J. 213
Lewis, A.S. 208, 210
Libni, son of Gershom 99
Licht, J.S. 164, 176
Lieberman, S. 43
Lomni, son of Gershom 99
Löw, I. 166, 167, 170
Lozachmeur, H. 153

Macuch, R. 213
Mahli, son of Merari 99
Malki-ṣedeq 30
Malki-reša' 30
Manasseh 183
Manasseh, tribe of 120
Mandel, P. 153, 154
Margulies, M. 149
Melcha, see Melka
Melchizedek 121, 149, 154, 155, 156
Melka, daughter of Bathuel see Milka
Menasce, J.P. de 142
Merari 35, 95, 97, 99, 182, 184, 189–192, 194, 196, 199
Methusaleh 125
Michmethath 120
Milik, J.T. 4, 17, 19, 25–31, 37, 121, 125, 128, 135–140, 169, 192, 193, 210, 216–218, 224, 225, 227–231
Milka 95, 97, 181
Mindel, T. 43
Miriam 160, 194
Montgomery, J.A. 132
Mooli, son of Merari 99
Moore, G.F. 183
Moreshet, M. 219

Morgan, M.A. 30
Morgenstern, M. 17, 121, 126, 145, 148, 162, 172, 180, 216, 218
Moses 30, 183, 193, 198
Moses the Preacher, Rabbi 26
Mosshammer, A.A. 153
Müller, H.P. 205, 207
Mushi, son of Merari 99

Naphtali (patriarch) 26
Nau, F. 5
Nauck, W. 163
Naveh, J. 43, 127, 130, 132, 155, 176
Nebe, W. 195
Nickelsburg, G.W.E. 19, 26, 136
Nippur 132
Noah 21, 30, 41, 125, 127, 180, 189, 218

Omousi, son of Merari 99
Oziel, son of Kohath 99

Papos (rabbi) 126
Pass, H.L. 1, 2, 6, 119
Payne Smith, R. 121, 143, 197
Philonenko, M. 12, 127, 128, 130, 133
Phineas 38, 140, 145
Porten, B. 155, 197, 210, 211
Powell, M.A. 44
Puech, E. 2, 6, 7, 25, 27–31, 34, 45, 110, 111, 117–120, 125, 143, 158–160, 164, 171, 183, 184, 196–198, 203, 211, 213, 224

Qahat see Kohath
Qimron, E. 126, 145, 172, 180, 216, 218

Rabin, I. 126
Rad, G. von 207
Raguel 120, 121
Rebecca 151
Reuben 37, 57, 59, 110, 112, 117, 119
Rimmon 28
Ringgren, H. 21

Salem 121
Sālīm 121
Samaria 137
Samaritans 137
Samuel b. Naḥman, Rabbi 156
Sandt, H. van de 127
Sarah 63, 131
Sarin (place) 137
Satan 130
Scharbert, J. 156
Schiffman, L.H. 41–42, 169, 175
Schorch, S. 185
Schürer, E. 221
Schwartz, J. 152, 162
Scythopolis 120
Sear, D.R. 43
Semei, son of Gershon 99
Senir (mountain) 135
Shaked, S. 127, 130, 132
Shechem (place) 12, 16, 59, 110, 112, 117–122, 136, 137, 140, 145, 151, 200
Shechem (person) 99, 101, 111, 142, 199
Shechemites 110, 113, 114
Shimei, son of Gershom 99
Si'on (mountain) 135, 136
Simeon 59, 110, 112, 118–120, 137, 138, 153
Simon, M. 156, 159, 198
Sirion (mountain) 135–137
Sivan, D. 126, 145, 172, 180, 216, 218
Smith, M. 38
Sokoloff, M. xi, 23, 25, 111, 113, 115, 121, 123, 142, 149, 155, 163, 166, 168, 176, 191, 192, 196, 197, 209–213, 219, 230
Sperber, D. 111
Sperling, H. 198
Starcky, J. 27, 31
Stec, D.M. 213
Steiner, R.C. 1, 126, 180
Stone, M.E. xi, 1–5, 8, 12, 14, 16–21, 23, 24, 26, 30, 31, 33–39, 45, 111–113, 115, 116, 121–123, 126, 128–130, 133, 135, 137, 139, 142, 144–148, 158, 161, 164, 165, 167, 170, 171, 172, 176, 180–186, 188, 189, 194, 197, 201, 204, 206, 208–211, 213, 222
Stuckenbruck, L.T. 124
Sukenik, E.L. 43

Talmon, S. 189
Tayāsīr (place) 120
Tel Balatah 121
Terah, father of Abraham 181
Thackeray, H.St.J. 174

Theodor, J. 115, 119, 149, 152, 156, 159, 185, 193
Theodosius, emperor 1, 43
Thomsen, R. 120
Tigchelaar, E. 30
Trans-Jordan 137
Tromp, J. 5, 6, 38

'Umm al-'Amud 155
Uzziel 99, 160, 194

VanderKam, J.C. 10, 15, 16, 19, 20, 41, 150, 152, 159, 165, 167, 169, 170, 187, 207, 210
Vasiliev, A. 116
Vermes, G. 221

Wacholder, B.Z. 20
Weiss, P.R. 22
Weitzman, S. 183
Wertheimer, S.A. 116
Wilkinson, J. 120
Wilson, C.W. 120
Wintermute, O. 121
Wise, M.O. 193, 195
Wright, W. 6

Yadin, Y. 143
Yahalom, J. 149
Yalon, H. 197
Yardeni, A. 111, 155, 197, 210, 211
Yeivin, Z. 43

Zeus 170
Zion 121

INDEX OF ANCIENT SOURCES

Hebrew Bible

Genesis **6:12** 221, **9:4–6** 180, **10:9** 143, **14:18** 121, 149, **14:19** 154, 155, **14:22** 154, 155, **15:13** 181, 182, **17:14** 113, **18:1** 113, **18:10** 131, 184, **18:14** 184, **18:6** 44, **20:5** 123, **21:1** 156, **21:33** 149, **21:4** 113, **22:17–18** 131, **24:48** 125, **24:49** 158, **28:22** 15, **31:29** 123, **33:18** 121, **34** 110, 113, **34:15** 113, 115, **34:16** 113, **34:22** 113, **34:25** 137, **35:1–5** 15, **35:11** 185, 188, **35:11b** 185, **35:18** 184, 191, **37:12–14** 118, **37:14** 118, **37:18** 118, **40:11** 123, **42–47** 27, **45** 27, **45:14** 27, **46:11** 181, **46:28** 196, **47:29** 158, **49** 118, **49:5–7** 110, **49:5** 138, **49:8** 184, **49:10** 35, 185–187, 194, **49:19** 184, **50:23** 200, **50:26** 206

Exodus **1:6** 206, **1:8** 206, **2:22** 182, **6:16** 200, **6:16–19** 198, **6:18–20** 200, **6:19** 198, **6:20** 193, **9:29** 124, **12:40–41** 200, **15:26** 180, **18:3** 182, **19:6** 140, 186, **28:41** 149, **29:4** 149, **32:28** 139, **32:29** 139, **34:6** 158, **40:15** 145, 222

Leviticus **1** 41, **1:7** 168, **1:8–9** 174, **1:12–13** 174, **1:13** 174, **2:15–16** 176, **3:3–4** 42, **5:9** 171, **17:13** 180, **19:35** 176, **20:21** 159, **21:9** 221

Numbers **3:19** 200, **6:22–27** 150, **6:27** 120, **8:21** 12, **18:13** 142, **25:7–8** 139, **25:11–13** 139, **25:12–13** 140, 145, **25:12** 145, **25:13** 145, 222, **26:57–59** 200, **26:59** 193, 198

Deuteronomy **3:8–9** 135, **10:16** 113, **18:3** 156, **29:9** 214, **33:5** 185, 188, **33:10** 34, 36, 132, 156, 158, 187, 208

Joshua **17:7** 120, **23:2** 214, **24:1** 214

Judges **8:31** 192, **18:30** 182, **21** 29

1 Samuel **1:13** 134, **2:8** 212, **2:13** 156, **5:4** 124, **25:18** 44

2 Samuel **21:20** 124, **24:1** 130

1 Kings **3:9** 36, **3:25** 113, **10:19** 187, **15:20** 135, **18:32** 44

2 Kings **4:16–17** 184, **4:16** 184, **6:4** 113, **9:13** 187, **9:35** 124, **11:14** 187

Isaiah **6:13** 160, **11:2** 128, **22:23** 212, **29:11f.** 208, **30:10** 158, **32:5** 211, **32:7** 211, **33:6** 213

Jeremiah **3:19** 142, **6:10** 114, **9:25** 114, **14:21** 212, **15:15** 156, **15:21** 124

Ezekiel **7:20** 159, **13:9** 1, **16:8** 197, **17:15** 212, **26:7** 212, **36:25** 122, **40:38** 174, **44:6–9** 113, 114

Micah **3:11** 214

Zechariah **3:1–10** 161, **3:1–2** 130, **4:1** 138, **4:14** 20, **7:14** 142

Malachi **2:4–9** 36, **2:5** 145, **2:6–7** 34, 128, **2:6** 34, 125, 128, **2:7** 208, **2:9** 219

Psalms **28:2** 124, **50:5** 115, **71:4** 124, **76:3** 121, **91** 127, **91:2** 132, **91:4** 132, **91:9** 132, **106:24** 142, **110:4** 111, 155, **119:133b** 129, 131, **119:160** 107, **123:1** 123, **123:3** 123, **155** 127, 129

Proverbs **3:35** 209, **8:11** 209, 213, **8:15–16** 203, **8:18–19** 203, **8:21** 203, **15:33** 208, **16:16** 213, **20:20** 197

Job **1–2** 130, **1:13** 124, **18:4** 111, **21:21** 113, **24:13** 218, **25:2** 145, **28:18** 213, **33:6** 120, **34:27** 218, **38:23** 119, **40:8** 111, **40:24** 123

Ruth **1:13** 190

Qohelet **3** 143, **7:14** 111

Esther **6:1** 144

Daniel **1:4** 208, **1:7** 192, **2:8ff.** 119, **2:29** 124, **2:30** 25, 111, 124, **2:45** 113, **4:16** 124, **5:14** 128, **5:23** 155, **6:12** 148, **6:13** 148, **6:14** 148, **6:19** 144, **9:20–21** 134

Ezra **4:12** 197, **4:15** 164, **4:19** 164, **5:2** 162, **6:2** 210, **9:2** 160, **9:5** 124

Nehemiah **9:7** 192

1 Chronicles **6:2–4** 198, **21:1** 130
2 Chronicles **4:6** 174, **9:18** 187, **16:4** 135, **17:12** 153, **27:4** 153, **29:5** 159, **30:9** 133

Ancient Versions and Translations

Aquila **Genesis 49:10** 185
Fragmentary Targum **Genesis 4:12** 120, **6:11** 120, **19:3** 115, **32:26** 142, **34:15** 115, **49:3** 37, **49:12** 120, **Exodus 17:16** 212
LXX **Genesis 14:22** 154, **15:13** 182, **Hosea 7:15** 127
Palestinian Targum **Ezekiel 7:19** 209
Targum Neofiti **Genesis 6:11** 120, **17:23** 113, **24:63** 123, **28:10** 152, **34:12** 111, **49:3** 37, **50:1** 142, **50:23** 200, **Leviticus 5:9** 171, **7:30** 175, **Deuteronomy 5:24** 158, **10:16** 113
Targum Onqelos **Genesis 1:31** 191, **4:23** 207, **17:20** 191, **31:40** 144, **33:3** 143, **35:11** 185, **50:23** 200, **Exodus 23:19** 142, **34:26** 142, **Leviticus 3:3** 172, **3:9** 172, **4:10** 172, **21:9** 221, **Numbers 23:18** 207, **Deuteronomy 33:5** 185
Targum **Psalms 119:8** 191
Targum Pseudo-Jonathan **Genesis 17:23** 113, **22:3** 168, **25:27** 143, **48:22** 119
Targum **Ruth 1:13** 190

Apocrypha and Pseudepigrapha

ALD **1** 18, 137, **1:1–3** 11, **1:1** 25, **1:2** 112, 211, **1:3** 25, **2** 12, 18, 28, **2:1–3** 11, **2:1** 18, 119, 122, 147, **2:2–3** 18, **2:4–5** 11, 12, 18, 117, 122, **2:4–4:6** 11, **2:4–4:4** 12, **2:4–3:18** 5, **2:4** 12, **2:6** 121, **3** 11, 12, 18, 139, 217, **3:1** 12, 122, 230, **3:2** 123, **3:4** 17, 34, 130, 217, **3:5–6** 33, **3:5** 24, 32, 229, 231, **3:6** 128, **3:9** 211, 229, **3:10** 4, **3:11** 129, 131, **3:13** 131, **3:14** 131, **3:15** 125, **3:16** 24, 133, **3:17** 36, 131, **3:18** 33, 133, **4** 18, **4:1–6** 14, 18, **4:1–2** 12, **4:3–6** 13, **4:3** 13, 14, **4:4–6** 133, **4:4** 12, 16, 135, **4:5–6** 15, **4:6–9** 16, **4:6** 230, **4:7** 15, 17, 18, 37, 140, 141, **4:8** 17, 18, 37, 224, **4:9–13:6** 11, **4:9–13** 15, 16, 18, **4:9–12** 13, 15, 140, **4:9–11** 16, 17, 139, 224, **4:9–5:8** 151, **4:9–5:5** 11, **4:9** 3, 11, 12, 15, 17, 25, 37, 140, 143 145, 146, 224, 232, **4:9a** 139, **4:9b–10** 139, **4:11** 3, 8, 16, 25, 142, 158, **4:12** 13, 16, 142, **4:13** 15, 17, 138, 148, **4:14** 3, **5** 18, 39, 204, **5:1** 3, 17, 39, 40, 150, 152, 154, 224, 225, 228, **5:2–8** 16, **5:2–5** 40, **5:2–4** 220, **5:2** 15, 146, 224, 228, **5:3** 3, **5:4** 150, 156, 186, **5:5–6** 37, 162, **5:5** 25, 40, 150, **5:6–8** 40, **5:6–9:1** 11, **5:6** 5, 40, 151, 154, **5:7–6:4** 157, **5:7** 17, 40, 150, 152, 159, **5:8–6:2** 180, **5:8** 3, 4, 21, 36, 149, 153, 156, 157, 158, 230, **6–10** 38, **6** 18, **6:1** 3, 144, 156, **6:2** 156, 157, 158, **6:3–10:13** 158, **6:3** 4, 5, 157, 159, 162, 229, **6:4** 4, 159, 162, 180, **6:5** 3, **7:1–2** 12, **7** 18, **7:1** 4, 163, 164, **7:2** 164, **7:3** 4, 25, 165, **7:4** 3, 21, 163, 164, 231, **7:5–6** 25, **7:5** 3, 25, 164, 169, **7:6** 170, 231, **7:7** 171, **8** 18, **8:1** 3, 171 **8:2** 12, 162, 171, 190, 224, **8:3** 211, **8:4** 3, 24, 163, **8:6** 4, 149, **8:7–9:16** 41, **8:7** 178, 211, **9** 19, **9:1–11:8** 171, **9:1** 178, **9:7** 204, **9:9** 77, **9:17–18** 42, 43, 44, **9:17** 44, **10** 19, **10:1–2** 157, **10:3** 36, 38, **10:5** 42, 158, **10:6** 12, **10:8** 156, **10:10** 21, 36, 38, **11** 19, **11:2–3** 194, **11:2** 4, 198, **11:3** 186, **11:4** 35, 183, **11:5–13:12** 11, **11:5–7** 35, 183, **11:5** 181, 183, 198, **11:6–7** 37, **11:6** 3, 37, 141, 181, 183, 198, **11:7** 3, 35, 199, **11:8** 3, 4, 5, 192, 196, 198, **11:10** 3, 24, 192, 198, 223, 234, **11:11** 3, 4, 194, 195, 196, 199, **12** 19, **12:1** 3, 119, **12:2** 3, **12:3** 194, **12:4** 192, **12:5** 194, **12:6–9** 6, **12:6** 3, 120, 196, 200,

12:7 3, **12:8** 194, 196, **12:9–13:13** 204, **12:9–13:2** 205, **12:9** 3, 233, **12:14** 4, **13** 19, 34, 35, **13:1–2** 207, **13:1** 3, 25, 199, 206, **13:2–11** 35, **13:2–3** 205, **13:2** 25 29, 202, 207, **13:2a** 206, **13:3** 3, 24, 25, 202, 205, 231, **13:4–14** 202, **13:4–6** 223, **13:4–5** 204, **13:4–5a** 205, **13:4** 3, 34, 202, 203, 209, 223, **13:4b** 208, **13:5** 3, 4, 24, 25, 203, **13:5a** 208, 209, **13:5b** 205, **13:6** 201, 203, 205, 208, 214, **13:7–10** 205, **13:7** 24, 119, 201, 203, 219, **13:7a** 209, **13:8** 29, 113, 203, **13:9–10** 223, **13:9** 3, 24, 25, 209, **13:10–11** 205, **13:10** 24, 25, 192, 202, 203, 209, 213, **13:11b** 209, **13:12** 24, 201, **13:13** 24, 203, 213, **13:14** 132, **13:15–16** 202, 203, 223, **13:15** 35, 202, 203, 208, **13:16** 4, 24, 35, 38, 140, 188, 203, **13:17** 211

ALD Bodleian **col. a, lines 1–13** 18, **col. a 2, 8, 9,** 45, **col. a, line 3** 3, **col. a, line 17** 3, **col. b** 11, **col. b, line 6** 3, **col. b, line 22** 3, **col. c, line 10** 3, **col. c, line 21** 3, **col. d, line 9** 3

ALD Cambridge **col. a, line 16** 147, **col. a, lines 18, 20, 21, 22, 23** 45, **col. b, lines 19, 20, 23** 45, **col. b, line 20** 2, **col. b, line 23** 118, **col. c, line 14** 3, **col. d, line 19** 3, **col. e, line 5** 3, **col. e, line 14** 3

ALD Greek **1–2** 18, **5:6–9:1** 11, **9:1–11:4** 11, **11:5–11:8** 11

Baruch **3:36–4:1** 204

2 Baruch **44:13** 212

ben Sira **6:19–20** 208, **10:30** 209, **11:1** 209, **15:1–6** 204, **15:1** 204, **24:23** 204, **29:11** 213, **29:12** 213, **39** 35, **39:4** 209, 211, **41:18** 113, **45:6–25** 139, **45:15** 150, **45:17** 208, **45:23** 139, **45:24** 38, 145, **51** 203, 204

Biblical Antiquities **8:7** 110, **9:1–10** 30, **50:5** 134

1 Enoch **3** 169, **6:6** 135, **8:1** 137, **10:11** 159, **17:4** 122, **40:7** 130, **65:6** 130, **74:12** 189, **78:10** 138, **91:4** 125, **91:18–19** 125, **91:19** 125, **93:10** 128, **94:1–4** 125, **106:11** 155

2 Enoch **50:5** 213

2 Esdras **1:31** 114

Greek Testament of Levi see *TPL*

Joseph and Asenath **11:19** 124, **18:8–9** 122, **23:14** 110, **26:6** 137

Jubilees **4:17** 208, **6:25** 189, **6:32** 189, **7:21** 159, **10:3–6** 127, **12:19–20** 127, **13:8** 189, **16:18** 37, **21:1** 93, **21:2** 188, **21:5–19** 42, **21:12–15** 168, **21:12** 165, 167, 169, **21:13** 165, 169, **21:16** 81, **21:17–18** 93, **22:24** 153, **24:22** 189, **27:19** 189, **27:27** 15, **28:14** 188, 189, **29:16–19** 153, **30** 110, **30:1** 121, **30:5–7** 220, **30:7** 221, **31–32** 151, 152, **31** 15, 37, 39, 154, **31:3** 15, 150, **31:5–6** 153, **31:5** 152, 153, **31:6** 153, **31:9** 154, **31:13–17** 202, **31:13–20** 187, **31:14** 160, **31:15** 156, 158, **31:16b** 161, **31:26–27** 40, **31:26** 15, 150, **31:29** 15, **32:1** 145, **32:2** 15, **32:10–15** 16, **32:17–19** 28, **32:20** 140, **32:21–22** 28, **32:2–3** 228, **32:3** 15, 16, 73, 152, **32:9** 15, 148, **33:20** 37, **33:21** 153, **34:1–9** 119, **34:1–2** 119, **34:9** 121, **34:10–11** 118, **34:15** 206, **34:20** 181, **36:12** 153, **36:20** 153, **37:14–17** 153, **37:14** 153, **37:16–17** 153, **38:4–9** 153, **38:4–8** 153, **38:24** 190, **42–46** 27, **43** 27, **45:1** 194, 196, **45:16** 38, **46:3** 206, **46:8** 206

Judith **9:2** 110, 137, **12:7** 12

Psalms of Solomon **18** 20

Paralipomena of Jeremiah **1:2** 132

Sibylline Oracles **4:152ff.** 124, **4:163–65** 13, **4:165** 12

Syriac Psalm **3** (Psalm 154) 129, **3:2** (Psalm 154) 124

Testament of Abraham **1 3:5** 153, **1 5:1** 153, **2 3** 153

Tobit **2:4** 121, **3**:12 123, **4:1** 160, **4:12** 159, **7:1** 212, **7:6** 120

TPBenjamin **3:1** 155, 206

TPDan **5:6** 127

TPGad **3:2** 204, **4:7** 204

TPJudah **3–7** 119, **3:4** 137, **4:3** 141, **5** 119, **5:1–2** 119, **7:7** 121, **9:5** 137, **12:11–12** 27, **12:11** 27, **21** 37, **21:2–4** 140, **21:4** 141, **24–25** 26

TPL

2–3 230, **2:2** 200, **2:3** 5, 12, 135, **2:4–5** 138, **2:4** 5, 14, 16, **2:5–6** 135, **2:5–5:1** 16, **2:5** 14, 135, 136, 138, **2:10** 65, **3–5** 14, **3:5–6** 69,

4:2 32, 33, 65, 127, 133, **5** 16, **5:1** 14, 69, 139, **5:1–2** 119, **5:2–3** 142, **5:3** 135, 137, **6:1** 135, 137, **6:3** 57, 110, 112, 229, **6:5** 161, **7:2** 5, **8** 16, 17, 140, 145, 146, **8:1** 151, **8:2–17** 16, **8:2** 142, **8:2b-3** 73, **8:5** 122, **8:10** 149, **8:10b** 73, **8:11–14** 37, **8:11** 39, **8:11a** 139, 140, **8:12** 139, **8:13** 139, **8:14–15** 215, **8:14** 39, 141, 204, **8:16** 69, 141, 142, **8:18–19** 17, 69, **9** 147, 170, **9:1–6** 151, **9:1–2a** 73, **9:1** 17, 40, 147, **9:2** 17, 40, **9:3–4** 148, **9:3** 147, **9:4** 73, **9:5–6** 204, **9:5** 152, **9:6** 154, 155, 156, 188, **9:7–14** 42, **9:7** 156, **9:7a** 73, **9:9** 159, **9:10** 160, **9:11** 81, 162, **9:12** 81, 170, **9:13** 89, **9:14** 89, **10** 217, **10:5** 34, 203, **11:1–2** 97, **11:2** 181, 182, **11:3** 181, **11:4** 97, **11:5–6** 184, 186, **11:5** 97, 181, 186, **11:5ff.** 145, **11:6a** 97, **11:7** 97, 191, 196, **11:8** 97, 193, **12:1–4** 99, **12:1–3** 198, **12:4** 198, **12:5–6** 101, **12:5** 194, **12:6–13:7** 204, **12:6–7** 205, **12:6** 200, **12:7** 107, 206, **12–13** 207, **13** 204, **13:1–5** 35, **13:1** 205, 206, 207, **13:1a** 107, **13:2–3** 107, 204, 205, **13:2–3a** 205, **13:2** 208, 209, **13:2b** 208, **13:3–4** 109, **13:3a** 209, **13:3b-4** 205, **13:4–5** 35, **13:4b** 209, **13:4c** 209, **13:5–6** 205, **13:6** 107, **13:7–8** 205, **13:7** 109, **13:7a** 209, **13:7c** 209, **13:9** 205, 211, **13:9b** 107, **14** 216, 217, **14:1** 34, 203, 216, **14:3** 216, **14:4** 217, **16–18** 35, 203, **16–17** 217, **16:1** 34, 35, 203, **17** 31, **18–19** 32, **18:2** 5

TPNaphtali **1:9–12** 26, **3:2** 204, **8:7** 204

TPSimeon **1:1** 206, **4:3–7** 27

TPZebulun **1:1** 206, **8:4** 27

Wisdom of Solomon **6–11** 203, 213, **7:14** 213, **8:10** 209, **10:13–14** 211

Dead Sea Scrolls

CD (Damascus Document) **4:15** 5, **4:17** 229, **12:23–13:1** 21, **14:19** 21, **20:1** 21

Cave 1

1QapGen (1Q20) **3:2** 120, **5:16–19** 125, **5:18** 120, **5:29** 1, 126, 180, **6:1–2** 218, **6:2** 218, **6:2–3** 126, **6:3** 218, **6:11** 115, **6:23** 144, **7:2** 216, **7:7** 155, **10:14** 172, **11:14** 120, **12:14** 195, **12:17** 155, **13:9** 115, **13:15** 191, **20:9** 115, **20:12–13** 155, **20:12** 192, **20:13** 111, **20:16** 133, **20:33** 191, **21:2** 154, **21:19** 121, **21:20** 154, **22:12** 154, **22:13** 121, **22:15** 154, **22:16** 154, 155, **22:17** 154, **22:19–20** 219, **22:21** 155, **22:22** 154, **22:29** 164, **22:32** 191

1QH[a] **7:19** 145, **17:33** 131, **19:27** 145, **22:6** 129

1QLevi (1Q21) **frag. 1** 15, 17, 18, 37, 139, 140, 156, 188, **frag. 2** 139, 140, **frag. 3** 143, **frag. 4** 147, **frag. 7** 17, 18, 139, 140, **frag. 8** 18, 117, **frag. 37** 145, **frag. 45** 171, **frag. 52** 144

1QM **1:9–10** 143, **67:12–15** 37

1QpHab **11:12–13** 114, **11:13** 114

1QS **2:4** 145, **3:13–4:26** 126, 128, **4:2** 125, 126, **4:2–8** 128, **4:10–11** 126, **5:5** 114, **6:6** 209, **9:11**, 20

1QSa (1Q28a) **2:12–15** 37

1QSb (1Q28b) **1:7–8** 127

Cave 2

2Q24 (2QNew Jerusalem) **1:3** 230

Cave 4

4Q196 (4QpapTobit[a]) **6:8** (Tobit 3:12) 123, **14 2:11** (Tobit 7:6) 120

4Q197 (4QTobit[b]) **4 2:1** 191, **4 3:4** (Tobit 7:1) 212, **4 3:8** (Tobit 7:6) 120

4Q198 (4QTobit[c]) **1:9** 119

4Q202 (4QEnoch[b]) **1 3:15** (*1 Enoch* 9:4) 212

4Q203 (4QEnochGiants[a]) **9:3** 124

4Q209 (4QAstronomical Enoch[b]) **25:3** (*1 Enoch* 78:10) 138

4Q212 (4QEnoch[g]) **1 2:17–21** (*1 Enoch* 91:18–19) 125 **1 4:13** (*1 Enoch* 93:10) 128

4Q213 (4QLevi[a]) **1–2 2:15–16** 188, **frag. 1** 19, **1 1–2** 201, **1 1:9** 214, **1 1:11** 209, 210, **frag. 1 col. 2** 11, **1 2:6** 201, **1 2:9** 201, **frag 2** 201, **2:5** 201, **frag. 4** 126, **4:5** 125, **4:6** 211, **4:7** 24, **4:8** 24
4Q213a (4QLevi[b]) **frag. 1** 22, **1 1–2** 11, **1 1:5–7** 117, **frag. 1 col. 2** 18, 131, **1 2:5** 132, **1 2:15–16** 115, **1 2:16–18** 138, **frags. 3–4** 17, **3–4:5–6** 24
4Q213b (4QLevi[c]) **1:1** 144, **frag. 3** 158
4Q214 (4QLevi[d]) **frag. 1** 8, **2:3** 171, 172, **2:4** 172, **2:5** 172, **2:6** 176,
4Q214b (4QLevi[f]) **2–3:8** 171, **5–6 1:4–5** 24, **5–6 1:5** 167, **frag. 7** 158, **8:2** 213
4Q219 **2:7–12** 169
4Q225 (4QPseudo-Jubilees[a]) **2 2:11–12** 39
4Q226 (4QPesudo-Jubilees[b]) **7:4** 39
4Q243 (4QPseudo-Daniel[a]) **7:3** 125, **33:1** 125
4Q244 (4QPseudo-Daniel[b]) **2:2** 229
4Q246 (4QApocryphon of Daniel) **1:5** 143, **2:5** 125
4Q252 (4QCommentary on Genesis A) **5:5** 186, **5:6**185
4Q266 (4QDamascus Document[a]) **10 1:12** 21
4Q269 (4QDamascus Document[d]) **1 51:2** 21
4Q394 (4QMMT[a]) **3–7 1:2–3** 189
4Q464 (4QExposition on the Patriarchs) **7:8** 112
4Q525 (Beatitudes) **2 3:2–3** 213, **2–3 2:9** 203
4Q534 (4QBirth of Noah[a]) **1 1:8** 124, **7:1** 208
4Q536 (4QBirth of Noah[c]) **2, 2 10–11** 208
4Q537 (4QTestament of Jacob?) **5:2** 217, **12:1–2** 217, **frag. 14** 28
4Q538 (4QTestament of Judah) **1:6** 27
4Q539 (4QTestament of Joseph) **2–3:2** 207, **3:2** 28
4Q541 (4QApocryphon of Levi[b]?) **frag. 7** 31, **frag. 9** 31, **13:3** 207, **frag 24** 32, **24 2:4** 164
4Q542 (Testament of Qahat) **1 1:4–6** 211, **1 1:6** 209–211, 219, **1 1:12** 207, **1 2:9** 29, **1 2:12** 30, **3 2:13** 229
4Q 543 (4QVisions of Amram[a]) **1a–c** 30, **1 a–c:1** 180, **1 a–c:2–4** 193
4Q544 (4QVisions of Amram[b]) **1** 30, **1:2** 191, **2** 30
4Q545 (4QVisions of Amram[c]) **1a 1:5–6** 160, 194
4Q558 (4QpapVision[b]) **63:2** 195
4Q559 (4QpapBiblical Chronology) **2:5–9** 194, **2:7** 199
4QEnoch[b] see 4Q202
4QEnoch[g] see 4Q212
4QAstronomical Enoch[b] see 4Q209
4QExposition on the Patriarchs see 4Q464
4QLevi[a] see 4Q213
4QLevi[b] see 4Q213a
4QLevi[c] see 4Q213b
4QLevi[d] see 4Q214
4QLevi[e] see 4Q214a
4QLevi[f] see 4Q214b
4QMMT see 4Q394
4QNaphtali see 4Q215
4QTobit see 4Q196, 4Q197
4QpGen[a] see 4Q252
4QPseudo-Daniel see 4Q243, 4Q244, 4Q245
4QTestimonia **12–16** 37
4QTobit see 4Q197, 4Q198

Cave 11

11Q11 (11Qapocryphal Psalms) **6:3–15** 127
11Q18 (New Jerusalem) **frag. 13** 173, **13:2** 163
11QPs[a] (11Q5) **6:3–15** 127, **18:12–15** 204, **19** (Plea for Deliverance) 127, **19:15** (Plea for Deliverance) 129, **19:16–17** (Plea for Deliverance) 128, **21–22** 204, **24** 127, **24:3–4** 124, 161, **24: 12–13** 129, **27:4–6** 189
11QtgJob (11Q10) **1:7** (Job 18:4) 111, **5:3** (Job 21:21) 113, **8:4** (Job 24:13) 218, **9:4** (Job 25:2) 145, **22:1** (Job 33:6) 120, **31:1** (Job 38:23) 119, **34:3–4** (Job 40:8) 111, **34:3** (Job 34:27) 218, **35:3** (Job 40:24) 123

New Testament and New Testament Apocrypha

Mark **14:36** 150
Romans **8:15** 150
Galatians **4:6** 150
Hebrews **7** 155, **11:22** 206
James **4:5** 5
Acts of Peter **39** 134
Gospel of Thomas **15:1** 208

Other Ancient Sources

Aḥiqar, Aramaic **line 12** 210, **line 89** 191, **line 139** 211
Aḥiqar, Syriac **ms 66v §10** 208, **ms 68r §28** 210
Augustine, **City of God 7** 206
Carpentras Stele (KAI 269) **line 4** 222
Clement of Alexandria, *Stromateis* **7:7** 134
Elephantini papyrus (Cowley) **No. 28** 197
Discorides **1.19** 167
Ephrem, *Opp. Gr.* **403B** 143
Eusebius, *Onomastikon* **26:22** 120
Eusebius, *Praeparatio evangelica* **9:22** 110
Geoponica xi:1 170
Josephus, *Antiquities* **1.212–217** 30, **1:337–342** 110, **3.227** 174
Josephus, *War* **3.353–54** 134
P. Murabbaʿât **20, l. 3** 111, **42:67** 210
Philo, *De gigantibus* **52** 134, *De migratione Abrahami* **223** 110, *De mutatione nominum* **193–195, 199–200** 110, *De plantatione* **126** 134, *De specialibus legibus* **1.272** 134, *Vita Mosis* **2.143** 122
Plutarch *Vitae decem oratorum* VI Aeshines (Mor. 840B) 208
Sefire Inscription **I A line 40** 113
Theodotus, *Work on Shechem* 110
Theognis **1, 19** 116

Rabbinic and Later Hebrew Sources

m. Middot **2:5** 164, 165, 168
m. Tamid **2:2** 42, **2:3** 167, 169, **3:1** 174, **4:2** 174
m. Yoma **2:3** 174, 175
t. Baba Batra **5, 11–12** 43
t. Menaḥot **9:14** 167, 169
b. Baba Batra **109b** 183
b. Baba Meṣia **23b** 176
b. Menaḥot **85b** 168
b. Qiddushin **9a** 168
b. Rosh Hashanah **23a** 170
b. Shabbat **137b** 116
b. Tamid **29b** 169
b. Yoma **25b** 175
j. Berakot **9 14a** 116
j. Demai **2:1 22c** 197
j. Gittin **43d (55)** 219; **47b (35)** 43, 120
j. Ketubot **1:2 25b** 197; **7 31d** 167, 170
j. Qiddushin **3:4 64a** 197; **64a (38)** 219
Genesis rabba **13:9** 115, **26:5** 159, **43:6** 156, **65:16** 152, **65:22** 149, **94:9** 193, **97:6** 119, **99:8** 185
Exodus rabba **19** 115
Leviticus rabba **30:6** 149
Mekilta d'Rabbi Ishmael, **Bešalaḥ 6:14–16** 126
Midrash Tadšē **viii** 189, 190
Midrash Wayissaʿu **2, line 54** 119, 121, **3, lines 5–7** 153
Seder ʿolam **2:35** 200, **3** 206
Tanḥuma **wa-yeḥi 10** 185
Tanḥuma Yelamdenu **wa-yera'** 116
Yalqut Shimʿoni **Shemot 162** 189, 206, **Pinḥas 772** 156, **Song of Songs 993** 116
Zohar **Exodus 19a** 198